W9-ABG-547

UNIVERSITY OF NEW HAVEN
EDUCATION
CURRICULUM CENTER

Better Schooling for the Children of Poverty:
Alternatives to Conventional Wisdom

Edited by

Michael S. Knapp
University of Washington

Patrick M. Shields
SRI International

McCutchan Publishing Corporation
P.O. Box 774, 2940 San Pablo Ave., Berkeley, CA 94702

LC
4091
.B 48
1991

ISBN 0–8211–1022–5
Library of Congress Catalog Card Number 91–60678

Copyright © by McCutchan Publishing Corporation
All rights reserved

Printed in the United States of America

Contents

Contributors

Richard L. Allington, State University of New York at Albany
Jere E. Brophy, Michigan State University
Walter Doyle, University of Arizona
Georgia Garcia, University of Illinois at Urbana-Champaign
Michael S. Knapp, University of Washington
Heather McCollum, Policy Studies Associates
Curtis McKnight, University of Oklahoma
Luis Moll, University of Arizona
Margaret Needels, California State University at Hayward
Barbara Neufeld, Education Matters, Inc.
P. David Pearson, University of Illinois at Urbana-Champaign
Andrew C. Porter, University of Wisconsin-Madison
Walter G. Secada, University of Wisconsin-Madison
Patrick M. Shields, SRI International
Brenda J. Turnbull, Policy Studies Associates
Andrew A. Zucker, SRI International

Acknowledgments

This book synthesizes many strands of research and represents the culmination of a process that involved experts in the field, U.S. Department of Education (ED) staff, and researchers carrying out the Study of Academic Instruction for Disadvantaged Students, a three-year investigation of the education offered in schools that serve large numbers of poor children.[1]

Many of the chapters contained in this volume were commissioned originally as discussion papers presented at three meetings of experts convened by SRI International in December of 1988 to consider what was known about effective classroom management, curriculum, and instruction in schools serving disadvantaged students. The discussion at these meetings has had a profound effect on our synthesis of themes in the literature, as reflected in the literature review chapters and concluding chapter. We are especially grateful to Lisa Delpit, Luis Laosa, Linda Winfield, Mary Lindquist, and Marcia Farr, whose participation in these meetings as critics/discussants

1 The study is being carried out by SRI International and Policy Studies Associates with support from the U.S. Department of Education, Office of Planning, Budget and Evaluation (Contract Number LC88054001).

broadened our perspective on the research problem in important ways.

Directly and indirectly, the ideas in this book have also been influenced by individuals who are part of the study's Advisory Panel, including Beatrice Birman, Gary Echternacht, Carolyn Evertson, Beverly Glenn, Marilyn Rauth, Robert Slavin, and Marshall Smith.

Certain staff of ED have been particularly instrumental in conceiving and supporting the work reflected in this book. The project monitor, Carol Chelemer of the Office of Planning, Budget and Evaluation (OPBE), deserves particular mention, as do others in OPBE—Alan Ginsburg, Val Plisko, Nina Winkler—and others elsewhere in ED—Martin Orland, Patricia Rennings, and Mary Jean LeTendre—whose interest, critical feedback, and participation in expert committee meetings helped refine our thinking.

Besides those who authored the literature review chapters, other members of the study team had an important role in shaping the thinking that is reflected in this book: Nancy Adelman of Policy Studies Associates and Deborah Swanson-Owens of Stanford University. Finally, we thank the SRI staff who edited and produced the book: Carolyn Estey, Dorothy Stewart, Marion Collins, and Klaus Krause.

Michael S. Knapp
Patrick M. Shields

Introduction

The Search for Effective Academic Instruction for the Children of Poverty

More than one in five of the schoolchildren in the United States come from families in poverty. For educators, policymakers, researchers, and the public, improving poor children's schooling is an increasingly urgent concern. While few are complacent about the quality of the education offered to any children in this country, the rate at which poor children leave school ill-equipped for adult life is particularly alarming. Despite extra resources from federal and state programs and despite recent educational reforms, the children of poverty experience failure disproportionately in their early school years. Many of them remain on track for failure, and some well-intentioned efforts to give them special help may even compound their difficulties. From their earliest years in school, these children find themselves *at a disadvantage* in the pursuit of learning, jobs, or personal fulfillment.

To improve the education that elementary schools offer poor children, we need both a clearer diagnosis of problems with the school program and clearer ideas about solutions. Current approaches reflect different assumptions about what is wrong and how to improve the situation, as illustrated by questions of basic skills, classroom order, and cultural differences:

- *Basic skills.* Recognizing that a large proportion of disadvantaged students have not mastered basic academic skills, some educators advocate programs that focus exclusively on these skills. Supplementary programs, like compensatory education supported by the federal Chapter 1 program, often have taken this approach. Other educators look for ways to embed the teaching and learning of skills in broader applications of knowledge.
- *Classroom order.* The difficulty of establishing and maintaining an orderly environment in classrooms with large numbers of disadvantaged students is well known. This difficulty leads some educators to devise systems of rules and behavioral controls that bring a uniform structure to the school day. Others urge that classroom order be derived more directly from, and sustained by, the kind of academic program in which students are engaged (see Chapter 10).
- *Cultural differences.* The fact that many disadvantaged students' culture and language differ from those of the school leads some educators to urge that schools accommodate these differences more directly, while others advocate more explicit teaching of "mainstream" culture and language (e.g., Davidson, 1988).

These are only a few dimensions of the debate about effective ways to teach disadvantaged students.

This book is meant to clarify the terms of the debate by probing and moving beyond what has come to be conventional wisdom about the instruction offered disadvantaged students. The book presents a set of commissioned papers and synthesizes existing scholarship in mathematics and literacy, and also with regard to instructional strategies and classroom management, viewed generically. The ideas summarized in this volume focus on the nature of educational problems, and solutions to them, in schools that serve large numbers of disadvantaged students.

At the same time, the book sets forth a research-based perspective to guide further studies, in particular, the Study of Academic Instruction for Disadvantaged Students, a three-year investigation (now in progress) of the education in selected academic subjects offered to children from impoverished families. This study, supported by the Office of Planning, Budget and Evaluation in the U.S. Department of Education, is an in-depth examination of curriculum and instruction in a sample of classrooms within elementary schools serving high concentrations of poor children.

This book is based on the first report to emerge from the study. Others will follow, based on the data we gather in sample classrooms. (The appendix to this book offers more detail about study assumptions, design, and likely contributions to understanding the issues under discussion.)

Some important principles have been established about schooling in the settings that serve the children of poverty. Folk wisdom among teachers and various lines of research have converged on important insights into the prerequisites for academic learning in these settings. The following insights have particular bearing on the academic instruction offered disadvantaged students:

- *Maximizing time on task.* Research on generic instructional strategies and classroom management has convincingly demonstrated that for certain kinds of learning goals (those measured by conventional standardized tests), teaching approaches that maximize students' time on task are likely to enhance student achievement (Cooley & Leinhardt, 1980; Brophy & Good, 1986). The point may seem obvious, but in classrooms serving the children of poverty, it is easy to overlook: there are many potential distractions from academic work in such classrooms.
- *Establishing high expectations and a school climate supporting academic learning.* More than a decade of research on "effective schools" has increased our understanding of how to build a supportive environment for teaching and learning. Initially directed at inner-city elementary schools serving large numbers of poor children, these studies suggest that a series of factors can boost student learning; among them are high expectations for the achievement of all children, active instructional leadership, and a school climate that ensures high priority is given to academics (see Purkey & Smith, 1983).
- *Strengthening the involvement of parents in support of instruction.* Research on the involvement of parents in instruction has led to another basic insight, once again coinciding with common sense: student learning can be greatly enhanced by active involvement of parents in support of their children's instruction (Becher, 1984; Leler, 1983; Stevenson & Baker, 1987). Although there are many things

that constrain poor parents' involvement with their children's education, numerous examples attest to their powerful influence on learning when they do become involved, with or without the active encouragement of the schools.

By maximizing student engagement in learning, building a school climate supportive of academic learning, and engaging parents in the education of their offspring, schools serving the children of poverty can accomplish a great deal. But these improvements establish only a foundation for academic learning; they have little to do with the nature of what is taught and how it is taught.

To date, the most widely accepted conception of what and how to teach disadvantaged students emphasizes "the basics" through skills-based, sequentially ordered curricula that maximize the teacher's direct control over learning opportunities (Calfee, 1986; Romberg, 1986; also see Chapters 6 and 8 in this book). In this view of academic instruction, the content of mathematics, reading, or writing is a sequence of discrete skills—for example, how to divide three-digit numbers with and without remainders, how to decode phoneme blends and syllables, how to begin a sentence with a capital letter and end it with a period.

This view of content appeals to those who teach students experiencing difficulty in school because it breaks reading, mathematics, or writing into small, manageable learning tasks that students can easily master. The learners, conceived as individuals with identifiable skill deficits, can then be guided toward attainment of the skills they lack. A structured, linear sequence of skills provides a template for diagnosing what students do and do not know, thus enabling teachers to pinpoint what should be taught next or retaught.

The most widely accepted approaches to conveying this content to disadvantaged children emphasize a great deal of teacher-directed instruction, rapid pacing, frequent feedback to students, repeated opportunities for practice and review, and homogeneous whole-class or small-group formats. This way of instructing children has various apparent benefits: children are kept on task, there are few opportunities for distraction, there are many opportunities to "revisit" the same skill or material until the child achieves mastery. Furthermore, teachers are able to monitor students' progress continually, making adjustments as needed.

In the hands of skillful teachers, these approaches bear obvious fruit: disadvantaged children can perform well on standardized achievement tests of reading and mathematics (Chapter 12 reviews evidence related to this point). But unintentionally, these approaches may limit the learning of children by not encouraging analytical or conceptual skills, by failing to nurture the ability to express oneself orally or in writing, by repetitively exposing children to the same material, or by failing to provide a larger meaning or purpose to learning (see Chapters 5 and 6).

An emerging set of ideas about teaching disadvantaged children, bolstered by research evidence, suggests that we can go beyond the limitations implied by the above approaches. First, we must look more carefully at our model of the learner—in particular, at what is implied by focusing on the "disadvantaged" children's presumed deficits. Second, we need to examine the nature of what is being taught to these children, to understand whether and how the content of instruction challenges children to acquire more than discrete skills. Third, we must reconsider how we organize and carry out instruction to achieve more ambitious instructional goals.

The chapters of this book review emerging conceptions of the learner, content, and instructional approaches that promise to offer more to the children of poverty. Although the chapter authors have restricted their discussion to the case of mathematics and literacy in elementary schools, and to instructional strategies or classroom management viewed generically, the ideas presented here have wide applicability to other content areas and to other levels of education.

REFERENCES

Becher, R. M. (1984). *Parental involvement: A review of research and principles of successful practice*. Washington, DC: National Institute of Education.

Brophy, J. E., & Good, T. L. (1986). Teacher behavior and student achievement. In M. C. Wittrock (Ed.), *Handbook of research on teaching* (3rd ed.). New York: Macmillan.

Calfee, R. (1986). Curriculum and instruction: Reading. In B. I. Williams, P. A. Richmond, & B. J. Mason (Eds.), *Designs for compensatory education: Conference proceedings and papers*. Washington, DC: Research and Evaluation Associates.

Cooley, W. W., & Leinhardt, G. (1980). The instructional dimensions study. *Educational Evaluation and Policy Analysis*, 2(1), 7–25.

Davidson, J. L. (Ed.). (1988). *Counterpoint and beyond*. Urbana, IL: National Council of Teachers of English.

Leler, H. (1983). Parent education and involvement in relation to the schools and to parents of school-aged children. In R. Haskins & D. Adams (Eds.), *Parent education and public policy*. Norwood, NJ: Ablex.

Purkey, S. C., & Smith, M. S. (1983). School reform: The district policy implications of the effective schools literature. *Elementary School Journal, 85*, 353–389.

Romberg, T. A. (1986). Mathematics for compensatory school programs. In B. I. Williams, P. A. Richmond, & B. J. Mason (Eds.), *Designs for compensatory education: Conference proceedings and papers*. Washington, DC: Research and Evaluation Associates.

Stevenson, D. L., & Baker, D. P. (1987). The family-school relation and the child's school performance. *Child Development, 58*, 1348–1357.

Part I

Toward Effective Curricula and Instruction in Literacy

— 1 —

Effective Literacy Instruction for At-Risk Children

Richard L. Allington

Disadvantaged children, the children of poverty, are at risk in our nation's schools. These children are those most likely to experience school failure and this school failure, more often than not, involves literacy learning difficulties. These are the children who travel predictable avenues once difficulties in maintaining on-schedule literacy acquisition appear. These predictable avenues for poor children are retention in grade, transition room placement, enrollment in remedial or special education programs, and placement in a "bottom track." Travel on any of these avenues increases the likelihood that one will never accomplish serious academic work, will leave school before completion, will achieve parent status prior to age eighteen, and will be unemployed as a young adult. Children of poverty are more likely to travel these avenues than are other, more advantaged children, and we can identify early in their school careers which will travel the high road and which will travel the low.

In our work (e.g., Allington, 1983, 1986; Allington et al., 1990; Stuetzel, Shake, & Lamarche, 1986; Allington & Johnston, 1986,

1989; Allington & McGill-Franzen, 1989a & b; Johnston, Allington, Afflerbach, 1985; McGill-Franzen, 1987; Broikou, Allington, & Jachym, 1989), we have examined the school experiences of poor children, with a particular interest in those who participate in remedial and special education programs. We have addressed the literacy instructional experiences of these children across the school day and across school settings. We have concluded that few schools have organized instructional resources such that children who need access to larger amounts of high-quality instruction actually experience such access. In other words, the routine finding that remedial and special education interventions rarely result in improved academic achievement (e.g., Birman, 1988; Ysseldyke, Thurlow, Mecklenburg, & Graden, 1984; Slavin, 1987) is predictable given the design of most of such instructional interventions. Too often, the instructional programs organized for children of poverty reflect concern for providing the minimum amount of the least expensive instruction allowed under federal and state program regulations (Allington & McGill-Franzen, 1989b).

I will sketch the components of our "plain vanilla" model of instructional efforts that facilitate the acquisition of literacy abilities in at-risk children, briefly report common findings about these components, and present current problems to consider in examining the usefulness of the components in a study of "effective literacy instruction." I will also pose additional elements that deserve inclusion in an expanded and more explanatory model.

INSTRUCTIONAL TIME

Instructional time allocated for literacy instruction is obviously important (Denham & Lieberman, 1980; Kiesling, 1978; Wiley & Harnischfeger, 1974) but few instructional programs for disadvantaged (or low-achievement) children reliably increase instructional time (e.g., Allington & McGill-Franzen, 1989a; Birman, 1988; Haynes & Jenkins, 1986; Ysseldyke et al., 1984; Zigmond, Vallecorsa, & Leinhardt, 1980). In fact, schools with high concentrations of poor children routinely schedule significantly less literacy instructional time than schools with few poor children (Birman et al., 1987). While it seems feasible that the small-group pullout instruction commonly found in remedial and special education could increase allocated time, it rarely does. It also seems feasible that a smaller size of instruction groups in pullout settings could result in higher student engagement (thereby improving on the classroom setting). The evidence, however, suggests that compared to classroom instruction, off-task behavior is more frequent (or not substantially different) during pullout instruction in remedial or resource rooms (Allington & McGill-Franzen, 1989a; Haynes & Jenkins, 1986). Low-achieving students tend to be off-task more than higher-achieving peers, although this often seems related to task difficulty or appropriateness (Gambrell, Wilson, & Gannt, 1981).

Another way of summarizing this component is to note that there exists little evidence to suggest that (1) schools with many poor children schedule more instructional time for literacy lessons than schools with few poor children, (2) remedial or special education programs are organized in ways that routinely enhance time allocated for literacy lessons, and (3) the literacy instruction provided low-achievement learners is differentiated in ways that improve on-task behavior.

More recently we have begun to consider an issue raised by Walter Doyle (1984) in another school context. That is the issue of the length of the scheduled instructional periods. It seems that small instructional time allocations (ten to twenty-five minutes) influence enormously the type of instructional episodes and instructional tasks that teachers select. A scheduled thirty-minute remedial session actually involves about twenty minutes of instructional time. During twenty-minute instruction periods, different activities can be accomplished than in sixty- to ninety-minute periods (with seventy-five to eighty minutes for instruction). Short periods seem conducive to small tasks, brief attempts at reading and writing, literal or locate tasks rather than comprehension or composition tasks. However, remedial and special education students have schedules that break their days into short segments. Teachers and administrators seem to believe that these learners need short scheduled periods (due to their attention spans and such) and often plan one or more different activities within these short periods.

There are several paradoxes in all this. First, we have the fixed-length school day and year. If all students attend school for the same amount of time, how do we find more minutes for some students? Obviously, most schools have not designed "add-on" (before- or after-school, summer school, Saturday school) programs. Most schools do not seem to have any clear policy on what core curriculum instruction should be replaced by the instructional support programs. Second, while at-risk student "attentional problems" are frequently mentioned by instructional staff and short segments of instruction are often scheduled, the relationship of the activity shifts to off-task behavior seems unnoticed. Additionally, the possibility that these shorter periods result in lower-level and less engaging tasks goes unnoticed. Finally, while "individualization" of instruction has been a key phrase in most educational interventions for at-risk learners, one finds little evidence that instructional time allocations are related to individual educational deficits (Allington & McGill-Franzen, 1989a; Thurlow, Ysseldyke, Graden, & Algozzine, 1984)—children with greater lags in achievement are scheduled for no more instruction than children with lesser lags.

To end this discussion of instructional time I want to note that in our "plain vanilla" model we assume, after Carroll (1963), that by comparing the amount of time spent with the amount of learning achieved, one can begin to estimate the varying rates of acquisition of literacy by different children. This is, of course, a very crude indicator of "opportunity" to learn, or "necessary opportunity." This model also assumes that most children receive a generally similar "plain vanilla" curriculum exposure. We have argued that some children will simply need access to larger amounts of instruction than others, if we are to achieve that abnormal state of attainment of "average" rates of acquisition by all (or more than half) of the learners. Simply put, unequal inputs could produce more equal outcomes. However, we find that low-achiever children are scheduled for fewer minutes of literacy instruction than their achieving peers and have argued that instructional interventions that reduce instruction are odd strategies for enhancing achievement (Stanovich [1986] labels this the "Matthew effect," the rich get richer . . .).

In our more recent conceptualizing we have attempted to consider how one might address the issue of "coherent blocks" of literacy instruction, that is, settings in which reading/writing/spelling/ language tasks cohere, or hang together as a set of interrelated activities. We suppose that coherent blocks facilitate literacy acquisition (see next section) and have been addressing how an observer might note coherent blocks (as opposed to unrelated sets of tasks) that occur during reading/language arts instructional time. In addition, out-of-school literacy experiences, especially voluntary reading (Anderson, Wilson, & Fielding, 1988), have demonstrated effects on reading achievement, and engagement in such activities seems related to school experiences, particularly the emphasis on voluntary reading and the accessibility of appropriate books.

On the other hand, allocated and engaged time are slippery variables that we have attended too heavily to (perhaps because counting minutes is easier than identifying quality instruction). The most efficient way to resolve a learning difficulty is not to double the amount of ineffective instruction.

INSTRUCTIONAL TASKS

The first forays away from the experimental laboratory led us to consider differences in the instructional tasks experienced by members of "good" and "poor" reader groups in classrooms (Allington, 1977, 1980, 1983, 1984). These reports focused on two primary differences: distribution of oral and silent reading opportunities and differences in text reading opportunities. The evidence indicated that poor readers were most likely to be assigned round-robin oral reading in reading groups, while good readers were more likely to be asked to read silently. The series of studies described how teachers interrupted poor readers more often, asked poor readers fewer comprehension questions, and so on. From these data it was argued that poor readers seemed to learn what was taught—and that what they were taught was fundamentally different from what better readers were taught. We argued, for instance, that fundamental differences in the oral and silent reading processes and practices created two fundamentally different types of readers—one group learned to read for personal purposes with self-monitoring of meaning and the other learned to pronounce words aloud while being monitored externally by their teacher or peers.

More recently we have attempted to integrate that view with the position expressed by Walter Doyle (1986) that the academic tasks that children do are good indicators of what they are likely to learn and with the extension by Marx and Walsh (1988) that the thinking children do during their academic work is the crux of the matter. Virtually all analyses of the instructional experiences of low-achievement children portray massive involvement in low-level task completion (e.g., Rowan, Guthrie, Lee, & Guthrie, 1986; Cole & Griffin, 1986; Oakes, 1987; Rohwer, 1980). At the same time, concern for the lack of "higher-order" and "critical thinking" abilities among at-risk pupils is a national concern (Adams, 1986). Our work has, like others, indicated that comprehension is not often the focus of the literacy lessons of low-achievement children and that reading or writing of extended texts rarely appears as academic work in the lessons of these learners (Walmsley & Walp, 1990).

In our earliest work, the importance of silent, comprehension-focused, extended text reading was emphasized (Allington, 1977, 1980, 1984). As we initiated our whole school day observations (Allington et al., 1986; Johnston et al., 1985), the issue of congruence of curricula between classroom and instructional support programs emerged. We argued that the common situation we encountered— low-achievement learners working in two different, and often philo-sophically incompatible, literacy curricula in the two settings—could not be supported with any existing theory or model of effective teaching. Remedial and special education clients were more likely to have cognitive confusion fostered (as opposed to cognitive clarity) as a result of this "planned fragmentation" of the curriculum (Allington et al., 1990).

We have begun to address the issue of curricular coherence (rather than congruence) across the literacy lessons in the regular education program, as well as the coherence in the lessons experi-enced in the regular and support programs (Allington et al., 1990). This coherence is not a new idea; a half-century ago it was called an "integrated language arts" approach and more recently proponents of the "whole language" philosophies have raised similar issues anew. Basically, coherence can be viewed as planned arrays of literacy lessons that offer interrelated academic tasks, with the whole language position emphasizing the primacy of experiences with extended texts for both reading and writing instruction.

Currently, the common classroom literacy curriculum offers planned fragmentation. The curricular materials (which typically represent the intended curricula) for reading, spelling, language arts, phonics, handwriting, and so on present no interrelated conceptual-ization or instruction. In a typical school day learners work in a basal reading series with brief text reading accompanied by several skill worktexts. The academic work in these latter materials occupies larger proportions of the reading instructional experience than the time spent reading the stories in the reader. Much has been written about the incoherence inherent in basal reader materials (e.g., Anderson, Brubaker, Alleman-Brooks, & Duffy, 1985; Beck, McKeown, Omanson, & Pople, 1984; Osborn, 1984)—lessons that often are not composed of interrelated activities. Less has been written about the incoherence of the array of literacy lessons across several literacy curricula found in most classrooms. As we have examined the literacy lessons of the regular education program, the fragmentation of literacy lessons is obvious. Word-level tasks, for instance, are found in reading, spelling, phonics, and language arts materials, but only by chance is there any relationship between these activities across a school day. When one examines the additional curricular materials and academic tasks presented low-achievement learners in remedial and special education during that same instructional day, the fragmentation is simply enhanced.

We suppose that this fragmentation is not purposely designed to make literacy learning difficult. However, we also suppose that such is the ultimate effect. Unfortunately, there exists slim empirical evidence for such a conclusion, although the revisions in several state curricula (e.g., California and New York) suggest that the logic of coherent curricular approaches must be compelling. We do know that when classroom and specialist teachers emphasize the same literacy skills in their instruction, learner attainment of mastery of those skills is enhanced (e.g., Winfield, 1986) and we have evidence in New York state that when classroom and remedial programs emphasize congruent skills and strategies, achievement improves (Bove, 1988). However, such coordination occurs only when it is part of a plan (as opposed to spontaneously or by chance) and the collaboration necessary is not easily achieved (especially when incoherent curricula are mandated) in schools (Allington & McGill-Franzen, 1989b).

Our "plain vanilla" model of effective literacy instruction is now becoming a "hot fudge sundae" model. We earlier emphasized allocations of instructional time and engagement in teacher-directed silent reading of connected text, particularly. Currently we are attempting to address the effects of coherent curricular plans for literacy instruction—plans that result in instruction that emphasizes text comprehension and composition, especially extended texts (e.g., trade books, stories, articles, etc.). We would focus on the "coherent blocks" of instruction noted earlier and on the relationship between the academic tasks that occupy children during these blocks. It is our yet unexamined hypothesis that at-risk children will benefit substantially from planned sets of instructional activities that foster awareness of the interrelationships across various literacy tasks (Walmsley & Walp, 1990). In other words, we argue that at-risk children have the least tolerance for the fragmentation that currently dominates the literacy instruction across the school day.

Concerns about the lack of effectiveness of the various categorical programs, in part a result of the curricular fragmentation and interference between regular education and instructional support programs (Allington & Johnston, 1989), have led to a variety of proposals for the reformulation of the current plethora of federal and state-funded efforts to enhance the academic achievement of at-risk learners. The regular education initiative (Wang, Reynolds, & Walberg, 1988; Gartner & Lipsky, 1987) proposes a merger of regular, remedial, and special education (for the two-thirds who are mildly handicapped) into a coherent system of instructional support. The pilot "unified" support programs (Jenkins, Pious, & Peterson, 1989) in Washington state treat all academic difficulties through a unified system, combining regular, remedial, special, and migrant education support efforts into a single comprehensive effort. The New York "congruence" model for state-funded remedial and Chapter 1 programs, the California School-Based Program Coordination Act, and revisions in guidelines for the Chapter 1 Schoolwide Projects all evidence policymakers' interest in moderating, if not eliminating, the fragmentation and segregation inherent in categorical programs today. We would go a step further, beyond "procedural" coordination to "instructional" and "philosophical" coordination within a school district (Idol, West, & Lloyd, 1988; Walp & Walmsley, 1989).

Such efforts would result in intended curricula that were philosophically compatible. This would result in an instructional staff that adhered to a common "point of view" about literacy learning. Philosophical and instructional coherence should result in an instructional plan that is also coherent across schools within a district, across classrooms and settings in a school (grade two, Chapter 1, resource room, bilingual, etc.), and across a school career. This may be too much to ask of our schools, especially in the near term. On the other hand, schools today vary in their proximity from this "ivory tower" standard. Some schools have different and incompatible mandated curricula for regular, remedial, special, and bilingual education literacy efforts. Others offer far less fragmentation and interference.

Some schools have segregated staffs for regular, remedial, special, and bilingual education. Others offer far more integrated efforts. If Moore and his colleagues are correct (1981), and our experience suggests they are, such differences reflect different plans developed in central administrative offices, rather than differences in schools, per se.

A final concern with instructional tasks involves the long-standing notion of "individualization" of instruction. Individualization has long held a position of primacy in discussions of interventions with low-achievement learners, regardless of category. On the other hand, few reliable effects for individualization have been reported in school-based research (e.g., Leinhardt, Zigmond, & Cooley, 1981). In a recent careful curriculum analysis, McGill-Franzen and Allington (1990) examined what "individualization" might mean for remedial and special education students. They concluded that individualization often meant working alone on low-level skills tasks. What it did not mean was individually appropriate instructional interactions or tasks. They characterized the remedial and resource room instruction as "routinized" (much like classroom instruction), wherein the learners had to adapt to another teacher's routine. Little evidence was found of differentiation of support instructional tasks by difficulty, task focus, or classroom curricula. What they found was children in support programs spending much time working alone (an odd form of individualization for the least able pupil).

In working through this issue we have puzzled over which features of academic tasks one should attend to when making judgments of "appropriateness." We have not found much guidance in earlier research efforts. It does seem that issues of task difficulty, curricular coherence, task quality, and so on need consideration. So too we would argue for individual instructional interactions between the teacher and the learner. We do know that some individualized programs do promote literacy acquisition (e.g., Boehnlein, 1987; Clay, 1983; Lyons, 1987), but we are unsure of the contribution of the one-to-one teacher/student ratio (as opposed to other factors).

Fraatz (1987) notes the "paradox of collective instruction"—that we teach each child similarly to ensure equity, but must teach each differently to assure individualization. She points out that individualization must differentiate between issues such as differences (more/less, preferred, etc.) in time allocated to different students, differences in instructional interactions, differences in curricula, differences in social interactions, and the like. At what point does "individualization" become discrimination (Lightfoot, 1973)? Much of what is done to low-achievement children in schools is done in the name of "individual needs," but less of this addresses an individual child's needs than we might expect. To address the issue of effective instruction we must sort out appropriate individual instructional differentiation from the wealth of instructional differences that emerge across a school day.

INSTRUCTIONAL INTERACTIONS

In our "plain vanilla" model we attempted a broad dichotomization of teacher instructional focus on "word and accuracy" versus "text and comprehension." We attempted to record, in our fieldnotes, instances of "strategic explanation" (Duffy, Roehler, & Rackliffe, 1986b) as opposed to simple procedural directions or assignment of tasks without instruction. It became clear that a word- and sentence-level focus dominated tasks for at-risk children and that explicit teaching was a rare occurrence (Allington et al., 1986; Allington & McGill-Franzen, 1989a). At-risk children spent the vast majority of their school day working alone on low-level tasks such that it seemed that their teachers believed that completing the materials would resolve the difficulty (and that they could complete these tasks without instruction).

However, our attempts at capturing important features of instructional interactions were not particularly satisfying. When we had audiotape (or video) recordings of the instructional session paired with the fieldnotes, observational data, and copies of the curricular materials in use, we could better address the issues of concern. But even here we were often left with no good idea of teachers' intentions or rationales for their behaviors. Shake (1984) used videotapes of instructional sessions as a stimulated recall procedure in an attempt to tap the intentionality of various instructional moves. But linking these data to other information gathered across observational sessions is difficult, indeed. We have been interested in this because we are convinced by the work of Duffy and his colleagues (1986a & b) that what teachers explain (and how successfully) is critical to the learning of at-risk learners. These children seem less likely than other children to incidentally acquire the knowledges, conventions, and strategies of fluent reading and writing.

This issue is under some substantial current reconsideration as a result of two lines of argument, which pull in opposite directions, it seems. On the one hand we have the current press for "whole language" programs and "process" approaches to writing (e.g., Altwerger, Edelsky & Flores, 1987; Cambourne & Turbill, 1987; Smith, 1981). Proponents of these positions have much to offer those interested in effective education of at-risk children. They are undoubtedly correct in the assertion that the current fragmentation and the lack of authentic literacy experiences work against the best interests of these children. On the other hand, proponents of the view have been criticized (Delpit, 1986, 1988) for what critics see as a too casual approach to teaching. Delpit makes the argument along social-class and ethnic-group lines—arguing that such approaches can work successfully with children from families of the "culture of power" (basically white middle-class children), but that these approaches are not successful with children outside that cultural group.

We are troubled unexpectedly, for we had, by and large, rejected previous process-product findings that suggested different teaching strategies were more effective with at-risk populations (Johnston et al., 1985; Allington & Johnston, 1989). We had rejected these findings because they were relatively rare, not particularly powerful (or reliable), and fit no good theory of either learning or instruction. More recently, though, reports of differences (among Native American populations primarily) in effective instructional methods with differing cultural groups have been appearing with some regularity (e.g., Au & Jordan, 1981; Au & Mason, 1981; Michaels & Collins, 1984; Phillips, 1983; Barnhardt, 1982; Cazden, 1988) and now Delpit (1988) argues so persuasively. Her voice seems supported, at least in part, by Comer (1988), who argues that previous efforts in the design of "effective" schools for the disadvantaged concentrated too exclusively on curriculum and instruction and not enough on "cultural incongruities." Cummins (1986) also notes the disabling effects of repetitive social interactions during instructional sessions, but discusses the disabling characteristics of the current structured and fragmented learning experiences. His position is that the current focus on curriculum and instruction deflects attention from more fundamental concerns about educational interventions.

Our "plain vanilla" model is obviously unable to address such issues. We are, however, convinced that explicit explanation is necessary, that enormous learner involvement in reading and writing of extended texts with a focus on meaning making is critical, that coherence across instructional tasks and settings facilitates and eases the acquisition of literacy. We are also convinced that the communicative interactions that occur during the school day between teachers and children, and between children, are powerful determinants of the effective schooling.

These issues need serious attention in any study of effective schools, particularly effective schools for the children of poverty and children of color. Traditional process-product instrumentation seems insufficient to the task, as have our more naturalistic attempts. Careful analysis of dialogue, teacher and student cognition, motive, responsibility, independence, choice, and other aspects of teaching and learning need to be addressed. Operationalization and instrumentation must not be biased toward locating a restricted set of teacher or student behaviors presumed related to effective instruction (Gage & Needels, 1989). For instance, drawing a picture could be considered an off-task behavior during reading or writing time, but the activity could also be "scaffolding" (McGill-Franzen & Allington, 1990) for reading or writing, or demonstration of comprehension after reading. Likewise, silent reading of a book can be considered seatwork, independent practice, or a literary experience. Does it matter whether the book is assigned or self-selected? Does it matter whether there is a standard assignment sheet to complete after each chapter? Does it matter whether writing or vocabulary activities later in the day are related to this text? Does it matter whether the reader presents the book to her teacher, or to her classmates? Does it matter whether the teacher and child explore "wonderful ideas" from the book (Duckworth, 1987)? Does minority status, poverty status, or low-achievement status have some added importance in such situations?

UNDERSTANDING EFFECTIVE PROGRAMS

Given the common findings concerning educational programs for at-risk learners, we have been interested in developing a better understanding of how such programs came to exist (and, conversely, why good people so often create ineffective programs). Ron Edmonds' work provided some basic insights, as did the work of Don Moore and his colleagues (Edmonds, 1979; Moore, Hyde, Blair, & Weitzman,

1981). Edmonds provided information on school-level issues, while Moore's work addressed district-level issues. These works and others (Levine & Leibert, 1987; Ligon & Doss, 1982; Vanecko, Ames, & Archambault, 1980) helped us understand the opportunities and constraints that operate on those who work in schools.

However, my candidate for the most influential factor is, very simply, district commitment to the effective education of all children—the poor, the handicapped, the minority, those different from the mainstream. We have discussed various potential measures (e.g., local funds spent on remedial or special education compared to local funds spent on football teams or advanced placement classes or new office furniture, etc.), but have found none fully satisfactory. Yet, too often we left a school district with the distinct feeling that local commitment extended only as far as applying for external funding for categorical programs. We found districts that had seemingly learned to optimize fiscal returns through excessive labeling, cross-subsidy, and triple- or quadruple-dipping into various external education pots for individual children. In these districts, though, children who earned money from multiple sources were typicallly served by only one (and often excluded from regular education instruction) and even then they were provided the minimum service required, not the services needed to resolve the difficulty.

To advance effective instructional practices for at-risk children we must do more than describe the features of the classroom and the curriculum. We must describe how those effective programs evolved and how they are maintained. We do know that significant and enduring change is difficult in schools. We know that offering simple platitudes is insufficient. A model for investigating effective academic instruction must include multiple components that attempt to tease out the "hows" of implementation and sustenance.

For instance, McGill-Franzen (1987) notes the effects of fiscal incentives or disincentives in state regulations on the distribution of enrollments in various categorical programs—especially intriguing is the apparent shift of 1.5 million children from Chapter 1 to the learning disabled special education category. We observed districts where 20 percent or more of the population was identified as handicapped and comparable districts where fewer than 5 percent were so identified. We studied districts where the Chapter 1 clients all had scores above the fortieth percentile and others where the same program served only children who fell below the twenty-third percentile.

We have observed learning-disabled populations with reading achievement equal to or better than the district Chapter 1 student achievement and others where these two populations differed more substantially. Like Kimbrough and Hill (1981), we observed cross-subsidization, but usually the subsidy went from externally funded programs to locally funded programs. On the other hand, we worked in a district that literally doubled the federal and state funds available with local contributions to support remedial and special education programs.

Local commitment is observable in other ways as well, but we found it perhaps most obvious in the interviews with local administrators and teachers. Edmonds wrote of "high expectations"; we have found it useful to examine attributions for success or failure of students. Winfield's (1987) study of urban teachers is instructive here. She found attribution varied on two dimensions: possibility and accountability. Her teachers reported that either (1) these children could be expected to learn to read or not or (2) it was or was not her responsibility to teach these children to read. Not surprisingly, those teachers who believe in and accept responsibility for children's learning are more likely to teach, and teach well. In one of our schools, for instance, two-thirds of the classroom teachers reported that the "primary responsibility for reading instruction" of Chapter 1 students was assigned to the Chapter 1 pullout teachers (these Chapter 1 teachers assigned responsibility to the classroom teachers, though). Likewise, 90 percent of the classroom teachers felt that the special education teacher had primary responsibility for the reading instruction of learning disabled mainstreamed children. These children routinely received less instruction and qualitatively inferior instruction compared to their peers. The teachers attributed the learning failure to family or child deficits even in the face of the evidence on instructional quantity and quality.

When a building principal disavowed responsibility for (and/or knowledge of) the Chapter 1 and special education instruction ("You'll have to ask Bill about that, that's his ballpark, not mine"), we usually found a segregated support program and a regular education staff less than wholly committed to resolving the learning failures of at-risk children. When district and building administrators attributed learning difficulties to parents, homes, or deficits in children (attention problems), we have found a similar response from the teachers. When district administrators responsible for the various instructional programs (regular education, Chapter 1, special education, bilingual) have little shared knowledge about the programs they each lead, principals and teachers typically reflect this situation in their admitted ignorance ("I don't really have any idea of what they do in that program").

The importance of discovering the district plan or plans is best demonstrated by our assertion that most teachers we observed were simply following the district plan (Allington & McGill-Franzen, 1989a). That is, when the district plan produced four separate and incompatible commercial reading/language arts materials, most teachers offered an incoherent array of instructional tasks drawn from these materials. When the district plan mandated a different and incompatible curricular approach to reading in remedial or special education, teachers followed that mandate. When districts attempted to maximize external funding, teachers referred many children for inclusion in special programs. On the other hand, when district plans called for coherent and collaborative approaches to remedial and special education, teachers offered the same. When districts included literature in their reading curiculum and made appropriate materials available, teachers used them. When books were unavailable, but workbooks and xerox machines were available, teachers filled up the day with low-level paper/pencil tasks.

This latter issue may deserve expansion. We have proposed an "accessibility" hypothesis to account for much of the teacher curricular choices we have observed (Jachym, Allington, & Broikou, 1989). In this analysis we had district personnel estimate seatwork costs for reading/language arts materials. We aggregated costs of workbooks, spelling books, phonics books (whatever commercial seatwork material was purchased), and also the costs involved in reproducing seatwork materials (copying equipment and supplies, maintenance contracts, personnel costs in duplicating, etc.). The variation between districts was substantial, as was the average cost per student ($38 to $105 per child, with an average of $53.50). However, school administrators typically estimated $8–$12 per student! The district with the highest concentration of poor children spent the most, even though we were continually told how little money was available to support instruction (the expenditure was approximately three times that of the two smallest expenditure districts).

When district plans, intended or accidental, make resources accessible to support certain activities, one should not be surprised to see those activities. The point here is one that Barr and Dreeben (1984) have addressed far more elegantly—that decisions made at other levels do have enormous potential for constraining the actions of teachers. Our point is even more direct—most teachers we have observed spend their days doing exactly what they believe those in charge want them to do. Good plan or bad—teachers follow the plan (or, in the absence of any agreed-upon plan, they invent their own—a more common case for remedial and special education teachers).

Another aspect of district plans is the use of various moves to keep achievement standards artificially high. For instance, one district used combinations of exclusion from kindergarten, retention in grade, and transition room or special education placement in such a way that only about one-third of the children finished grade three on schedule (the others were given the "gift of time"). Grade three is where the first state competency testing begins. In the district mentioned earlier with an excess of 20 percent of the students classified as handicapped, only the higher-achieving 80 percent of the students reported scores on the state exams (the handicapped student scores do not have to be included in the district report). In both these cases the "average" achievement levels reported were blatantly manipulated to make the schools look more effective. These are obviously more subtle methods than providing students with the answers and probably just as successful in achieving the intended goal—a better aggregate score reported to the community.

Thus one must be concerned about how "effective" schools and teachers are identified. Are schools, or teachers, that retain large numbers of children more effective than those who retain none? One might expect the former to present better average achievement levels by grade. Are schools or teachers who refer large numbers of children into special education more effective than those who identify few? Again, the former will present better "gains" for the regular education program. Are schools with higher test scores but lower parental satisfaction ratings more effective than schools with a different pattern? Are schools with higher achievement test scores but with few students who voluntarily engage in book reading more effective than schools that exhibit lower test scores but substantially higher levels of voluntary reading? Are standardized tests acceptable substitutes for wholistic evaluations of reading and writing abilities?

CONCLUSIONS

Previous efforts to capture the attributes of "effective" instruction have been narrowly cast and, ultimately, provided narrow answers. Effectiveness must be cast more broadly than group achievement test scores, although obviously these will play some role. However, whatever the role, one must examine what part of the expected school population is included in the tested pool ("expected" meaning age group cohorts including those left back, sent out, classified, etc.). Beyond standardized testing, I would argue that voluntary reading data, wholistic assessments of real reading and writing, surveys of parental satisfaction, and an analysis of the progress of all individuals toward academic goals are necessary data to be considered.

Earlier efforts also cast instruction narrowly and largely ignored curriculum. I have proposed a number of aspects of instruction that have been previously underemphasized and have suggested that instruction seems intricately linked to the curriculum of choice (or mandate). We have proposed an "accessibility" hypothesis to account for much of the variation (or sameness) found between schools. Because "individualization" has played such a central role in discussion of effective instruction for low-achievement learners (even though a small empirical base exists), clear criteria for describing instruction must be developed. A central problem will be that of defining "appropriateness" of instructional activities outside of an analysis of teacher intention.

The nature of the academic work that children do must be described satisfactorily, as must the texts that they use (or create) in completing this work. The interrelationship of the tasks across a school day (or week) must be considered, especially given concern for curricular coherence. Langer and Applebee (1987) suggest that reading shapes writing and vice versa, and that writing shapes learning from reading. In order to examine any of the several potential hypotheses about the nature of integrated literacy curricula, it will be necessary to produce far better descriptions.

We must be concerned with how schools found to be effective emerged in the educational community and whether they can be sustained. Our work has suggested the centrality of district-level plans rather than school or classroom-level efforts, especially in the literacy learning experiences of children who participate in remedial and special education programs. While principals and teachers are obviously important players, these participants seem to follow district-level plans more often than they create unique school or individual plans (although one does see such principals and teachers). This position is similar to that expressed by Barr and Dreeben (1984) and Moore, Hyde, Blair, and Weitzman (1981) and points to the need to understand the influence of district-level constraints and opportunities on school and classroom behavior.

Finally, literacy learning activity of disadvantaged children is invariably nested in layers of federal and state constraints and opportunities. Different state education agencies will structure such constraints and opportunities differently and these variations must be documented along with the effect on local design (e.g., New York's Congruence Initiative, California's Reading/Language Arts Framework, Ohio's Statewide Reading Recovery Implementation).

REFERENCES

Adam, M. J. (1986). Teaching thinking to Chapter 1 students. In B. I. Williams, P. A. Richmond, & B. J. Mason (Eds.), *Designs for compensatory education: Conference proceedings and papers* (pp. IV-85 – IV-119). Washington, DC: Research and Evaluation Associates.

Allington, R. L. (1977). If they don't read much, how they ever gonna get good? *Journal of Reading, 21*, 57–61.

Allington, R. L. (1980). Teacher interruption during primary grade oral reading. *Journal of Education Psychology, 72*, 371–374.

Allington, R. L. (1983). The reading instruction provided readers of different reading abilities. *Elementary School Journal, 83*, 549–559.

Allington, R. L. (1984). Content coverage and contextual reading in reading groups. *Journal of Reading Behavior, 16*, 85–96.

Allington, R. L. (1986). Policy constraints and effective compensatory reading instruction: A review. In J. Hoffman (Ed.), *The effective teaching of reading: From research to practice*. Newark, DE: International Reading Association.

Allington, R. L., & Broikou, K. (1988). Shared knowledge: New roles for classroom and specialist teachers. *Reading Teacher, 41*, 806–811.

Allington, R. L., Gaskins, R. W., Broikou, K., Jachym, N., & King, S., (1990). Improving school literacy programs for at-risk learners through instructional coordination. *Journal of Educational and Psychological Consultation, I*, 123–156.

Allington, R. L., & Johnston, P. (1986). The coordination among regular classroom reading programs and targeted support programs. In B. I. Williams, P. A. Richmond, & B. J. Mason (Eds.), *Designs for compensatory education: Conference proceedings and papers*. Washington, DC: Research and Evaluation Associates.

Allington, R. L., & Johnston, P. (1989). Coordination, collaboration, and curricular coherence. In R. Slavin, N. Madden, & N. Karweit (Eds.), *Effective educational programs for at-risk children*. Boston: Allyn-Bacon.

Allington, R. L., & McGill-Franzen, A. (1989a). Different programs, indifferent instruction. In D. Lipsky & A. Gartner (Eds.), *Beyond separate education*. Baltimore: Brookes.

Allington, R. L., & McGill-Franzen, A. (1989b, May). School response to reading failure: Chapter 1 and special education students in grades 2, 4, and 8. *Elementary School Journal, 89,* 529–542.

Allington, R. L., Stuetzel, H., Shake, M. C., & Lamarche, S. (1986). What is remedial reading? A descriptive study. *Reading Research and Instruction, 26,* 15–30.

Altwerger, B., Edelsky, C., & Flores, B. (1987). Whole language: What's new? *Reading Teacher, 41,* 144–154.

Anderson, L. M., Brubaker, N. L., Alleman-Brooks, J., & Duffy, G. G. (1985). A qualitative study of seatwork in first-grade classrooms. *Elementary School Journal, 86,* 123–140.

Anderson, R. C., Wilson, P., & Fielding, L. (1988). Growth in reading and how children spend their time outside of school. *Reading Research Quarterly, 23*(3), 285–303.

Au, K. H., & Jordan, C. (1981). Teaching reading to Hawaiian children: Finding a culturally appropriate solution. In H. T. Trueba, G. P. Guthrie, & K. Au (Eds.), *Culture and the bilingual classroom: Studies in classroom ethnography* (pp. 139–152). Rowley, MA: Newbury House.

Au, K., & Mason, J. (1981). Social organization factors in learning to read: The balance of rights hypothesis. *Reading Research Quarterly, 17,* 115–152.

Barnhardt, C. (1982). Tuning-in: Athabaskan teachers and Athabaskan students. In R. Barnhardt (Ed.), *Cross-cultural issues in Alaskan education* (Vol. 2, pp. 144–166). Fairbanks: University of Alaska, Center for Cross-cultural Studies.

Barr, R., & Dreeben, R. (1984). *How schools work*. Chicago: University of Chicago.

Beck, I., McKeown, M., Omanson, R., & Pople, M. (1984). Improving the comprehensibility of stories: The effects of revision that improve coherence. *Reading Research Quarterly, 19,* 263–277.

Birman, B. F. (1988). Chapter 1: How to improve a successful program. *American Educator, 12,* 36–42.

Birman, B. F., Orland, M. E., Jung, R. K., Anson, R. J., Garcia, G. N., Moore, M. T., Funkhouser, J. E., Morrison, D. R., Turnbull, B. J., & Reiser, E. R. (1987). *The current operation of the Chapter 1 program: Final report from the National Assessment of Chapter 1*. Washington, DC: U.S. Government Printing Office.

Boehnlein, M. (1987). Reading intervention for high-risk first graders. *Educational Leadership, 44,* 32–37.

Bove, R. (1988). Personal communication.

Broikou, K. B., Allington, R. L., & Jachym, N. (1989). The impact of the Felton decision in one archdiocese. *Remedial and Special Education, 10,* 29–34.

Cambourne, B., & Turbill, J. (1987). *Coping with chaos*. Portsmouth, NH: Heinemann.

Carroll, J. (1963). A model for school learning. *Teachers College Record, 64,* 723–733.

Cazden, C. (1988). *Classroom discourse: The language of teaching and learning*. Portsmouth, NH: Heinemann.

Clay, M. (1983). *The early detection of reading difficulties.* Exeter, NH: Heinemann.

Cole, M., & Griffin, P. (1986). A sociohistorical approach to remediation. In S. deCastell, A. Luke, & K. Egan (Eds.), *Literacy, society and schooling: A reader,* pp. 110–131. New York: Cambridge University Press.

Comer, J. (1988). Educating poor minority children. *Scientific American, 259,* 42–48.

Cummins, J. (1986). Empowering minority students: A framework for intervention. *Harvard Educational Review, 56*(1), 18–36.

Delpit, L. D. (1986). Skills and other dilemmas of a progressive black educator. *Harvard Educational Review, 56*(4), 379–385.

Delpit, L. D. (1988). The silenced dialogue: Power and pedagogy in educating other people's children. *Harvard Educational Review, 58*(3), 280–298.

Denham, C., & Lieberman, A. (1980). *Time to learn* (No. 1980-695-717). Washington, DC: U.S. Government Printing Office.

Doyle, W. (1984). How order is achieved in classrooms. *Journal of Curriculum Studies, 16*(3), 259–277.

Doyle, W. (1986). Vision and reality: A reaction to issues in curriculum and instruction for compensatory education. In B. I. Williams, P. A. Richmond, & B. J. Mason (Eds.), *Designs for compensatory education: Conference proceedings and papers.* Washington, DC: Reseach and Evaluation Associates.

Duckworth, E. (1987). *The having of wonderful ideas.* New York: Teachers College Press.

Duffy, G. G., Roehler, L. R., Meloth, M. S., & Varrus, L. G. (1986). Conceptualizing instructional explanation. *Teaching and Teacher Education, 2,* 197–214.

Duffy, G. G., Roehler, L. R., & Rackliffe, G. (1986). How teachers' instructional talk influences students' understanding of lesson content. *Elementary School Journal, 87,* 4–16.

Edmonds, R. (1979). Some schools work and more can. *Social Policy, 37,* 28–32.

Fraatz, J. M. B. (1987). *The politics of reading: Power, opportunity, and prospect for change in America's public schools.* New York: Teachers College Press.

Gage, N. L. & Needels, M. (1989). Process-product research on teaching: A review of criticisms. *Elementary School Journal, 89,* 253–300.

Gambrell, L., Wilson, R., & Gannt, J. (1981). Classroom observation of task attending behaviors of good and poor readers. *Journal of Educational Research, 74,* 400–404.

Gartner, A., & Lipsky, D. (1987). Beyond special education: Towards a quality system for all students. *Harvard Educational Review, 57*(4), 367–395.

Haynes, M. C., & Jenkins, J. R. (1986). Reading instruction in special education resource rooms. *American Educational Research Journal, 23,* 161–190.

Idol, L., West, J. W., & Lloyd, S. R. (1988). Organizing and implementing specialized reading programs: A collaborative approach involving classroom, remedial, and special education teachers. *Remedial and Special Education, 9,* 54–61.

Jachym, N., Allington, R. L., & Broikou, K. (1989). Estimating the cost of seatwork. *Reading Teacher, 43*(1), 30–35.

Jenkins, J., Pious, C., & Peterson, D. (1989). Categorical programs for remedial and handicapped students: Issues of validity. *Exceptional Children, 55,* 147–148.

Johnston, P. H., Allington, R. L., & Afflerbach, P. (1985). The congruence of classroom and remedial reading instruction. *Elementary School Journal, 85,* 465–478.

Kiesling, H. (1978). Productivity of instructional time by mode of instruction for students at varying levels of reading skill. *Reading Research Quarterly, 13*, 554–582.

Kimbrough, J., & Hill, P. T. (1981). *The aggregate effects of federal education programs.* Santa Monica, CA: Rand.

Langer, J. A., & Applebee, A. N. (1987). *How writing shapes thinking: A study of teaching and learning.* Urbana, IL: National Council of Teachers of English.

Leinhardt, G., Zigmond, N., & Cooley, W. (1981). Reading instruction and its effects. *American Educational Research Journal, 18*, 343–361.

Levine, D. U., & Leibert, R. E. (1987). Improving school improvement plans. *Elementary School Journal, 87*, 397–412.

Lightfoot, S. L. (1973). Politics and reasoning: Through the eyes of teachers and children. *Harvard Educational Review, 43*, 197–244.

Ligon, G. D., & Doss, D. A. (1982). *Some things we have learned from 6500 hours of classroom observations.* (Pub. no. 81.56). Austin, TX: Austin Independent School District, Office of Research and Evaluation.

Lyons, C. (1987, April). *Reading recovery: An effective intervention program for learning disabled first graders.* Paper presented at the annual meeting of the American Educational Research Association, Washington, DC.

Marx, R. W. & Walsh, J. (1988). Learning from academic tasks. *Elementary School Journal, 88*, 207–219.

McGill-Franzen, A. (1987). Failure to learn to read: Formulating a policy problem. *Reading Research Quarterly, 22*, 475–490.

McGill-Franzen, A., & Allington, R. L. (1990). Comprehension and coherence: Neglected elements of literacy instruction in remedial and resource room services. *Journal of Reading, Writing, and Learning Disabilities, 6*(2), 149–182.

Michaels, S., & Collins, J. (1984). Oral discourse styles: Classroom discourse and the acquisition of literacy. In D. Tannen (Ed.), *Coherence in spoken and written discourse.* Norwood, NJ: Ablex.

Moore, D. R., Hyde, A., Blair, K., & Weitzman, S. (1981). *Student classification and the right to read.* Chicago: Designs for Change.

Oakes, J. (1987). Tracking in secondary schools: A contextual perspective. *Educational Psychologist, 22*, 129–153.

Osborn, J. (1984). Workbooks that accompany basal reader programs. In G. Duffy, L. Roehler, & J. Mason (Eds.), *Comprehension instruction: Perspectives and suggestions.* New York: Longman.

Philips, S. (1983). *The invisible culture: Communication in classroom and community on the Warm Springs Indian Reservation.* New York: Longman.

Rohwer, W. D. (1980). How the smart get smarter. *Newsletter of the Laboratory of Comparative Human Cognition, 2*, 35–39.

Rowan, B., Guthrie, L. F., Lee, G. V., & Guthrie, G. P. (1986). *The design and implementation of Chapter 1 instructional services: A study of 24 schools.* San Francsico: Far West Laboratory for Educational Research and Development.

Shake, M. C. (1984). *Congruence between instructional philosophies and practices: A study of teacher thinking.* Dissertation completed at SUNY at Albany, NY.

Slavin, R. E. (1987). Making Chapter 1 make a difference. *Phi Delta Kappan, 69*(2), 110–119.

Smith, F. (1981). Demonstrations, engagement and sensitivity: The choice between people and programs. *Language Arts, 58*, 634–636.

Stanovich, K. (1986). Matthew effects in reading: Some consequences of individual differences in the acquisition of literacy. *Reading Research Quarterly, 21*, 360–407.

Thurlow, M. L., Ysseldyke, J. E., Graden, J., & Algozzine, R. (1984). Opportunity to learn for LD students receiving different levels of special education services. *Learning Disability Quarterly, 7*, 55–67.

Vanecko, J. J., Ames, N. L., with Archambault, F. X. (1980). *Who benefits from federal educational dollars?* Cambridge, MA: ABT Books.

Walmsley, S. A., & Walp, T. (1990). Integrating literature and composing into the language arts curriculum: Theory and practice. *Elementary School Journal, 90*(3), 251–274.

Walp, T., & Walmsley, S. A. (1989). Instructional and philosophical congruence: Neglected aspects of school reform. *Reading Teacher, 42*, 364–368.

Wang, M., Reynolds, M., & Walberg, H. (1988). Integrating the children of the second system. *Phi Delta Kappan, 70*(3), 248–251.

Wiley, D. E., & Harnischfeger, A. (1974). Explosion of a myth: Quantity of schooling and exposure to instruction, major educational vehicles. *Educational Researcher, 3*, 7–12.

Will, M. (1986). *Educating students with learning problems: A shared responsibility*. Washington, DC: OSERS, U.S. Department of Education.

Winfield, L. (1986). Teacher beliefs toward academically at-risk inner-urban children. *Urban Review, 18*, 253–268.

Winfield, L. (1987). Teachers' estimates of test content covered in class on first grade reading achievement. *Elementary School Journal, 87*, 437–454.

Ysseldyke, J. E., Thurlow, M. L., Mecklenburg, C., & Graden, J. (1984). Opportunity to learn for regular and special education students during reading instruction. *Remedial and Special Education, 5*, 29–37.

Zigmond, N., Vallecorsa, A., & Leinhardt, G. (1980). Reading instruction for students with learning disabilities. *Topics in Language Disorders, 1*, 89–98.

2

Modifying Reading Instruction to Maximize Its Effectiveness for All Students

Georgia Earnest Garcia and P. David Pearson

We think that reading instruction for all children—including those who have been labeled "at-risk" or "disadvantaged"—should be designed to facilitate the development of comprehension strategies. While we do not want to underestimate the importance of acquiring decoding skills as a part of a repertoire of reading strategies, we do want to make clear our dissatisfaction with stage models of reading (where students first learn to decode and then learn to comprehend), and our commitment to a focus on comprehension from the outset of

This chapter evolved out of an earlier paper commissioned by SRI International's Committee on Curriculum and Instruction for its Study of Academic Instruction for Disadvantaged Students. We want to thank Richard Allington, Jan Dole, Russell Gersten, Robert Jimenez, Steven Stahl, and an anonymous reviewer at the Center for the Study of Reading for their comments and suggestions.

31

schooling. We think that it is important for all students to understand that the main purpose of reading is to construct meaning. Data from the National Assessment of Educational Progress (Applebee, Langer, & Mullis, 1987) suggest that we have done a fairly good job of teaching children how to decode text. In fact, most children and young adults who participated in the assessment were able to decode and comprehend simple text. On the other hand, only small percentages of them were able to reason about what they read and wrote. Even more alarming was the finding that black and Hispanic children performed considerably poorer than their Anglo counterparts as early as fourth grade (Applebee et al.), a time when most children are expected to begin learning from text (Chall, 1983). It is with these findings in mind, along with our knowledge about the current instructional situation and current view of reading, that we recommend that all children—regardless of their level of skills mastery, dialect, or first language—receive reading instruction that will foster and promote the development of comprehension strategies.

In this chapter, we briefly describe the type of reading instruction that all too frequently is provided to low-achieving students in American schools. We discuss why a comprehension focus—more specifically a focus on the development of comprehension strategies—is important and how it is different from much currently available instruction. Then we suggest strategies that need to be developed and, in the search for an appropriate instructional model, review four delivery models: direct instruction, explicit instruction, cognitive apprenticeships, and whole language. Finally, based on this review, we delineate a new instructional model that we think will help to promote comprehension strategies. Within this framework, we identify issues that are especially relevant to the teaching and learning of children who frequently have been labeled "at-risk" or "disadvantaged."

THE CURRENT SITUATION

Classroom research has documented the influence of basal reading programs on elementary reading instruction (Durkin, 1978–79; Fisher, Berliner, Filby, Marliave, Cohen, Dishaw, & Moore, 1978;

Hatch & Bondy, 1984; Mason & Osborn, 1982). A common characteristic of most basal programs is that they attempt to reduce the complexity of learning to read by decomposing the "process" into a series of discrete and isolated skills. Although children may become proficient at performing these discrete tasks, they may not become proficient readers. In fact, one reason that children without extensive exposure to print prior to formal schooling may fail at reading is that the instructional focus on discrete tasks does not foster an understanding of what reading is all about (see Teale & Sulzby, 1986).

Current theoretical views of reading comprehension do not support a discrete skills perspective. The discrete skills assumptions of current basal programs hearken back to theoretical positions characteristic of the task analytic (see Gagne, 1965) and mastery learning (see Bloom, 1968; Carroll, 1963) traditions of the 1960s (see Pearson & Raphael, in press, or Pearson, Dole, Duffy, & Roehler, in press, for discussions of this movement). Even though the most recent entries into the basal market differ substantially from their predecessors, vestiges of the task analytic and mastery learning traditions are still seen in the pretests and posttests that dictate when an individual student is to study a particular skill, receive more practice, or move on to another skill or set of skills.

In such systems some students, particularly low achievers, never reach the skills at the higher end of the continuum because their teachers continue to have them work on unmastered "basic" skills at the lower end. Or, as Stanovich's (1986) "Matthew" effect has been colloquially interpreted, "them that has, gits." Dreeben's (1987) research, in particular, has revealed that the differential performance of black children as compared to white children frequently is determined by the amount of time spent on reading, the richness of the curricular material covered, and the appropriate matching of instruction to the ability level of the children.

It also is not uncommon for low-achieving students to receive reading instruction where the emphasis is on decoding at the expense of comprehension (Allington, 1983; Garcia, Jimenez, & Pearson, 1989). J. Collins (1982) documented this finding in a study in a first-grade integrated classroom in California and in a third-grade black classroom in Chicago. In both classrooms, children in the low groups received far less instruction and practice in reading comprehension than did those in the high groups. Moll, Estrada, Diaz, and Lopes (1980) discovered similar findings when they compared the reading instruction given to Spanish-English bilingual children in both Spanish and English. However, in this case, even children who were in the high and middle Spanish reading groups did not receive much comprehension instruction in their English reading classes. Instead, their English teachers emphasized decoding activities because they misinterpreted the children's nonnative English pronunciation as a symptom of decoding problems.

Many teachers tend to delay or de-emphasize comprehension instruction for language-minority children because they misinterpret the children's less-than-fluent oral reading of standard English as evidence that they are not ready to understand text. Despite strong warnings, based upon considerable sociolinguistic research, that they should not interpret a nonstandard dialect as a language deficit (Goodman, Watson, & Burke, 1987; Torrey, 1983; Troutman & Falk, 1982), some teachers still misinterpret black children's use of Black English Vernacular as evidence of a decoding problem (Burke, Pflaum, & Krafle, 1982; Cunningham, 1976–77).

Ironically, what little evidence we have about intervention programs for low-achieving primary-level first- and second-language readers demonstrates that increased access to a wide range of reading materials, in comparison to conventional programs, improves performance on both comprehension and decoding tasks (Elley & Mangubhai, 1983; Feitelson, & Goldstein, 1986). On the other hand, attempts to improve the comprehension of poor readers in the upper primary grades through extensive decoding training have had mixed results. Blanchard (1980) reported improved literal and inferential comprehension performance for a sample of sixth-grade poor readers as a consequence of pre-teaching them to read all the words that were in the experimental passages. However, in a study with fourth- and fifth-grade poor readers, Fleisher, Jenkins, and Pany (1979–80) found that while explicit decoding training improved the children's passage decoding, it did not improve their passage comprehension. A major limitation of these studies is that they involve teaching poor readers how to decode every new word that they encounter, a rather prohibitive task that contradicts our current knowledge about the generative nature of language acquisition and literacy. Such studies also do not present children with the type of exposure to print that they need to begin to understand the functions and features of written language and to move from cognitive confusion about written language to cognitive clarity (Downing, 1976, 1986).

THE COMPREHENSION FOCUS

Current views of reading, variously termed interactive, strategic, schema-theoretic, or social-cognitive, suggest that quality reading instruction for all children should focus on the development of comprehension strategies from the outset of schooling. Based on empirical research in cognitive psychology and the psychology of language, these views suggest that readers are involved in a recursive search for meaning.

Throughout this search, readers deploy their own knowledge in concert with perceptions from the text and context to create a dynamic interpretation. Each of these influences is multidimensional. Factors within the reader include knowledge of the topic, reading skills, and reasoning strategies. Factors within the text include remnants of the author's biases, goals, and intentions (see Winograd & Bridge, 1986), as well as structural characteristics, graphic characteristics, and adjunct aids. Factors within the context include the environment in which we read or learn to read; cultural values that reflect our ethnic, religious, and national identities; and specific purposes we develop for particular tasks.

Although contextual factors typically have not been highlighted as sources of influence in the reading process, findings from cross-cultural studies have indicated that beliefs affect not only how we determine levels of importance, but also how we group information into categories (Lipson, 1983; Reynolds, Taylor, Steffensen, Shirey, & Anderson, 1982; Steffensen, Joag-Dev, and Anderson, 1979). When subjects read text that is culturally familiar, they read it faster, remember more of it, and make fewer comprehension errors. Similarly, the purposes for which children read, how their interactions with text are shaped, and the settings in which they read are contextual factors that influence how they construct meaning (Bloome & Green, 1982; Cazden, 1985; Teale, 1986).

Expert as well as novice readers participate in this interactive process in which these three clusters of influence—reader, text, and context—converge to permit the construction of meaning. However, readers may operate at different levels of sophistication and may differ not only in the types of strategies they use but also in their awareness of what they are doing. In other words, all readers are predisposed to try to make sense of the texts we ask them to read, but some readers have better tools, can use the tools they have more adaptively and flexibly, and can apply those tools to more challenging texts.

COMPREHENSION STRATEGIES: BUILDING A CURRICULUM

The evidence available suggests that low achievers do not get the same access to comprehension instruction and activities that is afforded higher achievers. At the same time, we have argued that what is presented to any and all students in our current curricula is not as thoughtful or helpful as it could be. It's like saying that the apple is rotten to begin with, and, to make matters worse, certain students don't even get their share of that rotten apple. What should be our curriculum for low-achieving students, or, for that matter, for all students?

To answer this question, we have expanded upon a recent effort by Pearson, Dole, Duffy, and Roehler (in press). They present six interrelated strategies they think should comprise the scope of classroom reading comprehension instruction. Their claim is that these strategies are derived from studies that have tried to document the nature of "expert" reading. The logic that guided their search is that one way of determining curricular goals is to learn what it is that characterizes the successful performance of experts.

Their choice of the term *strategies* as opposed to *skills* is a deliberate one. In their discussion, they note that the term *skills* is too closely tied to the hierarchical sequencing of commercial reading programs and, therefore, is associated with the repeated practice of isolated activities with small units of text. The term strategy, on the other hand, connotes a flexible plan that is under the conscious control of the reader. Strategy is associated with the reasoning processes readers use to make sense of text. It includes a metacognitive emphasis and reflects the adaptive nature of the comprehending process.

The goal of strategy implementation is to "set in motion the learning processes which lead to expert performance" (Resnick, 1984, p. 443). Pearson and his colleagues eschew the notion of scope and sequence because this type of organization does not give everyone equal access to the strategies that are needed for "expert" comprehension. What changes over time is not the sequencing or type of strategy presented, but the facility with which the readers employ these strategies and the type and sophistication of content to which they apply them. Children's progress will vary, but if they are to learn how to construct meaning from text, they need to be exposed to instruction that facilitates the interrelated development of comprehension strategies.

Six Strategies

The first strategy is determining importance. This strategy is more than finding the main idea, but it surely includes attempts to find main ideas. In addition to reader-determined importance (see Williams, 1986a, 1986b; Tierney & Cunningham, 1984; and Winograd & Bridge, 1986), the reader needs to derive from the text what the author must have considered important in setting pen to paper in the first place. To do this, the expert reader relies on general world knowledge and domain-specific knowledge, text structure knowledge, and knowledge of author biases, intention, and goals (see Afflerbach, 1986; Resnick, 1984; Winograd & Bridge, 1986).

In the classroom, an emphasis on determining importance would require that a teacher focus on more than asking students to locate the main idea of a paragraph. The latter emphasis typically concentrates on text structure knowledge—how to use key words, phrases, graphics, summarizing statements, text organization, and other surface-level cues to determine what is important in the text. Teachers, as expert language users, should demonstrate the varied strategies and sources of information that they rely on to figure out what is important for them, as readers, to glean and remember from the text. Through a think-aloud procedure they might show students how they utilize general world knowledge, domain-specific knowledge, knowledge about the author's purposes, and text structure knowledge. This type of procedure moves students beyond a strictly "literal" interpretation of the text to one that requires them to think and reason about what they have read.

The second strategy is synthesizing information across large units of text to create summaries. This strategy is related to determining importance but goes beyond it in scope. The empirical work on summary training is quite encouraging. Working with students from middle school to college level, Brown and Day (1983; Brown, Day, & Jones, 1983) have successfully taught students to create text summaries by using five strategies: (a) deleting irrelevant information from a paragraph, (b) deleting redundant information from a paragraph, (c) creating a superordinate label for a list of things or actions, (d) locating topic sentences for paragraphs and knowing when it is appropriate to use them, and (e) creating topic sentences when none exist in order to "cover" a segment of the text.

While research has suggested that children's abilities to perform these summarizing operations may be developmentally linked (see Brown & Day, 1983), Palincsar and Brown (1984, 1986) have incorporated some of these operations into their successful reciprocal teaching approach with students who were accurate readers but poor comprehenders at the middle-school level. Their approach teaches students to apply four strategies to any text they read by (a) summarizing it, (b) asking a few questions that get at what is important in the text, (c) clarifying any parts of the text that prove difficult to understand, and (d) predicting what the author will talk about next. An important feature of their approach is that students are encouraged to share how they are constructing meaning from text. So, instead of just having the teacher as a model, the students begin to view each other as models.

Like so many other strategies that are intended to be highly adaptable, synthesizing may lend itself less to rules and decomposition and more to modeling and guided practice. Teachers can demonstrate how to synthesize by utilizing think-aloud demonstrations or by relying on the techniques like those used in reciprocal teaching.

The third strategy in the Pearson et al. scheme is drawing inferences. Even very young children can and do use their prior knowledge to make inferences about what they read (Kail, Chi, Ingram, & Danner, 1977). Instructional studies conducted by Pearson and his colleagues have demonstrated that children as young as second graders can benefit from teachers' guidance designed to improve their inferencing abilities (see Gordon & Pearson, 1983; Hansen, 1981; Hansen & Pearson, 1983; Pearson, 1985; and Raphael & Pearson, 1985).

In helping children to develop this strategy, teachers can begin by making them aware of many of the inferences they automatically make while reading. For instance, in the Kail et al. (1977) study, the children read sentences such as "Mary was playing in a game. She was hit by a bat." The children had no difficulty in drawing the inference that Mary was playing baseball even though the game of baseball is not mentioned in the sentences.

Teachers can also demonstrate how to use clues from the text along with background knowledge to answer different types of inferential questions. G.Garcia's (1988) research with second-language children enrolled in fifth- and sixth-grade classrooms indicated that these children primarily relied on a literal interpretation of the text to answer inferential questions. If children are to learn from what they read, then they need to know how to answer textually explicit and implicit questions as well as scriptally implicit questions, which require the children to integrate background knowledge with information in the text (see Johnston, 1984, and Pearson & Johnson, 1978). Raphael's work on question-answer relationships (Raphael & Pearson, 1985; Raphael & Wonnacott, 1985) suggests that children benefit from instruction helping them to adapt question-answering strategies to the demands of the questioning tasks they encounter.

The fourth comprehension strategy is asking questions. Not just teachers but students need to do this. Teacher-student discourse patterns in the American classroom consist primarily of teacher initiation–student response–teacher evaluation (TI-SR-TE) participant structures (see Mehan, 1979, and Cazden, 1988). Although this structure has dominated American classrooms for at least two decades (Guszak, 1967; Mehan, 1979; O'Flahavan, Hartman, & Pearson, 1989), it does not allow the children to monitor and control their own comprehension. Despite limited research on this topic, there is both theoretical (Craik & Lockhart, 1972) and empirical (Andre & Anderson, 1978–79) support for question generation as a student-controlled strategy. The work of Singer and Donlan (1982) and Wittrock (1983) provides direct examples of ways to involve students in question generation. Additionally, question generation is an integral part of both the reciprocal teaching (Palincsar & Brown, 1986) and question-answer relationship activities mentioned earlier (Raphael, 1982, 1984).

The fifth strategy in the Pearson et al. scheme is comprehension monitoring. Expert readers are more careful in their construction of meaning than are novice readers (for summaries of this work, see Baker & Brown, 1984, or Garner, 1987). Expert readers not only tend to know how well their reading is progressing but also alter their reading strategies to compensate for a problem once they realize one exists. Novice readers generally are less aware of the problems and are less able to compensate for them.

There is considerable evidence that all children can develop comprehension monitoring ability. Miscue research (see K. Goodman, 1968, 1976, 1978), in particular, has demonstrated that all readers, including novice readers, try to make sense of the text as they read aloud (see Y. Goodman, 1971 and Hudelson, 1981). Initial findings from the implementation of the Reading Recovery program also have demonstrated that with extensive tutoring, first-grade students in the bottom 10 percent of the achievement distribution can learn to monitor reading for meaning (see Boehnlein, 1987; Clay, 1987; and Columbus Public Schools, 1987).

Classroom teachers can help students develop comprehension-monitoring expertise. Young children should be encouraged to speak up when something does not make sense to them, whether they are listening to it or reading it. Older children need to understand why comprehension may go awry. By emphasizing how they, their teachers, and their classmates construct meaning from text, children enhance their metacognitive awareness and improve their own comprehension monitoring. To develop these competencies, teachers and students must go beyond correct answers given in a text or a workbook to discuss, in an environment of mutual respect, how different individuals arrived at different answers or interpretations.

We have included Pearson et al.'s notion of adapting resources as our sixth strategy. It is a logical successor to their fifth strategy, comprehension monitoring. Once a comprehension failure is detected, something can be done to repair it. There is considerable research supporting this kind of fix-up strategy. For example, expert readers tend to know when and how to study difficult text for longer times than do novice readers (see Masur, McIntyre, & Flavell, 1973, and Owings, Peterson, Bransford, Morris, & Stein, 1980). Expert readers also are more likely to look back at the text to resolve a problem than are novice readers (Alessi, Anderson, & Goetz, 1979; Garner, 1987). Finally, expert readers utilize a more varied repertoire of strategies to answer questions about the text than do novice readers (Raphael & Pearson, 1985).

Garner (1987), in particular, describes classic fix-up strategies that distinguish the expert from the novice reader. Students need to understand that there are times when the reader needs to speed up, slow down, look back, reread, skim, predict, generalize, or even resort to a dictionary. Somehow our instructional activities tend to breed a surface-processing attitude among students. Too many students are interested in getting through the text at the expense of understanding it.

Common Features

Central to all these strategies is the importance of activating students' prior knowledge, or schemata, and providing students with a comfortable context, or instructional environment, in which to develop these strategies. "Schemata" refers to the organizing frameworks within the mind that the reader uses to identify and integrate new information with previously learned information (Anderson, Spiro, & Anderson, 1978). The activation of this process is at the heart of comprehension and inherent in all of the strategies presented. Without the activation of prior knowledge, it would be difficult for readers to determine what is important in text, to draw inferences, or to monitor comprehension.

Expert readers are more adept at using their prior knowledge to help them make sense of text than are novice readers (among others, see Bransford, Stein & Vye, 1982; Gordon & Pearson, 1983; Hansen, 1981; Hansen & Pearson, 1983; Pearson, Hansen, & Gordon, 1979). On the other hand, there is some evidence that novice readers can be taught how to use and alter their prior knowledge, to improve their text comprehension (see Dole & Smith, 1987, and Roth, 1985). To learn how to use their knowledge to monitor and improve comprehension, all students, including those labeled "at-risk" or "disadvantaged," need to be given the opportunity to read both familiar and unfamiliar text. Content analyses of basal reading series suggest that these series, in and of themselves, do not contain enough material that reflects the cultural and background experiences of minority children (Butterfield, Demos, Grant, May, & Perez, 1979; Logan & Garcia, 1983). If these children are to become proficient readers, then they need to read text that allows them to integrate new knowledge with current knowledge.

One of the few comprehension-based instructional programs that has been developed specifically for language-minority children is that of the Kamehameha Early Education Program (KEEP) in Hawaii (Au, 1981; Au & Mason, 1981; Cazden, 1988; Tharp, 1982). KEEP is a reading program specifically designed for Hawaiian children of Polynesian descent. Based on current reading comprehension research, the program emphasizes students' discussion of what they already know about a topic before they read it; silent reading of the text to answer specific questions; and subsequent discussion that integrates the students' experiences with what they have read. In addition, the program recognizes that the social context in which the children learn to read also is important. Students are not constrained by the TI-SR-TE discourse pattern of interaction. Instead, they have been allowed to use a discourse pattern, termed "talk story," that approximates the type of verbal interaction to which they are more accustomed at home and in their speech community. Although educators interested in cultural differences have warned against overgeneralizing the success of individual programs and have pointed out the dangers of stereotyping (Cazden & Mehan, 1989), it does appear that awareness of cultural differences is important in the organization and development of literacy instruction. Nevertheless, the extent to which programs have been developed based on this awareness still is very limited and continues to be controversial. Heath's (1982) study of children from a black Southeastern community and Philips' (1983) study of Native-American children from the Warm Springs Indian Reservation demonstrated that these particular children also were accustomed to different participant structures than those used in the mainstream classroom. Similar to the KEEP findings (Au, 1981), Heath reported considerable success when teachers adapted classroom literacy instruction to the type of participant structures with which the particular children were more comfortable.

The curriculum proposed by Pearson et al. (in press) emphasizes strategies rather than skills, includes a clear metacognitive focus, entails prior knowledge activation and utilization throughout the strategies, and recognizes the influence that the classroom environment has on children's literacy development. Although this curriculum has not been tested in the classroom, we think that it is past time for it to be considered.

HELPING STUDENTS ACQUIRE EFFECTIVE STRATEGIES: THE QUESTION OF INSTRUCTION

Clearly, it is not enough to have a curriculum composed of excellent strategies; we also need a plan for helping students acquire those strategies (or, if you prefer, a plan for helping teachers teach those strategies). So we turn now to the issue of instruction: How shall we help students acquire the strategies they need in order to be active, strategic readers?

To review the instructional candidates available, we refer to a recent conceptualization by Pearson and Raphael (in press). Based upon a review of research and rhetoric, they identify four models as candidate delivery systems—direct instruction, explicit instruction, cognitive apprenticeships, and whole language. They view these four models as forming a continuum, where direct instruction is at the more curriculum-centered end, involving a high level of teacher control, and whole language is at the more child-centered end, involving a low level of teacher control. Discussion of these models has been marred by polemics; hence the inherent differences between them have been emphasized at the expense of any discussion of their similarities.

Direct Instruction

Gersten & Carnine (1986) have reviewed the comprehension research conducted within this paradigm. They present a host of skills and strategies that they feel are better learned in a direct instruction setting than in settings in which skills are merely practiced on their own by students, and errors are simply acknowledged by the teacher, a situation described and critiqued by Durkin (1978–79). Two underlying assumptions of direct instruction are that teachers need precise guidance in teaching reading comprehension and that principles of instructional design can be used to structure this type of instruction.

The basic position of direct instruction is that children seldom learn what we do not teach them directly. Left to their own devices—without benefit of step-by-step instruction, step mastery, guided practice, and extensive feedback—they are likely to develop maladaptive strategies. Hence, instruction must be well planned, deftly executed, and extensively supported with much guided practice, independent practice, feedback, and assessment. A common characteristic of direct instruction (whether intentional or artifactual) is the breakdown of strategies into smaller, more easily trackable subskills to accommodate the inherent complexity of reading.

Explicit Instruction

Pearson and his colleagues (Pearson & Dole, 1987; Pearson & Gallagher, 1983) use the term *explicit instruction* to distinguish their position from the direct instruction view. Duffy and Roehler and their colleagues (1987) use a similar construct they label *explicit explanation*. The basic differences between the direct instruction position and the explicit instruction position lie in task conceptualization and control over the learning environment. Neither Pearson nor Duffy sees any need to decompose skills into subskills. Indeed, because they see so much conceptual overlap among comprehension skills (finding main ideas often entails both drawing inferences and determining cause-effect relationships simultaneously), they find both theoretical merit and practical benefit (time-savings) to more holistic strategies. They also require that skill application occur with authentic texts (i.e., naturally occurring) instead of skill-driven texts (i.e., written specifically to facilitate skill application).

Control, in the explicit view, is more of a shared responsibility than a teacher responsibility (see Pearson & Dole, 1987, or Pearson, Dole, Duffy, & Roehler, in press, for a complete discussion). Teachers may begin an instructional cycle by accepting major responsibility for skill application; however, they soon release responsibility to students. The notion of "gradual release of responsibility" is central to their view (Pearson & Gallagher, 1983).

While they raise many unanswered questions about this paradigm, Pearson and his colleagues cite supportive research to establish the efficacy of the explicit instruction position. They include the questioning work of Raphael and her colleagues (e.g., Raphael & Pearson, 1985; Raphael & Wonnacott, 1985), the metacognitive training studies of Paris (see Paris, 1984), the comprehension skill work of Baumann (1984), and the explicit explanation work of the Michigan State group (Duffy, Roehler, Sivan, Rackliffe, Book, Meloth, Vavrus, Wesselman, Putnam, & Bassiri, 1987). They use the four facets of skill development suggested by Paris, Lipson, and Wixson (1983): What (what the skill is), How (how to perform it), When (when to apply it) and Why (why one would ever use it in the first place). Most convincing in this tradition is the research of Duffy and his colleagues. They have documented a positive relationship between the degree to which teachers are explicit about explaining the what, how, when, and why, and the degree to which students acquire and use comprehension strategies.

Components in an explicit instructional routine include teacher modeling (making public the secrets of invisible processing), guided practice (a kind of learning-through-problem-solving segment), independent practice (students do it on their own), consolidation (public review to see if students can handle it with minimal guidance), and application (using it with regular texts). Strategies need not be decomposed to reduce complexity; complexity is better handled, they suggest, by scaffolding, providing extra support when students experience difficulty doing it on their own. That is, in essence, what the construct of gradual release of responsibility (see Pearson & Gallagher, 1983) is for. A teacher slides up and down that continuum as necessary, providing precisely the amount of scaffolding necessary to support student success.

Scaffolding is a term borrowed from Bruner (Wood, Bruner, & Ross, 1976) and Vygotsky (1962) to characterize learning in social situations. The metaphor of the scaffold is apt because the teacher support, like a scaffold, is temporary and adjustable. While it can be used to explain the teacher's role in explicit instruction, it is even more commonly associated with the cognitive apprenticeship model.

Cognitive Apprenticeships

Further along the continuum is the cognitive apprenticeship model (see Collins, Brown, & Newman, 1989, and Brown, Collins, & Duguid, 1989). Collins and his colleagues discuss the difficulty of teaching complex cognitive processes that basically are invisible. They suggest that reading, writing, and mathematics are not easily learned through the learning-as-the-transmission-of-knowledge model of Western civilization. Instead, they contend that such activities are more easily learned through an apprenticeship model similar to that which historically characterized all instruction and which still characterizes entry into certain crafts and professions.

Similar to craft apprenticeships, the cognitive apprenticeship model is based on an expert—in this case, the teacher—helping novices of different abilities acquire expertise by first observing what the expert does and then trying it out under the expert's tutelage. Key components of the approach include modeling, coaching, and fading. Pearson and Raphael (in press) point out that these three elements are similar to the modeling, guided practice, consolidation, and gradual release of responsibility that characterize explicit instruction. Unlike the latter, however, the cognitive apprenticeship model emphasizes the importance of always presenting instruction within the context of higher order problem-solving activities that are genuine and authentic as opposed to activities that are developed solely to permit skill or strategy practice. Pearson and Raphael point out that a major advantage of this type of situated learning is that the issue of transfer is eliminated; students develop a repertoire of reading strategies as a means to completing functional and meaningful problem-solving activities.

Sequencing within the cognitive apprenticeship model involves two principles: (1) presenting global skills before local skills, and (2) completing activities in increasingly diverse and complex contexts. At every level of complexity, scaffolding—not subskill decomposition and sequencing—is the mechanism that helps students cope with complexity. Diversity, meeting the same task in new problems and new situations, should also increase over time so that students are able to acquire a "richer set of contextual associations" for the task. Although aspects of cognitive apprenticeship are reflected in a few reading (Palincsar & Brown, 1984), writing (Scardamalia & Bereiter, 1983), and mathematics (Schoenfield, 1983) programs, none of these provide a direct test of its efficacy.

Whole Language

In a relatively short period of time the whole-language movement has had an incredible impact on the field of reading. Based on first-language acquisition theory, advocates of the movement consider literacy development to be an interrelated facet of language development (see K. Goodman, 1986, and Altwerger, Edelsky, & Flores, 1987, for details about this movement). Children acquire literacy in the same way that they acquire oral language—naturally and over time through extensive and varied exposure to authentic literacy tasks. Children's emerging expertise and control over literacy tasks are viewed as a natural extension of their language development. Listening, speaking, reading, and writing are considered interrelated aspects of language development. There is no reason for one aspect of language development to be emphasized prior to the development of another. For this reason, separate instruction in reading or language arts does not occur in whole-language classrooms. Phonics instruction and basal readers are eschewed in favor of exposure to literacy events that have real functions and that may involve all four aspects of language development. With the emphasis on functional and real literacy tasks, there is no need to read materials that have been especially developed to practice or learn skills or subskills.

Whole language specifically differs from the cognitive apprentice-ship position in its definition of the teacher's role. In whole language, the teacher is the facilitator but not the expert, whereas in the cognitive apprenticeship model, the teacher is the expert, or the master craftsperson, while the children are the novices or apprentices. The whole-language literature implies that the students and not the teacher define the tasks to be undertaken as well as the materials to be read. The teacher's role is to provide a supportive classroom setting where children are encouraged to define what they want to read and write. All tasks must be functional and authentic, including the purposes for completing tasks, the content of what is read or written, and the audience for whom the communication is intended. Teachers should not tell anyone what to do or when to do it. While they may share their interpretation of text, or explain the use of standard conventions such as spelling or punctuation, they are not supposed to impose these standards on their students as evaluative criteria.

Pearson and Raphael (in press) point out that the limited research base behind whole language has hindered its evaluation as a complete instructional approach. Part of the problem is that whole-language proponents tend to be critical of standardized tests and quantitative experimental research (Edelsky & Harman, 1988; K. Goodman, 1986). As a result, they generally avoid using either of them to evaluate whole-language programs. To what degree whole language is effective at the different levels of schooling is not known, at least not from the "conventional" perspective that many educators are accus-tomed to in evaluative research. Neither is it known to what extent the whole-language approach can provide all children with the literacy development that they need to succeed in American schools (see Delpit, 1986, 1988, for a discussion of this issue).

What is known, however, is that some features of the whole-language model have been positively associated with other successful instructional approaches. Pearson and Raphael review these features and specifically note that there is considerable evidence to indicate that reading literature results in better reading comprehension than does isolated skill practice (Anderson, Hiebert, Scott, & Wilkinson, 1985; R. Anderson, Wilson, & Fielding, 1988; Taylor, & Frye, 1987). Similarly, children's knowledge about letter-sound correspondences is enhanced when they are allowed to use invented spelling (i.e., spell words on their own when they are unsure of the correct spelling) (see Clarke, 1986). Also, the quality and quantity of children's writing are improved when children are encouraged to participate in wide-ranging, unfettered writing activities from the outset of schooling (Calkins, 1983, 1986; Graves, 1983). In addition, the reliance on authentic, functional literacy tasks helps students to develop a more realistic view of the uses of reading and writing (Garcia, Flores, Prieto, & Moll, 1987; Freire, 1983).

It also may be that the whole-language approach reduces the cultural mismatch that frequently occurs in classrooms where linguistic- or cultural-minority children are in attendance because the students and not the teacher define the context of the learning situation (for a discussion of this mismatch, see Au & Mason, 1981; Heath, 1982; and Philips, 1983). This, along with the early emphasis on print awareness in the formal school setting, may be what helps to enhance the initial literacy acquisition of some linguistic- and cultural-minority children.

Choosing the Best Alternative

We began our review of instructional models with the clear intention of selecting, on the basis of the review, one of the four as the best alternative for children who have been labeled "at-risk" or "disadvantaged." However, the review has led us to a change of heart. First, we must confess that we really do not know the long-term effects of any of the programs on the reading comprehension of such children. Second, we are not sure that any program, in and of itself, provides the appropriate delivery system for the comprehension focus that we are advocating. Rather than select one of the models as clearly superior to the others, what we want to do is to identify features of each model that we think are especially appropriate for designing instruction for low-achieving students. In short, we will build our own consensus model of instruction. In doing so, we will parallel what good teachers do on a yearly, weekly, and daily basis—compile an "eclectic" model of instruction from available resources.

The first feature in our consensus model is teacher modeling. Teachers can and should show students how they themselves perform the tasks they ask students to perform. Interestingly, modeling as an instructional feature does not allow us to discriminate among our four models because it is an integral part of each. Even whole-language advocates support the practice, although they tend to prefer the term *demonstration* (Smith, 1984), and they require that only authentic, whole processes be demonstrated. One reason that modeling or demonstration is so important to good instruction is that comprehension processes are so hard to talk about in the abstract (in the sense of rules or steps) that one almost has to "see it to believe it." What is especially helpful are "reflective" demonstrations—demonstrations in which the modeler talks the students through the processes involved in his or her performance (what Paris, 1984, calls "making thinking public"). Like so many domains of inquiry in which knowledge is "ill-structured," it is easier and more instructive to present cases (examples of the process in action) than it is to deal with rules or guidelines (see Spiro, Coulson, Feltovitch, & Anderson, 1988, for a complete treatment of learning in ill-structured domains of knowledge). The first principle in our consensus model reads like this:

> Because reading comprehension is an ill-structured knowledge domain, it is more appropriate to provide students with demonstrations of how strategies are applied in real reading situations than it is to offer them either abstract sets of rules or multiple opportunities to practice the strategies. At the very least, rules and/or practice opportunities ought to be accompanied by reflective demonstrations.

A second feature in our consensus model is authenticity. Authenticity is the essence of the whole-language model. It would be an unspeakable act to ask a child to read an unauthentic text or to perform an unauthentic task (see Edelsky & Draper, in press, and Edelsky & Harman, 1988). Authenticity is an ultimate goal of the direct instruction model (direct instruction advocates do want students to apply what they have learned to real texts read primarily for purposes of comprehension, but they tolerate a lot of special texts during instruction), a required part of the explicit instruction model (but special texts are tolerated for demonstration purposes), and an implicit requirement of cognitive apprenticeships (there is no need to apprentice a student reader to a fake text or task when there are plenty of authentic ones lying around). Our particular version of the authenticity principle goes like this:

> Strategy instruction should occur within the context of trying to comprehend a particular text written by an author for the purpose of communicating a message (informational, enter-

taining) of some sort to an audience. For purposes of demonstrating or highlighting a particular feature of the strategy, it may be permissible to remove a text segment from its surrounding context (a teacher could put a paragraph on the overhead, for example, but make it a real paragraph from a real text), but both the strategy and the text segment should be immediately recontextualized.

The third feature in our consensus model focuses on the issue of reducing complexity during strategy acquisition. Essentially, education has adopted two principles for reducing complexity: task decomposition and scaffolding. We want to establish our position clearly on the side of scaffolding. Task decomposition, a critical feature of direct instruction, has had its "day in court" for the past thirty years. It is time, we think, to give equal time to scaffolding as an alternative strategy for coping with complexity. What we are saying is that our instructional practice of decomposing tasks and removing them from natural contexts in order to highlight critical features has not proven all that successful, especially for low-achieving students. It may be better to have students perform the task in contexts that are as close as possible to the situation in which they will ultimately have to apply it and, in that process, to provide them with support as they struggle through it. In summary, here is our principle:

> To help novices cope with the intrinsic complexity of reading tasks, it is better to provide extensive scaffolding for authentic tasks than it is to decompose and decontextualize those same tasks.

The fourth feature of our consensus model is an intrinsic bias toward student control of the instructional situation. We do not take quite the radical position advocated by whole-language devotees, who would claim that students should always be in charge of their own learning (selecting texts to read and topics for writing), but we do think control by "others" is too dominant in our current situation. Currently someone else—be it a teacher, an administrator, or a basal author—decides what gets taught when, what gets practiced when, and what the criteria for success and failure are; students have to rely on feedback from others to let them know whether they are becoming literate individuals. Everything we know about the importance of metacognitive control of cognitive processes and everything we know about intrinsic motivation demand that we let students participate in the planning and evaluation of the curriculum to which we subject them. The ultimate goal of teacher assessment should be student self-assessment; the ultimate goal of teacher planning should be to help students learn how to plan their own learning. These goals can only be accomplished in an atmosphere of shared responsibility for curricular decision making. The concept of gradual release of responsibility, applied so assiduously to task completion by the explicit instruction advocates, should be expanded to both the planning and assessment aspects of literacy curricula. Our principle reads like this:

> From the earliest stages of the school literacy curriculum, students of all achievement levels should be involved in planning reading and writing activities and in evaluating their own performance. With additional experience and expertise, students should take additional responsibility for planning and evaluating their own learning.

These are the four features of our consensus model—teacher modeling (to let students in on the secrets), task and text authenticity (to ensure purposefulness), scaffolding (to cope with complexity), and shared decision-making responsibility (to develop self-assessment skills). Looking back upon our four candidate models, one might conclude that we borrowed very little from the direct instruction tradition and a lot from whole language. But we see components from all these models, although we must admit that our consensus principles are more consistent with a liberal version of explicit instruction and cognitive apprenticeship and a conservative version of whole language than they are with direct instruction. Nevertheless, direct instruction advocates would surely claim our emphasis on modeling and feedback as theirs, just as whole-language patrons would consider authenticity and student control as theirs. Our emphasis on scaffolding would be applauded by advocates of cognitive apprenticeship and explicit instruction. On the other hand, we permit more deviation from principles of authenticity and shared decision making than we think advocates of whole language would like; conversely, we demand greater adherence to those same principles than explicit instruction advocates would demand (they would view them more as ultimate goals to work toward than as day-to-day operational tools).

A FINAL WORD

Clearly our approach requires teachers to move away from the "teacher-proof" model frequently offered in conventional programs to a model in which they make most decisions within their classrooms. Along with this independence comes considerable responsibility and commitment. For our approach to work, teachers must see themselves as readers and writers and be willing to widen their knowledge base about reading and writing. They must also understand that the development of literate individuals in school requires that literacy instruction be extended beyond the reading and language arts classes to include all domains of inquiry. And finally, if this process is to involve those groups of children who traditionally have been called "at-risk" or "disadvantaged," teachers need to be aware of and willing to accommodate the different language and literacy experiences that their students bring to the classroom. For literacy to flourish, all participants must share in its ownership.

REFERENCES

Afflerbach, P. P. (1986). The influence of prior knowledge on expert readers' importance assignment processes. In J. A. Niles & R. V. Lalik (Eds.), *Solving problems in literacy: Learners, teachers, and researchers* (pp. 30–40). Thirty-fifth Yearbook of the National Reading Conference. Rochester, NY: National Reading Conference.

Alessi, S. M., Anderson, T. H., & Goetz, E. T. (1979). An investigation of lookbacks during studying. *Discourse Processes, 2,* 197–212.

Allington, R. (1983). The reading instruction provided readers of differing reading abilities. *Elementary School Journal, 83,* 545–559.

Altwerger, B., Edelsky, C., & Flores, B. M. (1987). Whole language: What's new? *Reading Teacher, 41,* 144–154.

Applebee, A. N., Langer, J. A., & Mullis, I.V.S. (1987). *The nation's report card: Learning to be literate in America: Reading.* Princeton, NJ: Educational Testing Service.

Anderson, R. C., Hiebert, E. H., Scott, J. A., & Wilkinson, I. A. (1985). *Becoming a nation of readers.* Washington, DC: National Institute of Education.

Anderson, R. C., Spiro, R. J., & Anderson, M. C. (1978). Schemata as scaffolding for the representation of information in connected discourse. *American Educational Research Journal, 15,* 433–440.

Anderson, R. C., Wilson, P. T., Fielding, L. G. (1988). Growth in reading and how children spend their time outside of school. *Reading Research Quarterly, 23,* 285–303.

Andre, M.E.D.A., & Anderson, T. H. (1978–79). The development and evaluation of a self-questioning study technique. *Reading Research Quarterly, 14,* 605–623

Au, K. H. (1981). Participation structures in a reading lesson with Hawaiian children: Analysis of an appropriate instructional event. *Anthropology and Education Quarterly, 11,* 91–115.

Au, K. H., & Mason, J. M. (1981). Social organizational factors in learning to read: The balance of rights hypothesis. *Reading Research Quarterly, 17,* 115–152.

Baker, L., & Brown, A. L. (1984). Metacognitive skills of reading. In P. D. Pearson (Ed.), *Handbook of reading research* (pp. 353–394). New York: Longman.

Baumann, J. F. (1984). The effectiveness of a direct instructional paradigm for teaching main idea comprehension. *Reading Research Quarterly, 20,* 93–115.

Blanchard, J. S. (1980). Preliminary investigation of transfer between single-word decoding ability and contextual reading comprehension by poor readers in grade six. *Perceptual and Motor Skills, 51,* 1271–1281.

Bloom, B. S. (1968). Learning for mastery. *Evaluation Comment, 1*(2), 1–12.

Bloome, D., & Green, J. (1982). The social contexts of reading: A multidisciplinary perspective. In B. A. Huston (Ed.), *Advances in reading/language research: Vol. 1* (pp. 309–338). Greenwich, CT: JAI Press.

Boehnlein, M. (1987). Reading intervention for high-risk first-graders. *Educational Leadership, 44,* 32–37.

Bransford, J. D., Stein, B. S., & Vye, N. J. (1982). Helping students learn how to learn from written text. In M. H. Singler (Ed.), *Competent reader, disabled reader: Research and applications* (pp. 141–150). Hillsdale, NJ: Erlbaum.

Brown, A. L., & Day, J. D. (1983). Macrorules for summarizing texts. The development of expertise. *Journal of Verbal Learning and Verbal Behavior, 22,* 1–14.

Brown, A. L., Day, J. D., & Jones, R. S. (1983). The development of plans for summarizing texts. *Child Development, 54,* 968–979.

Brown, J. S., Collins, A., & Duguid, P. (1989). Situated cognition and the culture of learning. *Educational Researcher, 18,* 32–42.

Burke, S. M., Pflaum, S. W., & Krafle, J. D. (1982). The influence of Black English on diagnosis of reading in learning-disabled and normal readers. *Journal of Learning Disabilities, 15,* 19–22.

Butterfield, R. A., Demos, E. S., Grant, G. W., May, P. S., & Perez, A. L. (1979). A multicultural analysis of a popular basal reading series in the International Year of the Child. *Journal of Negro Education, 48,* 382–388.

Calkins, L. (1983). *Lessons from a child.* Portsmouth, NH: Heinemann.

Calkins, L. (1986). *The art of teaching writing.* Portsmouth, NH: Heinemann.

Carroll, J. (1963). A model for school learning. *Teachers' College Record, 64,* 723–733.

Cazden, C. B. (1985). Social context of learning to read. In H. Singer & R. B. Ruddell (Eds.), *Theoretical models and processes of reading* (3rd ed., pp. 595–610). Newark, DE: International Reading Association.

Cazden, C. B. (1988). *Classroom discourse: The language of teaching and learning.* Portsmouth, NH: Heinemann.

Cazden, C. B., & Mehan, H. (1989). *Context, code, classroom and culture.* Paper presented at the annual meeting of the American Educational Research Association, San Francisco.

Chall, J. S. (1983). *Stages of reading development*. New York: McGraw-Hill.

Clarke, D.L.K. (1986). *Invented versus traditional spelling in first graders' writing: Effects on teaching to spell and read*. Unpublished doctoral dissertation, Ontario Institute for Studies in Education, Toronto.

Clay, M. M. (1987). *The early detection of reading difficulties* (3rd ed.). Auckland, NZ: Heinemann.

Collins, J. (1982). Discourse style, classroom interaction and differential treatment. *Journal of Reading Behavior, 14*, 429–437.

Collins, A., Brown, J. S., & Newman, S. E. (1989). Cognitive apprenticeship: Teaching the craft of reading, writing, and mathematics. In L. B. Resnick (Ed.), *Knowing, learning, and instruction: Essays in honor of Robert Glaser*. Hillsdale, NJ: Erlbaum.

Columbus Public Schools. (1987). *Final evaluation report, language development component, CLEAR-Reading Recovery Program, 1985–86*. Columbus, OH: Author.

Craik, F.I.M., & Lockhart, R. S. (1972). Levels of processing: A framework for memory research. *Journal of Verbal Learning and Verbal Behavior, 11*, 671–684.

Cunningham, P. M. (1976–77). Teachers' correction responses to Black-dialect miscues which are non-meaning changing. *Reading Research Quarterly, 12*, 637–653.

Delpit, L. D. (1986). Skills and other dilemmas of a progressive black educator. *Harvard Educational Review, 56*, 379–385.

Delpit, L. D. (1988). The silenced dialogue: Power and pedagogy in educating other people's children. *Harvard Educational Review, 58*, 280–298.

Dole, J. A., & Smith, E. L. (1987, December). *When prior knowledge is wrong: Reading and learning from science text*. Paper presented at the annual meeting of the National Reading Conference, St. Petersburg, FL.

Downing, J. (1976). The reading instruction register. *Language Arts, 53*, 762–766.

Downing, J. (1986). Cognitive clarity: A unifying and cross-cultural theory for language awareness phenomena in reading. In D. B. Yaden & S.Templeton (Eds.), *Metalinguistic awareness and beginning literacy: Conceptualizing what it means to read and write* (pp. 13–29). Portsmouth, NH: Heinemann.

Dreeben, R. (1987). Closing the divide: What teachers and administrators can do to help black students reach their potential. *American Educator, 11*, 28–35.

Duffy, G., Roehler, L., Sivan, E., Rackliffe, G., Book, C., Meloth, M. S., Vavrus, L. G., Wesselman, R., Putnam, J., & Bassiri, D. (1987). Effects of explaining the reasoning associated with using reading strategies. *Reading Research Quarterly, 22*, 347–366.

Durkin, D. (1978–79). What classroom observations reveal about reading comprehension instruction. *Reading Research Quarterly, 14*, 481–533.

Edelsky, C., & Draper, K. (in press). *Authenticity: A purposeful notion*.

Edelsky, C., & Harman, S. (1988). One more critique of reading tests—With two differences. *English Education, 20*, 157–171.

Elley, W. B., & Mangubhai, F. (1983). The impact of reading on second language learning. *Reading Research Quarterly, 19*, 53–67.

Feitelson, D.K.B., & Goldstein, Z. (1986). Effects of listening to series stories on first graders' comprehension and use of language. *Research in the Teaching of English, 20,* 339–356.

Fisher, C. W., Berliner, D., Filby, N., Marliave, R., Cohen, L., Dishaw, M., & Moore, J. (1978). *Teaching and learning in elementary schools: A summary of the beginning teacher evaluation study.* San Francisco: Far West Laboratory for Educational Research and Development.

Fleisher, L. A., Jenkins, J. R., & Pany, D. (1979–80). Effects on poor readers' comprehension of training in rapid decoding. *Reading Research Quarterly, 15,* 30–48.

Freire, P. (1983). The importance of the act of reading. *Journal of Education, 165,* 5–11.

Gagne, R. (1965). *The conditions of learning.* New York: Holt, Rinehart & Winston.

Garcia, E. E., Flores, B., Prieto, A., Moll, L. (1987, April). *Effective schools for Hispanic bilinguals: An interdisciplinary empirical report.* Presentation at the seventeenth International Bilingual/Bicultural Education Conference, National Association for Bilingual Education, Houston, TX.

Garcia, G. E. (1988). *Factors influencing the English reading test performance of Spanish-English bilingual children.* Unpublished doctoral dissertation, University of Illinois, Urbana-Champaign.

Garcia, G. E., Jimenez, R. T., & Pearson, P. D. (1989). *Annotated bibliography of research related to the reading of at-risk children* (Tech. Rep. No. 482). Urbana-Champaign: University of Illinois, Center for the Study of Reading.

Garner, R. (1987). *Metacognition and reading comprehension.* Norwood, NJ: Ablex.

Gersten, R., & Carnine, D. (1986). Direct instruction in reading comprehension. *Educational Leadership, 43* 70–78.

Goodman, K. S. (1968). The psycholinguistic nature of the reading process. In K. S. Goodman (Ed.), *The psycholinguistic nature of the reading process* (pp. 13–26). Detroit, MI: Wayne State University Press.

Goodman, K. S. (1976). What we know about reading. In D. Allen & D. J. Watson (Eds.), *Findings of research in miscue analysis: Classroom implications* (pp. 157–262). Urbana, IL: National Council of Teachers of English.

Goodman, K. S. (1978). Miscue analysis and further research directions. In S. Hudelson (Ed.), *Learning to read in different languages* (pp. ix–xiii). Washington, DC: Center for Applied Linguistics.

Goodman, K. S. (1986). *What's whole in whole language?* Exeter, NH: Heinemann.

Goodman, Y. (1971). *Longitudinal study of children's oral reading behavior* (Grant No. OEG-5-9-325062-0046). Washington, DC: Office of Education, Bureau of Research. (ERIC Document Reproduction Service No. ED 058 008).

Goodman, Y. M., Watson, D. J., & Burke, C. L. (1987). *Reading miscue inventory.* New York: Richard C. Owen, Publishers.

Gordon, C., & Pearson, P. D. (1983). *Effects of instruction of listening comprehension research* (Reading Ed. Rep. No. 39). Urbana-Champaign: University of Illinois, Center for the Study of Reading.

Graves, D. (1983). *Writing: Teachers and children at work.* Portsmouth, NH: Heinemann.

Guszak, F. J. (1967). Teacher questioning and reading. *Reading Teacher, 21,* 227–234.

Hansen, J. (1981). The effects of inference training and practice on young children's reading comprehension. *Reading Research Quarterly, 16,* 391–417.

Hansen, J., & Pearson, P. D. (1983). An instructional study: Improving the inferential comprehension of fourth grade good and poor readers. *Journal of Educational Psychology, 75,* 821–829.

Hatch, J. A., & Bondy, E. (1984). A double dose of the same medicine: Implications from a naturalistic study of summer school reading instruction. *Urban Education, 19,* 29–38.

Heath, S. B. (1982). Questioning at home and at school: A comparative study. In G. Spindler (Ed.), *Doing the ethnography of schooling: Educational anthropology in action* (pp. 102–131). New York: Holt, Rinehart & Winston.

Hudelson, S. (Ed.). (1981). *Learning to read in different languages.* Papers in applied linguistics: Linguistics and literacy series: 1. Washington, DC: Center for Applied Linguistics.

Johnston, P. (1984). Prior knowledge and reading comprehension test bias. *Reading Research Quarterly, 19,* 219–239.

Kail, R. V., Chi, M.T.H., Ingram, A. L., & Danner, F. W. (1977). Constructive aspects of children's reading comprehension. *Child Development, 48,* 684–688.

Lipson, M. Y. (1983). The influence of religious affiliation on children's memory for text information. *Reading Research Quarterly, 18,* 448–457.

Logan, J. W., & Garcia, J. (1983). An examination of ethnic content in nine current basal series. *Reading Horizons, 23,* 165–169.

Mason, J., & Osborn, J. (1982). *When do children begin "reading to learn?": A survey of classroom reading instruction practices in grades two through five* (Tech. Rep. No. 261). Urbana-Champaign: University of Illinois, Center for the Study of Reading.

Masur, E. F., McIntyre, C. W., & Flavell, J. H. (1973). Developmental changes in apportionment of study time among items in multiple free recall task. *Journal of Experimental Child Psychology, 15,* 237–246.

Mehan, H. (1979). *Learning lessons.* Cambridge, MA: Harvard University Press.

Moll, L. C., Estrada, E., Diaz, E., & Lopes, L. M. (1980). The organization of bilingual lessons: Implications for schooling. *The Quarterly Newsletter of the Laboratory of Comparative Human Cognition, 2,* 53–58.

O'Flahavan, J., Hartman, D., & Pearson, P. D. (1989). *Teacher questioning and feedback practices after the cognitive revolution: Replication and extension of Guszak's (1967) study* (Tech. Rep. No. 461). Urbana-Champaign: University of Illinois, Center for the Study of Reading.

Owings, R. A., Peterson, G. A., Bransford, J. D., Morris, C. D., & Stein, B. S. (1980). Spontaneous monitoring and regulation of learning: A comparison of successful and less successful fifth graders. *Journal of Educational Psychology, 72,* 250–256.

Palincsar, A. M., & Brown, A. L. (1984). Reciprocal teaching of comprehension-fostering and comprehension-monitoring activities. *Cognition and Instruction, 1,* 117–175.

Palincsar, A. M., & Brown, A. L. (1986). Interactive teaching to promote independent learning from text. *Reading Teacher, 39,* 771–777.

Paris, S. G. (1984). Teaching children to guide their reading and learning. In T. E. Raphael (Ed.), *The contexts of school-based literacy* (pp. 115–130). New York: Random House.

Paris, S., Lipson, M., & Wixson, K. K. (1983). Becoming a strategic reader. *Contemporary Educational Psychology, 8,* 293–316.

Pearson, P. D. (1985). Changing the face of reading comprehension instruction. *Reading Teacher, 38,* 724–738.

Pearson, P. D., & Dole, J. (1987). Explicit comprehension instruction: A review of research and a new conceptualization of instruction. *Elementary School Journal, 88,* 151–165.

Pearson, P. D., Dole, J., Duffy, G. G., & Roehler, L. R. (in press). Developing expertise in reading comprehension: What should be taught? How should it be taught? In S. J. Samuels & A. E. Farstrup (Eds.), *What research says to the teacher* (2nd Ed.). Newark, DE: International Reading Association.

Pearson, P. D., & Gallagher, M. C. (1983). The instruction of reading comprehension. *Contemporary Educational Psychology, 8,* 317–344.

Pearson, P. D., Hansen, J., & Gordon, C. (1979). The effect of background knowledge on young children's comprehension of explicit and implicit information. *Journal of Reading Behavior, 9,* 201–210.

Pearson, P. D., & Johnson, D. (1978). *Teaching reading comprehension.* New York: Holt, Rinehart & Winston.

Pearson, P. D., & Raphael, T. E. (in press). Reading comprehension as a dimension of thinking. In B. F. Jones & L. Idol (Eds.), *Dimensions of thinking and cognitive instruction: Implications for educational change.* Hillsdale, NJ: Erlbaum.

Philips, S. U. (1983). *The invisible culture: Communication in the classroom and community on the Warm Springs Indian Reservation.* New York: Longman.

Raphael, T. E. (1982). Question-answering strategies for children. *Reading Teacher, 36,* 186–191.

Raphael, T. E. (1984). Teaching learners about sources of information for answering questions. *Journal of Reading, 27,* 303–311.

Raphael, T. E., & Pearson, P. D. (1985). Increasing students' awareness of sources of information for answering questions. *American Educational Research Journal, 22,* 217–235.

Raphael, T. E., & Wonnacott, C. A. (1985). Heightening fourth grade students' sensitivity to sources of information for answering comprehension questions. *Reading Research Quarterly, 20,* 282–296.

Resnick, L. B. (1984). Comprehending and learning: Implications for acognitive theory of instruction. In H. Mandl, N. L. Stein, & T. Trabasso (Eds.), *Learning and comprehension of text* (pp. 431–443). Hillsdale, NJ: Erlbaum.

Reynolds, R. E., Taylor, M. A., Steffensen, M. S., Shirey, L., & Anderson, R. C. (1982). Cultural schemata and reading comprehension. *Reading Research Quarterly, 17,* 353–366.

Roth, K. J. (1985). *Conceptual change learning and student processing of science texts.* Paper presented at the annual meeting of the American Educational Research Association, Chicago.

Scardamalia, M., & Bereiter, C. (1983). *The development of evaluative, diagnostic and remedial capabilities in children's composing.* Unpublished paper, the Ontario Institute for Studies in Education, Toronto.

Schoenfield, A. H. (1983). *Problem solving in the mathematics curriculum: A report, recommendations and an annotated bibliography.* The Mathematical Association of America, MAA Notes, No. 1.

Singer, H., & Donlan, D. (1982). Active comprehension: Problem-solving schema with question generation for comprehension of complex short stories. *Reading Research Quarterly, 17,* 166–186.

Smith, F. (1984). The creative achievement of literacy. In H. Goelman, A. Oberg, & F. Smith (Eds.), *Awakening to literacy: The University of Victoria symposia on children's response to a literate environment: Literacy before schooling* (pp. 143–153). Victoria, B.C., Canada: University of Victoria.

Spiro, R., Coulson, R. L., Feltovich, P. J., & Anderson, D. K. (1988). *Cognitive flexibility theory: Advanced knowledge acquisition in ill-structured domains* (Tech. Rep. No. 441). Urbana-Champaign: University of Illinois, Center for the Study of Reading.

Stanovich, K. E. (1986). Matthew effects in reading: Some consequences of individual differences in the acquisition of literacy. *Reading Research Quarterly, 21,* 360–406.

Steffensen, M. S., Joag-Dev, C., & Anderson, R. C. (1979). A cross-cultural perspective on reading comprehension. *Reading Research Quarterly, 15,* 10–29.

Taylor, B. M., & Frye, B. J. (1987). *Reducing time on comprehension skill instruction and practice and increasing time on independent reading in the elementary classroom.* Unpublished manuscript, University of Minnesota, Minneapolis.

Teale, W. H. (1986). Home background and young children's literacy development. In W. H. Teale & E. Sulzby (Eds.), *Emergent literacy: Writing and reading* (pp. 173–206). Norwood, NJ: Ablex.

Teale, W. H., & Sulzby, E. (1986). Emergent literacy as a perspective for examining how young children become writers and readers. In W. H. Teale & E. Sulzby (Eds.), *Emergent literacy: Writing and reading* (pp. vii–xxv). Norwood, NJ: Ablex.

Tharp, R. G. (1982). The effective instruction of comprehension: Results and descriptions of the Kamehameha Early Education Program. *Reading Research Quarterly, 17,* 503–527.

Tierney, R. J., & Cunningham, J. W. (1984). Research on teaching reading comprehension. In P. D. Pearson (Ed.), *Handbook of reading research* (pp. 609–655). New York: Longman.

Torrey, J. W. (1983). Black children's knowledge of standard English. *American Educational Research Journal, 20,* 627–643.

Troutman, D. E., & Falk, J. S. (1982). Speaking Black English and reading—Is there a problem of interference? *Journal of Negro Education, 51,* 123–133.

Vygotsky, L. S. (1962). *Thought and language* (E. Hanfmann & G. Vakar, Trans.). Cambridge, MA: M.I.T. Press. (Original work published 1934).

Williams, J. P. (1986a). Extracting important information from text. In J. A. Niles & R. V. Lalik (Eds.), *Solving problems in literacy: Learners, teachers, and researchers* (pp. 11–29). Thirty-fifth Yearbook of the National Reading Conference. Rochester, NY: National Reading Conference.

Williams, J. P. (1986b). Research and instructional development on main idea skills. In J. F. Baumann (Ed.), *Teaching main idea comprehension* (pp. 73–95). Newark, DE: International Reading Association.

Winograd, P. N., & Bridge, C. A. (1986). The comprehension of important information in written prose. In J. B. Baumann (Ed.), *Teaching main idea comprehension* (pp. 18–48). Newark, DE: International Reading Association.

Wittrock, M. C. (1983). Writing and the teaching of reading. *Language Arts, 60,* 600–606.

Wood, D., Bruner, J. S., & Ross, G. (1976). The role of tutoring in problem solving. *Journal of Child Psychology & Psychiatry, 17,* 89–100.

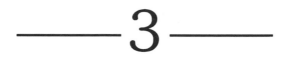

Social and Instructional Issues in Literacy Instruction for "Disadvantaged" Students

Luis C. Moll

This chapter addresses key issues in the academic instruction of "disadvantaged" students. Although I will focus primarily on Latino or Hispanic students, most issues discussed are equally relevant to other "linguistic minority" students. I take as my premise what I consider to be an obvious truism: There is nothing about minority children's language, culture, or intellect that should handicap their schooling. I therefore object to using the label "disadvantaged." These children are disadvantaged only to the extent that their parents and communities lack political power. That is, disadvantaged is not a characteristic or trait of the children, it is something done to the children. As McDermott (1987) has commented, "By making believe that failure is something that kids do, as different from how it is something done to them, and then by explaining their failure in terms of others things they do, we likely contribute to the maintenance of school failure" (p. 363).

Accordingly, in what follows I will elaborate on the following three points:

1. Any discussion of academic instruction for "disadvantaged" students must examine the societal context of schooling. The school experiences of "disadvantaged" students are intimately and complexly related to broader social, economic, and political factors. Viewing instruction in isolation from these factors helps distort explanations of school performance and limits suggestions for change to simply doing more of the same; after all, it works for other students, but in larger doses and better.

2. Current instructional practices seriously underestimate these children's intellectual capabilities and constrain their academic performance. When "disadvantaged" children are shown to succeed under modified instructional arrangements, it becomes clear that the problems these children face in school must be viewed, in great part, as a consequence of institutional arrangements that constrain children *and* teachers by not capitalizing fully on their talents, resources, and skills (Diaz, Moll, & Mehan, 1986; Moll & S. Diaz, 1987).

3. Given the limitations of current schooling practices, if we are to develop appropriate models for the instruction of "disadvantaged" students, most principles must come from elsewhere than schools (Tharp & Gallimore, 1988). In particular, the students' community represents a resource of enormous importance for educational change. As community-based studies have repeatedly shown, there is great diversity in the cultural and linguistic practices that form Latino and other language minority communities. Properly used, these diverse practices can serve as powerful assets to the children's schooling, especially to the development of literacy (see, e.g., Cazden, 1983; Cole & Griffin, 1986; Gallimore, 1985; Delgado-Gaitan, 1987; Heath, 1983, 1986; Jordan, 1985; LCHC, 1986; Moll & S. Diaz, 1987; Morris & Conan, 1983; Smith, 1981a, 1981b, 1987; Tharp, 1989; Vogt, Jordan, & Tharp, 1987).

I will start by presenting some demographic findings that help define the societal context of education. As will become clear, the issues we are addressing here under the rubric of academic instruction for the disadvantaged will not go away anytime soon. I will then summarize the literature on what goes on in classrooms.

There is ample evidence that academic instruction, especially for children whom we are calling the "disadvantaged," is severely restricted and restrictive. In this context it becomes clear that the so-called back-to-basics movement is a ploy. Cole and Griffin (1986) put it diplomatically when they wrote as follows: " . . . a continued imbalance in the educational mandates that guide the education of minorities and of white middle-class children deepens the problem: as schools serving minority children focus their resources on increasing the use of well-known methods for drilling the basics, they decrease the opportunities for those children to participate in the higher level activities that are needed to excel in mathematics and science." I will then review the findings of a recent study on outstanding teachers of Hispanic students. The instructional practices of these teachers highlight the importance of purpose and meaning in literacy instruction and stand in sharp contrast to the usual recommendations for more structure and control in the instruction of "low-SES-low-achieving" students (e.g., Brophy & Good, 1986).

I will conclude by summarizing a model of research and practice that examines how to build on community knowledge, practices, and values to change and extend classroom instruction.

THE SOCIETAL CONTEXT

Latinos and other linguistic minority populations, such as blacks, are at the bottom of the social order in practically every category (e.g., Reyes, 1987). For example, in 1986 almost 41 percent of Latino children under six years of age were living in poverty. The figure for blacks was 46 percent and for "whites" 17 percent. The median income level of Puerto Rican families in New York City in 1984 was $10,784 (compared with $31,000 for non-Latino whites). A similar distribution of income is found in other cities with Mexican-Americans and blacks. Health problems affecting Latino children are associated with poverty, including malnutrition, upper-respiratory diseases, lead poisoning, child abuse, and high rates of teenage pregnancy.

Equally distressing statistics characterize the educational situation of such linguistic minority students: high dropout rates and low academic achievement (Steinberg, Blinde, & Chan, 1982; Walker, 1987). Among all adults twenty-five or older in 1985, approximately 45 percent of Latinos and 47 percent of blacks had completed high school, compared with 76 percent for non-Latino whites. Further, those students who stay in school are doing poorly. For example, in New York City the percentage of students reading at grade level or above is less in predominantly Latino school districts than in the city as a whole at every grade. A similar gap holds for mathematics.

In addition to the above, however, we are in the midst of a striking and dramatic change in population, and many educators, including bilingual educators, seem to be oblivious to its consequences. Latinos, for example, are among the fastest growing population groups in the country. It is estimated that by the year 2000, there will be a total of over 22 million Latinos in this country. This would make us the fifth largest Latino population group in the Americas. Only Brazil, Mexico, Peru, and Venezuela are projected to have larger populations. By the year 2000 there will be over 400 million Spanish speakers in the Americas. Note that in this international context Latinos are not a "linguistic minority."

Furthermore, along with other political minorities, such as blacks, Latinos are now the majority or becoming the majority in many important urban educational school systems. Latinos, as a group, are predominantly urban, a change from only a few years ago. New York City, Los Angeles, Chicago, and San Antonio account for over 20 percent of all Latinos. We are, or will be, the majority in school systems in these as well as other major cities in this country. It follows that serving these students' needs will become the top item on any educational agenda within these locations.

Additionally, Latinos are overwhelmingly members of bilingual communities. Although it may be safe to conclude that there seems to be an intergenerational shift to English among Latinos, the acquisition of English may not be accompanied by a loss of Spanish (Language Policy Task Force, 1982, 1984). The great majority of individuals in Latino communities come into contact with both Spanish and English over their lifetimes, whether through contact with monolingual and bilingual members of the community or with persons outside the community. This "community bilinguality" is a prominent characteristic distinguishing Latinos from the dominant groups in society.

The Latino population also is very young (as is the black population), with a mean age of about twenty-two years, and the birth rate is very high (Latinos between eighteen and forty-four years old have the highest fertility rate in the nation—107 births per 1,000 women—compared with non-Latino whites—67 births per 1,000), not to mention increases in population because of immigration. This demographic profile means that the educational issues affecting Latinos, as well as other linguistic minority groups, are going to be around for a very long time, well into the next century.

We turn next to examining the nature of schooling for "disadvantaged" students.

THE CHARACTERISTICS OF SCHOOLING

It is inarguable that the classroom instruction working-class and poor children receive is very different from the instruction students from wealthier classes receive. In general, these children receive rote, drill-and-practice instruction, and do work that is mechanical, highly structured, and redundant (Anyon, 1980, 1981; Lubeck, 1984; Page, 1987; Wilcox, 1982; Willis, 1977; Gamorans & Berends, 1987). For example, Anyon's (1980, 1981) research examined classroom instruction in five elementary schools in contrasting social-class communities (Ramsey, 1983, 1985). She designated the schools according to, among other variables, family income and occupation, with the schools ranging from "Working-class" (with most family incomes at or below $12,000) to what she labeled "Executive Elite Schools," (with most family incomes exceeding $100,000, with some in the $500,000 range). Anyon provided examples from fifth-grade classrooms to illustrate differences in instruction among the schools. She collected data through classroom observations; interviews with teachers, principals, and district administrators; and assessment of instructional materials in each classroom. All teachers in her sample were described by their principals as good or excellent instructors.

Work in the working-class classrooms, as described by Anyon (1980, 1981), was almost robotic, involving rote behavior and very little student decision making or choice: "The teachers rarely explain why the work is being assigned, how it might connect to other assignments, or what the idea is that lies behind the procedure or gives it coherence and perhaps meaning or significance" (1980, p. 73). Accordingly, work is often evaluated according to whether the children followed the right steps of a procedure.

Language arts, for example, involved the mechanics of simple punctuation, with the rules often displayed in a ditto that the students followed. One teacher commented that simple punctuation is all that working-class students would ever use (p.74). There was no expository writing; most classroom writing involved answering questions provided in a ditto sheet. Social studies was also largely mechanical, rote work, with little connection to larger societal contexts. Individual activities were often fragmented and without inherent meaning, other than that the students were instructed to perform them. In one school, social studies consisted of copying the teacher's notes from the board. As the students finished copying the sentences, the teacher would erase the board and write more. Similar rote work was done in oral work, science, and mathematics.

The teachers controlled the students' work and movement closely and rarely explained the basis for their decisions. They would often shout directives and stress the need for quiet. The children would often resist the teachers' orders and the work assigned. Teachers, in turn, would make the lessons easy or not demanding to minimize the students' resistance. In sum, working-class schooling is depicted by Anyon as a continuous struggle between teachers and students.

In contrast, children in wealthy communities experienced a very different curriculum. For example, work in those classrooms was to develop one's analytical intellectual powers. The teachers asked the children to reason through problems and produce intellectual products of top academic quality. Language arts involved the analysis of language as a complex system that should be mastered, and writing assignments involved research reports for social studies and science. Social studies involved the discussion of concepts and independent research. Social life was not shunned but included for analysis.

Classroom discussions related to realistic and difficult social issues, such as reasons for inflation, the contamination of foods, or workers' strikes.

The teachers exercised little control over the students' movement and monitored the level of difficulty of lessons carefully to make sure they were intellectually challenging and satisfying to the students.

Although Anyon was careful not to generalize beyond her sample, subsequent work by others suggests the validity of her characterizations. For example, recent research by Oakes (1986), focusing on tracking and using a national data base (Goodlad, 1984), reached a similar conclusion about the social context of schooling: there is an unequal distribution of schooling that favors the already-privileged; white and affluent students receive more of what seems to be effective teaching than do other groups; minority and poor students receive an emphasis on low-level basic literacy and computational skills. As the social class of the community increases, there is a concomitant shift in instruction from rote to more process-oriented teaching, from simplicity to complexity, and from low to high expectations. As Oakes (1986) noted, "There is no presumption that high-status knowledge is equally appropriate for all" (p.74).

We get a sense of the pervasiveness of this phenomenon from the research on the uses of computers in schools: in general, poor children do drill and practice; affluent children do programming and problem solving (Center for the Social Organization of Schools, 1983–1984). A similar reduction of the curriculum occurs in classrooms for limited-English-proficient children. In these classrooms there is the additional tendency to simplify the curriculum's complexity to match the limited-English speaker's level of English proficiency. This simplification or watering-down of the curriculum may occur in several ways; for example, by relegating limited-English-proficient students to low-level academic work, regardless of their literate competence in their first language, or by not allowing these students to participate in what are perceived as cognitively demanding activities, such as expository writing (Diaz et al., 1986; Goldenberg, 1984; Moll, 1986; Walsh, 1987).

In sum, the schooling of "disadvantaged" students is intimately linked to their social-class standing. This schooling can be characterized as atomistic, highly structured, repetitive, and emphasizing the learning of low-level skills. This form of instruction is so common that, as Edelsky (1986) has suggested, it is easy to assume that it is just how schooling must be if children are having difficulty. Note the recommendations of two leading educational psychologists (Brophy & Good, 1986, as cited in Ralph, 1988, p.7):

> low-SES-low-achieving students need more control and structuring from their teachers: more active instruction and feedback, more redundancy, and smaller steps with higher success rates. This will mean more review, drill, and practice, and thus more lower-level questions. Across the school year, it will mean exposure to less material, but with emphasis on mastery of the material that is taught and on moving students through the curriculum as briskly as they are able to progress.

OUTSTANDING TEACHING OF "DISADVANTAGED" STUDENTS

The classroom analysis reported herein provides an important contrast to the forms of instruction described above. The study formed part of a larger project on "effective" schooling conducted in three elementary schools and seven classrooms in a major metropolitan area of the Southwest.[1] The schools were nominated to participate in the study by educational administrators and teachers from twelve metropolitan school districts. The classrooms selected for study were highly rated by the educators and the students had scored at or above grade level for at least two years on measures of academic achievement.

I will summarize our observations of two fifth-grade teachers, one Spanish-English bilingual and the other an English monolingual, concentrating on the characteristics of reading and writing instruction. Both classrooms were located in working-class communities and most students in both classrooms were Hispanic. We conducted approximately one hundred hours of observation, and every teacher was videotaped monthly for a period of five hours. In addition, we collected data through formal and informal interviews and compiled classroom documents and records, including samples of the students' work.

---

1. This work was supported by a grant to Eugene Garcia from the Inter-University Program for Latino Research and the Social Science Research Council.

Central to the teachers' approach was a view of literacy as the understanding and communication of meaning. In particular, they believed that reading comprehension and written expression must be developed through functional, relevant, and meaningful language use. Therefore, one of their major instructional goals was to make their classrooms literate environments in which many language experiences could take place and different types of "literacies" could be practiced, understood, and learned. These teachers rejected rote instruction or reducing reading and writing into skill sequences taught in isolation or in a successive, stage-like manner. Rather, they emphasized the creation of social contexts in which children actively learned to use, try out, and manipulate language in the service of making sense or creating meaning. The teachers saw their role as providing the necessary guidance or social arrangements so that children, through their own efforts, could assume control of diverse purposes and uses of oral and written language. Their approach is consistent with the recommendations of recent studies of effective literacy and language learning, which consistently point out the importance of students interacting frequently, purposefully, and meaningfully with language and text (Edelsky, 1986; Farr, 1986; Goodman, 1986; Langer & Applebee, 1986; 1987; Moll & R. Diaz, 1987). These studies stress the importance of children learning language and literacy as a medium of communication instead of as a static subject with sets of isolated topics, facts, or skills that must be learned, as is common in most classrooms (Goodlad, 1984; Langer, 1984; Oakes, 1986).

The students learned the curriculum through different social arrangements that teachers facilitated. The teachers strategically *mediated* these social arrangements to engage students or to give them practice with different aspects of the process (Moll, 1989; Vygotsky, 1978). Further, regardless of individual differences in teaching or in children, including differences in English language proficiency, the teachers mediated in similar ways the children's interaction with the classroom content. They facilitated learning through creating related tasks or activities, rather than controlled learning by imposing a single model of learning for the children to follow (Moll, 1988).

For example, reading was integrated into almost all of the students' classroom activities. No basal readers were ever used; the teachers relied on trade books that were interesting and challenging to the students. As well, the teachers did not group children by ability, a common practice in classrooms (Goodlad, 1984); instead they grouped them by interest or by activity, such as grouping students reading about dinosaurs or about volcanos for the science project. Students read in many different ways: silently to themselves or to other students, either in a small group or to the whole class. The teachers also read to the children daily. Throughout, the teachers encouraged the students to make sense of what they read, and to be critical readers of others' work and of their own.

The following example is illustrative. In a lesson the teacher and seven students of mixed reading abilities discussed a novel they had been reading about the U. S. revolutionary war. The teacher pointed out to the students the different personal relationships presented in the novel to capture how the war was affecting people's lives In what resembled a conversation, with the students more actively involved than in the usual recitation that makes up lessons (Durkin, 1978–1979; Goodlad, 1984; Tharp & Gallimore, 1988), the discussion included the teacher's and students' observations about the role of women in society, how different political allegiances could disrupt a family, the role of religious beliefs and family discipline, how a novel can make history more understandable, and the nature of colonialism. None of these topics formed part of any curricular script; they arose and evolved through the participants' joint discussion of text. The teacher would monitor casually, but carefully, the students' participation, contributions, and understanding of the text, providing more time to some students as needed.

During regularly held reading conferences, students summarized what they had read, expressed their feelings about the story, indicated what they liked most or least about the story and why, predicted what would happen next, and explained the basis of their predictions, confirmed or disconfirmed past predictions, and compared the text to books they had read before. The students often selected, depending on their interests, what books they wanted to read; the teacher selected the books she read aloud to the students. The students would also meet once a week with younger students, usually first graders, to read to them and to listen to them read.

As with reading, children were involved in writing activities for a major part of the day. Students would write almost every day on a topic of their choice. They would develop drafts and ask classmates to read their work and provide feedback, or sought the teacher's comments to help with their editing. Sometimes students would read aloud what they were writing to the whole class to obtain their feedback. The class would comment on the introduction of the story, character development, dialogue, and what they liked about the story or essay. Students also wrote literature logs on their readings, where they would comment on stories or articles they had read, wrote in daily journals or diaries, and wrote poetry and letters. In the bilingual classroom, the students could read or write in either language. We observed students reading a story in English and writing in their logs in Spanish, and vice versa. The teachers encouraged their students to write original and creative pieces, in either language.

Writing also formed part of other sections of the curriculum. For example, in one class the students were involved in science projects for a considerable amount of time. They selected their topics and worked individually or with a group of students. They researched their topic by going to the library, interviewing people in the field, reading, and viewing films, and then wrote a final research report accompanied by visuals and other products of their research. The students produced drafts of the report and edited them with the assistance of the teacher and other students in the class. The teacher asked the students to use descriptive language so that the "non-experts" in their field of research could understand their project. The students then edited their final drafts for spelling, punctuation, syntax, and clarity.

KEY ELEMENTS IN THE TEACHING

As illustrated above, the teachers assumed that the children were competent and capable and that as instructors it was their primary responsibility to provide the students with a challenging, innovative, and intellectually rigorous curriculum. The teachers considered the idea of "watering down" the curriculum as unacceptable or, as one of the teachers expressed it, "degrading and disrespectful to the children." Accordingly, the teachers emphasized the lessons' substance and content in teaching and in motivating the students' learning. What children read mattered and the teachers emphasized high-quality trade books that contained stories that were meaningful and interesting to the students, or relevant to the academic topic they were examining.

Reading and writing always involved analysis of text and the comprehension of content, with special emphasis on the students' examination of the authors' and their own use of language and how it influenced their thinking. This means not only reading comprehension, but understanding how meaning is created and communicated. For example, the teachers helped the students understand strategies authors used to convey meaning. Through their questioning, the teachers helped the students examine the writers' strategies in some depth: how writers manipulate words, phrases, descriptions, or dialogue to influence readers. The teachers also helped the students analyze the strategies they used as readers to understand text by having them make predictions and guesses about what would happen next in a story and explain why. In short, the teachers' emphasis on substance and content facilitated the frequent occurrence of what were in essence metalinguistic and metacognitive events: *the conscious examination of others' and one's own use of language and thinking.*

It also was the case that meaningful content was a key in facilitating the learning of English. In both the bilingual and monolingual classrooms, the teachers concerned themselves primarily with organizing learning activities that involved students substantively in the class. One of the teachers put is as follows: "The richer the content, the more the students had something they connected to." This idea is similar to Genesee's (1986) suggestion that second-language learners will learn a second language to the extent that they are motivated by the curriculum to learn the academic material. It is the students' interest in things academic that motivates them to learn the second language or to retain and develop their first language. Thus, in both classrooms, learning English was a residual goal of academic performance.

As part of lessons, the teachers encouraged students to use their personal experiences to make sense of the classroom content. The children would regularly introduce topics that came from their home or community experiences and the teacher used their comments to expand the children's understanding of the lessons (e.g., Tikunoff, 1985; Wong-Fillmore & Valadez, 1985). This was most evident in reading lessons where the children often contributed personal observations and anecdotes to make a point or comment about the text.

In contrast to the usual recommendations for a highly structured curriculum, we observed a diversity of learning arrangements in the classrooms. Reading and writing, for example, took place in many ways, and they were usually integrated as part of a broader activity. The teachers also used the different instructional situations to assess children, relying on observations of the students' performance in several contexts to reach conclusions about their progress and the type of assistance they might need. Regardless of instructional arrangement or of student characteristic, the essence of instruction in these classrooms was the understanding and communication of meaning.

INVESTIGATING COMMUNITY-MEDIATED SCHOOLING

The instructional approach described above emphasizes literacy learning and development in the service of various academic goals. It also makes use of the students' experiences and interests to facilitate literacy learning at the highest level possible, thus avoiding the "watered-down" curriculum typical of working-class schooling. We believe that this approach can be extended much further, however, to link systematically what goes on in classrooms with family activities and community life; that is, to situate the schooling of children in the sociohistorical specifics of the community. Our goal is not only to facilitate family and community involvement in classroom instruction, but to explore the possible influence of school learning on home activities (e.g., Levin, 1987; Philips, 1983; Pousada, 1987).

We are particularly interested in elaborating the relationship between what Vygotsky (1987, ch. 6) called "everyday" and "scientific" (academic or scholarly) concepts. In brief, Vygotsky believed that the processes for developing each type of concept depend on, and influence, each other. Everyday concepts provide the "living knowledge," "conceptual fabric," and motivation for acquiring scientific concepts, which, in turn, provide a more conscious way of operating on everyday concepts. One extends the other; the everyday concepts give meaning to the scientific, and the scientific transforms the way the child perceives the everyday concepts. As Vygotsky (1987) wrote, "In receiving instruction in a system of knowledge, the child learns of things that are not before his eyes, things that far exceed the limits of his actual and even potential immediate experience" (p. 180).

How can we use community knowledge to enhance classroom learning and classroom knowledge to enhance community learning? The key, Vygotsky seemed to suggest, is to embed both academic and social knowledge within a system of instruction; to create meaningful connections between scientific and social life through the concrete learning activities of the students. These meaningful connections develop and build on the conscious awareness of the student; in particular, the awareness of how she or he can use the everyday to make sense of the classroom content and use the classroom activities to understand social reality (e.g., Freire, 1983). Vygotsky (1987) wrote that "conscious awareness enters through the gate opened up by the scientific concept" (p. 191). But scientific concepts always form part of a specific system or social organization of instruction. We hardly believe that rote instruction of low-level skills is the system of instruction that Vygotsky had in mind. Rather, the sources of conscious awareness are found in instructional systems that facilitate the types of conceptual discourse described above, and in a social system where the role of the teacher is to provide the necessary support and guidance so that children, through their own efforts, assume conscious control of the purposes and uses of oral and written language.

We are conducting a research project intended to introduce innovations into the teaching of literacy by facilitating close collaboration between researchers and practitioners, community members and educators, and students and teachers. The project consists of three main, interrelated activities: (1) an ethnographic analysis of the transmission of knowledge and skills among households in a Latino community of Tucson, (2) creation of an after-school "lab" where researchers and teachers use community information to experiment with literacy instruction, and (3) classroom observations in which we both examine existing methods of instruction and explore how to change instruction by applying what is learned at the after-school lab (Moll, Velez-lbanez, & Greenberg, 1988).[2] All activities in lab and classrooms are documented through participant observations and the administration of other instruments. The goal is to create a "model system" in which diverse social, material, and intellectual resources are coordinated to advance the literacy instruction of Latino and other students. In what follows I will present a brief description of each component.

---

2. This project is supported by a contract from the Office of Bilingual Education and Minority Language Affairs, U.S. Department of Education.

Household Analysis

Our field work is guided by an important principle derived from previous community-based studies: *The Latino community represents a resource of enormous importance for educational change.* The research components described here are designed to help us identify and capitalize on these resources for literacy instruction. We are focusing on a broad and significant sociocultural practice or activity, which we have called "mechanisms of exchange" (see Greenberg, 1984; Velez-Ibanez, 1988). By this term we mean the wide and prevalent use, particularly among Mexican-American households, of reciprocal exchange relations to recruit persons into clusters of social networks. These flexible, social networks facilitate two important functions: (1) enable economic- and labor-related exchanges and (2) form social contexts for the transmission of knowledge, skills, and cultural values and norms.

We are presently analyzing two important aspects of these social networks. One is the prevalence and extent of these networks among our study sample (N = 30). Our preliminary analysis of the data indicates that each household has an average of six members and is connected to approximately seven related (kin) households in the general community. In addition, 88 percent of our sample report assisting others with tasks or chores, including child care and household repairs, suggesting an ongoing exchange. For example, 31 percent of the families report other friends or relatives taking care of their child daily or up to twice a week. This extended familism incorporates people who are not kin, occurs despite class standing or language preference, and seems to become more extensive with generational advancement and socioeconomic mobility. That is, instead of these networks dissipating with "acculturation," they seem to get even more involved and extensive.

Our initial observations also suggest that these networks are transnational: households in Tucson are closely linked through these social networks to households in Mexico. There is a constant exchange of information, capital, and visits. One goal of these inter-town contacts is the "cross cultural" socialization of children. As one family put it, they value the trips to Mexico so that their son can interact with his cousins and learn how to take care of himself in the Mexican context (*para que pueda hablar y platicar con sus primos y defen-*

derse); they also expect their son to readapt when he returns to Tucson.

These data highlight the multidimensional, thick social relationships that constitute life outside the classroom. These multiple relationships contrast with the singular teacher-child relationship common in classrooms. Our initial analysis, therefore, indicates the importance of the *social character of learning*: how the acquisition, use, and transmission of knowledge is deeply embedded in diverse social relationships.

The second aspect that we are elaborating is the nature of the "funds of knowledge" that these households exchange. These clustered households, distinct from nuclear-based families prominent in the Anglo middle-class, share knowledge regarding not only repair of homes and automobiles, home remedies, planting and gardening, and sales, but also access to institutional assistance, school programs, transportation, occupational opportunities, and other services. Briefly put, the *households' funds of knowledge are wide-ranging and abundant*. They are central to home life, and we are convinced that they can be central to the children's schooling.

Our present analysis is trying to articulate further this theoretical concept to clarify its instructional utility. For example, we are tracing the history of specific funds of knowledge; most are related to the households' rural origins and modes of economic production. We are also analyzing what specific household activities make use of these funds of knowledge; that is, how they are learned, organized, and transmitted. We have found there is an identifiable household pedagogy; there is an identifiable organization to learning (e.g., Anderson & Stokes, 1984; Greenfield & Lave, 1982; Levin, 1987; Levin, Brenner, & Mehealani McClellan, 1987). For project purposes, we are differentiating whether the knowledge is taught explicitly or is tacitly learned. Knowledge that is taught explicitly often involves a sequence of instruction; for example, how to assemble a bicycle or repair an appliance. (This example is not trivial. One of the boys in the study assembles bicycles from discarded and used parts and sells them to children in the neighborhood.) These events are characterized by the *conscious* attempt to transfer knowledge to someone else and are school-like in their organization. These teaching attempts contrast with the implicit acquisition of "folk" knowledge, usually obtained by being in the household environment (e.g., knowledge about plants). The social networks and their exchanges provide a motive and a context for applying much of this knowledge. This knowledge may remain "hidden" until activated for purposes of assisting others (e.g., knowledge about self-medication). To be sure, folk knowledge can be taught explicitly, but a special time is not usually set aside for the deliberate instruction in these matters, it is not as school-like.

A third differentiation is knowledge that requires further institutional support, say, from school or work, such as knowledge about accounting, sales, or computers. An important activity in the households is the learning of English. Several families in the study are taking English classes or know somebody who is studying English. The learning of English is an activity that seems to require considerable institutional support.

We are addressing several questions based on our deepening understanding of these funds of knowledge. How can we take full advantage of both tacit and explicit knowledge to improve instructional practices? How are the household social relations similar to or different from the social relations teachers establish with children in schools? What is the role of school-based knowledge in the households?

Another set of questions involves the role of literacy in these household practices. How is literacy used? What is the community's perception of literacy? More specifically, what is the role of literacy in the formation and function of these mechanisms of exchange? How does literacy in school differ from literacy out of school, and how are they related? And, particularly, what links can we create between learning in school and learning out of school; between using literacy in school and out of school (see Moll & R. Diaz, 1987)?

Third, how do these networks, as coping mechanisms, shape the families' perceptions of how the broader social system operates? How do they influence groups' perceptions about success? In particular, how do they shape the community's view of schools and their functions? According to Ogbu (e.g., Ogbu & Matute-Bianchi, 1986), notions about success are an important part of a group's socialization process and their relations to the broader social system. These attitudes or beliefs may influence decisively the importance placed upon schooling and the effort students may exert in school.

In summary, our household study is collecting data on three main areas of inquiry: the social basis of teaching and learning in the homes; the uses of knowledge and literacy in the family and their social networks; and folk theories about society, schools, and schooling.

The After-School Lab

Previous research has shown that it is very hard to transport community information directly into classrooms. Sometimes the relevance of the information is not apparent; sometimes the information does not make sense to teachers. Therefore, conditions must be created that ease the integration of community data into instruction in ways academically beneficial to the students (Moll & R. Diaz, 1987).

Our after-school lab serves as an intermediate structure between the community and the classrooms. At this lab researchers, teachers, and students meet weekly to experiment with the teaching and learning of literacy. This idea has much in common with Berliner's (1985) notion of creating pedagogical laboratories where teachers would have "students to teach concepts to, where expert teachers can provide critiques of the lessons, and where the peers of the novice teacher and the children themselves can join in the analysis of the teaching activities that just occurred" (p. 6). Our study, however, combines an educational laboratory with community field studies and classroom analyses.

The main characteristics of this lab are derived from our theoretical position, which emphasizes the prime importance of social context in literacy learning and the interactive role of adults and peers in creating such contexts (Langer & Applebee, 1986; Moll & S.Diaz, 1987; Scribner & Cole, 1981). In particular, we are stressing the active participation of students in learning literacy. Therefore, one of our main tasks at the after-school setting is to create social environments that allow students to use reading and writing in many forms and ways; to organize communicative relationships and social transactions where adults help children understand and master different types of literacy (see Heath, 1986; Wells, 1986).

For example, in our current work we are implementing four related activities. First, the children are doing a survey of community literacy. They are recording where literacy is found, who uses it, and for what. A goal is for the children to become consciously aware of the many uses of literacy within their environment. Second, building on a genealogical activity that the children are doing in their classrooms, they are creating a fictitious family, complete with roles and descriptions for each family member and friends, including a description of the family's social network. Note that we are using the children's funds of knowledge to develop the activity. Third, we are using the school's computers to write and edit and to communicate. We are currently linked to children and teachers in San Diego, Puerto Rico, and New York City. As part of these connections, the students are comparing the results of their activities with similar activities conducted at these other sites. They are also analyzing educational software and communicating the results of their analysis to their peers. In short, the students use their reading and writing extensively to participate in the social (communicative) system of the lab.

Classroom Research

The third and final part of our study involves classroom research. Our goal here is twofold: analyze the existing organization of instruction and establish a relationship between the classrooms and the after-school site as a way of introducing innovations into teaching practices.

To achieve the first goal, we are observing in classrooms to describe and analyze literacy instruction and other classroom events. We are currently observing or initiating observations in twelve classrooms. We will be addressing questions such as How are teachers organizing instruction? What is the extent of English and Spanish literacy instruction? How are they teaching reading? How are they teaching writing?

What sort of outcomes do we foresee? We fully expect teachers to improve their teaching of literacy. We expect that working collaboratively with peers and researchers will influence their perceptions about teaching, about how children learn, and about the nature of schooling for limited-English-proficient students. We also will assess changes in the students' literacy learning. We expect that students in both the lab and classrooms will demonstrate improvement in their literacy acquisition and development and that the students in the implementing classrooms will outperform the comparison classrooms in all of the project's literacy measures.

We plan to assess the degree to which the literacy modules helped teachers and schools take advantage of community resources. We expect teachers to make use of these resources as part of their daily classroom instruction and to use ethnographic modes of inquiry with their students in identifying and utilizing hidden resources for the teaching of literacy. We also expect teachers to form networks to help other teachers use the lab to address problems and issues in literacy learning. We anticipate that there will develop considerable parental interest and participation in their children's schooling as parents become important resources for their children's literacy development. Finally, we will develop a model system that is replicable by teachers and school personnel in other locations for purposes of teacher training, parental participation, and to address specific issues in the teaching and learning of literacy.

CONCLUSION

I have reviewed several issues regarding the education of minority students. I have emphasized the importance of broader circumstances of living in understanding the nature of their schooling and described the severe instructional constraints they face. In contrast to their wealthier peers, minority students are subjected to a "disabling" education. I also highlighted, however, the possibilities of reorganizing instruction in ways that are much more enabling, and described a research project that attempts to combine school and community resources to advance literacy instruction and learning.

REFERENCES

Anderson, A. B., & Stokes, S. (1984). Social and institutional influences on the development and practice of literacy. In H. Goelman et al. (Eds.), *Awakening to literacy*. New York: Heinemann.

Anyon, J. (1980). Social class and the hidden curriculum of work. *Journal of Education, 162*(1), 67–92.

Anyon, J. (1981). Elementary schooling and the distinctions of social class. *Interchange 12*, 118–132.

Berliner, D. C. (1985). Laboratory settings and the study of teacher education. *Journal of Teacher Education, 36*(6), 2–8.

Brophy, J. E., & Good, T. L. (1986). Teacher behavior and student achievement. In M. C. Wittrock (Ed.), *Handbook of research on teaching* (3rd ed.). New York: Macmillan.

Cazden, C. (1983). Can ethnographic research go beyond the status quo? *Anthropology and Education Quarterly, 14*(1), 33–41.

Center for the Social Organization of Schools. (1983–1984). *School uses of microcomputers: Reports from a national survey (Issues 1 through 6)*. Baltimore, MD: Johns Hopkins University.

Cole, M., & Griffin, P. (Eds.). (1986). *Contextual factors in education.* Final report to the Carnegie Corporation. San Diego: University of California, Laboratory of Comparative Human Cognition.

Delgado-Gaitan, C. (1987). Traditions and transitions in the learning process of Mexican children: An ethnographic view. In G. & L. Spindler (Eds.), *Interpretive ethnography of education: At home and abroad.* Hillsdale, NJ: Erlbaum.

Diaz, S., Moll, L. C., & Mehan, H. (1986). Sociocultural resources in instruction: a context-specific approach. In California State Department of Education, *Beyond language: Social and cultural factors in schooling language minority children* (pp. 187–230). Los Angeles: Evaluation, Dissemination and Assessment Center, California State University.

Durkin, D. (1978–1979). What classroom observations reveal about reading comprehension instruction. *Reading Research Quarterly, 14,* 481–533.

Edelsky, C. (1986). *Writing in a bilingual program: Habia una vez.* Norwood, NJ: Ablex.

Farr, M. (1986). Language, culture, and writing: Sociolinguistic foundations of research on writing. In E. Z. Rothkopf (Ed.), *Review of research in education* (pp. 195–224). Washington, DC: American Educational Research Association.

Freire, P. (1983). The importance of the act of reading. *Journal of Education, 165*(1), 5–11.

Gallimore, R. (1985). *The accommodation of instruction to cultural differences.* Paper presented at the University of California Conference on the Underachievement of Linguistic Minorities, Lake Tahoe, CA.

Gamorans, A., & Berends, M. (1987). The effects of stratification in secondary schools: Synthesis of survey and ethnographic research. *Review of Educational Research, 57*(4), 415–435.

Genesee, F. (1986). The baby and the bathwater or, what immersion has to say about bilingual education. *NABE Journal, 10*(3), 227–254.

Goldenberg, C. N. (1984). *Roads to reading: Studies of Hispanic first graders at risk for reading failure.* Unpublished doctoral dissertation, University of California at Los Angeles.

Goodlad, J. (1984). *A place called school.* New York: McGraw-Hill.

Goodman, K. (1986). *What's whole in whole language?* Portsmouth, NH: Heinemann.

Greenberg, J. B. (1984). *Household economy and economic sector participation in Douglas, Arizona and Agua Prieta, Sonora.* Unpublished manuscript.

Greenfield, P., & Lave, J. (1982). Cognitive aspects of informal education. In D. Wagner & H. Stevenson (Eds.), *Cultural perspectives on child development.* San Francisco: Freeman & Co.

Heath, S. B. (1983). *Ways with words: Language, life, and work in communities and classrooms.* New York: Cambridge University Press.

Heath, S. B. (1986). Sociocultural contexts of language development. In California State Department of Education, *Beyond language: Social and cultural factors in schooling language minority children* (pp. 143–186). Los Angeles: Evaluation, Dissemination and Assessment Center, California State University.

Jordan, C. (1985). Translating culture: From ethnographic information to educational program. *Anthropology & Education Quarterly, 16,* 106–123.

Langer, J. (1984). Literacy instruction in American school: Problems and perspectives. *American Journal of Education, 93,* 107–132.

Langer, J., & Applebee, A. (1986). Reading and writing instruction: Toward a theory of teaching and learning. In E. Z. Rothkopf (Ed.), *Review of research in education* (pp. 171–194). Washington, D.C.: American Educational Research Association.

Langer, J., & Applebee, A. (1987). *How writing shapes thinking: A study of teaching and learning* (NCTE Research Report No. 22). Urbana, IL: National Council of Teachers of English.

Language Policy Task Force. (1982). *Intergenerational perspectives on bilingualism: From community to classroom.* New York: Hunter College, Centro de Estudios Puertorriquenos.

Language Policy Task Force. (1984). *Speech and ways of speaking in a bilingual Puerto Rican community* (Report No. NIE-G-81-054). Washington, DC: National Institute of Education.

LCHC (Laboratory of Comparative Human Cognition). (1986). The contributions of cross-cultural research to educational practice. *American Psychologist, 41*(10) 1049–1058.

Levin, P. (1987). *The impact of preschool on teaching and learning in Hawaiian families.* Paper presented at the annual meeting of the American Anthropological Association, November.

Levin, P., Brenner, M., & Mehealani McClellan, J. (1987). *The social context of early literacy in Hawaiian homes.* Unpublished paper.

Lubeck, S. (1984). Kinship and classrooms: An ethnographic perspective on education as cultural transmission. *Sociology of Education, 57,* 219–232.

McDermott, R. P. (1987). The explanation of minority school failure, again. *Anthropology and Education Quarterly, 18*(4), 361–364.

Moll, L. C. (1986). Writing as communication: Creating strategic learning environments for students. *Theory Into Practice, 25*(2), 102–108.

Moll, L. C. (1988). Key issues in teaching Latino students. *Language Arts, 65*(5), 465–472.

Moll, L. C. (1989). Teaching second language students: A Vygotskian perspective. In D. Johnson & D. Roen (Eds.), *Richness in writing: Empowering ESL students.* New York: Longman.

Moll, L. C., & Diaz, R. (1987). Teaching writing as communication: The use of ethnographic findings in classroom practice (pp. 195–221). In D. Bloome (Ed.), *Literacy and schooling* (pp. 55–65). Norwood, NJ: Ablex.

Moll, L. C., & Diaz, S. (1987). Change as the goal of educational research. *Anthropology and Education Quarterly, 18*(4), 300–311.

Moll, L. C., Velez-Ibanez, C., & Greenberg, J. (1988). *Project implementation plan. Community knowledge and classroom practice: Combining resources for literacy instruction* (Technical report, Development Associates Subcontract No. L-10). Tucson, AZ: University of Arizona, College of Education and Bureau of Applied Research in Anthropology.

Morris, R., & Conan, L. (1983). *A writing of our own: Improving the functional writing of urban secondary students* (final report). Philadelphia: University City Science Center. (ERIC Document Reproduction Service No. 241 668).

Oakes, J. (1986). Tracking, inequality, and the rhetoric of school reform: Why schools don't change. *Journal of Education, 168,* 61–80.

Ogbu, J., & Matute-Bianchi, E. (1986). Understanding sociocultural factors: Knowledge, identity, and school adjustment. In California State Department of Education, *Beyond language: Social and cultural factors in schooling language minority children* (pp. 73–142). Los Angeles: Evaluation, Dissemination and Assessment Center, California State University.

Page, R. (1987). Teachers' perceptions of students: A link between classrooms, school cultures, and the social order. *Anthropology and Education Quarterly, 18*(2), 77–99.

Philips, S. U. (1983). *The invisible culture: Communication in classroom and community on the Warm Springs Indian Reservation.* New York: Longman.

Pousada, A. (1987). *Puerto Rican community participation in East Harlem bilingual programs* (Working paper #11, Language Policy Task Force.) New York: Hunter College, Centro de Estudios Puertorriquenos.

Ralph, J. (1988, March). *Planning paper for the Center on the Study of the Education of Disadvantaged Students.* Washington, DC: Office of Educational Research and Improvement, U.S. Department of Education.

Ramsey, P.D.K. (1983). Fresh perspectives on the school transformation-reproduction debate: A response to Anyon from the antipodes. *Curriculum Inquiry, 13,* 296–320.

Ramsey, P.D.K. (1985). Social class and school knowledge: A rejoinder to Anyon. *Curriculum Inquiry, 15,* 215–222.

Reyes, L. (1987). *Demographics of Puerto Rican/Latino students in New York and the United States.* New York: Aspira.

Scribner, S., & Cole, M. (1981). *The psychology of literacy.* Cambridge, MA: Harvard University Press.

Smith, D. (1981a). Ethnographic monitoring of children's acquisition of reading/language arts skills in and out of the classroom: General findings. *The Generator, 12*(2), 37–68.

Smith, D. (1981b). Ethnographic monitoring: A way to understanding by those who are making schooling work. *The Generator, 12*(2), 69–92.

Smith, D. (1987). Illiteracy as social fault: Some principles of research and some results. In D. Bloome (Ed.), *Literacy and schooling* (pp. 55–65). Norwood, NJ: Ablex.

Steinberg, L., Blinde, P. L., & Chan, K. (1982). Dropping out among minority youth. *Review of Educational Research, 54*(1), 113–132.

Tharp, R. (1989). Psychocultural variables and constants: Effects on teaching and learning in schools. *American Psychologist, 44*(2), 349– 359.

Tharp, R., & Gallimore, R. (1988). *Rousing minds to life: Teaching, learning and schooling in social context.* Cambridge, MA: Cambridge University Press.

Tikunoff, W. (1985). *Applying significant bilingual instructional features in the classroom.* Rosslyn, VA: National Clearinghouse for Bilingual Education.

Velez-Ibanez, C. G. (1988). Networks of exchange among Mexicans in the U.S. and Mexico: Local-level mediating responses to national and international transformations. *Urban Anthropology, 17*(1), 27–51.

Vogt, L., Jordan, C., & Tharp, R. (1987). Explaining school failure, producing school success: Two cases. *Anthropology and Education Quarterly, 18*(4), 276–286.

Vygotsky, L. S. (1978). *Mind in society.* Cambridge, MA: Harvard University Press.

Vygotsky, L. S. (1987). Speech and thinking. In L. S. Vygotsky, *Collected works, Vol. 1* (pp. 39–285) (R. Rieber & A. Carton, Eds.; Minick, N., Trans.). New York: Plenum.

Walker, L. C. (1987). Hispanic achievement: Old views and new perspectives. In H. Trueba (Ed.), *Success or failure: Learning and the language minority student* (pp. 15–32). Cambridge, MA: Newbury.

Walsh, C. (1987). Schooling and the civic exclusion of Latinos: Toward a discourse of dissonance. *Journal of Education, 169*(2), 115–131.

Wells, G. (1986). *The meaning makers: Children learning language and using language to learn.* Portsmouth, NH: Heinemann.

Wilcox, K. (1982). Differential socialization in the classroom: Implications for equal opportunity. In G. Spindler (Ed.), *Doing the ethnography of schooling.* New York: Holt, Rinehart & Winston.

Willis, P. (1977). *Learning to labor.* New York: Columbia University Press.

Wong-Fillmore, L., & Valadez, C. (1985). Teaching bilingual learners. In M. C. Wittrock (Ed.), *Handbook of research on teaching* (3rd ed.). New York: Macmillan.

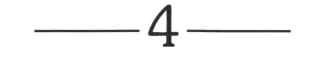

4

Review of Research on Curriculum and Instruction in Literacy

Michael S. Knapp and Margaret Needels

In this chapter, we focus primarily on curriculum and instruction in literacy, as it is—and can be—taught to disadvantaged students. Our emphasis is on instructional practices that are unique to this content area. Findings that reflect more generic knowledge about teaching are not discussed extensively here (see Chapter 12 for a more extended review of this research).

We divide literacy into two parts, one dealing with reading and the other with writing, but note that the two are closely related. Popular notions view the two as similar processes of constructing meaning. Reading and writing not only share a common communicative function, but also provide the basis for developing a system of personal thought (Langer, 1986). Both reading and writing involve an interaction between mind and text, and it is this interplay that leads to new knowledge, interpretations, and conceptualization.

This view of the role of reading and writing in the development of personal thought suggests a broad definition of literacy—one that goes beyond the set of functional skills required by routine life experience to include the capacity for thinking and reasoning that has come to be associated with highly developed literate behavior. At this level of proficiency, literate individuals are expected to be able to read many kinds of text with ease, understand their overt and covert messages, interpret them, and reason effectively with the written material at hand. They are also expected to be able to move beyond narrative and summative writing to more lengthy analytic writing.

However defined, underlying conceptions of literacy have a great deal to do with what one views as appropriate curricular content, teaching approach, and measures of effectiveness, even at the earliest grades in school. These in turn represent something more fundamental: what we deem to be sufficient skills in literacy. Because narrow functional conceptions of literacy can easily lead to a truncated curriculum that limits the future growth of disadvantaged students, we have approached this review assuming that literacy curriculum and instruction for disadvantaged students can and should include a broad set of competencies in the use of language, though not so broad as to sacrifice depth of coverage.

OVERARCHING ISSUES

Before discussing the literatures that pertain to teaching reading and writing, we note five issues that apply to all aspects of literacy instruction for disadvantaged students. The issues concern: (1) the purposes of literacy instruction for disadvantaged students, (2) the relative emphasis on (and relationships among) "basic" and "higher-order" skill components in the literacy curriculum, (3) the accommodation of students' linguistic and cultural backgrounds in literacy curriculum and instruction, (4) the integration of different elements in the literacy curriculum, and (5) the amount of literacy instruction low-achieving disadvantaged students receive. A few words about each issue serve to introduce the discussions of curriculum content and instructional practice that follow.

The Goals for Literacy Instruction Aimed at Disadvantaged Students

It is easy to assert that disadvantaged students should all receive the same curriculum and instruction in reading and writing as other students, but the practical realities of teaching—especially in schools serving large proportions of such students—often lead educators to adopt more modest goals. Either explicitly or implicitly, literacy instructors in such settings are often satisfied if they can get most students to a level of minimal, functional literacy. Critics, on the other hand, worry about the "watered-down" or "differentiated" curriculum available to such students who, they assert, are capable of more (Chapter 3). Research on the effects of differential expectations by teachers suggests that the critics' concerns are in some degree warranted. The crucial issue is whether to aim high or low when dealing with a population of students who appear, at first glance, to have little proficiency in literacy skills.

The Relative Emphasis on "Basic" and "Higher-order" Skill Components in the Literacy Curriculum

There is no universally accepted distinction between higher- and lower-order skills in literacy, or, for that matter, in any other area of the curriculum. Some scholars even dispute whether the distinction is useful at all (Resnick, 1987; Schrag, 1989). Nonetheless, most literacy scholars and educators would agree that when students draw inferences from written text, interpret what they read, or construct extended, coherent text, they are involved in a higher-order—that is, intellectually more demanding—activity than when they reproduce the sounds that correspond to commonly encountered phonemes, write simple descriptive sentences, or match vocabulary words with their definitions. Also, at any level of complexity, novel or unfamiliar reading and writing tasks require a more sophisticated capacity to construe and solve the problems posed by the tasks—that is, a "higher-order" skill—than do routine tasks.

At issue is the degree of emphasis to be placed on each level of skill, the desirability of teaching these skills separately from one another, and the timing of teaching them. At one pole of debate on this issue, scholars contend that disadvantaged students tend to need more attention to "basic" literacy skills (e.g., decoding, grammar, vocabulary recognition), of which they typically demonstrate less mastery, and that these skills must be acquired before higher-order skills (e.g., comprehension, text construction). At the other pole, scholars assert that basic skills are not a prerequisite to higher-order skills and that too much attention to basic skills may be counter-productive—by leaving too little time for work on comprehension or composition, providing few opportunities for applying spelling or phonic skills, or reducing student motivation to learn to read or write.

Accommodating the Students' Linguistic and Cultural Backgrounds

Because disadvantaged students include a disproportionate number from linguistic minority or nonmainstream backgrounds (e.g., ethnic minority as well as poor white children), literacy instruction, which centrally involves the use of language, must take account of these facts. At issue are (1) ways to make instruction in decoding, spelling, and so on, intelligible to those whose sound systems do not correspond to standard English; (2) the degree to which dialects or other languages should be permitted in literacy instruction; (3) the manner in which errors that stem from these sound systems are handled, for example, in ways that respect—or denigrate—the student's background (Scott, 1988; this volume, Chapter 3); and (4) the inclusion of content in literacy instruction that is meaningful in terms of the student's own experience. The spectrum of approaches to these issues is wide, ranging from strict insistence on correct English to the inclusion of other languages in bilingual education approaches.

Integration of Elements in Literacy Curriculum and Instruction

The more literacy programs focus on skill deficiencies and pre-scriptions for overcoming them, the more segregated or "fragmented" the curriculum is likely to become (other factors discussed below also encourage the fragmentation process). Embedded in such programs is the assumption that a systematic attack on the component skills, which disadvantaged students often have not mastered, is precisely what these students need. On the other hand, making the different elements of the literacy curriculum work together seems especially important for disadvantaged learners, who may have fewer chances outside of school to integrate and apply what they are learning about writing sentences, pronouncing phonemes, analyzing story structure, and so on (Johnston, Allington, & Afflerbach, 1985). Some observers argue that this is doubly important for those among the disadvantaged population who receive part (or all) of their literacy instruction from a supplementary program of some kind: the incoherent nature of the curriculum may be as much a cause of disadvantaged students' failure to learn as anything (see Chapter 1).

The Amount of Literacy Instruction for Low-achieving Disadvantaged Students

A simple way of approaching the matter is to assert that by providing low-achieving disadvantaged students more literacy instruction than is typically offered the student population as a whole, schools will overcome the disadvantage such students encounter. This position states in the starkest terms the theory underlying compensatory education, which by law and intention seeks to offer extra instructional help to disadvantaged students who are also poor readers or writers. On the whole, such programs do not appear to increase reliably the amount of time students spend in literacy instruction (e.g., Rowan, Guthrie, Lee, & Guthrie, 1986; Allington in Chapter 1 of this book). Schools with the highest concentrations of poor children tend to put less time into literacy instruction than other schools (Birman et al., 1987). In addition, there appears to be less time devoted to teaching writing to all students than many believe to be optimal, as recent NAEP findings suggest (LaPointe, 1986). Clearly, however, the absolute amount of time in instruction is not the only critical variable. As one scholar has observed, "The most efficient way to resolve a learning difficulty is not to double the amount of ineffective instruction" (see Chapter 1).

READING

Within the vast literature on the content, teaching, and learning of reading, a good deal of research bears on curriculum and instruction that is appropriate to disadvantaged students. We begin by reviewing briefly the principal categories of approaches to teaching reading and the conceptions of learning to read that underlie them. From there we turn to typical content and practices in reading programs for the general population as well as for disadvantaged students. Last, we summarize and synthesize what is known about effective instruction and curriculum in this subject area.

Approaches to Teaching Reading

Approaches to designing and implementing reading instruction can be arrayed along a continuum ranging from those that disaggregate reading into its component skills to those that emphasize the integration of language skills in activities aimed at the purposeful use of language. We distinguish three points on this continuum, although in practice a greater number of permutations exist within the field. We also note that the differences between particular approaches are neither simple nor unidimensional; nonetheless, the continuum we describe serves to capture some of the most salient distinctions as these apply to the task of teaching disadvantaged students.

- *Discrete-skills approaches.* At one end of the continuum, a pervasive set of approaches treats reading as the mastery of specific skills (e.g., Osborn, Wilson, & Anderson, 1985), the assumption being that once these "building blocks" are in place, the student will be able to make sense out of written text. These approaches put great emphasis on decoding—that is, breaking words and simple sentences into recognizable sound patterns and then reassembling these to decipher meaningful words and thoughts. Students need to be taught these skills in a systematic, formal way, although some scholars (e.g., Chall, 1983) assert that learners can pick up these skills more readily at certain developmental stages. Within this tradition, text materials are typically designed to expose students to skills in a sequential, ordered fashion. This is exemplified by the published series of phonetically controlled basal readers. Decoding skills, vocabulary, and comprehension are typically taught in a step-by-step, "direct instruction" mode (see Chapter 2).
- *Meaning-oriented reading approaches.* In the middle of the continuum, other scholars (e.g., Duffy et al., 1987; Collins, Brown, & Newman, 1989) emphasize the search for meaning in written text from early in the process of learning to read and deemphasize (or sometimes ignore altogether) practice with decoding skills. The types of text to be read can vary considerably in this tradition and

may include basal readers, child-appropriate literature, or text generated by the students themselves (e.g., stories transcribed by the teacher). Within this tradition, teaching approaches vary considerably but include a good deal of explicit, active teaching alongside student-initiated activity.

- *Integrated language approaches.* At the other end of the continuum, approaches also emphasize reading as the construction of meaning, but do so as part of activities that integrate reading, writing, and other forms of communication. Instruction based on "whole language" philosophies are the principal example of this category of approach (e.g., Altwerger, Edelsky, & Flores, 1987). These approaches seek to embed reading in a broader set of communicative activities that convey to the learner clear and important purposes for communication. Students' motivation for learning to read and the practice they get in reading skills arises naturally out of activities that involve written and other forms of expression. The teacher's role becomes more that of a facilitator; students are given greater responsibility for mastering and creating authentic texts.

The relative appropriateness of these approaches for disadvantaged students is a matter of debate. Although it is tempting to resolve the debate in favor of one or another approach, this is probably not a fruitful exercise. The actual payoff to students of any given instructional approach probably depends on more than the distinguishing attributes of the approach itself; factors discussed in other chapters (e.g., classroom management and instructional strategy factors reviewed in Chapter 12) have as much to do with the net benefit to a given group of students as does the approach.

Nonetheless, some observations can be made about assumptions and trade-offs implied by the different categories of approach. First, the approaches typically rest, explicitly or implicitly, on different assumptions about the process of learning to read. Integrated language approaches, for example, tend to assume that learning to read is a natural process; by repeated exposure to authentic reading material in properly motivated circumstances, most learners will acquire the appropriate skills (Goodman & Goodman, 1979).[1] Other

---

1. Some integrated language approaches, however, structure the learning process considerably—see Clay (1987).

categories of approach tend to assume that the learning process occurs in response to formal instruction that provides learners what they otherwise would not come by—in particular, discrete skills (e.g., Osborn et al., 1985) or structures for thinking and knowing (Calfee & Drum, 1986). Second, different instructional approaches structure the content of the curriculum differently: discrete-skills approaches fractionate the content, leaving the integration of skills up to the learner—a possible sacrifice of the whole for the parts. At the other end of the continuum, integrated language approaches maintain the integrity of the content as a meaningful whole, but with the possible loss of mastery of particular skills—a sacrifice of the parts for the whole. Third, the approaches typically put the locus of responsibility for managing the learning process in different places, with discrete-skills approaches placing it with the teacher and integrated language approaches placing it with the student while the teacher assumes a facilitative, enabling role. Finally, as one moves along the continuum toward integrated language approaches, more is required of the teacher. To share with students control over learning tasks, to push students beyond the surface reading of words to their meanings, to set up and facilitate situations in which reading (and writing) arise as natural and purposeful acts—all these goals assume sophistication on the teacher's part, which in the real world of schools is not always present.

The Typical Pattern of Reading Curriculum and Instruction in Grades 1 Through 8

The three categories of approach are not found in equal proportion among schools. For a variety of reasons, the typical pattern of reading instruction in grades 1 through 8 favors discrete-skills approaches, and, to a lesser extent, meaning-oriented approaches (although there is gradual movement in that direction). This happens both in the intended reading curriculum—the design of instruction embedded in published materials, frameworks and syllabi, and tests—and the enacted reading curriculum—the delivery of instruction within classrooms.

The Intended Reading Curriculum

To understand what schools set out to teach students in reading, one needs to look at the curriculum designs embedded in published reading materials, the district and state curricular frameworks or syllabi that govern what teachers are expected to do, and the tests that reinforce and account for the results of teaching.

The design of most contemporary reading materials (workbooks, readers, teachers' manuals, software) rests on the assumptions and learning theories implied by discrete-skills or meaning-oriented approaches. Although reading materials in current use for grades 1 through 8 take a great many forms, by default or by design their content falls into a predictable pattern (see Calfee, 1986, for an overview of this pattern). First, the materials structure the content in terms of a fixed sequence of skills to be learned. The materials often heavily emphasize phonetic decoding skills, the assumption being that these skills form the strongest foundation for later reading. Alternatively, the materials deemphasize decoding—for example, by introducing new words that do not correspond to a phonetic sequence—but still maintain a fixed structure for introducing increasingly complex text. Second, the materials include a great many repetitive, out-of-context drills to establish these skills, typically through workbook exercises designed for individual seatwork (Anderson, Hiebert, Scott, & Wilkinson, 1985). Third, the materials provide either few stimuli to help students probe text for meaning or a great many "comprehension" questions that may detract from the reading itself. Fourth, vocabulary-controlled and graded basal readers form the primary text to which students are exposed in the lower elementary grades (see Chapter 2); in the upper elementary and junior high school grades, the reading fare is more varied but generally has a dearth of interesting texts available to the disadvantaged reader.

Although they are clearly a major factor, the designs of contemporary reading materials alone do not determine what is taught to disadvantaged students. Other forces play an important role, among them (1) instructional philosophies and curricular decisionmaking at both the teacher and district levels; (2) the "content" of tests, to which curriculum planners and teachers often orient their instruction (Carbo, 1988); (3) state curricular guidelines and mandates; and (4) the fact of extensive government investment in remedial and compensatory reading programs. For various reasons, these forces tend to reinforce the same "discrete-skills" assumptions about the teaching and learning of reading that are embedded in published materials. For one thing, teachers often take the textbook as the basic structure for their teaching (published reading materials include teachers' manuals that encourage this practice). For another, multiple-choice standardized testing can most easily capture discrete skills (Carbo, 1988). In addition, accountability-minded educational agencies at the state and local levels tend to create reading/language arts frameworks and syllabi that are easily tested.

The Enacted Curriculum

The teaching of reading to all students, disadvantaged or otherwise, tends to emphasize the discrete-skills emphasis of the materials, tests, frameworks, and syllabi. In brief, the predominant pattern of reading instruction in lower elementary grades can be summarized as follows (based on Calfee, 1986):

1. "Reading" is a separate subject from "language arts" (which typically include various topics such as spelling, grammar, story writing, etc.).
2. Instruction tends to follow the sequence laid out in basal reading series and related materials, in particular, student workbooks and teachers' manuals.
3. A large proportion of instructional time is devoted to individual seatwork aimed at practicing these skills—perhaps two-thirds of the typical reading period (which allows the teacher to work with small reading groups one at a time).
4. Students typically receive reading instruction in small ability-based groups for a portion of the reading period. In groups, students take turns reading aloud to the teacher. The relative proficiency of these groups is well known to the class as a whole and is a basis for social ranking among students.
5. Instruction in reading "comprehension" is not extensive, and does not involve much thinking about, or working with, the text.
6. Assessment of reading instruction (a) reinforces the discrete-skills emphasis of instruction; (b) emphasizes recall and the location of information rather than understanding; and (c) tells relatively little about what students really know.

In the upper elementary grades, many elements of this pattern continue, especially for the poorer readers, who are felt to need further work in building their "basic" reading skills. For the better readers, the "reading" and "language arts" classes become increasingly more oriented to literature and composition, and the two are combined in a subject called "English." In addition, reading becomes a tool in other areas of the curriculum, especially social studies and science, but also mathematics. By junior high school, the transition is complete. Students typically are attending separate, tracked classes in "English," which generally are differentiated by the students' proficiency in reading and writing and which pursue curricula aimed at different ends. At the high end of the student proficiency continuum, the curriculum aims at preparing students for high school college preparation tracks (whether or not such tracks are formally declared), and at the low end for participation in vocational educational or other equivalent activities.

There are, of course, many variations on the theme, as well as substantial deviations from the pattern where educators subscribe to approaches that emphasize a meaning orientation or whole-language approach, but the practices we have described are widespread enough to form a conventional wisdom about the teaching of reading that is often unquestioned.

Taken together, the pattern of intended and enacted curriculum just described is a source of concern to many educators. Efforts to reform the teaching of reading have zeroed in on a number of assumptions underlying this pattern and have advocated a substantial shift away from discrete-skills approaches (Anderson et al., 1985). Findings from the National Assessment of Educational Progress (LaPointe, 1986; Applebee, Langer, & Mullis, 1988) further support the contention that, overall, current curriculum and instruction in reading may not challenge students sufficiently. These concerns have prompted some states to develop altogether different frameworks emphasizing meaning-oriented or integrated language approaches (e.g., California State Board of Education, 1987).

Curriculum and Instruction for Disadvantaged Students

The pattern is more pronounced in schools and classrooms serving large numbers of disadvantaged students, and is complicated by the various remedial or compensatory arrangements for helping students in these schools who have trouble learning to read and write. As critics have pointed out, this instructional pattern appears to work less well for disadvantaged students than for others (see Chapter 2).

Much of what we know about the curriculum and instruction to which disadvantaged students are exposed derives from studies of compensatory reading programs and from the literature on poor readers. From this literature, we can construct the following picture of the enacted curriculum in reading available to this student population.

The primary content of the reading curriculum, as conveyed to most disadvantaged learners, is a set of disaggregated language skills that lack meaning and coherence. The disaggregation or "fragmentation" of reading that all students experience in some degree is more pronounced, for several reasons, in classes serving large numbers of disadvantaged students. First, these classrooms have a high proportion of students who have not mastered the discrete skills that many teachers presume to be the building blocks of reading facility. Naturally enough, teachers often redouble their efforts to teach these skills. Second, disadvantaged students are less likely to have been exposed to certain prerequisites for reading skill—for example, the Standard English vocabulary that appears in written text. Accordingly, teachers set out to teach this vocabulary in a more systematic way, which typically means more vocabulary lists, more workbook assignments. Third, teachers' failure to take into account the sound systems students bring to school—such as those embedded in non-Standard English dialects or other languages spoken at home—makes the learning of skills such as phonics more difficult for many disadvantaged students (Scott, 1988). Once again, teachers' most natural response is to work even harder on the phonic skills in ways that confuse students or deprive them of opportunities to acquire other reading skills. Finally, disaggregating the content of reading into discrete skills lends itself to the multiple-setting instructional arrangements encouraged by separately funded supplementary programs, for example, by giving students help with decoding in the Chapter 1 resource room and leaving comprehension to the regular classroom. The result is that disadvantaged students have relatively less chance to "put it all together" and to apply what they are learning to meaningful and engaging activities involving written text.

Disadvantaged students are exposed to reading curricula that reflect limited resources and generally low expectations for their performance. Schools that serve large numbers of working-class and poor children typically provide instruction that differs qualitatively from what is offered to children from more affluent backgrounds. One observer summarized a series of studies that indicate that "in general [working-class and poor] children receive rote, drill and practice instruction, work that is highly structured and redundant" (Chapter 3). Studies that compare instruction across social-class lines suggest that, by contrast, students in affluent communities are more likely to receive instruction that promotes analytical abilities and a higher level of literacy skills (Anyon, 1981; Oakes, 1985). Resources for reading instruction—for example, readers, workbooks, computer software—are often less plentiful in schools serving large concentrations of disadvantaged students (see Chapter 5).[2] This has the effect of narrowing the range of reading content or the types of learning experiences these students may have. In addition, it is well established that teachers often expect less of students who bear some distinguishable sign of disadvantagement (e.g., limited English proficiency, ethnic background).

Teachers tend to treat poor readers in ways that may compound the problems these students have with reading. Research on poor readers suggests that they are taught differently from their more advantaged counterparts. Some might argue that these differences are justified; students who feel defeated by a page of text, for example, are not necessarily ones who should be asked to read long works. But a number of scholars are concerned that differences in instructional practices such as the following may work against poor students' learning to read:

- Teachers tend to interrupt poor readers more often than good readers to correct the same kinds of mistakes, with the effect that poor readers get less practice developing fluency and less chance to learn self-correction skills (see work summarized in Chapter 1).
- Teachers tend to ask poor readers fewer comprehension questions, so these students need to think less about what they are reading (e.g., Garcia & Pearson in Chapter 2 of this book; Moll, Estrada, Diaz, & Lopes, 1980).
- Poor readers typically have fewer opportunities for silent reading (Applebee et al., 1988); their oral reading experiences put them "on show"—which exposes their failures to others on a regular basis.

---

2. Supplementary materials purchased through federal or state categorical programs may be in abundance, but these are typically kits, games, exercise books, tapes, and the like, designed for discrete-skills practice rather than for extended text reading.

- Poor readers tend to have a narrower range of appropriate texts to read and are allowed to exercise less discretion in selecting what they will read than good readers. This pattern reflects, in part, the paucity of good, interesting materials for beginning readers; for example, basal reading series still do not contain sufficient material that reflects life experiences of minority and disadvantaged children (see Chapter 2).

These practices are understandable, if misguided. Teachers are naturally wary of asking too much of a poor reader, but in trying to correct errors and construct manageable learning tasks, they risk asking too little or depriving the activity of intrinsic interest or meaning. Because disadvantaged students include a disproportionate number of poor readers, this danger has grave consequences for this student population.

Supplementary instruction adds different materials, instructors, settings, and group contexts and, as a result, makes the reading program for disadvantaged students more complex. Poor readers among the disadvantaged population are often exposed to two sets of reading materials, with varying degrees of congruence between them (Johnston et al., 1985). Moreover, supplementary program instructors—whether reading specialists, aides, or others—represent another set of adults with whom students must establish a relationship. Some evidence suggests that these individuals are not always knowledgeable about what is being done in the regular reading classroom (see Chapter 1). More often than not, supplementary instruction takes place in a separate setting from the regular classroom, such as a pullout or resource room, though there are various in-class models for conducting this kind of instruction. Typically, students are assigned to supplementary instruction in small groups that, in effect, label the student a "poor reader."

Effective Reading Curriculum and Teaching for Disadvantaged Students

There is more agreement among scholars about the typical state and inadequacies of current reading practices than about what to do to improve the situation. Three streams of research serve to summarize variables believed to be related to effective reading curriculum and instruction for disadvantaged students. The three streams of research focus on (1) "direct instruction" approaches, (2) ways to improve remedial reading instruction, and (3) active, comprehension-focused reading instruction. Taken together, these studies point to different variables, depending on the teachers' and schools' instructional goals.

Research on the efficacy of "direct instruction" in reading to disadvantaged students has its roots in the national Follow Through Evaluation of the early 1970s; a number of studies picked up the findings of this research and explored them further. The approaches studied took the teaching of basic reading skills as the principal goal of instruction. The model of reading instruction espoused or implied by these works emphasizes:

- *An emphasis on lower-level literacy skills.* Thorough grounding in decoding skills and vocabulary, as a first step, to compensate for students' nonstandard linguistic backgrounds or presumed lack of exposure to the vocabulary typical of introductory reading materials.
- *Rapid pacing and small, manageable increments of new material.* Carefully sequenced instruction that introduces new skills in small, manageable steps at a relatively rapid pace (Barr & Dreeben, 1984; Allington, 1984).
- *A directive role for the teacher.* Whole-group instruction actively controlled by the teacher.
- *Demonstration-practice-feedback cycle.* A repeated cycle of demonstration of new reading skills, such as the recognition of phonetic patterns, practice with these skills, and frequent corrective feedback to the student regarding the mastery of these skills (Rosenshine & Stevens, 1984).
- *Maximized opportunity to learn.* School decisions (e.g., regarding time allocation) and efficient teaching practices that maximize students' opportunity to learn reading and their engaged learning time in the pursuit of this set of skills.

Recent research and commentary call into question some of the elements of this model. This approach to teaching reading is probably effective at teaching basic decoding skills and the recognition of vocabulary words to disadvantaged students, but it may do little to improve comprehension and may even inhibit it (Calfee, 1986; Garcia & Pearson in Chapter 2 of this book). For poor readers in particular, the approach may also lead unwittingly to the pattern noted above of repetitious instruction in decoding skills. Increasingly, reading scholars are abandoning the linear/sequential view of the language-learning process that underlies this model for an interactive, constructivist view (Bridge, 1988; Anderson et al., 1985). In this view, the learner constructs meaning from text, drawing on various sources of information. The process simultaneously involves higher-order and lower-order skills, even for students at the earliest stages in learning to read (Resnick, 1987). Thus, designing curricula that proceed in a linear way from simple, basic skills to higher-order skills may fail to engage students sufficiently.

Research that focuses on the poor reader and remedial or compensatory programs suggests ways to improve on this model without contradicting it altogether. Implicit in much of the research on remedial and compensatory reading instruction to date is the assumption that these programs are concerned primarily with increasing students' basic skills in reading. While reinforcing the emphasis on certain variables from the first tradition (e.g., the amount of time allocated to reading: poor readers need more of it than others), this body of work concentrates on other variables, among them the following:

- *The nature of corrective feedback.* The manner of the teacher's corrective behavior; for example, reducing the number of interruptions during oral reading (Allington, 1980).
- *An emphasis on sustained silent reading and the development of fluency.* The opportunity for daily silent reading in addition to, or in place of, oral reading as well as a focus on developing reading fluency (Allington, 1983).
- *Deemphasis on lower-level decoding skills.* Relatively less time spent on worksheet-based practice in decoding skills, vocabulary, and the like.
- *Curricular congruence.* Coherence in regular and supplementary reading curricula and instructional approaches (Johnston et al., 1985).

The adjustments to curriculum and instructional approach implied by the preceding list may not go far enough if schools and teachers take comprehension, which many take as fundamental to successful reading (Anderson et al., 1985), as the primary goal of reading. That goal—facilitating the students' construction of meaning from written text—may be better served by active attempts to teach comprehension strategies as well as to provide opportunities for students to interact with a wide range of written text (Pearson, Dole, Duffy, & Roehler, in press). In particular, such instruction might be characterized by explicit efforts to teach students to (1) determine what is important, to the reader and the author, in written text (see Chapter 2); (2) synthesize information across large units of text (Brown & Day, 1983); (3) use and alter prior knowledge in seeking to understand text (Roth, 1986); (4) draw inferences from text (Pearson, 1985); (5) pose questions to each other during and following the reading of text (e.g., Palincsar & Brown, 1984); and (6) monitor their own comprehension (e.g., Clay, 1987).

This kind of strategic focus implies further amendments to the research-based model of effective reading instruction described above. From this perspective, disadvantaged students are likely to be better served by the following:

- *Active, comprehension-focused curricula that emphasize meaning from the earliest stages.* This does not mean, however, that teaching decoding skills is unimportant, but rather that decoding is not the primary focus of instruction; instead, decoding is viewed as one of several tools to help students construct meaning.
- *Exposure to a wide variety of text,* with less (or no) use of phonetically controlled or vocabulary-controlled basal readers.
- *Instruction in which students are a resource for one another's learning,* for example, as reading partners or as group critics and facilitators in "reciprocal teaching" approaches (Palincsar & Brown, 1984).
- *Instruction in which teachers play an active role, as in direct instruction models, but with greater emphasis on explicit teaching of comprehension strategies* (Duffy et al., 1987).
- *Learning activities that place reading in the context of a real task or application,* thus providing the student with a compelling reason to read.

Many of these elements are found in integrated language approaches, but there remains little evidence to date regarding the positive or negative effects of such approaches on disadvantaged students. Some critics wonder whether the implied teaching approach, which is often indirect and facilitative, will work well with this student population (see Chapter 1).

WRITING

In many respects, the literature on the content and teaching of writing in elementary and junior high schools parallels that of reading. As discussed above, reading and writing share a common cognitive core; thus, we approach the review in a similar fashion, although with some differences, which reflect the fact that writing and reading involve different cognitive process behaviors (Langer, 1986). We begin with presenting alternative ways scholars approach writing and argue that a sociocognitive perspective on writing is the most useful for understanding writing curriculum and instruction for students in general and for disadvantaged students specifically. Next, we review alternative approaches to writing instruction, examine the theoretical basis for each, and assess their applicability to instructing disadvantaged students. We then examine the writing curriculum in elementary schools and junior high schools and the patterns of typical practice. Finally, we review what is known about the effective teaching of writing and draw implications from it for teaching disadvantaged students.

Scholarship in writing over the last decade has helped to articulate the intellectual processes writers employ and has documented to some extent the relationships between these processes and the context in which the learning takes place. Four major strands of research in the field have contributed to this understanding by approaching writing as follows:

- *Writing as a cognitive process.* Researchers following this strand view writing as mainly a problem-solving task (Hayes & Flower, 1980; Beaugrande, 1984; Cooper and Matsuhashi, 1983). From observing and interviewing writers, a cognitive model of the writing process has been developed. Subsequent research attempts to identify the manner in which writers with varying characteristics follow this model. Much of this research has focused on differences between expert and novice writers.
- *Writing as a developmental process.* Closely related to the cognitive perspective, this area of research is concerned with the acquisition of written language. Work by such researchers as Graves (1981), Calkins (1979), and Dyson (1983) has increased our understanding of the developmental stages of learning to write. Langer

(1986) and others argue that this view is different from the expert/novice studies described above—that an inexperienced (novice) writer should not be equated with a young child who is in the process of acquiring written language.

- *Writing and learning to write in social context.* The view of writing espoused by another group of researchers has focused on the context within which persons learn to write. This view recognizes the importance of the home, the workplace, the community, and the classroom. Researchers following the contextual view have shown that children learn much about writing before they come to school, and this early context must be acknowledged in any discussion of the acquisition of written language (Cochran-Smith, 1984; Heath, 1983; O. Taylor, 1983; Teale and Sulzby, 1986). These researchers argue that learning to write is not simply skill acquisition, but is learning to enter into discourse communities, which have their own rules and expectations (Freedman, Dyson, Flower, & Chafe, 1987).
- *Writing as a sociocognitive process.* Still other scholars have sought to integrate cognitive and social processes; they recognize that cognitive processes are influenced, in part, by the particular context within which the learning occurs (Langer, 1986; Freedman et al., 1987). The writing process is shaped by both the writer's prior knowledge and the purposes and audiences of a given writing task. This view thus attempts to integrate the theoretical perspectives of both the cognitive and social context traditions.

Of these strands, we believe the last offers the most powerful concepts for understanding writing curriculum and instruction for disadvantaged students. It explicitly acknowledges the impact of student background and of social context on writing processes or learning to write, while including a conception of writing as a problem-solving task that calls for an intellectually complex set of responses.

Given this view of writing, two sets of concerns must be considered before a picture of effective writing curriculum and instruction for disadvantaged students can be developed. As in the case of reading, assumptions about the students' linguistic backgrounds must be considered, since this background provides students not only with a context for but with varying forms of expression that shape their view of written communication. And, like reading, writing may serve fundamentally different purposes, depending on the audience, the genre (e.g., storytelling, expository writing, personal communication, etc.) within which the students are working, and the level of intellectual performance they are expected to achieve.

Assumptions About Linguistic Background

Deficit models typically assume that differences in the students' linguistic backgrounds are a major cause of weak writing performance, and that students of nonmainstream linguistic backgrounds will achieve higher levels of writing if teachers effectively teach the discrete skills needed to write correctly. However, many writing scholars believe that student performance is influenced by factors other than the lack of grammatical and syntactical similarities between the students' linguistic backgrounds and the linguistic conventions expected in school-sponsored writing.

Heath (1981) believes students' lack of achievement is influenced, in large part, by the lack of fit between the functions of writing outside school and those served by most methods of writing instruction. Heath maintains that to build effective programs of writing instruction, these out-of-school functions need to be integrated into school-sponsored writing. Hendrix (1981) agrees with Heath and argues that uses of writing outside school as well as the students' motivation and needs should be considered in school-sponsored writing—that is, school-sponsored writing should not be separated from the personal, social, or political aspects of life. He writes that the most effective instructional efforts will be those that stress "human validity" as well as correctness and clarity.

Others argue that the functional mismatch between community and school tasks is too simplistic an account of disadvantaged students' failure to acquire adequate literacy. Cook-Gumperz, Gumperz, and Simons (1981) argue that all children learning to read and write must learn new communicative strategies. However, learning these new strategies will be especially difficult for children who come from homes where most communication is oral, as compared with those who come from homes where printed language is common. In light of such theory and commentary, it is clear that instruction that focuses on only discrete skills of grammar and mechanics will not address the needs of the disadvantaged child.

Assumptions About Types of Writing and Levels of Literacy

It is widely accepted that the types of writing that are to be learned and the level of literacy to which instruction is aimed greatly affect the content and approach to teaching writing, and ultimately the skills learners acquire. In the case of disadvantaged students, especially those experiencing difficulties in learning how to write, it is tempting for schools to assume that these students need only to learn the kinds of writing associated with lower levels of functional literacy, as discussed at the beginning of this chapter.

These assumptions can severely limit the kinds of skills that disadvantaged students develop in writing instruction and the uses to which they may put the writing. Scholars have long established that different genres of writing are associated with task structures that require the writer to convey different meaning to the reader. More recent writing research indicates that different genres of writing place different cognitive demands on the learner (Langer, 1986). The perceived appropriateness of these demands for particular learners influences beliefs about the goals of teaching writing. That is, the kinds of writing assigned to students and associated instructional goals are influenced by the teachers' perception of the student's ability to master the demands required of the task.

Thus, in several ways, writing instruction for disadvantaged students is influenced by beliefs about the appropriateness of certain kinds of writing tasks and about the way students will use writing outside school. The writing instruction provided to disadvantaged students may not promote what some authors have described as "high literacy" (Scardamalia & Bereiter, 1986). High literacy, as described by Resnick and Resnick (1977), has been a tradition in the education of the elite. Such a level of literacy is aimed at developing students' linguistic and verbal *reasoning* abilities. On the other hand, low literacy promotes the minimum level of reading and writing and reflects the education that is typically available to the disadvantaged.

Approaches to the Teaching of Writing

The most common approaches to the teaching of writing draw in varying degrees on the base of scholarship about the acquisition of writing skills. Although there are many instructional alternatives associated with particular methods (e.g., freewriting, conferencing, sentence combining, etc.), three broad categories of approach to the teaching of writing can be distinguished that parallel the approaches to teaching reading described earlier:

- *Component skills approaches.* This category of approaches focuses on the discrete skills that are assumed to be the "building blocks" of writing facility: penmanship, spelling, punctuation, grammar, paragraphing, and so on. Instruction in this tradition places great emphasis on drills and practice exercises aimed at conveying to students the sets of rules by which written language is correctly rendered.
- *Process approaches.* Another, more recent category of approaches seeks to teach students the process of writing described by expert writers. This category of approach to teaching writing is based on the above-mentioned "writing as a cognitive process" strand of research on writing. This process includes stages such as prewriting, generation of text, critical review of written text, and revision. Instruction in this tradition tends to place much more attention on getting students to generate text and subsequently refine it, during the course of which the "mechanics" of writing are gradually learned. This teaching practice focuses primarily on learners' cognitive activities, rather than on the substance of their texts (Scardamalia & Bereiter, 1986).
- *Whole-language approaches.* A third category of approaches, noted previously in discussing reading, shifts the emphasis onto the meaningful use of language. Following the "whole-language" philosophy (Altwerger, Edelsky, & Flores, 1987), instruction is typically designed to integrate writing with reading and oral expression and to create situations in which students have "authentic" reasons to communicate with the written word. The substance and structure of the writing are of primary concern.

The three categories rest on different theoretical bases and concerns about the teaching of writing. The first presumes that the ability to write grows out of a grasp of mechanics. Rather like discrete-skills approaches to reading, this set of approaches presumes that one must learn "the basics" first, and then one can engage in meaningful and more complex expression. As mentioned above, the belief that the quality of the writing produced by linguistically different students can be enhanced through instruction in grammar still prevails in much of the writing instruction offered to K-12 students.

The second category acknowledges that writing is a complex process and that the stages within this process can serve as the framework for appropriate learning activities. An avalanche of recent research has developed the view that writing is iterative: the writer moves back and forth between the general stages in the writing process. Moreover, subprocesses have been identified under this superordinate process. How to help less competent writers to understand and internalize these processes is a central issue for curriculum developers and for classroom teachers implementing instruction that is driven by a process view of writing.

The third category assumes that without a meaningful context for communication, neither the mechanics nor the process will be well learned. In this tradition, teachers seek to highlight the contextual components of a given writing task. Among these components are audience concerns and expectations, the writer's purpose, and the conventions associated with a particular form of writing. All of these factors inform the cognitive demands of, and subsequent strategies employed in response to, a writing assignment.

As with the approaches to the teaching of reading, we can make some observations about the appropriateness of these approaches to the instruction of disadvantaged learners. Assuming that "high" literacy is the goal for teaching this student population, as it is for the student population as a whole, the first category of approaches appears to have the least to offer. There is little built into these approaches that guarantees anything beyond a grasp of mechanics. By contrast, the second and third categories seem to suggest teaching approaches more likely to yield higher levels of literacy. In a curriculum aimed at developing such literacy, what is to be learned would most likely come from a purposefully guided construction of, and interaction with, text rather than from the teacher's direct instruction or exercise activities (Scardamalia & Bereiter, 1986).

Writing Curriculum and Instruction in Grades 1 through 8

Curriculum and instruction in writing tend to fall into a predictable pattern that parallels the focus of reading instruction on discrete skills. The pattern appears both in the intended curriculum and as it is enacted in classrooms; however, unlike reading instruction, which has been greatly influenced by textbooks, writing instruction has not relied as heavily on the structure of published materials.[3]

The Intended Curriculum

As in the case of reading, the predominant pattern of curriculum designed for elementary and junior high schools displays the component-skills approach discussed above. Unlike reading, however, writing does not always occupy a central position in the curriculum. It has often been observed that in elementary schools, at least, relatively little writing is done at all, and that writing instruction primarily emphasizes component skills—the "mechanics" of writing (Pearson & Gallagher, 1983; Graves, 1978). With the exception of language arts materials that deal with language mechanisms, textbooks exert relatively little influence on the writing curriculum, which brings both an advantage and a disadvantage. The advantage is that writing instruction is not so bound by the structure of the texts (except in traditional "language arts" programs), as is frequently the case in reading instruction. The disadvantage is that the classroom teacher has access to minimum guidelines for teaching writing; without a textbook to structure their teaching, many teachers are less likely to offer writing instruction.

The typical writing program in grades 1 through 8—often described as, or subsumed within, "language arts"—seeks to inculcate a set of skills related to the surface features of written text: spelling, punctuation, grammar, paragraphing, etc. The structure of the curriculum varies somewhat from district to district and from state to state, but the following ingredients are commonly emphasized: (1) grammar, including sentence parts, sentence structure, and sentence types; (2) parts of speech; (3) paragraph writing; and (4) a hierarchy of genres, for example, writing a letter at the first-grade level and writing a newspaper editorial at the eighth-grade level. A substantial emphasis is given to mechanical correctness. Restricted writing activities (short answer or fill-in-the-blanks) are by far the most common activities and extended writing activities remain infrequent (Applebee, 1984).

---

3. The statement does not hold for traditional "language arts" materials, of which there are a great many and which are heavily used in the classroom.

The curriculum in many widely used language arts textbooks today reflects whole-language principles; however, in practice, the integration of writing into the language arts curriculum is minimal. For example, some of these textbooks make practically no connections among the various components of the language arts program. Although such texts may note the relationships between grammar instruction and writing instruction, they make no connection between reading assignments and students' writing. Writing is thus treated separately, thereby decreasing the authenticity of the writing assignments.

By contrast, some textbooks that follow a literature-based approach to teaching language arts treat writing as an integrated part of the program, offering students instruction in the writing process and an opportunity to interact with a reading text through writing.

It is not unusual for textbooks to advocate a process approach to teaching writing, within a whole-language framework, and at the same time, in particular lessons, to treat writing as a discrete skill, relegated to the end of each chapter.

Typically, state and district frameworks and curricular guidelines reinforce the pattern of skills-oriented writing instruction just described. Some states have undertaken an ambitious restructuring of the writing curriculum through frameworks, model curriculum guides, and assessment programs. For example, the state of California has developed (1) a curriculum framework intended to serve as the framework for all district curricula within the state, (2) a statement of curriculum standards intended to give assistance to districts in translating the framework into more specific curriculum goals, and (3) a statewide testing program that is directly related to the state framework and curriculum standards. Several features of this framework illustrate an attempt to redefine the intended curriculum in ways that incorporate principles of writing instruction espoused by whole-language and some process-oriented theorists.

Other state frameworks are beginning to display a similar emphasis, but this has yet to work its way into common practice. In reviewing three states' frameworks (California, Maryland, Virginia), we found striking similarities among the stated goals of these frameworks. All three emphasized the following goals:

• Students will understand and use the stages in the process of writing.

- Students will write for a variety of purposes, developing an under-standing of voice, audience, form, and content.
- Students will value writing for personal and social reasons (e.g., as a vehicle for self-discovery and also as a means of empowerment).

Virginia was the only state to identify, as a separate goal, writing for creative expression. Thus, it appears that the formal curriculum, as designated by the frameworks, reflects much of what is popular in current thinking about the teaching of writing. Yet, the teaching strategies for implementing this curriculum have yet to reflect this emphasis.

The Enacted Curriculum

Few studies are available that provide us with a comprehensive picture of how the intended curriculum in writing is translated into classroom writing instruction. The results of the National Assessment of Educational Progress for 1984 (Applebee, Langer, & Mullis, 1986), included results of questionnaire data asked of fourth-, eighth-, and eleventh-grade students about the management of the writing process and the writing instruction they received. The data from the fourth and eighth graders provide some indication of the enacted writing curriculum occurring in elementary school and junior high school classrooms.

The highlights of these results are listed below:

- Most students, majority and minority alike, are unable to write adequately except in response to the simplest of tasks.
- American students can write at a minimal level, but cannot express themselves well enough to ensure that this writing will accomplish the intended purpose.
- Students had less difficulty with tasks requiring short responses based on personal experiences; however, less than 19 percent of the eighth graders and 2 percent of the fourth graders wrote adequate or better responses.
- Few students understood and considered strategies of the writing process. During revision and editing, a large proportion of students reported that they focus on mechanics, such as spelling and punctuation.

- Students reported that their teachers are more likely to mark mistakes than to show an interest in what they write or to make suggestions for the next paper.
- Students who report doing more planning, revising, and editing are better writers than those who report doing less.

Students who reported writing three or more reports and essays during a six-week period had higher achievement levels than students who reported doing no writing during the time period. Twenty-two percent of the fourth graders and 12 percent of the eighth graders reported doing no writing.

Applebee et al. conclude that activities oriented toward the writing process have begun to be incorporated into writing instruction; however, the results indicate that these activities have not been carried out in a way that facilitates students' higher-order thinking and their ability to think about what they are writing. These scholars offer two major recommendations:

1. Students need broad-based experiences in which reading and writing tasks are integrated into their work throughout the curriculum.
2. Instruction in the writing process needs to focus on teaching students how to think more effectively as they write.

The state frameworks that we reviewed contain goals in alignment with these recommendations; however, the textbooks, although moving in that direction, have not, for the most part, provided instructional guidelines that would promote more complex and elaborated text.

Effective Teaching of Writing to Disadvantaged Students

In contrast to reading research, little research has examined effective approaches to teaching writing to disadvantaged students. However, some studies of the efficacy of instructional strategies for all students and on strategies for teaching writing to linguistically different students give clues to appropriate approaches to use with disadvantaged students.

Effective Instructional Strategies

Numerous claims are advanced about the efficacy of particular methods of writing instruction, for example, holding conferences (Graves, 1978), freewriting (Elbow, 1973), teaching rhetoric of invention (Young, 1976), and providing opportunities for sentence combining (Mellon, 1969). Others have argued that instead of discussing these specific kinds of instruction, it is more useful to try to develop more general categories of instruction. Hillocks (1986) does this in his meta-analysis of research on the teaching of writing over the past twenty years. He compares four modes of writing instruction:

1. *The presentational mode* is characterized by (1) clear and specific objectives, (2) lecture and teacher-led discussions, (3) the study of models that illustrate a concept, and (4) specific assignments.
2. *The natural process mode* is characterized by (1) generalized objectives, (2) freewriting, (3) writing for audiences of peers, (4) opportunities to revise, and (5) high levels of interaction among students.
3. *The environmental mode* is characterized by (1) clear and specific objectives, (2) materials selected to engage students with each other in specific processes important to some aspect of writing, and (3) high levels of peer interaction.
4. *The individualized mode* is characterized by (1) students receiving instruction through tutorials, and (2) programmed instruction.

In his meta-analysis, Hillocks (1986) included only studies that used both pre- and posttest student writing samples to assess effectiveness. Thus, only a small proportion of the available research was included; this review is limited by the small number of studies included in each category. These small numbers did not allow more discrete meta-analysis of these categories by age of students, economic status, or other student characteristics. Overall, his meta-analysis indicated that the environmental mode was far superior to the other three approaches. The distinguishing characteristics of this mode of instruction—in particular, the emphasis on group interaction and clear and specific objectives—apparently seem more able to engage students in activities that promote good writing skills. However, an effective, balanced program is likely to draw appropriately from all four modes.

Whatever the category of writing instruction, Applebee and Langer (1983) argue for a "substantive" rather than "procedural" approach to teaching writing. Rather than stressing the component skills of writing, the authors advocate focusing on the language task that is to be carried out by the student (Bruner, 1978; Cazden, 1980). Teachers following this approach must (1) identify the difficulties that particular students will have when approaching a writing task, (2) select appropriate strategies that will help students overcome these difficulties, and (3) structure the task in such a way that these strategies are explicit, thus allowing students to learn the strategies needed when encountering a certain kind of difficulty (Applebee & Langer, 1983). Teachers following such an approach do not segregate the many skills involved in the writing process, but teach each as it is needed for a particular task.

Principles for Teaching Writing to Disadvantaged Students

Although relatively little work has been done that specifically addresses writing instruction for disadvantaged students, several principles can be inferred from the preceding discussion that have relevance for disadvantaged students (as well as for the student population in general):

- *Because many come to school without much experience with extended text, disadvantaged students need more opportunities to write, from the earliest time in their school careers.* Applebee et al. (1986) reported that disadvantaged urban students showed lower writing skills. For these students especially, opportunities to write can play a crucial role in developing their writing skills.
- *Curriculum and instruction for this segment of the population should deemphasize instruction in the component skills as a prerequisite for meaningful writing.* Research consistently showed that component skill instruction does not facilitate writing skills (Hillocks, 1986). However, this type of instruction persists, and textbooks are written following the approach. The instructional approach discussed above would integrate the use of component skills with the purposeful use of language. Because this approach requires the teacher to address the specific needs of the student, less emphasis

can be given to textbooks that present a fixed instructional plan
and more emphasis placed on training teachers in this approach
(Bruner, 1978; Cazden, 1980).

• Writing should be learned in contexts that emphasize the meaningful use of language. This does not necessarily mean a wholesale
adoption of curricula built on whole-language philosophies, but it
does mean creating opportunities for using written language to
communicate things of value to the students. Some movement has
been made in this direction (Applebee et al., 1986); however,
more thought needs to be given to specific ways that will benefit
the student. Work on the writing needs of the Hispanic student,
for example, maintains that the student can use writing as a tool
for expressing cultural and personal identity. The students must
feel that the language they use will be honored. Writing topics
that allow students to express opinions, moods, aspirations, and
descriptions of self can be effective (although some cultures and
settings make it more difficult for students to expose their inner
thoughts). Thus, the role of the teacher is to help students
discover that they can write and feel the power that the written
word can give.

• *Writing teachers need to acknowledge and connect with the students' cultural
and linguistic backgrounds,* so that the students' learning needs are
not misinterpreted and so that meaningful contexts for learning
to write can be better constructed. For example, the writing of
students speaking Black English will be influenced by the dialect
they speak. Teachers need to become aware that Vernacular
Black English is a rule-governed language system that is different
from but not deficient by comparison with Standard English (Farr
Whiteman, 1980). Rather than treating the deviations from Standard English as simply errors in grammar, the teacher can consider such writing as part of the student's primary language
system and conduct instruction accordingly.

SUMMARY: PRINCIPLES UNDERLYING EFFECTIVE LITERACY CURRICULA AND INSTRUCTION FOR DISADVANTAGED STUDENTS

Several themes run through the literature on literacy curricula
and instruction, although there are differences in the focus and extent

of research on reading and writing. We group these themes under the following headings: (1) the shortcomings and prevalence of curricula that emphasize discrete, component skills; (2) movement toward an emphasis on meaning in literacy instruction; (3) the integration of curricular elements and instructional services in the teaching of literacy; (4) accommodating differences of linguistic background in literacy instruction.

The Shortcomings and Prevalence of Curricula That Emphasize Discrete, Component Skills

There is a tendency for literacy curricula available to most disadvantaged students to teach discrete, component skills in a linear sequence, from what are viewed as the "basics" to more complex skills. Remedial and compensatory programs are especially prone to this tendency, the assumption being that low achievers have to get their basics first, before they can move on to more challenging (and interesting) tasks. But core program instruction in classrooms serving large concentrations of disadvantaged students shows a similar tendency. The generally low levels of literacy for this student population suggest that the current emphasis is not working well, although it may be teaching some discrete skills effectively.

- This means that in reading instruction disadvantaged students are heavily exposed to decoding, with relatively little chance to acquire skills in comprehension.
- In writing instruction, it means that these students typically get a heavy dose of the mechanisms of "language arts"—spelling, grammar, punctuation, penmanship, and the like—and relatively little chance to learn to compose written text.
- Research suggests that basic and higher-order skills can be taught to this student population simultaneously, in ways that engage students more effectively—for example, reading instruction that focuses on comprehension strategies as well as skills or writing instruction that focuses on the process and purposes of writing, as well as on its mechanisms.
- At the least, an instructional diet that includes many more opportunities for extended reading and text writing from the earliest stages can improve considerably on the current imbalance in literacy curricula available to this population.

Movement Toward an Emphasis on Meaning in Literacy Instruction

Curricula and instruction that promote the meaningful use of language have much to offer disadvantaged students of all ability levels.

- In reading, comprehension-focused curricula and instruction show particular promise for teaching students to read and understand what they read. This approach implies explicit teaching of comprehension strategies, and an approach to teaching decoding in the context of the application of these skills.
- Chances to write text that communicates things of importance to students in various genres lead students more quickly to a facility with the written word. This implies instruction that creates a variety of opportunities for written expression, and provides the appropriate substantive support for students to be able to accomplish these writing tasks.
- Integrated language approaches (e.g., predicated on "whole-language" philosophies), which combine reading, writing, and oral expression, place a particular emphasis on the meaningful use of language and may have particular benefits for disadvantaged student populations. However, they require a great deal of teachers and may sacrifice some skillbuilding if not done well. The potential of these approaches is not well demonstrated yet in the full range of schools serving disadvantaged students.

The Integration of Curricular Elements and Instructional Services in the Teaching of Literacy

Both the design and implementation of literacy curricula for disadvantaged students exhibit a great deal of "planned fragmentation" due to (1) the discrete-skills emphasis discussed above, (2) the separation and compartmentalization of reading and writing curricula from each other and from other subjects, (3) poor articulation across grades, and (4) frequent lack of connection between regular instruction and the supplementary services that remediate poor achievement in literacy for large numbers of disadvantaged students.

- Curricula and instruction are preferable that connect (1) the different skills with one another (decoding with reading, punctuation with the expression of written thoughts, etc.), (2) the learning of literacy skills with the various subject areas in which these skills can be used, and (3) the learning of reading with writing.

- Coordination of regular and supplementary literacy instruction, where appropriate, can simplify the learning task for low-achieving children and enhance the chance of their developing good literacy skills.

Accommodating Differences in Sociolinguistic Background in Literacy Instruction

The sociolinguistic differences between many disadvantaged students and the teachers or curricula they encounter in school are a major stumbling block confronting literacy education for this student population. Effective literacy instruction appears to acknowledge these differences and communicate to students an understanding and respect.

- Literacy instruction thus must be designed to recognize the language strengths students bring and at the same time must seek to teach them what for most is a significantly different language from the one they know at home, whether it is an English dialect or a non-English language.
- In reading, effective instruction (1) avoids persistent correction of dialect-based "errors" and repetitive teaching of decoding skills when dialect differences are the source of a student's apparent error and (2) includes a sufficient amount of reading material (including student-generated material) that relates to the base of experience students bring to school.
- In writing, effective instruction (1) recognizes the rules that govern students' speech and language use, then (2) seeks to teach alternate rules for Standard English, rather than treating students' natural language as "errors," and (3) encourages writing that allows students to express and reflect on their experiences (while not limiting them to their experiences).

REFERENCES

Reading

Allington, R. L. (1980). Teacher interruption during primary grade oral reading. *Journal of Educational Psychology, 72,* 371–374.

Allington, R. L. (1983). The reading instruction provided readers of different reading abilities. *Elementary School Journal, 83,* 549–559.

Allington, R. L. (1984). Content coverage and contextual reading in reading groups. *Journal of Reading Behavior, 16,* 85–96.

Altwerger, B., Edelsky, C., & Flores, B. (1987). Whole language: What's new? *Reading Teacher, 41*(2), 144–154.

Anderson, R., Hiebert, E., Scott, J., & Wilkinson, I. (1985). *Becoming a nation of readers.* Washington, DC: National Institute of Education.

Anyon, J. (1981). Elementary schooling and the distinctions of social class. *Interchange, 12,* 118–132.

Applebee, A. N., Langer, J. A., & Mullis, I.V.S. (1988). *Who reads best?* Princeton, NJ: Educational Testing Service.

Barr, R., & Dreeben, R. (1984). *How schools work.* Chicago: University of Chicago.

Birman, B. F., Orland, M. E., Jung, R. K., Anson, R. J., Garcia, G. N., Moore, M. T., Funkhouser, J. E., Morrison, D. R., Turnbull, B. J., & Reisner, E. R. (1987). *The current operation of the Chapter 1 program: Final report from the National Assessment of Chapter 1.* Washington, DC: U.S. Government Printing Office.

Brown, A., & Day, L. (1983). Macrorules for summarizing texts: The development of expertise. *Journal of Verbal Learning and Verbal Behavior, 22,* 1–14.

Bridge, C. A. (1988). Focusing on meaning in beginning reading instruction. In J. L. Davidson (Ed.), *Counterpoint and beyond: A response to becoming a nation of readers.* Urbana, IL: National Council of Teachers of English.

Calfee, R. (1986). Curriculum and instruction: Reading. In B. I. Williams, P. A. Richmond, & B. J. Mason (Eds.), *Designs for compensatory education: Conference proceedings and papers.* Washington, DC: Research and Evaluation Associates.

Calfee, R., & Drum, P. (1986). Research on teaching reading. In M. C. Wittrock (Ed.), *Handbook of research on teaching* (3rd ed.). New York: Macmillan.

California State Board of Education. (1987). *English-language arts framework.* Sacramento, CA: California State Board of Education.

Carbo, M. (1988, October). What reading tests should measure to increase literacy in the U.S. *Research Bulletin,* No. 7, Phi Delta Kappa Center on Evaluation, Development and Research.

Chall, J. S. (1983). *Stages of reading development.* New York: McGraw-Hill.

Clay, M. M. (1987). *The early detection of reading difficulties* (3rd ed.). Auckland, NZ: Heinemann.

Collins, A., Brown, J. S., & Newman, S. E. (1989). Cognitive apprenticeship: Teaching the craft of reading, writing, and mathematics. In L. B. Resnick (Ed.), *Knowing, learning, and instruction: Essays in honor of Robert Glaser.* Hillsdale, NJ: Erlbaum.

Duffy, G., Roehler, L., Sivan, E., Rackliffe, G., Book, C., Meloth, M. S., Vavrus,

L. G., Wesselman, R., Putnam, J., & Bassiri, D. (1987). Effects of explaining the reasoning associated with using reading strategies. *Reading Research Quarterly, 22*(3), 347– 366.

Garcia, G. E., & Pearson, P. D. (1988). *Modifying reading instruction to maximize its effectiveness for disadvantaged students.* Urbana: University of Illinois, Center for the Study of Reading.

Goodman, K. S., & Goodman, Y. M. (1979). Learning to read is natural. In L. B. Resnick & P. A. Weaver (Eds.), *Theory and practice of early reading.* Newark, DE: International Reading Association.

Johnston, P., Allington, R., & Afflerbach, P. (1985). The congruence of classroom and remedial reading instruction. *Elementary School Journal, 85*(4), 465–478.

Langer, J. (1986). *Children reading and writing.* Norwood, NJ: Ablex.

LaPointe, A. (1986). The state of instruction in reading and writing in U.S. elementary schools. *Phi Delta Kappan, 68*(2), 135–138.

Moll, L. C., Estrada, E., Diaz, E., & Lopes, L. M. (1980). The organization of bilingual lessons: Implications for schooling. *The Quarterly Newsletter of the Laboratory of Comparative Human Cognition, 2*(3), 53–58.

Oakes, J. (1986). *Keeping track: How schools structure inequality.* New Haven, CT: Yale University.

Osborn, J., Wilson, P. T., & Anderson, R. C. (Eds.). (1985). *Reading education: Foundations for a literate America.* Lexington, MA: D. C. Heath.

Palincsar, A. S., & Brown, A. L. (1984). Reciprocal teaching of comprehension-fostering and monitoring activities. *Cognition and Instruction, 1*(2), 117–175.

Pearson, P. D. (1985). Changing the face of reading comprehension instruction. *Reading Teacher, 38*(8), 724–738.

Pearson, P. D., Dole, J., Duffy, G. G., & Roehler, L. R. (in press). Developing expertise in reading comprehension: What should be taught? How should it be taught? In S. J. Samuels & A. E. Farstrup (Eds.), *What research says to the teacher* (2nd ed.). Newark, DE: International Reading Association.

Resnick, L. B. (1987). *Education and learning to think.* Washington, DC: National Academy Press.

Rosenshine, B., & Stevens, R. (1984). Classroom instruction in reading. In P. D. Pearson (Ed.), *Handbook of reading research.* New York: Longman.

Roth, K. J. (1986). *Conceptual change learning and student processing of science texts.* Paper presented at the annual meeting of the American Educational Research Association, Chicago.

Rowan, B., Guthrie, L. F., Lee, G. V., & Guthrie, G. P. (1986). *The design and implementation of Chapter 1 instructional services: A study of 24 schools.* San Francisco: Far West Laboratory.

Schrag, F. (1989). Are there levels of thinking? *Teachers College Record, 90*(4), 529–534.

Scott, J. C. (1988). Nonmainstream groups: Questions and research directions. In J. L. Davidson (Ed.), *Counterpoint and beyond.* Urbana, IL: National Council of Teachers of English.

Writing

Altwerger, B., Edelsky, C., & Flores, B. (1987). Whole language: What's new? *Reading Teacher, 41*(2), 144–154.

Applebee, A. (1984). *Contexts for learning to write: Studies of secondary school instruction.* Norwood, NJ: Ablex.

Applebee, A. N., & Langer, J. A. (1983). Instructional scaffolding: Reading and writing as natural language activities. *Language Arts, 60,* 168– 175.

Applebee, A., Langer, J., & Mullis, I. (1986). *The writing report card.* Princeton, NJ: Educational Testing Service.

Beaugrande, R. de. (1984). *Text production: Toward a science of composition.* Norwood, NJ: Ablex.

Bruner, J. (1978). The role of dialogue in language acquisition. In A. Sinclair (Ed.); *child's conception of language.* New York: Springer-Verlag.

Calkins, L. M. (1979). Andrea learns to make writing hard. *Language Arts, 56,* 569–576.

Cazden, C. (1980). Peekaboo as an instructional model: Discourse development at home and at school. *Papers and Reports of Child Language Development, 17,* 1–29.

Cochran-Smith, M. (1984). Looking like readers, talking like readers. *Theory Into Practice, 24,* 22–31.

Cook-Gumperz, J., Gumperz, J., & Simons, H. (1981). *School-home ethnography project.* Final report to the National Institute of Education. Washington, DC: U.S. Department of Education.

Cooper, C., & Matsuhashi, A. (1983). A theory of the writing process. In M. Martlew (Ed.), *The psychology of written language.* London: John Wiley and Sons.

Dyson, A.H. (1983). The role of oral language in early writing processes. *Research in the Teaching of English, 17,* 1–30.

Elbow, P. (1973). *Writing without teachers.* London: Oxford University Press.

Farr Whiteman, M. (Ed.). (1980). *Reactions to Ann Arbor: Vernacular Black English and education.* Washington, DC: Center for Applied Linguistics.

Freedman, S., Dyson, A. H., Flower, L., & Chafe, W. (1987). *Research in writing: Past, present, and future.* Berkeley, CA: Center for the Study of Writing.

Graves, D. H. (1978). *Balance the basics: Let them write.* New York: Ford Foundation.

Graves, D. H. (1981). Research update: Writing research for the eighties: What is reread. *Language Arts, 58,* 197–206.

Hayes, J. R., & Flower, L. S. (1980). Writing as problem solving. *Visible Language, 14,* 383–399.

Heath, S. B. (1981). Toward an ethnohistory of writing: American education. In M. Farr Whiteman (Ed.), *Writing: The nature, development, and teaching of written communication.* Hillsdale, NJ: Erlbaum.

Heath, S. (1983). *Ways with words: Language, life and work in communities and classrooms.* New York: Cambridge University Press.

Hendrix, R. (1981). The status and politics of writing instruction. In M. Farr Whiteman (Ed.), *Writing: The nature, development, and teaching of written communication.* Hillsdale, NJ: Erlbaum.

Hillocks, G. (1986). *Research on written composition.* Urbana, IL: National Council of Teachers of English.

Langer, J. (1986). *Children reading and writing*. Norwood, NJ: Ablex.

Mellon, J. C. (1969). *Transformational sentence combining: A method for enhancing the development of syntactic fluency in English composition* (Research Report No. 10). Urbana, IL: National Council of Teachers of English.

Pearson, P. D., & Gallagher, M. C. (1983). The instruction of reading comprehension. *Contemporary Educational Psychology, 8,* 317–344.

Resnick, D. P., & Resnick, L. B. (1977). The nature of literacy: An historical exploration. *Harvard Educational Review, 47*(3), 370–385.

Scardamalia, M., & Bereiter, C. (1986). Research on written composition. In M. C. Wittrock (Ed.), *Handbook of research on teaching* (3rd ed.). New York: Macmillan.

Taylor, O. (1983). Black English: An agenda for the 1980's. In J. Chambers (Ed.), *Black English: Educational equity and the law*. Ann Arbor, MI: Karama Press.

Teale, W., & Sulzby, E. (Eds.). (1986). *Emergent literacy*. Norwood, NJ: Ablex.

Young, R. E. (1976). Invention: A topographical survey. In G. Tate (Ed.), *Teaching composition: Ten bibliographical essays*. Fort Worth, TX: Texas Christian University Press.

Part II

Toward Effective Curricula and Instruction in Mathematics

5

Good Teaching of Worthwhile Mathematics to Disadvantaged Students

Andrew C. Porter

In the United States, education is a cornerstone of society, seen as the key to the nation's economic, political, and social future. Unemployment, crime, and illiteracy are all problems that schools are to solve. They are also problems that plague our nation's poor at much higher rates than for middle- and upper-income families. At least at present, strengthening the teaching and learning of academic content in K-12 schools is believed by many to be the appropriate strategy for solving the larger problems. The goal for our schools, then, is to maximize the probability of good teaching of worthwhile content to all students. The biggest challenge to realizing this goal is the currently inadequate success rates with disadvantaged students, students from low-income families, high percentages of which are minorities: blacks, Hispanics, and Native Americans. The purpose of this chapter is to identify some of the issues in studying the incidence of and causes for good teaching of worthwhile mathematics to disadvantaged students.

Generally, elementary schools and perhaps to a somewhat lesser extent, junior high schools, are doing a good job. Elementary school students perform quite well on basic knowledge and skills that have been stressed. There are some important weaknesses, too. Students do significantly less well on problem solving and higher-order thinking (Champagne & Klopfer, 1977; National Assessment of Educational Progress, 1983). Students who enter elementary school with a keen interest in learning and enthusiasm for all subjects, especially mathematics, all too often leave junior high school with little motivation for academic learning (National Center for Educational Statistics, 1977, p. 201). These inadequacies in our elementary and junior high schools, student acquisition of problem solving and higher-order thinking knowledge and skills, and students' attitudes toward learning and subsequent study, while general problems, are acute for disadvantaged students from poor urban and rural families. Paradoxically, these disadvantaged students have potentially the most to gain from school (e.g., National Science Foundation, 1982).

A GENERAL MODEL FOR CLASSROOM TEACHING AND LEARNING OF MATHEMATICS

Schwab defines the commonplaces of education as learner, teacher, curriculum, and milieu. These four characteristics of any educational experience are useful to keep in mind when thinking about models and/or criteria for studying and assessing mathematics curriculum and instruction as applied to disadvantaged students.

The Learner

When characterizing teaching and learning of mathematics for disadvantaged students, sex, ethnicity, and school composition variables should be taken into account so that averages do not obscure important variation. In mathematics, gender effects are an important issue to be addressed. While gender differences are not prevalent during the elementary school years, they emerge in junior high school and become substantial at the time when students exercise choice in whether or not to study mathematics and what kind of mathematics to study. If girls are to have an equal opportunity in mathematics in further study and in jobs with mathematics prerequisites, presumably corrective actions must begin before the problems are manifest. They must begin in the elementary grades. Similar statements can be made for minority students, especially blacks, Hispanics, and Native Americans (although family socioeconomic status (SES) is a serious confounding factor in most of the work that shows achievement gaps between minority and majority students in mathematics). Finally, the educational experiences of disadvantaged youth attending schools with high percentages of students from low-income families is known to be substantially different from the educational experiences of similar students attending schools serving predominantly middle- and upper-income families.

The Teacher

The 1980s education reform movement sees strengthening teachers and the teaching profession as the key to improving the quality of education for all students. "The key to success lies in creating a profession equal to the task, a profession of well-educated teachers prepared to assume new powers and responsibilities to redesign schools for the future" (Carnegie Forum on Education and the Economy, 1986, p. 2).

In virtually all elementary schools and junior high schools, it is teachers who ultimately decide what students will study and how they will be taught. Teachers are relatively free to draw on instructional materials in ways they deem appropriate and to design assessment strategies and standards for achievement that they deem appropriate. In short, teachers negotiate between their understanding of the ideal curriculum and the constraints within which they must work. These constraints include strengths and limitations of the teacher's subject matter knowledge, pedagogical skills, and repertoire for assessment practices as well as the constraints that come from having to teach a variety of subjects to classrooms of from twenty to thirty students with varying abilities and interests. Clearly then, variation in teacher knowledge, skills, and dispositions needs to be systematically studied when attempting to understand the mathematics education of disadvantaged students.

Curriculum

When Schwab listed curriculum as a commonplace, he had in mind the curriculum as experienced by students. As will be elaborated later, relatively little is known about this curriculum, and in fact, until recently, the curriculum as experienced by students has largely been taken for granted, both in policy setting and in educational research. What has received attention has been statements of idealized curricula such as The National Council of Teachers of Mathematics' (NCTM) standards for mathematics (NCTM, 1989) or the curriculum as it exists in published materials, primarily textbooks, or the curriculum as tested in norm-referenced published tests, state and district minimum competencies tests, and national assessments (e.g., Barr & Dreeben, 1983; Freeman, Kuhs, Porter, Floden, Schmidt, & Schwille, 1983; Stodolsky, 1988, 1989). There is a modest amount of research to show that, at least for elementary school mathematics, each of these types of curricula has important uniquenesses from the other, and none serve as good proxies for the curriculum as actually experienced by a particular student in a particular classroom (e.g., Porter, Floden, Freeman, Schmidt, & Schwille, 1988). They are, however, potential influences on what is taught and learned and so represent tools that might be employed to strengthen the curricula for disadvantaged students.

Milieu

The milieu commonplace highlights the importance of attending to the context in which educational experiences take place. For disadvantaged students, an important piece of that context is the special programs and services that they receive above and beyond or in place of the programs and services provided to nondisadvantaged students. Probably most important among these is their participation in pullout programs that may, on the one hand, provide important mathematics instruction outside the regular classroom experience and may, on the other hand, deprive them from mathematics instruction (or other kinds of important instruction) that they otherwise would have received.

Other potentially important attributes of the educational context distinguish the educational experiences of disadvantaged students from those of less disadvantaged students. For example, schools serving high percentages of disadvantaged students often have fewer resources than schools serving high percentages of students from middle-income and high-income families (e.g., Porter et al., 1988). This may mean that a disadvantaged student cannot take his or her textbook home for homework (because the school must protect instructional materials so that they will last longer and reduce replacement costs). Similarly, disadvantaged youth, when using workbook materials, may be required to copy problems from the materials and work them on a separate sheet of paper (rather than the much more efficient writing directly in their workbooks). This allows a workbook to be reused, and so cuts down on instructional costs. There are other examples where financial constraints may limit the instructional options for disadvantaged students: access to hand-held calculators, microcomputers for drill and practice of computational skills and for problem solving, equipment for applied problems in measurement, equipment for constructions in geometry.

Obviously, milieu need not be a negative constraint on the teaching and learning of mathematics by disadvantaged students. It is important to consider ways in which the context of education can enhance what is learned (in addition to identifying constraints that might be eliminated) (e.g., Porter, 1989).

A Macro-Level Model

Schwab's commonplaces suggest that any attempt to define the teaching and learning of mathematics for disadvantaged students will, at a minimum, need to characterize (a) the content of instruction, (b) the pedagogical practices of the teacher, (c) the curriculum materials used, including the assessment procedures, both in class and as a part of the formal educational hierarchy, and (d) the context within which student learning is embedded. This model is not a theory; yet it can serve to inform a research agenda.

WORTHWHILE MATHEMATICS CONTENT

Surprisingly, there is not clarity about what constitutes the most important mathematics for elementary and junior high school students to learn. Probably more than any other subject matter area, mathematics has received attention in defining the content of the discipline and how the discipline should be treated in schools. Typically, mathematicians and mathematics educators have taken the lead in creating published statements, curriculum guides, and frameworks (e.g., NCTM, 1980, 1989). But these statements have thus far had relatively little impact on creating a consensus among parents, teachers, school administrators, and education policymakers.

The goals for school mathematics learning are not constant over time. Just five years ago basic skills (and direct instruction) were the focus of state policies, school improvement programs, and state testing programs (e.g., Purkey & Smith, 1983). Today, this concern for basic skills is common among teachers and parents, but academics and policymakers have shifted their attention away from basic skills and on to higher-order thinking and problem solving (e.g., Costa, 1985). Assessment practices have not yet caught up with this shift, but if the technological problems can be solved, they will. Whether teachers and parents will be drawn along or not remains to be seen.

Within this confusion about what constitutes the most worthwhile mathematics for students to learn is the possibility that different students are best served by learning different mathematics (or must learn different mathematics because of limits in their motivation and/or abilities). To date, published statements of desired mathematics learning make relatively few, if any, distinctions among types of students—boys versus girls, majority versus minority students, or students from poor families versus students from rich families. However, these distinctions not being made in published statements is no guarantee that they are not made in practice. What little information is available concerning the implemented curriculum (i.e., the curriculum as experienced by students) points to children from poor families, minority children, and girls receiving more instruction on the mastery of basic skills and less instruction on developing conceptual understanding and learning how to apply that conceptual understanding to solve novel problems (e.g., Porter et al., 1988).

Defining Content

Regardless of judgments about what content is most worthwhile, the content of instruction is one of several key determinants of what students learn. In defining the content of mathematics instruction in elementary and junior high school, it is necessary to consider the following attributes (Porter et al., 1988):

- How much instructional time is allocated to mathematics teaching and learning in elementary school? Does a student study mathematics for thirty minutes every day or for thirty minutes each of three days a week? Are there other times during the school day, other than the instructional period labeled "mathematics," in which students are free to study mathematics or are encouraged to work on mathematics assignments? Is homework assigned in mathematics, and in what ways are students encouraged to spend time at home studying mathematics? How much mathematics is actually studied at home? Are there pullout programs in which mathematics is taught? How long are these pullout periods, and is there mathematics instruction in the regular classroom that is missed during pullout periods? In junior high school, where instructional periods are typically formal with students moving from classroom to classroom, keeping track of instructional time is somewhat easier; the questions of homework and pullout programs also apply. (For both elementary and junior high school mathematics instruction, there is the issue of engaged time versus allocated time, but that will be considered later in this chapter in the discussion on pedagogy.)
- What topics are covered during the instructional time? Does instruction emphasize basic computational skills, conceptual understanding, or applications? Is geometry taught? Is measurement taught? (E.g., Kuhs, Schmidt, Porter, Floden, Freeman, & Schwille, 1979.)
- When and in what order is content presented to students? To some extent, it is less important whether certain geometric concepts are taught in third grade or fifth grade, so long as somewhere during the elementary school experience those geometric concepts are taught. Care must be taken when interpreting differences among classrooms in the mathematics covered during instruction; over time, differences among classrooms (and so among students) may disappear, due to compensating differences at other grade levels in other years.
- What students receive what content? It must not be assumed that all students within a class receive the same mathematics instruction. Teachers may form groups for mathematics or they may

individualize mathematics instruction. Teachers may also treat students differently, even within whole-group instruction, such that the net result is a difference from student to student in the mathematics studied. There is some reason to believe that students perceived by the teacher to have low aptitude for mathematics receive instruction on definitions and computational skills only, leaving problem solving to the high-aptitude students (Porter et al., 1988). There is also evidence that students' aptitude for mathematics as perceived by teachers correlates with whether or not the students are from a low-income family (Good, 1987).

- What are the standards for student achievement? Teachers may hold strict or lenient standards for student achievement. They may teach content simply to expose students to that content, or they may teach content, demanding student mastery (e.g., Bernstein, 1985). To some extent, the standards for student achievement translate into the pace of instruction and, ultimately, how many topics are covered during an instructional period or school year. But teacher standards for student achievement also communicate to students what is to be learned and can result in students attending more or less well, studying harder or less hard, and ultimately learning different things.

Mathematical Content as Problematic

The content of mathematics instruction is not a straightforward concept. One difficulty is that the term "content" implies a form of instruction where what is to be learned is clearly specified *a priori*, where teachers present the content to be learned, and where students learn that content (more or less well). The image that may come to mind is learner as an empty vessel, to be filled with knowledge and skills. But students come to the classroom already "knowing" a great deal of mathematics. They have ideas about numbers, quantity, shapes, problem solving, and the like. The task of their learning is more one of knowledge construction and reconstruction than the above linear model suggests.

This conception of mathematics learning as knowledge construction shows the content of instruction to be something negotiated among teacher, student, and materials (e.g., Fennema, Carpenter, & Peterson, 1990; Lampert, 1985). The implications are several. First, the content of instruction from a student's eyes is probably not the same as the content of instruction from a teacher's eyes, and neither of these two may be in correspondence with the content of instruction as seen by an external observer, such as a researcher. Some teachers plan and deliver mathematics instruction as activities for students to experience; they do not select activities in pursuit of clearly defined goals for student achievement. In short, teachers don't always think in terms of particular learning outcomes, but rather think in terms of "interesting" activities that seem likely to enhance student knowledge construction (Clark & Yinger, 1977, 1979). Sometimes, this results in effective instruction where students learn a great deal of worthwhile content; other times, the activities become ends in themselves, with students taking away very little mathematics knowledge. The distinction between content and pedagogy breaks down or becomes blurred when viewed from the perspective of student as knowledge constructor.

When building educational programs or formulating educational policy, student knowledge is the ultimate goal. Yet, research has shown that teachers' intended content and students' understanding of what is to be learned are two intervening variables that are predictive of what is ultimately learned. Studies of the mathematics disadvantaged students are taught must take this multiple perspectives dilemma into account.

Other Important Outcomes of Mathematics Instruction

Mathematics content suggests kinds of mathematics to be learned, such as geometry, algebra, computation with whole numbers, decimals, and the like. But there is another domain of student outcomes that may be even more important. Unless students are able to use their conceptual understanding and skills in mathematics to solve novel problems, the value of their mathematical knowledge and skills will be severely limited. But problem solving and reasoning are capabilities that require having the disposition to be a problem solver in addition to having the knowledge and skills. Also, a student's ability to apply conceptual knowledge and skills to solve problems may be a function of the degree to which he or she possesses relevant metacognitive strategies, such as comprehension monitoring (e.g., Anderson, 1983; Brown, 1978; Brown & Burton, 1978; Palincsar & Brown, 1984). Finally, if students, in learning mathematics during their elementary school and junior high school years, come to hate mathematics, the knowledge and skills that they have acquired will be of substantially less value than if, in the process, they come to think of mathematics as both interesting and useful. There is evidence to suggest that these interest and motivation outcomes are even in more need of attention than are the outcomes of conceptual understanding and skills. Students enter school enthusiastic about learning, and mathematics is the single most preferred subject, yet by the end of their junior high school experience, many students have learned to hate mathematics and will study no more mathematics than is required. Unfortunately, this dislike for mathematics is more prevalent among girls and minority students than among white males (e.g., National Science Foundation, 1983).

GOOD TEACHING

Identifying the characteristics of good teaching of mathematics is at least as difficult as is deciding what mathematics is most important for disadvantaged students to learn. The search for prescriptive statements of good teaching has gradually given way to calls for teacher professionalization and teacher empowerment. Paradoxically, just at the time when popular opinion about good teaching has shifted in the direction of professional judgment, attempts at teacher assessment have increased dramatically. It is too soon to know how the calls for teacher empowerment and the calls for teacher assessment will negotiate a common ground. Much of the research on teaching, however, has moved away from empirical searches for prescription and instead in the direction of identifying principles of good teaching (Porter, 1988).

Prescriptions for good teaching are micro-level detailed statements about behaviors of effective teachers. Rowe's three-second wait time is an example of a prescription (1974). In contrast, principles of good teaching are general guidelines and predispositions that point teachers in productive directions. Principles of good teaching stop short of explicit advice about appropriate behaviors. A principle of good teaching is to make sure that each student knows what is to be learned, the intended outcome of study as opposed to the activity to be completed (Porter & Brophy, 1988). No one specific set of teacher behaviors is implied. Obviously, there are many different sets of behaviors that teachers might employ consistent with this principle. Whether or not teachers are employing certain principles in their teaching is difficult to assess; assessment of principles is a classic problem of implementation studies. In contrast, prescriptions are relatively easy to assess; a teacher either waits three seconds for a student to give an answer to a question, or does not.

While research on teaching is still in its infancy, a great deal of useful work has been completed over the course of the last fifteen to twenty years (e.g., Wittrock, 1986). This research has identified many important principles of good teaching and long lists of prescriptions for good teaching. Figure 5-1 provides a model of good teaching that can be used to characterize what is now known from research and to chart areas where further work is needed (taken from Porter, 1988). The model moves from left to right, representing good teaching as generally a rational, goal-oriented process. The model is dynamic, showing good teaching to be a self-monitored activity (e.g., teacher reflection). The model shows that good teaching is a function of a great many different kinds of knowledge, skills, and dispositions, which in turn have their origins from a potentially wide variety of prior experiences and present circumstances.

A study of the teaching and learning of mathematics for disadvantaged students can, perhaps, avoid same of the complexities of studying the antecedents of teachers' practice. But if these antecedents are completely ignored, the findings will be seriously limited. It is one thing to know what constitutes good teaching. It is quite another thing to know how to create teachers who do good teaching (e.g., Porter, 1986). Similarly, characterizing the nature of teaching of mathematics to disadvantaged students may identify strengths and weaknesses, but will not be sufficient to point ways in which strengths can be enhanced and deficiencies removed. Proposed remedies require research on probable causes of behavior.

A great deal of the recent research on teaching has focused on teacher decisionmaking. The work has attempted to characterize key decisions teachers make in delivering instruction and assessing the results, as well as the antecedents and consequences of each type of decision. This work, which characterizes teacher as thoughtful practitioner, has led to a rich literature of insights and findings about good teaching. From that work it is possible to extract what now appear to be a number of the most important principles (Porter & Brophy, 1988).

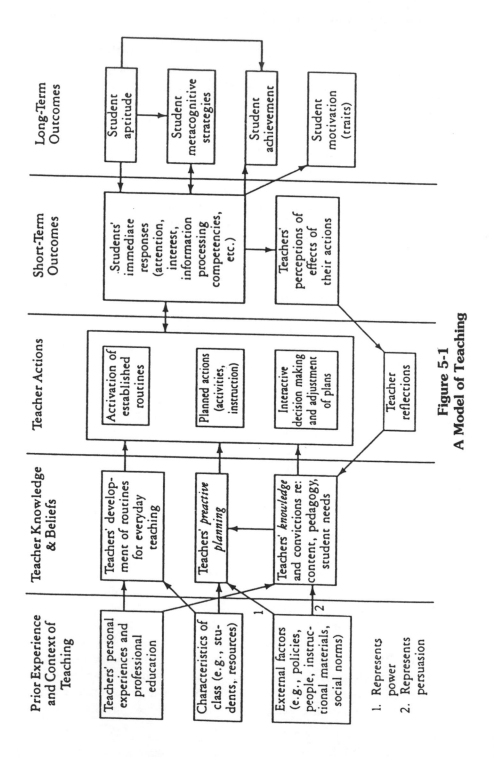

Figure 5-1
A Model of Teaching

Principles of Good Teaching

Good Teaching is Foreshadowed by Clear and Appropriate Goals for Student Achievement. The goals that teachers hold for their instruction cannot be taken for granted. Important differences exist among teachers in their goals, and these differences translate into differences in behaviors and subsequently into what students learn. There is not a one-to-one relationship between teacher goals for student achievement and student outcomes. On the other hand, students are much more likely to learn what it was that the teacher intended them to learn than they are likely to learn other things. That the relationship between teacher goals and student outcomes exists is not surprising. What is surprising is the nature of differences among teachers in the goals that they hold. In elementary school, it is a minority of teachers who hold student achievement of academic material as primary. The majority of elementary school teachers place primary emphasis upon student socialization into an orderly school environment and enhancing student interpersonal and citizenship knowledge and skills (e.g., Prawat, 1985; Prawat & Nickerson, 1985). Considering just teachers' goals for student academic achievement, much greater attention is placed on acquisition of facts and skills than on understanding key concepts in sufficient depth that they can be used to solve novel problems (e.g., Porter, 1989). For most teachers at least part of the time, the goal in mathematics content coverage is for exposure, not mastery. A great many mathematical topics are just touched on in instruction, with no expectation for any lasting effect upon what students know. There exists, however, a minority of teachers who (a) put primary emphasis on student academic achievement, (b) emphasize conceptual understanding and application, and (c) teach a limited range of content, but in doing so, demand student understanding and ability to solve novel problems. Too little is known about how such teachers overcome the constraints that prevent the majority of teachers from teaching in this way. Whatever those constraints, they seem to be especially difficult to overcome in schools and classrooms serving high concentrations of disadvantaged students.

Good Teachers Accept Appropriate Responsibility for Student Learning. Another important difference among teachers is the extent to which they accept appropriate responsibility for student outcomes. For example, in a study of teachers unusually effective in dealing with each of several difficult-to-teach types of students, one finding was ubiquitous. Regardless of the type of student difficulty, the more effective teachers saw the difficulty as something to be corrected. The less effective teachers saw the student difficulty as something over which they could have little control, something to be contained and, if possible, tolerated, not something to be corrected (Brophy & Rohrkemper, 1981). A similar result comes from international comparisons in mathematics. Among countries participating in the recently completed IEA study of mathematics achievement, Japanese students had the highest student achievement (McKnight et al., 1987). At the same time, Japanese teachers were much more likely to accept responsibility for low student achievement and to take credit for high student achievement than were teachers in the United States or other Western countries. This correlation between teacher acceptance of responsibility for student achievement and student achievement is not by itself evidence of a causal relationship, but taken together with similar findings is supportive of that conclusion. Studies of high school science teaching represent yet a third example of the importance of teachers' accepting responsibility for student achievement (Lee & Gallagher, 1986). Studies of high school science teaching characterize teachers as seeing their task as one of presenting content and the students' task one of learning content. Clearly, teachers who approach their teaching in this way see low student achievement as a student problem, not a teacher problem. Study after study has shown that high school science achievement in the United States is unacceptably low.

This finding of teacher responsibility is especially important in studying the teaching and learning of disadvantaged students. When expectations for student learning are low, as they typically are for low-income and minority students (e.g., Good, 1987), the likelihood of seeing low achievement as a student-owned problem would seem to be high.

Good Teachers Make Clear to Their Students What Is to Be Learned and Why Learning It Is Worthwhile. Here again, this principle of good teaching is not as surprising as is the fact that a substantial number of teachers do not appear to teach with the principle in mind. Studies of reading instruction in elementary school (e.g., Anderson, Brubaker, Alleman-Brooks, & Duffy, 1985) reveal that when interrupted during their studies and asked what they are doing, students typically answer by stating what task it is they are completing. When pressed, they can rarely articulate the purpose of the task—what it is they are to learn from completing the task. Like reading instruction, elementary school mathematics instruction is heavily dominated by seatwork. Students spend hours completing exercises, probably all too often with little thought as to what is to be learned and little knowledge as to why learning it would be useful. Studies of the teaching of elementary school social studies (Brophy, 1990) reveal that teachers rarely introduce instructional segments with clear statements about what is to be learned, and virtually never attempt to articulate why the learning is worthwhile. Again, mathematics instruction, with its heavy emphasis upon drill and practice of whole number computational skills, is likely characterized in the same way.

Good Teaching Promotes Learning of Comprehension Monitoring Strategies and Other Study Skills and *Allows Practice of These Skills and Acquisition of Appropriate Dispositions Through Structured Opportunities for Independent Learning.* The literature on metacognitive strategies is impressive in documenting the degree to which student learning can be enhanced through teaching and learning the knowledge, skills, and dispositions necessary for independent learning (Pressley, Snyder, & Cariglia-Bull, 1987). Disadvantaged students are several times more likely to lack needed metacognitive strategies than are their more advantaged counterparts. Thus, disadvantaged students have potentially the most to gain from teachers who make such strategies an explicit goal for their teaching. There may also be an interaction between the frequency with which instruction is oriented toward higher-order thinking and problem solving and the extent to which students possess the knowledge, skills, and dispositions necessary for them to function as semiautonomous (from the teacher), independent knowledge constructors. The less a student is capable of independent learning, the less likely the student is to receive instruction on problem solving. Perhaps the opposite should be true, however, since problem solving is far more difficult for students to learn than are basic mathematical skills.

Good Teaching Requires Teachers Who Know Their Subject Matter and Also Know the Preconceptions of the Subject Matter That Their Students Bring to the Classroom. Most of the research on relationships between teacher subject matter knowledge and student learning is weak, and so are the findings. Intuitively, good teaching requires that the teacher knows what is being taught. This leads to such sayings as, "I didn't really know (subject x) until I had to teach it." Yet, only recently has research been able to catch up with intuition. Studies of high school social studies teaching (e.g., Wineburg & Wilson, 1988) and elementary school science (Anderson & Smith, 1987) are documenting ways in which profound differences among teachers in their knowledge of a subject matter translate into important differences in instructional strategies. These, in turn, translate into differences in student achievement. Similarly, now that testing teacher subject matter knowledge is no longer taboo, surprising deficiencies in teacher subject matter knowledge are being documented. A Michigan study (Michigan Council of Teachers of Mathematics, 1982) found that a minority of elementary school teachers could correctly divide 24 by .3, despite the fact that respondents knew division facts. Their difficulty was with understanding place value, the only mathematical concept virtually certain to be taught during elementary school.

The remedies for serious shortcomings in teacher subject matter knowledge are less clear than the shortcomings themselves. Teacher assessment is on the rise, but if all individuals lacking in subject matter knowledge were eliminated from the teacher corps immediately, a serious teacher shortage would occur. Perhaps in the long run, strengthening teacher preservice education is the solution (e.g., The Holmes Group, 1986), but the challenge is substantial. There are approximately 2.4 million teachers in United States K-12 schools; if the top 20 percent in aptitude of every college graduation class were to elect teaching as a profession, for example, there would still be a shortage of about 20,000 new teachers each year. Other approaches to solving the problem are either to restructure the teaching profession so that fewer subject matter knowledge specialists are needed, or restructure the support provided teachers (through materials and technology), so that less teacher subject matter knowledge is required. Good teaching also requires teachers who understand the preconceptions that their students bring with them to instruction. Much of elementary and junior high school mathematics is about concepts and problems that students have experience with prior to formal instruction. Solving problems involving quantity and number is a matter of intense interest to very young children. All children care about matters of winning and losing and getting their fair share. Children enjoy comparing the size or amount of all sorts of things (Who is bigger? Who has more?). For reasons of out-of-school experiences or previous instruction, students begin a lesson or school year with beliefs that may be more or less consistent with the mathematics they are to learn. Research in a variety of fields, including mathematics, has revealed that these preconceptions must be identified and confronted directly if instruction is to be successful in the intended ways (e.g., Anderson & Smith, 1987; Brown & Burton, 1978).

Good Teaching Typically Makes Heavy Use of Published Instructional Materials. This principle is in direct contrast to the widely held belief, at least among teacher educators, that good teachers are not textbook followers. This belief makes little sense, however, in the world of real schools. Teacher time is limited, and so is teacher energy. Yet materials development is extremely time-consuming. Even if time were not a problem, teacher subject matter knowledge would be. Nor are most teachers knowledgeable about materials production. There is little reason to believe that one teacher with limited time, knowledge, and resources can develop a curriculum and supporting materials better than those available from the multi-million-dollar efforts of the publishing industry (Ball & Feiman-Nemser, 1986).

Good teaching is more likely to occur when the teacher makes heavy use of published instructional materials. A teacher's limited time is then more available for providing useful feedback to students on completed exercises and tests, and additional instruction to students who are confused or who require additional opportunities to see problem-solving behaviors modeled.

Curriculum Materials

Curiously, just as it is conventional wisdom that a good teacher is not a textbook follower, it is also conventional wisdom that what gets taught is what is in the textbook. What little empirical research is available, however, indicates that the mathematics content of the textbook being used is not a good indicator of the mathematics that is taught. Teachers using the same mathematics textbook vary substantially in the amount of time they allocate to mathematics instruction and to a considerable extent the mathematics content they cover within that time (e.g., Barr, 1988; Freeman & Porter, 1989; Porter,

1989). The mathematics instruction of teachers in the same school using the same textbook have been found to differ by the equivalent of eight full weeks of instruction (using fifty-minute lessons as the metric). Even teachers who follow their textbook closely, beginning with lesson one and working their way systematically through the book as the year progresses, fail to use from 30 percent to 50 percent of the lessons in the book, largely because they run out of time before completing the book. Many teachers, however, skip lessons and whole chapters as they follow their own predilections and sense of students' needs and interests in selecting material from the book. Surprisingly, most teachers spend from 10 percent to 20 percent of their instructional time on content that is not to be found in the textbook they are using.

Unfortunately, these deviations from the textbook typically compound the shortcomings of the published materials. For example, an already heavy emphasis upon computational skills in elementary school mathematics textbooks is typically increased by teachers who proceed somewhat independently from their text (or, put another way, those teachers who follow their textbooks most closely tend to offer a more balanced curriculum across the content areas of concepts, skills, and applications) (Freeman & Porter, 1989).

Content analyses of elementary school textbooks have revealed that, at least among the more heavily used textbooks, there are both important similarities and differences in content emphasis. For example, in an analysis of fourth-grade textbooks (Freeman et al., 1983) nineteen topics accounted for approximately 50 percent of the student exercises in each of four commonly used textbooks. However, the other half of each textbook covered a much larger number of topics, many of which are represented with only a very few exercises each. For example, 357 different topics were covered in one or more of the four books, yet only 20 percent of these topics were to be found in all four books. Not surprisingly, the nineteen common topics are heavily facts and skills oriented; solving story problems was not among these nineteen topics.

This feature of nineteen core topics in popular elementary school mathematics textbooks, most of which are facts and skills topics, and the finding that teachers emphasize definitions and computations in their instruction, may help to explain correlations between topic coverage in textbooks and topic coverage in classroom instruction. At least for middle elementary grade classrooms, the correlation between textbook and instruction is approximately .7; textbook topic emphasis accounts for 50 percent of the variation in topic emphasis within instruction. Nevertheless, when the topic emphasis in a textbook not used by the teacher is used to predict a teacher's topic emphasis, the correlations are only slightly lower. When a teacher uses a text covering substantially different mathematics content from that of most books and most teachers, that textbook can have a substantial impact upon what is taught. In a study of thirty-six fourth- and fifth-grade teachers in eighteen Michigan schools, two teachers were using CSMP (Armstrong et al., 1985). Of all the teachers in that study, the two CSMP teachers stood out in their content practices (Porter, 1989). While most teachers spent over 90 percent of their instructional time on computational skills, the two CSMP teachers spent only roughly half their instructional time on skills. These two teachers were also teaching in schools serving highly affluent neighborhoods, however, which makes it difficult to know whether the same shift in content emphasis would be likely in a school serving predominantly disadvantaged students.

The content emphases of published standardized tests of elementary school mathematics represent a much more balanced curriculum across concepts, skills, and applications than do textbooks or instructional practice (Freeman et al., 1983). Typically, these tests consist of three subtests, one for concepts, one for skills, and one for story problems. But these standardized tests have relatively little influence on instructional practices (e.g., Kuhs, Porter, Floden, Freeman, Schmidt, & Schwille, 1985). Rarely do standardized tests get used in ways that connect them to important rewards and sanctions for teachers and/or students. Most typically they are given in the spring of the year, and results are not available until the next year when students have moved on to another teacher. Tests that do appear to influence the content of instruction are, by contrast, embedded within the instruction. They are, for example, tests used to make grade-to-grade promotion decisions, or tests available as a part of a management-by-objectives system, or tests found at the end of the chapter in textbooks. Like textbooks and instructional practice, these curriculum-embedded tests place a great premium upon computational skills. They rarely require demonstration of student understanding of key concepts and students' ability to solve novel problems.

Textbooks and tests both have potential for substantially strengthening the quality of mathematics instruction for disadvantaged students. To have this effect, they would need to be changed substantially from their present form. Mathematics textbooks would need to put a much greater emphasis upon conceptual understanding and problem solving than is currently the case. In covering problem solving, care would need to be taken that the materials confront students with novel problems. A list of twenty-five story problems, all of which involve multiplication of single-digit numbers as the solution, lose their novelty somewhere after the third or fourth problem. Textbooks would need to have greater focus on fewer topics (topics balanced across concepts, skills, and applications). Currently, textbooks present hundreds of topics by just mentioning them, a problem that also characterizes teachers' classroom content practices (Freeman & Porter, 1989). It is difficult to see how students profit from this sort of superficial instruction. Textbooks also need to decrease the redundancy in content from one grade level to the next (Flanders, 1987). For example, the computational skill of multiplication of multiple-digit numbers is an emphasized topic in third, fourth, fifth, sixth, seventh, eighth, and ninth grades. As a result, the reward for learning this tiresome but rather straightforward skill (that is more dependably and quickly done by an inexpensive calculator) is to be bored with drill and practice in subsequent years.

Tests also need substantial revision if they are to serve the best interests of disadvantaged students. What teachers and students need are high-quality tests that place appropriate emphasis upon conceptual understanding and the solving of novel problems, which are readily available and which can be embedded within instruction. Test construction of this type is hard work and demands a high degree of technical skill and substantive knowledge. Teachers cannot be expected to develop such tests, at least not on any systematic and sustained basis. Large pools of exercises and items organized by a content outline that teachers could access electronically to build tests tailored to their instruction and their students would be extremely helpful. These are not currently available.

CONCLUSION

Mathematics in elementary school is in desperate need of change. This is true for all students, but the situation is worse for students from low-income families and worse yet in schools serving high concentrations of students from low-income families. Mathematics instruction places too much attention on computation skills and not enough on conceptual understanding and the ability to solve novel problems. Students' attitudes about mathematics and students' understanding of the role that mathematics plays in future study and in career options is not addressed. As a result, students leave junior high school bored with mathematics, and only knowing how to compute.

The explanations for this weak curriculum are many. The curriculum as taught is largely the curriculum one finds in popular textbooks and in the bulk of assessment practices. It is the curriculum typically emphasized as a part of the so-called effective schools movement. State and district frameworks typically specify minimum standards for what should be taught, standards that also take a heavy skills orientation. Perhaps most important of all, the mathematics taught today is very much like the mathematics taught in elementary school when today's teachers were students. It is the mathematics that most parents expect their children to study.

What is needed is revolutionary change. State and district curriculum policies must be reformulated (as some states such as California and districts such as San Diego appear to be doing). Textbooks need more than revision; they need a complete redesign. The same can be said for curriculum-embedded assessment devices. Nevertheless, the locus for real and lasting change lies ultimately with the individual classroom teacher. Fortunately, there are emerging professional development efforts that hold promise (e.g., Fennema, Carpenter, & Peterson, 1990), but such efforts are expensive. Disadvantaged students are most in need; that is where the limited resources should be invested.

REFERENCES

Anderson, C. W., & Smith, E. L. (1987). Teaching science. In V. Richardson-Koehler (Ed.), *The educator's handbook: A research perspective*. New York: Longman.

Anderson, J. R. (1983). *The architecture of cognition*. Cambridge, MA: Harvard University Press.

Anderson, L., Brubaker, N., Alleman-Brooks, J., & Duffy, G. (1985, November). A qualitative study of seatwork in first-grade classrooms. *Elementary School Journal,* *86,* 123–140.

Armstrong, R., Giamdrone, T., Harpel, J., Heidema, C., Kaufman, B., Pederson, P., Papy, F., & Schneider, J. (1985). *CSMP mathematics program for the intermediate grades.* Kansas City, MO: Mid-Continent Regional Education Laboratory.

Ball, D. L., & Feiman-Nemser, S. (1986). *Using textbooks and teachers' guides: What beginning elementary teachers learn and what they need to know* (Research Series No. 174). East Lansing: Michigan State University, Institute for Research on Teaching.

Barr, R. (1988). Conditions influencing content taught in nine fourth-grade mathematics classrooms. *Elementary School Journal, 88*(4), 387–411.

Barr, R., & Dreeben, R. (1983). *How schools work.* Chicago: University of Chicago Press.

Bernstein, H. T. (1985). When more is less: The mentioning problem in textbooks. *American Educator, 9*(2), 26–29, 44.

Brophy, J. (1990). Teaching for conceptual understanding and higher order applications of social studies. *Elementary School Journal, 90,* 351–417.

Brophy, J., & Rohrkemper, M. (1981, June). The influence of problem ownership on teachers' perceptions of and strategies for coping with problem students. *Journal of Educational Psychology, 73,* 295–311.

Brophy, J., Rohrkemper, M., Rashid, H., & Goldberger, M. (1983). Relationships between teachers' presentations of classroom tasks and students' engagement in those tasks. *Journal of Educational Psychology, 75*(4), 544–552.

Brown, A. L. (1978). Knowing when, where, and how to remember: A problem of metacognition. In R. Glaser (Ed.), *Advances in instructional psychology* (Vol. 1, pp. 77–165). Hillsdale, NJ: Erlbaum.

Brown, J. S., & Burton, R. R. (1978). Diagnostic models for procedural bugs in basic mathematical skills. *Cognitive Science, 2,* 153–192.

Carnegie Forum on Education and the Economy. (1986). *A nation prepared: Teachers for the 21st century* (the report of the Task Force on Teaching as a Profession). New York: Author.

Champagne, A. B., & Klopfer, L. E. (1977). A sixty-year perspective on three issues in science education: I. Whose ideas are dominant? II. Representation of woman. III. Reflective thinking and problem solving. *Science Education, 61,* 431–452.

Clark, C. M., & Yinger, R. J. (1977). Research on teacher thinking. *Curriculum Inquiry, 7,* 279–304.

Clark, C. M., & Yinger, R. J. (1979). Teachers' thinking. In P. L. Peterson & H. J. Walberg (Eds.), *Research on teaching* (pp. 231–263). Berkeley, CA: McCutchan.

Costa, A. L. (1985). *Developing minds: A resource book for teaching thinking.* Alexandria, VA: Association for Supervision and Curriculum Development.

Fennema, E., Carpenter, T. P., & Peterson, P. L. (1990). Learning mathematics with understanding: Cognitively guided instruction. In J. E. Brophy (Ed.), *Advances in research on teaching. Vol. 1: Teaching for meaningful understanding and self-regulated learning.* Greenwich, CT: JAI Press.

Flanders, J. R. (1987, September). How much of the content in mathematics textbooks is new? *Arithmetic Teacher,* 18–23.

Freeman, D. J., Kuhs, T. M., Porter, A. C., Floden, R. E., Schmidt, W. H., & Schwille, J. R. (1983). Do textbooks and tests define a national curriculum in elementary school mathematics? *Elementary School Journal, 83,* 501–513.

Freeman, D. J., & Porter, A. C. (1989, Fall). Do textbooks dictate the content of mathematics instruction in elementary schools? *American Educational Research Journal, 26,* 403–421.

Good, T. L. (1987, July-August). Two decades of research on teacher expectations: Findings and future directions. *Journal of Teacher Education, 32–47.*

The Holmes Group. (1986). *Tomorrow's teachers: A report of the Holmes Group.* East Lansing, MI: Author.

Kuhs, T., Porter, A., Floden, R., Freeman, D., Schmidt, W., & Schwille, J. (1985). Differences among teachers in their use of curriculum-embedded tests. *Elementary School Journal, 86,* 141–154.

Kuhs, T., Schmidt, W., Porter, A., Floden, R., Freeman, D., & Schwille, J. (1979). *A taxonomy for classifying elementary school mathematics content* (Research Series No. 4). East Lansing: Michigan State University, Institute for Research on Teaching.

Lampert, M. (1985). How do teachers manage to teach? Perspectives on problems in practice. *Harvard Educational Review, 55*(2), 178–194.

Lee, 0., & Gallagher, J. J. (1986, March). *Differential treatment of individual students and whole classes by middle school science teachers: Causes and consequences.* Paper presented at the annual meeting of the National Association for Research in Science Teaching, San Francisco.

McKnight, C. C., Crosswhite, F. J., Dossey, J. A., Kifer, E., Swafford, J. O., Travers, K. J., & Cooney, T. J. (1987). *The underachieving curriculum: Assessing U.S. school mathematics from an international perspective.* Champaign, IL: Stipes.

Michigan Council of Teachers of Mathematics (MCTM). (1982, February). *A report to the executive board on the test of concepts and skills in elementary mathematics previously authorized by the board, and administered to 392 prospective elementary teachers in five Michigan universities in December, 1981* (a report of the MCTM Teacher Preparation Committee). Unpublished manuscript, MCTM, Lansing.

National Assessment of Educational Progress. (1983). *Reading, science, and mathematics trends: A closer look.* Denver: Education Commission of the States.

National Center for Education Statistics. (1977). *The condition of education.* Washington, DC: U.S. Government Printing Office.

National Council of Teachers of Mathematics. (1980). *An agenda for action: Recommendations for school mathematics of the 1980's.* Reston, VA: Author.

National Council of Teachers of Mathematics. (1989). *Curriculum and evaluation standards for school mathematics.* Reston, VA: Author.

National Science Foundation. (1982). *Science and engineering education: Data and information.* Washington, DC: Author.

National Science Foundation. (1983). *A revised and intensified science and technology curriculum for grades K-12 urgently needed for our future: Recommendation of conference on goals for science and technology education, K-12* (Report to the NSB Commission on Precollege Education in Mathematics, Science, and Technology). Washington, DC: Author.

Palincsar, A., & Brown, A. L. (1984). Reciprocal teaching of comprehension-fostering and comprehension-monitoring activities. *Cognition and Instruction, 1*(2), 117–175.

Porter, A. C. (1986). From research on teaching to staff development: A difficult step. *Elementary School Journal, 87*(2), 159–164.

Porter, A. C. (1988). Understanding teaching: A model for assessment. *Journal of Teacher Education, XXXIX*(4), 2–7.

Porter, A. C. (1989). A curriculum out of balance: The case of elementary school mathematics. *Educational Researcher, 18*(5), 9–15.

Porter, A., & Brophy, J. (1988). Good teaching: Insights from the work of the Institute for Research on Teaching. *Educational Leadership, 45*(8), 74–85.

Porter, A., Floden, R., Freeman, D., Schmidt, W., & Schwille, J. (1988). Content determinants in elementary school mathematics. In D. A. Grouws & T. J. Cooney (Eds.), *Perspectives on research on effective mathematics teaching* (pp. 96–113). Hillsdale, NJ: Erlbaum; and Reston, VA: National Council of Teachers of Mathematics.

Prawat, R. S. (1985, Winter). Affective versus cognitive goal orientations in elementary teachers. *American Educational Research Journal, 22*, 587–604.

Prawat, R. S., & Nickerson, J. R. (1985). The relationship between teacher thought and action and student affective outcomes. *Elementary School Journal, 85*, 529–540.

Pressley, M., Snyder, B. L., & Cariglia-Bull, T. (1987). How can good strategy use be taught to children?: Evaluation of six alternative approaches. In S. M. Cormier & J. D. Hagman (Eds.), *Transfer of learning: Contemporary research and applications*. Orlando, FL: Academic Press.

Purkey, S., & Smith, M. (1983). Effective schools: A review. *Elementary School Journal, 83*, 427–452.

Rowe, M. B. (1974). Wait-time and rewards as instructional variables, their influence on language, logic, and fate control: Part 1. Wait time. *Journal of Research in Science Teaching, 11*, 81–94.

Stodolsky, S. S. (1988). *The subject matters: Classroom activity in math and social studies*. Chicago: University of Chicago Press.

Stodolsky, S. S. (1989). Is teaching really by the book? In P. W. Jackson & S. Haroutunian-Gordon (Eds.), *From Socrates to software: The teacher as text and the text as teacher*. Eighty-eighth Yearbook of the National Society for the Study of Education, edited for the Society by K. J. Rehage. Chicago: University of Chicago Press.

Wineburg, S. S., & Wilson, S. M. (1988). Models of wisdom in the teaching of history. *Phi Delta Kappan, 70* (1), 50–58.

Wittrock, M. C. (Ed.). (1986). *Handbook of research on teaching* (3rd ed.). New York: Macmillan.

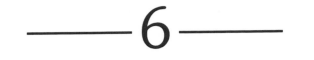

Selected Conceptual and Methodological Issues for Studying the Mathematics Education of the Disadvantaged

Walter G. Secada

That schools work differentially for students as a function of student demographic characteristics is a well-known and established fact. These characteristics include student socioeconomic status (SES), race, ethnicity, language background, and gender. Less clear is precisely what this "fact" means and, hence, what constitutes an appropriate response to it.

One set of responses dates back to the Great Society and they are tied to notions of cultural deprivation. Children growing up in poor homes and relatively impoverished community environments were said to have been deprived during their formative years of the school-related experiences, resources, and values that are common to middle- and upper-class families. Through no fault of their own, these children were disadvantaged. In response to this disadvantage, the Great Society through the Elementary and Secondary Education Act (ESEA) focused resources on providing poor children with compensatory educational experiences that were intended to make up for deficits from their earlier years.

Recently, disadvantage has returned to prominence in discourse in education. The Great Society's programs may have lost credibility in some quarters, but the problems they attempted to solve remain with us. If anything, these problems have become exacerbated over the recent past. Moreover, changes in the demographic composition of the U.S. school-age population mean schools are facing increasing numbers of students—both in absolute terms and proportionately—from precisely these backgrounds for whom schools have not worked (Hispanic Policy Development Project, 1988; Hodgkinson, 1985).

Schools and their related publics have had to take note of these changing demographic realities (National Research Council, 1989) and so have business and the military (Johnston & Packer, 1987; National Alliance for Business, 1986a, 1986b). With smaller numbers of white males entering the workforce and with increasing demands for a highly educated workforce, business and the military have found themselves competing for the same sorts of young people. If ever we could, no longer can we afford to educate a small portion of our student population and "train" the balance. Unless our educational systems do a better job of educating everyone, the United States will face an economic and military crisis as it will be unable to meet these demands from industry and the military for a technically educated workforce.

Also, our society is becoming an increasingly complex place in which to live (Grubb, 1986; National Research Council, 1989; Zarinnia & Romberg, 1987). Though the link between jobs and education may be important, there is a no less important link between education and the need for an informed citizenry who can participate fully in that society. This participation includes the ability to make judgments about complex social, moral, and legal issues; the ability to exercise those judgments within our country's democratic institutions; and, finally, the ability to control one's life within society (Secada, 1990).

It is at the intersection of these contexts that I would like to couch this discussion on mathematics education of disadvantaged students. Taken separately, any one of these forces—historical and for the future—could lead to research and policies that fail to address serious concerns had another force been considered simultaneously. As Cole and Griffin (1987) note, there is enormous pressure placed upon students in compensatory programs to master basic skills as prerequisite for other sorts of knowledge. Hence, these historical pressures might result in disadvantaged students' being denied access to the more advanced parts of a school's mathematics and science curricula—precisely the parts of that curriculum that are thought to be essential in order for students to participate in our evolving society.

Alternatively, concerns for the future often ignore the past. For example, there has been a general dissatisfaction with the "underachieving curriculum" (McKnight et al., 1987) and with disparities in the achievement of women and of some minority groups in mathematics. Yet it was a new and futuristic world view of mathematics (Zarinnia & Romberg, 1987), the future need for a mathematically literate populace (Romberg & Stewart, 1987), and advances in research on the learning and teaching of mathematics (Romberg & Carpenter, 1986) that were used in fashioning a set of Curriculum and Evaluation Standards for School Mathematics (National Council of Teachers of Mathematics [NCTM], 1987, 1989). Thus, in spite of calling for sweeping reforms in what and how mathematics is taught in the United States, the draft Curriculum Standards very specifically excluded the historically pressing issue of equity from its concerns (NCTM, 1987, p. 17). Only after the NCTM membership provided feedback concerning the importance of such concerns did equity find its way into the final document (NCTM, 1989).

The underlying assumption of this chapter is that research involving mathematics education for the disadvantaged must build on the real advances that have occurred in the past. Also, it must attend to changes that are taking place within schooling in general. New research, if it is to matter, must live within the tension that exists between the traditions of history that are focused on basic skills development for the disadvantaged and the forces for change that are based on projections in the kinds of mathematical literacy that will be required to participate in our future society. Otherwise, there is a very real danger that this research will be largely irrelevant to the true educational needs of disadvantaged students, or, worse yet, that it will legitimate practices that essentially do not prepare an increasingly larger segment of our population for meaningful participation in that society.

THE PROBLEMATIC NATURE OF DEFINING DISADVANTAGE

Key issues for any research are the definitions and validity of the constructs being used. Without concern for such issues, our sub-sequent ability to generalize across populations using these constructs becomes severely limited. In this section, I wish to note that the notion of disadvantage is problematic.

Certainly, any research that seeks to understand the schooling of disadvantaged children should have a clear definition of the population under consideration. "Disadvantaged," while conjuring politi-cally palatable visions of a group of students for whom schools have not worked as well as they might, needs to be unpacked so that we can understand the suppositions that undergird work based on that and similar notions.

There is no uniform consensus about what disadvantage means, even when it is used by the same writer. For example, in discussing the to-be-funded Center on the Study of the Education of Disadvan-taged Students, Ralph (1988) followed Slavin in "defining the disad-vantaged population to include those students who are likely to leave school (at whatever level or age) with an inadequate level of basic skills" (pp. 3–4). In this conception, disadvantage might be seen as focusing on the effects of leaving school unprepared for later life. Ralph built upon this notion by drawing from Wilson (1987) to further refine the notion of disadvantage.

> [There is a] population that suffers from the cumulative disadvantages of independent at-risk factors—growing up in poverty, in a single-parent family, or in an inner-city neighborhood—any one of which may be weakly correlated with school failure, but together form a qualitatively more potent set of obstacles for academic success. This latter group has been identified as Ameri-ca's urban underclass or the "truly disadvantaged." [Wilson, 1987; Ralph, 1988, pp. 4–5]

Discussing the same Center in the FY 1989 Application for Educational Research and Development Centers Program, Scope of

Work (U.S. Department of Education, 1988), Ralph linked the disadvantage to being "at risk."

> Most researchers use the term at-risk interchangeably with disadvantaged to describe various combinations of poor, minority, English-as-second-language, or sometimes urban children. The currency of the at-risk label comes from the belief that social science can reliably predict from an early age which youngsters run the danger of academic failure.... For a working definition, I use the following: A student at risk is a child who is likely to experience the problems associated with drug abuse, unwed pregnancy, suicide, dropping out of school, or chronically low academic performance. These problems are increasingly symptomatic of school-age youngsters.... [They] are . . . alterable so while schools may (or may not) be blameless, they could certainly affect these outcomes if they knew how.... For our purposes, we are focusing on disadvantaged children—children from low-income, minority families—as the general population most likely at risk. [P. 2]

In this conception, being disadvantaged is tied to the danger of suffering from problems that may or may not be the focus of schooling, but that certainly affect the ability to schools to meet their missions. In his former conception, Ralph (1988) attributed disadvantage more clearly to school failure, although acknowledging external factors, as well.

Prediction and Causation

In both of Ralph's formulations, disadvantage is tied to the prediction of school failure. That prediction is itself problematic, since it represents a shift in how poverty is viewed. It is one thing to note that children whose families are poor are, on the whole, not well served by schools or even that their mathematics achievement is less than it is for children from middle- and upper-SES backgrounds. Describing a given state of affairs, such claims undergird all of our concerns.

However, a shift from description to prediction is another matter altogether. What was the indication of a social problem becomes the prediction of an event. The focus of that event can shift the responsibility as well as render events more or less inevitable. Note how, in Ralph's formulation, a student as a function of his or her membership in multiple groups becomes "truly disadvantaged" and seems inevitably doomed to fail. The role of schools in constructing these events has become hidden.

One way around this problem might be to frame the prediction more complexly. Perhaps the better prediction is that, unless something is done, schools are at-risk of failing to educate students from "disadvantaged" backgrounds.

Moreover, when students are thought to perform poorly at school because of the specific socioeconomic factors such as poverty, language background, and so forth and those factors simultaneously define what it means to be disadvantaged, then the notion of disadvantagement has moved beyond being predictive to being, at least implicitly, causal. Such assumptions are evident in any study wherein authors use terms like "the effects of poverty on..." It is one thing to predict that, based on certain indicators, something is more likely to happen in one context than in another. It is another to claim that because of those indicators, an event will take place.

At first glance, a causal formulation of the problem might not be too far off target. After all, since the time of the Coleman Report (Coleman et al., 1966), we have known how strong a predictor student SES is of later school achievement. Our pervasive inability to break the predictive power of SES on that achievement must be acknowledged. Indeed, the effective schools movement is based on controlling for SES when identifying outlier schools for study (Brophy & Good, 1986). Given the strength of the relationship and our inability to break it, it becomes plausible to claim that the relationship between poverty (and whatever other factors compose disadvantage) and academic failure is causal in nature.

There are two problems with such a conception. First, a causal claim is based on the notion that we can manipulate an event in order to make another one occur (Cook & Campbell, 1979). The manipulated event attains the special status of being an independent variable, while its outcomes become dependent. I know of no studies where student demographic characteristics have been manipulated and the purported outcomes of such manipulation have been studied. Indeed, such a study seems impossible. Though poverty is conceivably manipulable, attempts to do so (through programs such as the Great Society) have failed. If anything, rates of poverty have increased over the past years.

Second, although individual student SES is known to predict mathematics achievement, a stronger predictor by far is the school's SES. In his meta-analysis, White (1982) found an average correlation between student SES and mathematics achievement of .22 in studies where the student was the unit of analysis; in studies where the school or community was the unit, the correlation rose to .73. Though this is, at least in part, an artifact of the aggregation, one could still argue that a student's SES is not what "causes" his or her low academic achievement. Rather, the stronger causal agent is the school and/or the community.

Couching a study in terms of causal language where the evidence does not support such language is dangerous. The discourse—that is, how we speak about the phenomenon—has been determined so that what is being sought are the mechanisms by which the causal linkages were forged. In a real sense, there is little new to be learned. On the other hand, the discourse of prediction, though itself problematic, allows some conceptual room for learning something new. However, the predictions themselves must be carefully constructed.

Loss of Theoretical Anchoring

In the 1960's Great Society usage, disadvantage was clearly linked to something that individuals or groups lacked, that is, experiences of a sort. Researchers, policymakers, and practitioners believed, somewhat naively, that what was needed was to compensate for what was missing, and that the problems associated with disadvantage would be attenuated, if not eradicated.

In current usage, disadvantage does not have such theoretical antecedents. The notion has been stripped of much explanatory power. Instead, it has been relegated to referring to the composition of a set of indicators that, individually and/or acting in consort, increase the likelihood of school failure. The naming of something does not really explain it.

Failure to articulate a set of theoretical antecedents for disadvantage could lead to the term's being expanded or used in strange ways. For example, gender differences in mathematics achievement and course taking are known to begin as early as middle school (Fennema, 1984; Oakes, 1990). In this sense, gender is certainly predictive of later school achievement, but it is not clear that we would want to claim that girls are educationally disadvantaged.

The interaction of gender, race, and poverty on mathematical achievement are well-established facts (Secada, 1990). Again, without some theoretical anchoring, it is not clear under what conditions one would wish to claim disadvantage for some specific groups and not for others.

Relativity of Terms

Disadvantage, even in current usage, is a relative term. Students from different backgrounds are construed as being disadvantaged when compared with other students. But these comparisons are made along a set of indicators that are highly value laden. Typically, they are academic in nature. Yet, in other contexts, disadvantaged students are able to do more and/or to do other things than their more advantaged peers. Terms such as "cultural discontinuity," or even "cultural conflict," convey this broader sense that in some situations, one is actually advantaged relative to those against whom one is considered as disadvantaged in other situations.

Terms like cultural discontinuity and cultural conflict convey the constructed nature of events. For example, African American students enter schools wanting to learn, yet as Grant (1989) and others (e.g., Ogbu, 1978) have noted, many students from oppressed groups actively begin to resist schooling sometime before high school. Labeling these students "disadvantaged" conveys an *a priori* explanation and inevitability to their resistance and eventual failure. Using the terms "discontinuity" and "conflict" does not.

THE METHODOLOGICAL LEGITIMATION OF CURRENT PRACTICE

Three related lines of current research have the potential for providing insights into the mathematics education of disadvantaged students.[1] First is the idea of proceeding from intended to enacted to received curriculum. By following a similar line of inquiry, we have learned much about the failure of the mathematics curriculum that currently is used in the United States (McKnight et al., 1987). That effort provided another piece of evidence that the mathematics curriculum is out of line with the need for educating a mathematically literate population.

---

1. In view of my previous critique of this term, I must note that I am using it as a *facon de parler*. The previously noted caveats on the use of this term should be kept in mind.

Second, sampling that permits comparisons across schools that systematically differ from one another can expand the range of practices under consideration. For example, sampling schools without compensatory programs, those with compensatory programs but low concentrations of disadvantaged students, and those with compensatory programs and high concentrations of disadvantaged students could provide us with opportunities to understand how the alignments between programs and classroom processes facilitated—or failed to facilitate—the learning of mathematics. Minimally, in view of White's (1982) findings about the correlations of school-level SES to mathematics achievement, it would be surprising were school-level effects not found.

Third, the selection of high-, average-, and low-achieving schools extends the effective schools research in two ways. It extends research throughout the continuum of achievement and does not just restrict achievement at one extreme end. It also allows us to discriminate effective practice from ineffective practice from practice that doesn't really matter one way or the other.

Currently, these research strategies are being implemented in combination via the Study of Academic Instruction for Disadvantaged Students. Yet these strategies, while providing insights about current practice, would seem unable to provide the sorts of information we need to ensure that the mathematics curriculum, as it should be, is accessible to all students. Rather, these research strategies constrain research to legitimate current practice that may not be aimed for the future needs of all students.

The Current Versus the Future Curriculum

Let us assume that schools where there was high achievement showed little variation among themselves. Further, let us assume that they showed strong curricular alignments: intent, implementation, and student learning. On the basis of these findings, one might argue that schools with disadvantaged students should replicate the sorts of structures and practices that the high-achieving schools have.

Yet, what McKnight et al. (1987) have argued is precisely that the present-day mathematics curriculum has been found wanting! Recommendations that fail to question the validity of the intended curriculum for disadvantaged students would be recommendations based on a flawed curriculum. Should we want to replicate practices that have been found to be wanting, even if they result in somewhat improved achievement for a particular group of students? This is precisely the sort of event that I have in mind when I refer to the moving target (Secada, 1990). We should aim for where the target is moving to, not for where it is moving from.

One way of addressing this issue would be to add a layer of analysis to curriculum assessment. That layer would precede the intended curriculum and represent an effort to gauge the quality of the current mathematics curriculum that is provided to disadvantaged students as judged against what they should be learning. The Curriculum and Evaluation Standards (NCTM, 1989), the California Framework (California State Department of Education, 1985), the characterization of curriculum from other countries where achievement is greater than in the United States, or a similar set of criteria could be used to create this added layer of analysis. Although we should expect there to be a strong misalignment between criteria drawn from the reform movement and subsequent curriculum manifestations, research should be designed so that features of high-achieving schools that tie into the reform movement can be identified—to aim to where curriculum will be, not where it has been.

The Best of the Worst?

One researcher has commented that the effective schools research looks at the best practices among the worst schools (Carter, personal communication). There is a kernel of truth within this bit of hyperbole. By looking at the practices of disadvantaged schools only, the vision of mathematics education for students in those schools becomes commensurately constrained.

Selection of Schools for Study Based on Mathematically Relevant Criteria

The use of academic achievement test scores as a criterion in sample school selection should be approached carefully. Mathematics achievement tests are typically weighted toward computational skills. High-achieving schools will be those whose students tend to be good at doing computations. In light of the widespread availability of pocket calculators, one should question such emphasis on low-level and narrow definitions of achievement.

A methodological alternative might be to select schools based on the purposeful omission of computational items from mathematics tests, or on giving computation a very low weight when selecting schools for study. Tests weighted toward problem solving and applications would be preferable for selecting schools. If such tests are unavailable, then the subtests from existing instruments that included such items might be used. In any case, selection of schools should be modified to focus more specifically on problem solving, applications, conceptual understanding, and similar sorts of mathematically important constructs.

Moreover, it would be desirable to have the pocket calculator readily available for all students who take these tests.

THE LIMITS OF STUDYING EXEMPLARY PRACTICE

Nowhere does the tension between defining students as disadvantaged versus seeing the issues as those of cultural variation become more pronounced than in the sorts of classroom processes that often are the focus of study for the education of the disadvantaged. Even something as seemingly neutral and demonstrably beneficial as "effective practice" contains cultural and linguistic components that must be taken seriously if we are to address the mathematics education of students who are labeled "disadvantaged." At the very least, there may be features in such practices that might result in differential effectiveness. At worst, these features might work against the very students whom they are meant to help. Teachers, administrators, policymakers, and even the researchers who recommend specific practices may try to implement them without having understood their inherently problematic natures.

Take, for example, the following, which are commonly thought of as "good practice" in mathematics instruction (or any subject area, for that matter): setting an atmosphere conducive to learning, maximizing engaged learning time, grouping students to accommodate differences in their academic proficiency, and maximizing family support. In each, the cultural and linguistic dimensions are often unappreciated.

Atmosphere Conducive to Learning

Certainly one cannot learn very much in a school that resembles a war zone. Yet, an atmosphere conducive for learning for many minority students might include features that are not part of a conducive climate for other students. Also, an atmosphere conducive for learning by the disadvantaged might exclude features that have been included elsewhere.

For example, minorities seem to learn better when there is a clearly communicated sense of caring for students that gets expressed on a personal and individual basis. Among Hispanics especially, the extended family and the nurturing the family provides to its members are highly valued and highly motivating. Such social and affective components are typically missing from mainstream definitions of "atmosphere."

Maximizing Engaged Learning Time

With any learning activity, there is a point of diminishing returns vis-à-vis time on task, engaged or not. The time-on-task studies have typically been restricted to a modest variation in time; very few students could be said to be engaged in tasks 100 percent of the time, nor could we claim that they maintained such a level of engagement for extended periods of time. This matches intuition, as anyone who has been in a non-English-speaking country will testify. After a few hours of trying to understand and to speak the language, a nonfluent speaker of the language will be very tired, if not exhausted. We do not know what that point is across or even within curricular subjects.

How the task in which one is engaged gets defined is also problematic. For example, consider the case of students of limited English proficiency (LEP). If all (or even most) mathematics instruction is carried out in English, the student has been given not one task but two: to learn the English language and to master the mathematics. If the student is engaged in the language aspects of such an instructional task, it seems very unlikely that he or she will have the time, the energy, or the desire to engage in the mathematics of the task.

The alignment between task content, how teachers communicate those demands, and student perceptions of the task at hand also would seem to be in need of study. The actual content of a given classroom task might be problematic in terms of its ability to engage a student from a different cultural group (where he or she has built up certain expectations about what tasks are important and worth engaging in), the conditions for display of task mastery, and the rewards associated with completion of the task in question (Fillmore, 1987; Secada, in press). If there is not an alignment along these dimensions, it seems unlikely that students will get engaged in the mathematical tasks that are at hand.

Ability Grouping

There seems to be uniform agreement among researchers, if not practitioners, that curriculum tracking and fixed, long-term ability grouping are undesirable (Slavin, 1989). Yet, there are ways by which such practices might take place other than through the formation of formal tracks in secondary school or through the assignment of students to homogeneous-ability grouped classrooms in elementary school.

Elementary mathematics curricula typically provide three pacings in their scope and sequence charts: basic, regular, and advanced. Recommended homework assignments also mimic a similar arrangement. Supplementary materials are organized along lines of remediation (which tends to focus on low-level activities) and enrichment. Teachers who follow such practices, as recommended in their text series, may have formed *de facto* tracks without meaning to do so.

There are other classroom practices that tend to group students by ability or teacher judgments of who is educable. In science education, it appears that teachers often pitch their lessons to a select number of students who compose a steering group (Lundgren, 1972). There are anecdotal accounts of middle-school mathematics teachers trying to select the few students who are worth "saving." I, myself, have spoken with many mathematics teachers of students from limited-English-proficient backgrounds. Many of these teachers question why they should help "those" students when their other students need assistance and when they (the LEP students) will receive assistance in their bilingual and/or ESL programs anyway. Such withholdings of instruction and assistance represent extreme forms of ability grouping, since students are sorted as to who are worth the effort of teaching versus those who are not, based on notions of ability.

Maximizing Family Support

This particular maxim provides an example of how those who are labeled "disadvantaged" often are blamed for being the victims. It is true that middle-class parents tend to be more involved in their children's educations than lower-SES parents. But, we need to be careful about ascribing differential valuing of schooling by parents based on such involvement. Assume that two sets of parents (or families) give a valence of 1 to a child's participation in school. This value takes meaning only in relationship to the valence given to other important familial needs and obligations. For middle-class families, items like food, clothing, and negotiating one's way in our society have significantly less importance, since they are taken-for-granted aspects of life. For the poor, or for non-English-speaking parents, these and other pressures take on a valence much greater than 1 because of their pressing nature. However, both sets of parents place equal value on their children's education.

The issue of family support is further problematic because certain kinds of support represent the subordination of parental concerns to the school's. For instance, parents of Title VII (bilingual education) and/or Chapter 1 children often are asked to serve on special advisory committees for those programs. This effectively rules out their participation in the school's PTA, or in other bodies that have more power within the schools.

Parents with limited English-speaking skills often find school personnel unwilling to make the time or effort to understand them. Instead, teachers, principals, and other administrators automatically refer these parents to the school's bilingual program. Again, parents find themselves shunted into marginal interactions with their children's schools.

Moreover, there are limits to the sorts of support that schools will validate as being useful. We all know of the busybody parent whose help is frankly seen as interference in the school. Whether similar judgments are made concerning the limits of appropriate involvement by parents of "disadvantaged" students is an open question. There is a strong folklore in the field of bilingual education that such judgments are often made, and that they are culturally, as well as linguistically, biased.

CULTURAL DIVERSITY, DISCONTINUITY, AND RESISTANCE

One view of why schools work differentially for students as a function of demographic characteristics lies at the intersection of notions of cultural diversity, discontinuity, and resistance. This view, and work associated with it, can be tied to the fact that disadvantage is inherently relativistic, and that the claim of primacy for a specific dimension represents the fundamental legitimation of a social arrangement that works to the advantage of the group that has been defined as advantaged.

According to a view of cultural discontinuity, students are thought to enter school having had a wide range of experiences. These experiences are tied to the socialization patterns followed in the children's homes, which are, in turn, a function of the cultures to which the parents and children belong.

Schools, on the other hand, are thought to be organized around other principles. Not only do they convey academic content, but they are thought to do so in a manner that is closely aligned to socialization patterns of specific cultural groups: of whites, of students from middle-class backgrounds, and of males. Moreover, teachers—who are predominantly white and female and have, themselves, been socialized along lines that are gender bound—often find themselves unable to respond as flexibly as they need to in order to adapt their instructional styles to match the diversity of what their students have come to expect.

For instance, children from middle-class backgrounds are taught how to understand and to respond to commands that are couched in the "polite" form of a question: "Wouldn't it be a good idea to pick up your toys?" Alternatively, children from poor and from non-white backgrounds are often given very direct instructions on what to do: "Pick up your toys." Moreover, children of limited English proficiency will understand the latter form of commands earlier in their learning of English. However, middle-class teachers often engage in such "polite" forms of giving commands, and, then, they become understandably upset when some children do not respond to these tacit commands (Heath, 1983).

There is some evidence to suggest that the elementary school mathematics curriculum, as it is currently organized, is biased against children raised in traditional Hispanic and American Indian families (Fillmore, 1987). These children are expected to engage in large, meaningful, and well-situated tasks at home, under adult supervision. Among Hispanics, failure at getting such a task right is not a concern, since the goal is for the child to come closer to mastery during his or her later trials. Among traditional American Indians, a task is never put on public display before the individual determines that it is ready for display (Deyhle, 1987). Moreover, neither Hispanic nor American Indian children are prepared for engaging in the small, repetitive, and (frankly) meaningless activities that they are expected to engage in as part of the mathematics curriculum (see my discussions of Fillmore, in Secada, 1990, in press). Over time, because of the ongoing conflicts caused by the discontinuity between what is validated in the student's home versus that which is validated at school, students begin to withdraw and come to resist, actively, the school's efforts (see Metz, 1988).

Ogbu (1978; Ogbu & Matute-Bianchi, 1986) provides another analysis that would seem to complement the one above. According to Ogbu, children learn from the adults in their home communities whether or not schooling is worth the effort. African-Americans, Mexican-Americans, Puerto Ricans, and American Indians have historically been oppressed in their interactions with representatives from the dominant culture. Although this oppression's most egregious forms have been removed, traditional barriers against these groups remain in the workplace and in terms of their complete participation in our society. According to Ogbu, parents from these groups value schooling highly, and they communicate these values very directly to their children. Yet, also, their children receive contradictory messages when they see examples of how, even with an education, individuals from their communities do not have access to well-paying jobs, or to other forms of participation in our society.

In Ogbu's view, children of oppressed groups come to define themselves in opposition to the dominant culture's norms of behavior. One such set of norms, of course, is to do well in school.[2] Hence, children belonging to groups that have been historically oppressed in our society not only will develop attitudes that set them in opposition to doing well in school (and they will interpret their school experi-

---

2. Ogbu's analysis, of course, is much more complex than I have been able to summarize.

ences in a manner that supports such interpretation), but also will exert pressure on their peers not to do well either.

Taken together, these analyses suggest that research on the mathematics education of disadvantaged students needs to take into consideration how students' home cultures and cultural values are consistent with or opposed to the norms of the schools they attend. For instance, one might start by asking a student—or a group of students—about what happened in their mathematics class. The discussion might focus on things like how meaningful the work was, what the cues were that children used to alert them to transitions in the lesson, how they perceived evaluation of their efforts, and the like. Next, these same children might be asked the same (or a similar) series of questions concerning tasks at home. Such a line of questioning might begin by asking children if they ever have had to engage in work that can be described like they had described the mathematics lesson in question. Follow-up questions would then focus on how those sorts of tasks were organized, and the kinds of rewards that they get for succeeding. These questions might be followed up with interviews with parents, followed by some actual home observations to check on the validity of the self-reported data. There might be other ways of pursuing these issues.

Of critical importance would be efforts that tried to determine when students begin to shift from being somewhat confused about the mismatch between school and home to their having oppositional attitudes about and behaviors in their schools. We might find practices that arrest the shift in some cases, that lead to alienation from home in others, and that exacerbate the process in yet others. The challenge, of course, would be to trace such a process within the context of the teaching and learning of mathematics.

CONCLUDING COMMENTS

One of the most critical concerns of any study should be the validity of the constructs that it attempts to use in explicating the phenomenon under consideration. In this chapter, I have tried to articulate a series of ways in which many constructs that have been used to study the mathematics education of disadvantaged students are problematic. They are problematic not only because they may be

based on faulty premises, but also because they may serve to legitimate ways of seeing things and practices based on those ways that are,
simply, maladaptive in terms of the need for a mathematically literate
populace.

   I have argued that research should be aware of the problematic
nature of its inquiry, and that care in interpreting results is essential.
Overall, the goal of ensuring that mathematics education is for
everyone—and not just for a select few—is an admirable one. Yet, as
we go about studying how we might make that happen, we must be
careful that we do not inadvertently use notions that are, in fact,
conceptual blinders. It is that spirit that should guide efforts to study
the mathematics education of disadvantaged students.

REFERENCES

Brophy, J., & Good, T. L. (1986). Teacher behavior and student achievement. In
   M. C. Wittrock (Ed.), *Handbook of research on teaching* (3rd ed.). New York:
   Macmillan.

California State Department of Education. (1985). *Model curriculum standards: Grades 9
   through 12*. Sacramento, CA: Author.

Cole, M., & Griffin, P. (Eds.). (1987). *Contextual factors in education: Improving science and
   mathematics education for minorities and women.* Madison: Wisconsin Center for
   Education Research, University of Wisconsin-Madison.

Coleman, J. S., Campbell, E. Q., Hobson, C. J., McPartland, J., Mood, A. M.,
   Weinfeld, F. D., & York, R. L. (1966). *Equality of educational opportunity.* Washington, DC: U.S. Government Printing Office.

Cook, T. D., & Campbell, D. T. (1979). *Quasi-experimentation.* Chicago: Rand McNally.

Deyhle, D. (1987). Learning failure: Tests as gatekeepers and the culturally different
   child. In H. T. Trueba (Ed.), *Success or failure? Learning and the language minority
   child* (pp. 85–108). Cambridge, MA: Newbury House Publishers.

Fennema, E. (1984). Girls, women, and mathematics. In E. Fennema & M. J. Ayer
   (Eds.), *Women in education: Equity or equality?* (pp. 137–164). Berkeley:
   McCutchan.

Fillmore, L. W. (1987, September 24). *Is effective teaching equally effective across diverse
   cultural learning styles?* Presentation made at the Upper Great Lakes Multifunc-
   tional Resource Center, Wisconsin Center for Education Research, University of
   Wisconsin-Madison.

Grant, C. A. (1989). Equity, equality, teachers, and classroom life. In W. G. Secada
   (Ed.), *Equity in education* (pp. 89–102). Philadelphia, PA: Falmer Press, Taylor &
   Francis.

Grubb, N. (1986). *Educational reform and the new orthodoxy: The federal role in revitalizing
   the U.S. labor force.* Unpublished manuscript prepared for the Joint Committee,

U.S. Congress. Available from the author at University of Texas at Austin or University of California at Berkeley.

Heath, S. B. (1983). *Ways with words.* Cambridge: Cambridge University Press.

Hispanic Policy Development Project. (1988). *Closing the gap for U.S. Hispanic youth: Public/private strategies.* Washington, DC: Author.

Hodgkinson, H. L. (1985, June). *All one system: Demographics of education, kindergarten through graduate school.* Washington, DC: Institute for Educational Leadership.

Johnston, W. B., & Packer, A. E. (1987, June). *Workforce 2000: Work and workers for the twenty-first century.* Indianapolis: Hudson Institute.

Lundgren, U. P. (1972). *Frame factors and the teaching process.* Stockholm: Almquist and Wiksell.

McKnight, C. C., Crosswhite, F. J., Dossey, J. A., Kifer, E., Swafford, J. O., Travers, K. J., & Cooney, T. J. (1987). *The underachieving curriculum: Assessing U.S. school mathematics from an international perspective.* Champaign, IL: Stipes.

Metz, M. (1988). *Some reflections on qualitative research concerning low achievement of poor children.* Unpublished manuscript available from Department of Educational Policy Studies, University of Wisconsin-Madison.

National Alliance for Business. (1986a). *Employment policies: Looking to the year 2000.* Washington, DC: Author.

National Alliance for Business. (1986b). *Youth 2000: A call to action* (Report on a National Leadership Meeting, June 10, 1986, Washington, DC). Washington, DC: Author.

National Council of Teachers of Mathematics. (1987). *Curriculum and evaluation standards for school mathematics* (draft). Reston, VA: Author.

National Council of Teachers of Mathematics. (1989). *Curriculum and evaluation standards for school mathematics.* Reston, VA: Author.

National Research Council. (1989). *Everybody counts.* Washington, DC: National Academy Press.

Oakes, J. (1990). Opportunities, achievement, and choice: Women and minority students in science and mathematics. In C. B. Cazden (Ed.), *Review of Research in Education, 16,* 153–222.

Ogbu, J. U. (1978). *Minority education and caste: The American system in cross-cultural perspective.* Orlando, FL: Academic Press.

Ogbu, J. U., & Matute-Bianchi, M. E. (1986). Understanding sociological factors: Knowledge, identity, and school adjustment. In Bilingual Education Office, California Department of Education, *Beyond language: Social and cultural factors in schooling language minority students* (pp. 73–142). Los Angeles: Evaluation, Dissemination, and Assessment Center, California State University.

Ralph, J. (1988, March). *Planning paper for the Center on the Study of the Education of Disadvantaged Students.* Washington, DC: Office of Educational Research and Improvement, U.S. Department of Education.

Romberg, T. A., & Carpenter, T. P. (1986). Research on teaching and learning mathematics: Two disciplines of inquiry. In M. C. Wittrock (Ed.), *Handbook of research on teaching* (3rd ed., pp. 850–873). New York: Macmillan.

Romberg, T. A., & Stewart, D. M. (1987, March). *The monitoring of school mathematics: Background papers* (3 vols.). Madison: Wisconsin Center for Education Research, University of Wisconsin-Madison.

Secada, W. G. (1990). Student diversity and mathematics education reform. In L. Idol & B. F. Jones (Eds.), *Dimensions of cognitive instruction* (pp. 295– 330). Hillsdale, NJ: Erlbaum.

Secada, W. G. (in press). Equity, student diversity, and cognitivist research. In T. P. Carpenter, E. Fennema, & S. Lamon (Eds.), *Teaching and learning mathematics*. Albany, NY: SUNY Press.

Slavin, R. E. (Ed.). (1989). *School and classroom organization*. Hillsdale, NJ: Erlbaum.

U.S. Department of Education. (1988). *FY 1989 application for educational research and development centers program, scope of work*. Washington, DC: Author.

White, K. R. (1982). The relation between socioeconomi status and academic achievement. *Psychological Bulletin, 91*(3), 461–481.

Wilson, W. J. (1987). *The truly disadvantaged: The inner city, the underclass, and public policy*. Chicago: University of Chicago Press.

Zarinnia, E. A., & Romberg, T. A. (1987). A new world view and its impact on school mathematics. In T. A. Romberg & D. M. Stewart (Eds.), *The monitoring of school mathematics: Background papers* (Vol. 1: The monitoring project and mathematics curriculum, Chapter 2, pp. 21–61). Madison: Wisconsin Center for Education Research, University of Wisconsin-Madison.

7

Mathematics Education, the Disadvantaged, and Large-Scale Investigation: Assessment for Stability Versus Assessment for Change

Curtis C. McKnight

Research on education for minority and disadvantaged students has too often settled for small, incremental additions to our understanding of instruction for this group. In the area of mathematics education, such research is far too limited. One of the messages of the Second IEA Mathematics Study (e.g., McKnight et al., 1987) is that incremental change has not worked. Considering feasible and realistic change as coming only in small increments can at times be nothing more than a corollary to the axiom, "if it's not broken, don't fix it." Unfortunately, in U.S. mathematics education, for the mainstream as well as the disadvantaged, things are broken.

The criterion for academic performance that underlies the design of many studies—achievement gains on standardized tests—further limits what these studies can tell us about instruction for the disadvantaged. Achievement outcomes are certainly one important product of the educational process, and parity in these outcomes is a seemingly obvious goal for education of the disadvantaged. Nevertheless, a narrow focus on such outcomes as a measure of effectiveness can limit the potential for effective change.

An incremental approach and the focus on achievement gains as measured by standardized tests seem to have some undesirable implications. It was this combination of approach and criterion in process-product research that elevated the model of direct instruction into an instructional model synonymous with effectiveness. Yet, the strategy of direct instruction has embedded in it serious issues of control and the possibility for politicizing education as a process of pacification. Further, such a narrow focus of criterion and approach would seem to imply a conception of learning as reception learning, a conception that is increasingly at odds with what we know about learning and teaching mathematics.

These concerns lead me to the role of provocateur and, as I look at research designed to improve mathematics education, to ask the question, "Does it encourage the continued stability of the status quo or does it aim at identifying and furthering needed change?" As a provocateur, I claim the right to exaggerate as a stimulus to useful, moderating discussion and, for purposes of fostering that discussion, to take positions I am not prepared to support as boldly as they are stated.

What is most needed in research on mathematics education for the disadvantaged (or any children, for that matter) are better models of the learning environment for mathematics and criteria for determining the effectiveness of instruction that reflect true change in educational practice. I will put forth my ideas on these matters in this chapter, but first, to provide context for my remarks, I review principles that underlie my thinking.

FIVE MAXIMS REGARDING MATHEMATICS EDUCATION FOR THE DISADVANTAGED

For the sake of discussion, I seek here to take a leap rather than a step, a leap that it is hoped will reveal issues that might make for assessment that leads to change. As a part of this leap, I wish to discuss five "maxims" arising from familiar issues in effective education for the disadvantaged. In the following paragraphs I state these maxims and some of what I see to be their implications.

1. *Parity of mediocrity is an unacceptable goal for education of the disadvantaged in mathematics or any other subject.* Only working for the potential for all to excel to the maximum of their capabilities is acceptable. Stated in this form the maxim seems truism, yet its implications are not. For example, this maxim certainly suggests that the use of achievement gains on standardized tests and achieving parity in such gains are inappropriate criteria for educational planning for the disadvantaged, when cross-national benchmarks in mathematics achievement (e.g., McKnight et al., 1987) show that the brightest and most expert of U.S. mathematics students manage to achieve mediocrity at best when compared to students from other countries by means of such tests. Certainly such narrow criteria lead almost straightaway to solutions in terms of the direct instruction model (with all its attendant concerns about stabilization of the status quo, pacification of minorities, etc.) and run the risk of letting conventional wisdom (e.g., traditional process-product research) determine the boundaries of the feasible. Further, the maxim suggests that parity, at best a secondary goal, is the wrong basis (or at least as a single basis) for a critique of tracking, sorting, and grouping in U.S. schools.

2. *Instructional delivery has "driven" content rather than vice versa.* It is the difficulties of effective instructional delivery that has often led to the conception of incremental change and set the boundaries for which reforms are feasible. This concern for what is feasible in instructional delivery has been used to decide which mathematical content was appropriate in school mathematics reform; it also has led to the tracking and grouping practices now under attack.

Yet, it can be argued that maximizing engaged time on inappropriate content tasks is at least as big a mistake as having inordinately low levels of engaged time. It is certainly a mistake to learn the wrong mathematics, even if it is done effectively. Both the mainstream and the disadvantaged must learn the mathematics needed for tomorrow, such as the prerequisites of the newly emerging computer-intensive applied mathematics that make up much of current research mathematics.

The academic and research mathematics of today should help determine school mathematics of tomorrow, and even of today. Hence, it is at least as appropriate for content to have an impact on instructional delivery as it is for instructional delivery to drive content. Certainly, it reinforces the belief that it is a tactical mistake to separate issues of content from issues of instructional delivery.

3. *Beliefs, concepts, and attitudes determine persistence and participation.* Sufficient research has been done on the importance of conceptions of mathematics to mathematics achievement to make it clear that there is a strong relationship between the two. The work of Erlwanger (1973, 1975) has provided one of the most damning critiques of Individually Prescribed Instruction, a particular individualized instruction program in mathematics, by carefully analyzing the cognitive processes of individual students through interviews as they carried out the tasks of the program and talked about what they were learning. These analyses revealed both systematic errors in student information processing on mathematical tasks from the program's workbooks (e.g., generalizing rules from the materials to derive .7. as the answer to ".3 + 4. = ?") and systematic misconceptions of the nature of mathematics that emerged from student experiences with program materials.

The series of detailed interviews by which Erlwanger uncovered the cognitive processes for individual students (e.g., those he calls "Benny" and "Mat") are frightening in what they document of children's implicit conceptions of mathematics gained as incidental learning from their curricular experiences in mathematics and determined in part by the mode by which those experiences were provided. For example, Erlwanger (1973), in discussing "Benny," points out that

> because a large segment of the material in [the Individually Prescribed Instruction mathematics program materials] is presented in programmed form, the questions often require filling in blanks or selecting a correct answer.

Therefore, this mode of instruction places an emphasis on answers rather than on the mathematical processes involved. . . . Benny is aware of this. He also knows that the key is used to check his answers. Therefore the key determines his rate of progress. But the key only has one right answer, whereas he knows that an answer can be expressed in different ways. This allows him to believe that all his answers are correct "no matter what the key says." . . . [T]he programmed form . . . was forcing Benny into the passive role of writing particular answers in order to get them marked right. [P. 15]

Truly devastating misconceptions of mathematics are revealed by the insightfulness of Erlwanger's interviews, as shown in the following excerpt ("E" is Erlwanger; "B" is "Benny"):

E: It [i.e., finding answers] seems to be like a game.
B: [Emotionally] Yes! It's like a wild goose chase.
E: So you're chasing answers the teacher wants?
B: Ya, ya.
E: Which answers would you like to put down?
B: [Shouting] Any! As long as I knew it could be the right answer. You see, I am used to check [sic] my own work; and I am used to the key. So I just put down 1/2 because I don't want to get it wrong." [P. 16]

Perhaps the true tragedy of such misconceptions is best revealed by "Benny's" comment at the end of an interview segment on fractions when he says, ". . . I would really like to know what happens. You know what I'll do today? I'll go down to the library . . . I am going to look up fractions, and I am going to find out who did the rules, and how they are kept" (p. 19).

While these investigations reveal that conceptions (and serious misconceptions) about the nature of mathematics are formed by children during mathematics instruction, they do not point out the impact of such conceptions, or of student beliefs and attitudes, on continued participation in the study of mathematics. McKnight et al. (1987, pp. 36–49) presents at least suggestive evidence that students' experiences in school mathematics help form both their conception of mathematics and their perceptions of its importance *to them* and thus, indirectly, help determine their willingness to persist in the continued study of mathematics into school grades when such participation becomes voluntary and on into college.

It seems clear that issues of persistence and continued participation in the study of mathematics are especially important in the context of progress for minorities and the disadvantaged. Thus, this maxim reminds us that matters of student beliefs, attitudes, and conceptions of mathematics are of direct relevance to progress toward equality for the disadvantaged in mathematics learning.

This reasoning, in turn, suggests the importance of monitoring the students' beliefs and attitudes, at least those relevant to continuing involvement in mathematics study. It also suggests the importance of monitoring student cognitive processing in the accomplishing of mathematical tasks and using this information to model the concepts and misconceptions of mathematics that emerge. Surely these student beliefs, attitudes, and conceptions that emerge from curricular experiences in mathematics are at least as important as achievement outcomes in measuring the effectiveness of mathematics education programs that serve the disadvantaged.

4. *Mathematics cannot be learned appropriately in a ghetto of isolation from work in other disciplines.* Traditional school mathematics has consisted of an academic lockstep through a sequence of fragmented increments of skill development, with each course preparatory for later work in the sequence and with the motivation for each step justified primarily in terms of preparation, with other motivation deferred to the (often indefinite) future. This version of school mathematics certainly communicates to students a specific conception of mathematics.

This conception of mathematics, which typically emerges from experiences with school mathematics, is far from the conception of mathematics held by citizens and workers who make extensive use of mathematics, let alone by academic and research mathematicians. A more appropriate conception might be to see mathematics as a set of conceptual and computational tools, of thought processes, that have broad application in many situations.

Such a tool-providing conception of mathematics as broadly applicable has obvious utility in convincing students to persist in participating in mathematics study, and this is of *obvious importance* to disadvantaged students. Yet this kind of conception of mathematics, unlike that embedded in traditional school mathematics curricula, cannot easily be communicated by the study of mathematics in isolation from the study of other subjects for which mathematics can provide descriptive and analytical tools, even in the early grades. In view of this crucial distinction in potential school mathematics experiences, it seems important that differences in curricular intentions and implementations relevant to this distinction should be carefully documented and investigated in research on mathematics education for disadvantaged students.

5. *Students extract incidental messages—meta-messages—from their learning environments and experiences.* At least since the pioneering work of Dreeben (1968), it has been clear that students learn not only from the intentional messages of instruction but also from the incidental messages—the meta-messages—of their learning environments and experiences. This is particularly important to consider when investigating the learning opportunities provided the disadvantaged, particularly in schools with a high concentration of the disadvantaged. Often these meta-messages conflict with the official messages (e.g., "mathematics is important," "it is important for you to learn mathematics," "you can learn mathematics") injected into the school setting and classroom learning environment. These contradictions may overcome deliberate efforts to shape student beliefs, conceptions, and attitudes toward persistence and continued participation in the study of mathematics.

One possible source of undesirable meta-messages comes from premature sorting and tracking that not only sets limits to students' opportunities to learn but also sends meta-messages to some students about lowered status, the futility of individual effort, and so on. This is particularly likely to have serious effects on the disadvantaged and their motivation to continue their involvement with mathematics.

Some aspects of the effects of sorting and tracking in U.S. schools in mathematics education were discussed in McKnight et al. (1987, pp. 102–111), from which Figure 7-1 here is taken. The analysis represented in Figure 7-1 suggests that not only does considerable variation in mathematics accomplishment (measured by an achievement pretest at the beginning of grade eight) exist in U.S. schools, but more than half (more than any other country investigated) of it is attributable to differences among schools and among classes within schools. There is thus less of the "pie" left to be affected by individual effort (differences between pupils within classes) than for any other country studied. Differences between schools and classes, and this inappropriate grouping and tracking, would seem to be a potent source of meta-messages about the point of student participation and effort in learning mathematics. This would seem to be particularly debilitating for the disadvantaged, since, by definition, they more often receive messages about lack of advantages and opportunities

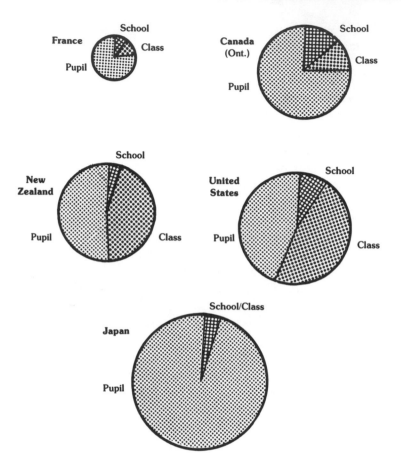

These circles depict for each country the variance components associated with the core pretest. (For most countries, this test consisted of forty items. For Japan, it had sixty items.) The areas of the circles are roughly proportional to the total amount of score variation. The slices represent the amount of total variation that is attributable to differences between students, classrooms, and schools. Since these are pretest data, the variance components represent how students were allocated to schools and classrooms and not to differences in teaching during the school year. Very similar patterns were found in the posttest data, as well.

Figure 7-1
Sources of Achievement Variance in Five Countries

(Taken from McKnight et al., 1987, p. 108)

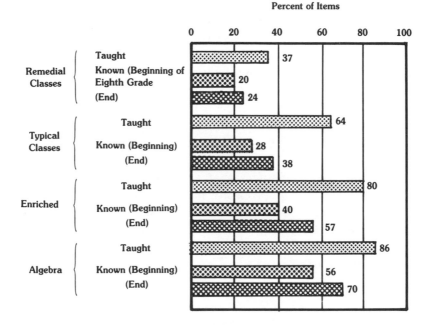

Percent of Items

Four different class types are found in eighth-grade mathematics in the United States, each with a different mathematics curriculum. In this graph, the amount of algebra taught and learned by students in each class type is shown. Students in the Remedial classes were taught only about one-third of the algebra on the international test, and very little algebra was learned during the year. On the other hand, students in the Algebra classes were taught almost all of the algebra on the test, and a great deal was learned. More extensive tracking was found at this level in the United States than in any other country in the study.

Figure 7-2
Achievement Effects of Tracking in U.S. Classrooms

(Taken from McKnight et al., p. 106)

and also because such messages reinforce beliefs identified in locus-of-control research that suggest that minorities and the disadvantaged already consider they are unable to control their future. Figure 7-2, which portrays the accumulated differences among class types of grades 1– 8, also suggests that issues of meta-messages are of importance and are directly related to achievement differences.

Past studies of "Pygmalion effects" also suggest that teachers' beliefs and expectations for their students are a potentially powerful source of further meta-messages. The Second/IEA Mathematics Study also suggests (e.g., McKnight et al., 1987, p. 66) that teacher beliefs about mathematics are not what might be desired and, thus, may contribute to inappropriate conceptions of mathematics in students with the attendant consequences of such misperceptions.

Thus, the fifth maxim and the issues it summarizes suggest that it is of critical importance to assess aspects of learning environments that are the sources of meta-messages that may be counterproductive in securing more effective participation in mathematics learning by the disadvantaged.

Obviously, meta-messages that are being sent cannot be measured directly, but an appropriate model of learning environments may be used to point out the sources of meta-messages that will allow for the indirect documentation of likely meta-messages. The concept of the meta-message should help identify critical elements of learning environments to assess.

A MODEL OF THE LEARNING ENVIRONMENT

The previous discussion suggests that a model of the learning environment may be helpful in identifying criteria of mathematics education of particular salience in assessment that leads to useful changes for the disadvantaged. Figure 7-3 presents schematically the elements of one such model.

Central to this model is the idea that the learning environment may be considered as made up of three interacting subenvironments: motivational environments, conceptual environments, and working environments. Further, these environments are embodied in three "nested" communities: the classroom, the school, and the larger community of town, neighborhood, and family.

The *motivational environment* may be considered as all those aspects of a particular community that affect the motivation of students to participate and excel in the study of mathematics. These motivational aspects include the (perceived or stated) view of the importance of mathematics (especially for the students involved); the (stated or perceived) expectations for achievement and persistence; the presence of explicit broad goals for mathematics learning; the presence of specific mastery milestones throughout the years of schooling; and the

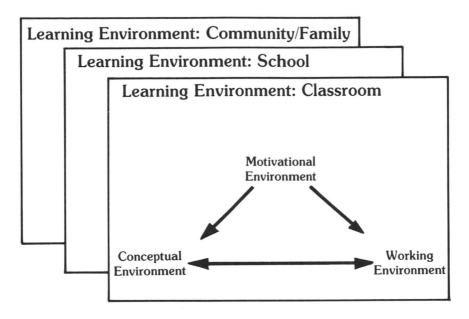

Figure 7-3
**The Learning Environment: Three Subenvironments and Three
Communities**

realization of these goals and the preparation for these milestones in
explicit objectives in the classroom. McKnight et al. (1987, pp.
84–101) discussed the importance of such milestones in decreasing
redundancy and fragmentation, while increasing focus and the sharing of explicit communal expectations in the curriculum and the
classroom. McKnight (1987) suggested that current practice is often
an undifferentiated myriad of educational objectives, behaviorally
stated, which often replace broad, substantive goals in today's mathematics education. Some of these motivational aspects are communicated, explicitly and/or implicitly, by all those in the nested
communities identified earlier as contributing to the learning environment. Table 7-1 indicates a possible model for the embodiment of the
motivational environment in the three communities.

The *conceptual environment* consists of the often implicit conceptual
framework that underlies students' work in mathematics learning.
Elements of this conceptual framework certainly include the conception of mathematics implicit in the broad community, shared implicitly and intentionally in the school community, and enacted in the
content-related activities of the classroom. Also included are similar

Table 7-1
Interactions of Three Subenvironments of the Learning Environment with Three Communities

Three Communities	Motivational Environment	Conceptual Environment	Working Environment
Community and Family	Importance	Implicit conceptions of mathematics	Support of and provision for resource environment
	Expectations	Implicit conceptions of societal role of mathematics	Standards for activity environment·
	Goals	Explicit conceptions of students' relation to mathematics	
School	Importance	Intentional conceptions of mathematics	Distribution of resource environment
	Expectations	Explicit, communicated conceptions of societal role of mathematics	Intentions for activity environment and structures
	Goals	Intentional conceptions of students' relation to mathematics	
	Achievement milestones		
Classroom	Importance	Enacted conceptions of mathematics	Control of access to resource environment
	Expectations	Embedded conceptions of societal role of mathematics	Implementation of activity structures and creation of activity environment
	Goals	Implicit and explicit conceptions of students' relation to mathematics	
	Achievement milestones Specific learning objectives		

complex communications of the societal role of mathematics and the conception of the involvement of mathematics in the lives of the particular students involved. Table 7-1 summarizes some of this realization of the conceptual environment.

The *working environment* consists of the resource environment, activity structures, and working conditions available to students in the study of mathematics. Certainly involved are the resources available, their proximity to the typical learning spaces of students, and the freedom of access to these resources during the study of mathematics and other subjects. Included also is the activity environment of mathematics learning through mathematical tasks and activity structures. Table 7-1 suggests some of the complex ways in which the working environment is supported, made available and intentional, and controlled and implemented by the three communities.

SOME NAIVE FUTUROLOGY

The model above explicates some of the generic elements important to mathematics learning that have implications for assessment aimed at useful change in mathematics education for the disadvantaged. As we move to make this model more specific and to identify criteria for investigation, there is some danger of unintentionally locking ourselves into the "small-step," incremental-change view of the feasible and realistic.

To aid in avoiding this, I have indulged in some admittedly naive futurology by sketching two scenarios for mathematics learning and then considering the issues raised by the contrasting scenarios. The first scenario, while risking caricature, is not too great an oversimplification of much of current practice in elementary school mathematics classrooms. The second scenario, while risking entry into the Twilight Zone, is based on a concretization of standards and hopes for the future even now being embodied in written form by the mathematics education community (NCTM, 1987). The contrast is, I think, enlightening.

Scenario One

Imagine, if you will, a lower-grade classroom in your neighborhood in which today's lesson concerns making and using bar graphs. The teacher, who is somewhat anxious about teaching mathematics at all, nevertheless feels responsible to do so and is comforted by a textbook that is very complete in describing what students are to do. The textbook is supplemented by a teacher's edition that tells her almost exactly what to do in teaching this lesson. She faces a fairly homogeneous group, a 4B class that has trouble with mathematics.

But at least most of them have the same sorts of trouble and the book deals with many of these.

She faces a group of thirty-five students, and because she has nothing other than textbooks, a blackboard, and paper and pencils for the students, she is naturally concerned that she maintain control in the class. Being well trained, she knows the mechanics of direct instruction, and briskly moves the group through their mathematical activities for the day. She states clearly the objective for today's lesson and what students should be able to do when it is over. She demonstrates the making of bar graphs, covering the three examples from the text, which are chosen to show something of the usefulness of bar graphs in the "real world," as well as how to construct them. She summarizes, after about fifteen minutes, the procedure for making a bar graph by writing a series of steps on the board, steps provided in her teacher's edition of the text. She carefully makes an assignment of twenty bar graph exercises by writing the page and exercise numbers on the board in a space reserved for recording the day's mathematics assignment. There is time for about thirty minutes of seatwork on the assignment, so she briskly moves the students into this activity and circulates among them, answering a few questions.

Fortunately, the students are used to irrelevant and meaningless mathematics assignments, so they are not too restive throughout these activities. A few subversives manage to pass notes, talk to their friends, or read a paperback book. A few others find the activities mildly interesting. Besides, these few are good at mathematics and enjoy doing something that makes them look good even if it is useless, as their less-skilled friends are quick to remind them. Few wonder what topic they will study tomorrow because they know they have only to turn the page to find out. Soon the forty-five minutes allotted for mathematics is over and they move on to social studies, where they will study how the population of the world has changed over the years because that's what's on the pages of the book for today.

Scenario Two

Imagine, if you will, a classroom in the distant future (perhaps in a galaxy far, far away). We are about to boldly go where no human has ever gone before (perhaps, without knowing it, even into the Twilight Zone). Today the work groups in this class will continue to work on group reports to share with the whole class on how the population of the world has changed over the last fifty years. They are six groups of five students each, but each group is very diverse. They have been working on this theme of change in the everyday world for over a week now. The teacher circulates from group to group, answering questions, encouraging students to follow up on ideas, and reminding them that they all must contribute to the group's written report and that one person should be chosen to present it orally to the class.

We focus on the "Bluebirds" group over in the corner. Of course, the five students in the Bluebirds for this project will not be the same ones in the group for the next project, but for some strange reason the name for the group has been around far longer than these students and they pay little attention to it.

They have been arguing over (discussing) how to show in their report how the population of the United States has changed differently in different parts of the country. Benny, who is good at mathematics, thinks they might do something with "before-and-after" bar graphs for different parts of the country and has suggested making such graphs and including them in their report. They have argued about this, but decided it was a good idea. They are just not sure how to go about dividing up the country for the graphs. Obviously, it is too much to make a separate bar graph for each state, but one graph for the whole country seems like it would show nothing about how the parts have changed differently. The teacher, who has just stopped by, suggests they think about why the changes have taken place and that might tell them how to group the states. Mary, who loves science fiction and has read a lot of it, likes thinking about things like this and comes up with the idea of the fact that the changes might be related to how states get most of their electricity. Remembering an article that she read in the encyclopedia about electric power in the United States, she goes to the back of the room to the computer hooked to the CD-ROM encyclopedia and soon locates the article. After a quick review of the article, she comes back to the group with a list of states that divides the United States into six areas.

Mat, who is into computers, goes to another PC hooked to a database about the United States and soon has the population figures, before and after, for the six areas. He looked up the population figures for each state, and Marita, who is working with him, adds up the numbers for each area on a calculator, then goes to a microcomputer with a graphing package to make the graphs, and, after a few changes suggested by Mat, prints out the completed set of six pairs of "before-and-after" bars. Mat and Marita explain the graphs to the rest of the group, who have been working on other parts of the report. Two people who pay special attention are Karen, who will use the word processor to write the first draft of the report because she likes to write and is good at it, and Juan, who has been chosen to present the group's report to the class, because the teacher has indicated that he needs more practice on oral communication skills and, besides, he is beginning to discover that he enjoys making speeches.

The teacher discovers that work on the projects has gone on over an hour, but she is not particularly worried. The task has been successful. The students were interested and busy (except Jefferson, who always daydreams a lot, no matter what a group is doing). Further, she has been educated to be aware that the project involves language arts, social studies, geography, and mathematics, as well as computers and information skills. She enters the time amount and a few notes on her desk computer, which helps manage her week's time for different tasks and keep evaluation notes on what individual students have contributed to their group. She also records strengths and weaknesses of each student that have been revealed during the day's work on the project.

Issues Raised by the Contrasting Scenarios

While the two scenarios sketched above serve the purpose of concretization and are suggestive rather than systematic, they do provide a contrast that, considered more systematically, can serve to identify issues and distinctions that may lead to investigative criteria aimed at assessment that makes for change. Table 7-2 summarizes a more systematic comparison of the learning environments implied by the two scenarios.

If talent is viewed as something that emerges gradually and is not easily identified at early stages, clearly the issue is raised of prolonging heterogeneity in classroom settings rather than forcing homogeneities at an early stage. Also, it is clear that the scenarios involve vastly different conceptions of the nature of mathematics and differing goals/objectives governing the classroom. The basis for motivation differs, but perhaps the largest differences are in the richness and accessibility of the resource environments of the two classrooms. The style of learning differs, as does teacher role, instructional and evalua-

Table 7-2
Contrasts Between Aspects of Two Learning Scenarios

Aspect	Scenario One: Todays' Mathematics Lesson	Scenario Two: Tomorrow's Mathematics Project
Basis for Determining Participants	Early homogeneity	Prolonged homogeneity
Conception of Mathematics	Mathematics as a body of knowledge	Mathematics as tools and processes for tasks in many subjects
Communication of Instructional Goals	In-class, often implicit outcome objectives	Widely explicated, broad goals
Motivation Basis	Preparation as motivation	Applicability as motivation
Working Environment	Resource-poor auditorium	Resource-rich workshop
Learning Style	Passive reception learning	Active discovery learning
Instructional Center	Teacher	Student groups; teacher as resource and monitor
Instructional Strategy	Direct instruction	Task force approach, groups and reporting
Instructional Grouping	Whole group, teacher led	Task forces, peer academic leadership
Content Orientation	Skills oriented	Problem oriented
Basis of Content Organization	Text determined	Combination of application and content determined
Level of Content Integration	Fragmented, separate topics	Task-integrated topic mixtures
Basis of Content Sequencing	Incremental skill development	Sequenced task-determined activities; serendipity
Instructural Time Determinants	Preallocated time amounts	Task-determined time amounts

tion strategies, and the mechanisms for the distribution of time and content.

Obviously, the orientation and level of integration of the mathematics content differs.

Perhaps the "farthest out" element of the second scenario is the conceptualization of small groups that function as "task forces" for the duration of one project and in which peer leadership and complementary skills are given a chance to emerge.

CRITERIA OF INSTRUCTIONAL EFFECTIVENESS RELATED TO TRUE CHANGE

The combination of the model explicated (Figure 7-3, Table 7-1) and the distinctions raised by the contrast between the two scenarios (Table 7-2) leads to a list of criteria of instructional effectiveness likely related to producing change in mathematics education for the disadvantaged. Some have obvious ways of assessment; others are more problematic. What follows is a list for consideration that summarizes the concerns raised by the earlier discussions.

1. Conceptions of importance of mathematics for the targeted students, as explicitly stated or implicitly held by the community, families, the school, the classroom environment, and the teacher.
2. Expectations for achievement and continued participation in the study of mathematics as explicitly stated or implicitly held by the community, families, the school, the classroom environment, and the teacher.
3. The broad goals for mathematics learning as explicitly stated or implicitly held by the community, families, the school, the classroom environment, and the teacher.
4. Content mastery milestones as explicitly communicated in the classroom and in the broader school environment.
5. Specific learning objectives, explicitly stated in instruction or stated in instructional materials and guides (but not communicated explicitly to the students) and the congruence of these objectives with the broad goals identified.
6. Content redundancy across grades (e.g., pages of review for each mathematical topic for each grade).
7. Teacher beliefs and attitudes (societal role of mathematics, student relationships to mathematics, etc.).
8. Teacher conception of mathematics (process vs. rules; body of knowledge vs. tool for work in other subjects, etc.).
9. Tracking policies and procedures; heterogeneous vs. homogeneous grouping; basis and timing of sorting.
10. Bases and means of explicit motivation in the classroom: preparation, vocational, applicability of mathematics, etc.

11. Richness of resource environment (variety and extent of resources; power of resources, etc.).
12. Accessibility of resources in environment (policies on time for resource use [special times vs. continuous accessibility], proximity of resources, freedom of use [direct supervision or not]).
13. Activity structures in implemented instruction (features of direct instruction, features of discovery learning and problem-solving activities; predominance of seatwork, etc.).
14. Teacher classroom processes (e.g., symbolic vs. perceptual emphasis; conceptual vs. procedural vs. application emphasis; resource demonstration or not, etc.).
15. Teacher centrality to instruction (director vs. facilitator—teacher conception, principal's conception, implemented patterns).
16. Grouping practices (whole vs. small groups, permanence of groups, basis of groups, potential for peer leadership in academic tasks).
17. Flexibility of time allocation (fixed time structure in classroom with fixed allocation for mathematics vs. opportunistic adaptation of time devoted to various subjects; teacher mechanisms for time tracking and balance).
18. Curriculum unit organization (lessons and incremental content segments vs. mathematical projects and tasks).
19. Mathematical content orientation (skills vs. applications and problem solving).
20. Basis of content organization (text determined, combination of applications and content determined, etc.).
21. Level of mathematical task integration (sequential fragmented, incremental subtopics vs. task-integrated subtopic mixtures).
22. Evaluation (product vs. process oriented; isolated evaluation activities vs. embedded evaluation).
23. Student beliefs and attitudes (social role of mathematics, nature of mathematics, mathematical self-concept, engagement with mathematics study).
24. Student cognitive process monitoring with modeling of conceptions of mathematics (as in Erlwanger).

CONCLUDING REMARKS

As stated in the beginning, I chose to be a provocateur, to raise questions rather than to answer them. While I would endorse the research questions posed in many studies, it seems important to raise a broad range of (perhaps idealistic) issues so that many facets of instructional practice are documented and assessed. Doing so will make the data of maximum usefulness in producing meaningful change for the disadvantaged. Investigators have the task of screening issues and setting priorities for the research. Ultimately, researchers must decide for themselves—and be able to demonstrate to others—how they can best contribute to this process of change.

REFERENCES

Dreeben, R. (1968). *On what is learned in school*. Reading, MA: Addison-Wesley.

Erlwanger, S. H. (1973). Benny's conception of rules and answers in IPI mathematics. *Journal of Children's Mathematical Behavior, 1*(2), 7– 26.

Erlwanger, S. H. (1975). Case studies of children's conceptions of mathematics, I. *Journal of Children's Mathematical Behavior, 1*(3), 157–283.

McKnight, C. C. (1987, April). *The U.S. mathematics curriculum: Spiral or circle?* Paper presented at the annual meeting of the American Educational Research Association, Washington, DC.

McKnight, C. C., Crosswhite, F. J., Dossey, J. A., Kifer, E., Swafford, J. O., Travers, K. J., & Cooney, T. J. (1987). *The underachieving curriculum: Assessing U.S. school mathematics from an international perspective*. Champaign, IL: Stipes.

NCTM (National Council of Teachers of Mathematics). (1987). *Curriculum and evaluation standards for school mathematics*. Reston, VA: Author.

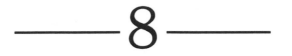

Review of Research on Effective Curriculum and Instruction in Mathematics

Andrew A. Zucker

The research literature on the teaching of mathematics to disadvantaged or other students is more limited than that related to literacy. For various reasons, which are not the concern of this review, the scholarly community has devoted itself primarily to research on mathematical learning, along with a range of investigations examining particular classroom practices. Practically nothing has been done to examine content (Romberg & Carpenter, 1986), and relatively little has been done to zero in on the particular needs, circumstances, or proper instruction of disadvantaged students.

Similarly, investigations that are comprehensive, longitudinal, and naturalistic are relatively sparse—little has been done, for example, to describe teaching practices over a whole year (Porter, Floden, Freeman, Schmidt, & Schwille, 1988). More than a decade ago, a leading mathematics educator wrote that research in this field must begin "with careful descriptions of a specified set of teachers teaching a specified set of topics to a specified set of pupils" (Kilpatrick, cited in Romberg & Carpenter, 1986). To date, it seems that this goal has not been reached. The frequency of such statements about the need for additional mathematics education research is, itself, an important finding of this review.

The consequence of these gaps in the literature is that we must often extrapolate from what is known to develop a picture of what is appropriate for disadvantaged students. In many respects, research will be breaking new ground.

In this chapter, I will review research relevant to curriculum and instruction in mathematics for disadvantaged students, focusing on what is (and should be) taught and how. The discussion commences with a review of overarching issues, then an examination of the typical pattern of mathematics curriculum and instruction in grades 1–8, followed by what is known about curriculum and instruction aimed at disadvantaged students. The chapter concludes with a review of what is known about effective practices.

OVERARCHING ISSUES

Some of the issues noted in discussing literacy curriculum and instruction (see beginning of Chapter 4) apply to mathematics as well. But certain issues can be restated and others added that capture the focus of scholarly discussions in this subject area. I highlight the following.

Relative emphasis on "basic" versus "higher-order" skill components in the mathematics curriculum for disadvantaged students—As in the case of literacy instruction, the question of whether to concentrate on "basic" computational skills or a broader mathematics curriculum is difficult to answer for educators who face children appearing to have little exposure to formal mathematics. A natural response to this situation is to emphasize highly structured curricula that feature repetitive drill-and-practice in computational algorithms, but that leave little or no room for other aspects of mathematics—that, for example, require and stimulate analytical or problem-solving skills—which are widely agreed to be important.

Focusing on curriculum for the disadvantaged versus curriculum for all— The primary locus of the problem in mathematics education for disadvantaged students may differ from the situation in literacy education. By broad agreement, the principal problem in mathematics education is the inefficient and narrow curriculum provided to the great majority of students. The National Assessment of Educational Progress (NAEP), international comparisons, and other sources indicate that American students as a whole are doing poorly in mathematics; disadvantaged students are the worst off, but other students are not so far ahead of them. It would be a grave error to take the norm in American classrooms as some kind of ideal for disadvantaged students (see argument in Chapter 6).

An implied hypothesis is that disadvantaged students presented with a mathematics curriculum *well* designed for typical students will achieve at significantly higher levels (the same could be said of many subject areas, undoubtedly). A direct analogy can be found in science, where the Science Curriculum Improvement Study (SCIS) curriculum, designed for "average" elementary school students, was later found to be especially effective for disadvantaged students (Knapp, St. John, Zucker, Needels, & Stearns, 1987). Similarly, recent NSF-supported research on mathematics instruction began with typical learners, but has shown some outstanding results in classrooms with large numbers of disadvantaged students (Peterson, 1988a; and personal communication).

*Addressing differential conditions for mathematics learning—*Improvements in the curriculum for all students will not obviate entirely the need to address the adverse conditions for mathematics learning that differentially affect disadvantaged students. Many of the worst features of American mathematics education (e.g., an overemphasis on arithmetic computation through grade 8) are intensified for disadvantaged students. In effect, disadvantaged students show the most severe ill effects of a system of mathematics education that is badly flawed for all students. In this view, a central issue is understanding the differential impact on disadvantaged students of the systemic problems/conditions that affect American mathematics education as a whole, such as poor textbooks, low expectations, insufficient home-work, or inappropriate goals.

The basic assumptions and structure of the current mathematics curriculum appear to intensify certain students' disadvantagement as they get older. It is well established that the mathematics achieve-ment of racial and ethnic subpopulations (excluding Asian Ameri-cans) shows increasing divergence from the national average with increases in the age of the population tested (Dossey, Mullis, Lind-quist, & Chambers, 1988), and this pattern would seem to generalize to the disadvantaged population as a whole. Disadvantage seems to grow worse as students get older. School-based practices appear to contribute to this lower growth trajectory. Whether school-based practices can equalize growth trajectories remains an unanswered question, but many would agree that schools can, and should, narrow the gap.

The problem of what instructional strategies should be applied to prevent students' disadvantage from increasing over time includes many subissues, such as the efficacy and effects of tracking; the balance of depth versus breadth of topical coverage in the curriculum; the extent and kind of access to instructional technologies; and the expectations for achievement that should be established for these students in the first place.

Maximizing the transfer of mathematical skills learned in schools to other applications—There is fairly clear evidence that the mathematics chil-dren *do* learn in school does not necessarily transfer well to other situations (Resnick, 1987b). The transfer of skills from school to real-world applications is especially lacking for disadvantaged stu-dents; the value of these students' "native" mathematical thinking may not be used sufficiently well as a building block.

It is not clear exactly how to maximize transfer, but at least two possibilities present themselves. First, curriculum and instruction can embed the learning of mathematical skills in a context in which these skills can be applied, either in simulated situations or in solving actual problems. Second, curriculum and instruction may make greater efforts to recognize and draw on the mathematical knowledge chil-dren bring to school. Research has clearly demonstrated that, inde-pendent of school, disadvantaged children can develop effective mathematical strategies and thinking to cope with the world in which they live. For example, studies of disadvantaged youngsters in Brazil who must use mathematics extensively for work-related activities such as selling candy show that these children use strategies different from those taught in school, with greater accuracy than when they apply strategies learned in school (Carraher, Carraher, & Dias-Schliemann, 1985; Saxe, 1988). Schools probably take insufficient notice of these kinds of everyday mathematical skills.

Good curriculum and instruction for disadvantaged students can no longer (if it ever could) ignore conceptual understanding or applications in favor of rote skills, which have limited transferability. Effective mathematics instruction for this population thus mixes concepts, skills, and applications; whether it should do so in exactly the same way as for more advantaged students, however, remains an open question.

The content of remedial or compensatory mathematics instruction—What to teach in specialized mathematics programs serving low-achieving students is also at issue. To the extent these programs concentrate on further practice with the computational skills that students appear to lack, they may only compound the problem, by failing to provide students with a basis for understanding what they are doing or visualizing how it might apply to their lives. On the other hand, given the small amounts of time typically available to students who participate in these programs (e.g., three or four 20-minute sessions a week), it may be difficult to do much more. Ultimately, the combination of regular classroom instruction and remedial services are responsible for conveying mathematics to low-achieving students. Achieving the right relationship and division of labor between these two is a major question for instructing the large numbers of disadvantaged students who appear to have limited proficiency in this area of the school curriculum.

MATHEMATICS CURRICULUM AND INSTRUCTION IN TYPICAL ELEMENTARY AND JUNIOR HIGH SCHOOLS

In mathematics education, what happens in classrooms—the "enacted curriculum"—tends to follow closely what is intended for these classes. By general agreement, both intended and enacted curricula are too limited.

The Intended Curriculum

A first step in understanding typical practices in grades 1-8 is to examine the intended curriculum as revealed by texts, frameworks or syllabi, and tests. A simple but very important study of K-8 mathematics textbooks helps to understand the curriculum as laid out by publishers (Flanders, 1987). This study analyzed popular textbook series page by page to determine what content in each is new and what is practice of material already taught. The principal finding was as follows:

> A relatively steady decrease occurs in the amount of new content over the years up through eighth grade, where less than one-third of the material is new to students. This decrease is followed by an astounding rise in the amount of new content in the texts of the most common ninth-grade course, algebra. [Flanders, 1987, p. 18]

Overall, the intended curriculum in mathematics is repetitive, unchallenging, and (for many) boring. Cross-national comparative research on mathematics confirms that the U.S. curriculum at the eighth-grade level (for all tracks) is substantially less challenging than in most other nations, and especially so for students at the "low" end (McKnight et al., 1987).

A few states have tried to adopt significantly different approaches. Connecticut, for example, has plans to make calculators available to every student in the eighth grade. California adopted a new state framework, rejected all elementary mathematics texts, and made publishers revise books before the state would adopt them (Knapp et al., 1987). This approach, however, is not typical of most states.

Some major tests used at the K-8 level have been focused more carefully in recent years on higher-order thinking skills, for example, NAEP tests and some state proficiency tests. As far as I am aware, most testing in mathematics at this level—especially teacher-made tests—is focused on arithmetic computation and other lower-order skills. The common, day-to-day tests that teachers use with their students may be especially poor in this respect.

In summary, despite abundant rhetoric about teaching problem-solving and other higher-order skills, an examination of the intended curriculum in grades 1-8 mathematics shows that a focus on arithmetic computation is the dominant norm.

The Enacted Curriculum

Investigations of the enacted curriculum paint a complementary picture. Studies have shown that in grades 1-8 by far the majority of time in mathematics is spent focusing on arithmetic computation and lower-level skills (Peterson, 1988b; McKnight et al., 1987; Dossey et al., 1988). Yet the transfer of lower-level skills to problem solving and higher-order thinking is not very good, suggesting a mismatch of goals and strategies. In addition, problem solving is not a major focus of the curriculum. Increasing numbers of researchers believe that students don't just "pick up" problem-solving strategies; rather, they must be explicitly taught, and to a much greater degree than is currently the case (Resnick, 1987a & b; Peterson, 1988a). Generally speaking, most grade 1-8 mathematics instruction is not focused on higher-order thinking; for example, the introduction of even simple word problems may be postponed until children have reached a high level of mastery of computational skills. To exaggerate the situation somewhat, a comparable situation might be not allowing children to engage in real conversations until they have mastered sufficient numbers of grammar exercises.

NAEP data confirm this bleak view. The most recent national assessment in mathematics finds the following:

- Mathematics classrooms are "more concerned with students' rote use of procedures than with their understanding of concepts and development of higher-order thinking skills" (Dossey et al., 1988). While NAEP shows performance gains since 1978, these are primarily for lower-order skills.
- The typical range of instructional techniques used in mathematics classes is limited. For example, use of small-group activity, laboratory work, or special projects is rare (Dossey et al., 1988).

Recent comparative research has demonstrated striking differences between the way mathematics and the way other subjects are taught in school. In one study, researchers found that about half the time students are learning mathematics they are engaged in solitary seatwork, while the comparable figure for social studies is only one-third (Stodolsky, 1985). The key contrasts researchers discovered between fifth-grade mathematics and social studies teaching are summarized this way:

In math, one way of teaching and learning dominated: students watched a teacher demonstrate a procedure—such as how to multiply fractions—then practiced it alone at their desks. . . . Except for rulers in a few classrooms, students used only pencils, paper, and textbooks. . . . Although taught by the same teachers, social studies lessons varied much more—from day to day within classrooms and from one classroom to the next. Group work complemented whole class instruction, and children spent less time laboring alone at their desks. The curriculum explicitly stressed independent learning and the development of research skills, so students consulted maps, encyclopedias, and newspapers, as well as textbooks. [Featherstone, 1986, p. 3]

Others confirm that mathematics seems to be characterized by especially heavy reliance on textbooks and teacher presentations, and by very limited access to manipulatives, social support, or small-group work (Dossey et al., 1988). As one researcher summarized the pattern: "In essence, the traditional math classes contain only one route to learning: teacher presentation of concepts followed by independent student practice" (Stodolsky, 1985, p. 123).

International comparisons provide further perspective on the typical pattern just described. In the early grades, one study found that relatively difficult addition and subtraction problems are introduced very late in American textbooks compared to when those topics are introduced in Soviet, Taiwanese, Mainland Chinese, and Japanese texts (Stigler & Perry, 1988). At the eighth-grade level, the United States, unlike most other nations involved in the Second International Mathematics Study (SIMS), is still emphasizing instruction in arithmetic; nonetheless, the achievement of American students in arithmetic is still below the average for all participating countries (McKnight et al., 1987). The SIMS also found that:

- U.S. mathematics instruction (at the eighth-grade level) seems to be more tied to the textbook than instruction in most other countries.
- Given a choice between more abstract and more perceptual approaches to teaching a topic (such as fractions), American teachers more often chose the abstract representations; this might pose particular difficulties for disadvantaged students.
- Americans' expectations of what students can learn in mathematics are relatively low. American parents, more than Chinese and Japanese parents, for example, seem to believe that ability in mathematics is "inborn," and therefore that hard work is less important. (Stigler & Perry, 1988)

An intriguing finding from international studies concerns the continuity of instruction and ease of understanding mathematics. One study investigated changes in instructional "segments"—that is, the smallest unit of instruction or a sequence of activity on a single topic. Segments in mathematics were defined as changing if there was a change in topic, materials, or type of activity. In Japan, only 6.9 percent of segment changes are marked by changing topic; in Taiwan, 16.1 percent; and in the United States, 24.8 percent (Stigler & Perry, 1988). (This parallels a finding by Porter et al. [1988] that 70 percent to 80 percent of the topics taught during a school year receive thirty minutes or less of instructional time.) The researchers suggest that "it appeared to us that the Chinese and Japanese classes were in some sense more comprehensible than were the U.S. classes" (Stigler & Perry, 1988, p. 214). Students' comprehension of individual lessons has not been measured directly, but if Stigler and Perry's hypothesis is correct, it would help to explain why American students' achievement is lower than we would wish.

Given these patterns of enacted curriculum, it is not surprising that many research findings show that students become "turned off" to mathematics in large numbers. In the higher grades (junior high school and above), most students apparently hold negative views on the nature of the discipline, and have limited expectations for the relevance of mathematics to their own futures (Dossey et al., 1988). This view represents a significant change from earlier grades when mathematics is among the subjects most liked by students (though, perhaps, they like mathematics at this level because it presents them with easy lower-level tasks). There also seems to be a significant gap in the minds of students between mathematics as it is taught (e.g., as a mechanical set of procedures) and mathematics as it is applied (e.g., as a way of thinking about problems in new situations). Various features with high motivational appeal are not yet common practice, such as microcomputers and "real-world" applications. Improvements recommended by many influential groups include appropriate—and appealing—technology (notably calculators and computers) and increased use of cooperative learning approaches (National Council of Teachers of Mathematics, 1987; Knapp et al., 1987).

Taken together, these and many other research findings have motivated a wave of efforts to change American mathematics instruction. Although experts still disagree on the precise prescription that can be formulated on the basis of research, the field is not content to wait until "all the answers are in." The National Council of Teachers of Mathematics has recently adopted, for the first time, a comprehensive set of standards put forth in *Curriculum Evaluation Standards for School Mathematics*, which includes many recommendations for departure from prevailing practices (National Council of Teachers of Mathematics, 1987). The following summarizes widely held views on the state of research on mathematics instruction and the overall direction of change:

> Current research is beginning to establish sufficient findings so that significant changes are called for in the teaching of mathematics. The traditional classroom focuses on competition, management, and group aptitudes; the mathematics taught is assumed to be a fixed body of knowledge, and it is taught under the assumption that learners absorb what has been covered. The research shows that learning proceeds through *construction*, not *absorption*, and that good teaching involves more than management. We believe that the task of this next decade will be to bring the variety of constructs from [research on] both [cognitive science and classroom teaching] together and relate them to an appropriate view of the mathematics to be taught. [Romberg & Carpenter, 1986, p. 868]

CURRICULUM AND INSTRUCTION FOR DISADVANTAGED STUDENTS

Some scholars have examined the particular situation of disadvantaged students more directly. As alluded to earlier, the available evidence suggests that the deficiencies of current curriculum and instruction in mathematics apply to the disadvantaged, only in greater degree.

Schools enrolling low-SES students emphasize more computation and less instruction focusing on applications and concepts than do other schools. As a group, therefore, these students spend far more time learning facts and computational skills, and cover fewer topics in mathematics (Porter et al., 1988).

This state of affairs partly reflects the assumption on which many traditional mathematics curricula are based, that computational skills must be learned before children are taught to solve even simple word problems. A growing body of research, however, indicates that this is a misguided assumption, and that "higher-order" skills should be embedded at all levels of instruction from novice through expert (Peterson, 1988b; Romberg & Carpenter, 1986).

Thus, under current assumptions, for those disadvantaged students slow to learn "basic skills," the curriculum may remain relatively impoverished for many years, contributing to a vicious cycle of reduced interest, expectations, and achievement. Although the curriculum is by no means the only culprit in this situation, recent evidence suggests that it is a prime target for change (McKnight et al., 1987; Flanders, 1987). As already stated, this problem exists across the board in U.S. mathematics education and, while exaggerated for disadvantaged students, is a problem for all.

Schools serving disadvantaged students tend to have less capable teachers and inadequate resources for mathematics education. Disadvantaged students are typically exposed to the least-trained teachers (Darling-Hammond & Green, 1988). Schools enrolling lower-SES students have fewer resources available for mathematics instruction, and in some of those schools conditions and morale are at pitifully low levels (Porter et al., 1988; Corcoran, Walker, & White, 1988).

Schools tend to have low expectations of disadvantaged students' ability to learn mathematics. A growing body of opinion and research suggests that the expectations set for students are important determinants of achievement and that expectations may be harming disadvantaged students in several ways. For example, some researchers, on the basis of many studies, suggest that we know that in as many as a third of all mathematics classes, teacher behavior sustains the poor performance of low achievers (Good & Biddle, 1988). These authors also assert that research shows that low expectations generally are projected to entire classes, that is, that low expectations are associated with particular teachers' views of whole groups—a factor that can be especially detrimental in schools serving high concentrations of disadvantaged students. Similarly, some researchers have suggested that tracking in effect becomes a self-fulfilling expectation imposed on students, resulting in little movement from lower to upper tracks (Oakes, 1985).

Disadvantaged students' families, and their communities, are typically less able to provide concrete assistance to students for mathematics learning. This is presumably one premise on which such successful programs as "Family Math" are designed. The very assumptions about what constitutes "mathematics" (e.g., that it is merely arithmetic) and its role in society are likely to be different among varying communities, and such assumptions, if overly narrow, can create significant problems for students. Parental encouragement and support provide another source of information to students, closely related to expectations. The High School and Beyond Study data show that such parental support is more important than SES as a predictor of achievement, especially for blacks (Committee on Research in Mathematics, Science, and Technology Education, 1985).

There is disagreement about the nature and effects of compensatory mathematics programs for the disadvantaged; at best, these programs appear to improve basic skills proficiency but do not narrow the overall achievement gap. At one extreme, some scholars assert that little is accomplished by such programs:

> Most programs probably widen the gap of knowledge about mathematics between those who are affluent in our society and those who are not. . . . There is nothing in the [compensatory] programs I have reviewed that would give low-income students an opportunity to do any important mathematics. [Romberg, 1988, pp. IV-11 and IV-14]

The recent National Assessment of Chapter 1, on the other hand, led to different conclusions. Basic skills instruction in mathematics is, of course, one of the major services provided by Chapter 1, and the study presents evidence that, at least to some degree, these services are effective. The Chapter 1 study reported that

> students receiving Chapter 1 services experience larger increases in their standardized achievement test scores than comparable students who do not. However, their gains do not move them substantially toward the achievement levels of more advantaged students. [Kennedy, Birman, & Demaline, 1986, p. vii]

The same volume also reported that "students participating in Chapter 1 mathematics programs gain more than those participating in Chapter 1 reading programs." The fact that black and Hispanic students' scores have risen significantly on NAEP tests during the past decade may be partially attributable to the influence of these programs.

SUMMARY: PRINCIPLES UNDERLYING EFFECTIVE CURRICULUM AND INSTRUCTION IN MATHEMATICS FOR DISADVANTAGED STUDENTS

Even though relatively few studies have examined mathematics programs aimed specifically at disadvantaged students, the research and commentary I have reviewed point to several themes regarding effective curriculum and instruction in mathematics for this student population. Three themes capture the most important implications for disadvantaged students and serve to organize the principles supported by the literature:

1. Ineffective curricula available to all students are the most important factor inhibiting mathematics learning of disadvantaged students.
2. Effective mathematics curricula in grades 1-8 include a broader range of topics than is currently taught and emphasize conceptual understanding and the application of mathematics skills.
3. Improved curricula require more than direct-instruction models have to offer, although these models can enhance some aspects of students' mathematical learning.

Focus on the Mathematics Curriculum for All Students

It appears that the largest improvement in curriculum and instruction for disadvantaged students in mathematics will come from a basic change in the structure of mathematics curricula available to all students. I have already commented on the limitations and remarkable uniformity of mathematics curricula to which most first through eighth graders are currently exposed; its deficiencies need not be repeated here.

The key point for schools serving disadvantaged students is that no amount of incremental adjustment to overcome the relatively impoverished state of such schools will make much difference in the mathematics abilities these students take away from school. To be sure, with better teachers and more resources, these students will add and subtract with more confidence and greater accuracy, at least in situations that present them with arithmetic operations in the format they have learned in school. But their ability to comprehend what they are doing and to apply it to the solution of novel problems will remain distinctly limited. Neither these students nor their more affluent counterparts will be adequately prepared for the mathematical challenges they will encounter in the future (see Chapter 6).

This is not to say that the conditions that distinguish schools in affluent and less affluent communities are unimportant in mathematics education. As in the case of reading, schools serving large numbers of disadvantaged students tend to teach an even more restricted form of mathematics, and there is clearly a need to address the conditions that make this the case (professional background, family understanding and support, resources for learning, etc.). But remedying all these factors will make only a marginal difference in students' exposure to important mathematical ideas and development of sophisticated mathematical skills.

Emphasis on Conceptual Understanding and Skills Application

The broad contours of an improved mathematics curriculum for disadvantaged (and other) students in grades 1 through 8 are fairly clear, but educators have yet to translate these ideas into specific, workable programs on a wide scale. The following principles are especially important:

- *The curricula place emphasis on students' developing a conceptual understanding of the mathematics they are learning.* That means, for instance, that before, during, and after the learning of multiplication tables, students are helped to see that multiplication is an extension of addition, multiplication is commutative, and so forth. This understanding develops as students approach the topic of multiplication in a variety of ways, including the use of manipulable objects and exposure to manual systems of multiplication, among other techniques.
- *The curriculum is designed so that mathematical skills are learned and practiced, wherever possible, in situations that allow students to apply the skills to actual situations and problems.* Using mathematical ideas and operations to accomplish something appears to enhance mathematics learning in a variety of ways: (1) motivation is increased; (2) students are helped to see how skills transfer to a variety of situations; and (3) understanding of mathematical concepts is

increased, as students appreciate the utility and range of application of mathematical ideas and operations. Applications are especially important for disadvantaged students, for whom what is learned in school often seems remote from the world they experience outside school.

- *From the earliest grades, the mathematics curriculum includes a range of topics often reserved for later years or even ignored by current curricula.* Of particular importance in grades 1-8 are a series of topics that many current curricula only touch on, if that: problem solving (which is implied by an emphasis on applications), estimation and measurement, geometry, and probability and statistics are the four topics most often mentioned in this regard.

There are other desirable ingredients in the curriculum that should be mentioned, chief among them the incorporation of the calculator and the computer into mathematics instruction. This is beginning to happen in certain states and localities, but the net improvement in schools serving disadvantaged students appears to be relatively small to date. Indications are that when these technologies do appear in such settings, they are typically used to reinforce the current limited curricula, as evidenced by the use of drill-and-practice software in mathematics instruction (for example, see Ragosta et al., 1982, regarding the use of computers to boost computation skills of inner-city children).

Expanding the Teacher's Pedagogical Repertoire

As a result of a great deal of research on teacher behavior, much of it research investigating aspects of "direct" and "active" instruction in various subject areas, certain basic principles of instruction in mathematics seem to be well established.[1] Time-on-task, or engaged learning time, should be maximized, with little time devoted to nonacademic pursuits. Work should be structured so that students

---

1. I do not treat "direct" and "active" instruction as the same, although they share the characteristic that teachers actively control most of the learning activities most of the time. The former are more limited than the latter and follow some variation of the original Follow Through Direct Instruction model. See more detailed discussion in Chapter 12.

experience frequent success and receive feedback about their work relatively quickly. A businesslike but supportive environment is called for in classrooms, and in the school as a whole.

Some research has focused explicitly on instructional practices that are successful with disadvantaged students. For example, one review article reported that

> data indicate that it was especially essential for teachers in low-SES classes to regularly monitor activity, supervise seatwork, and initiate interactions with students who needed help or supervision. Teachers in high-SES classes did not have to be quite so vigilant or initiatory, and could mostly confine themselves to responding to students who indicated a need for help. Positive affect, a relaxed learning climate, and praise of student responses were also more related to achievement in low-SES settings. [Brophy & Good, 1986, p. 349]

As in the case of reading, the research referred to in the quote indicates that active, teacher-directed instruction can be effective in teaching mathematics to this population of students. Studies have documented relationships between the features of instruction implied by these models—continuous control of learning by the teacher, the emphasis on whole-class instruction, the repeated cycle of demonstration-practice-feedback, and regular assessment—and student achievement in mathematics (e.g., Good, Grouws, & Ebmeier, 1983).[2] Because this approach to instruction emphasizes the teacher's active role, it contrasts favorably with common practices in mathematics teaching, which rely too heavily on individual seatwork.

But, as in other subject areas, there are clear drawbacks to the teaching approaches of the original direct-instruction model for conveying much of the mathematical content that appears important. Especially when teachers instruct their classes in a "direct" instruction mode, their pedagogy tends to limit the teaching of higher-order thinking skills and lends itself to highly proceduralized forms of mathematics teaching: so many minutes for review, so many minutes for development of new concepts, and so on. As such, these models are likely to encourage a correspondingly proceduralized view of mathe-

---

2. Chapters 4 and 12 contain further discussions of the research on "active" and "direct" instruction, much of which is relevant to mathematics.

matics as a set of procedures for manipulating numbers or mathematical problems.

Research suggests that the following ways of expanding teachers' pedagogical repertoire are especially important to consider in the case of instruction for disadvantaged students:

- *Instruction that promotes self-monitoring and study skills.* Though much of it requires active instruction by teachers at the outset, explicitly teaching students to monitor their own work coupled with the chance to use these skills can significantly build the students' ability to learn independently (see Chapter 5).
- *Teacher-student and student-student discourse about mathematical ideas and applications.* Increasing evidence links the development of the ability to think mathematically with the presence of sustained conversation between students and teachers, and among students, about the content of mathematical activities (e.g., Fennema, Carpenter, Keith, & Jenkins, 1989; Russell & Friel, 1989). Although this work has not been extensively applied to disadvantaged populations, there is reason to believe that it makes sense there, too.
- *Multiple representations of mathematical ideas.* With thoughtful use of manipulatives, graphic displays, and other ways of representing mathematical ideas, teachers can help students grasp the concepts behind symbols and operations, though the materials alone will not teach the connections between object and idea; teachers must do that (Schram, Feiman-Nemser, & Ball, 1989).
- *Instruction that provides experience with educational technologies as problem-solving tools.* When teachers integrate technologies such as computers and calculators into their instruction, students acquire powerful problem-solving tools, not to mention the motivational influence of these tools. This means that teachers must engineer the use of technology in ways that go beyond the widespread practice of emphasizing drill-and-practice software for disadvantaged learners.
- *Project-centered teaching* that encourages the use of structured student task groups and peer academic leadership (Chapter 7).

However, unequivocal research findings confirming effective instructional practices are relatively sparse, and many "commonsense" beliefs are not easily confirmed by research. For example, researchers have not definitely associated extensive knowledge of mathematics as a discipline (for example, the content knowledge possessed by individuals who hold a master's degree in mathematics) with higher student achievement, even though in the extreme cases, lack of subject matter knowledge clearly reduces what a teacher can do (see Chapter 5). Another example is provided by the increasingly large body of research showing that instruction does not take full advantage of the initial knowledge of mathematics with which students come to school. Some have gone so far as to state that "children's invented strategies for solving addition and subtraction problems are frequently more efficient and more conceptually based than the mechanical procedures included in many mathematics programs" (Romberg & Carpenter, 1986). While debate continues on the frequency with which student-developed problem-solving strategies work—and the practicality of instruction that promotes this—the possibility of expanding the instructional repertoire in mathematics seems especially important to pursue.

REFERENCES

Brophy, J. E., & Good, T. L. (1986). Teacher behavior and student achievement. In M. C. Wittrock (Ed.), *Handbook of research on teaching* (3rd ed.). New York: Macmillan.

Carraher, T. N., Carraher, D. W., & Dias-Schliemann, A.D. (1985). Mathematics in the streets and in schools. *British Journal of Developmental Psychology, 3*, 21–29.

Committee on Research in Mathematics, Science and Technology Education of the National Research Council. (1985). *Mathematics, science and technology education: A research agenda*. Washington, DC: National Academy Press.

Corcoran, T. B., Walker, L. J., & White, J. L. (1988). *Working in urban schools*. Washington, DC: Institute for Educational Leadership.

Darling-Hammond, L., & Green, J. (1988, Summer). Teacher quality and educational equality. *College Board Review*, 16–41.

Dossey, J. A., Mullis, V. S., Lindquist, M. M., & Chambers, D. L. (1988). *The mathematics report card: Are we measuring up?* Princeton, NJ: Educational Testing Service.

Featherstone, H. (ed.). (January 1986). Taking more math but enjoying it less. *The Harvard Education Letter, 2* (1).

Fennema, E., Carpenter, T., Keith, A., & Jenkins, M. (1989, March). *Cognitively-guided instruction*. Paper presented at the annual meeting of the American Educational Research Association, San Francisco.

Flanders, J. (1987, September). How much of the content in mathematics textbooks is new? *Arithmetic Teacher*, 18–23.

Good, T. L., & Biddle, B. J. (1988). Research and the improvement of mathematics instruction: The need for observational resources. In D. A. Grouws & T. J. Cooney (Eds.), *Perspectives on research on effective mathematics teaching*. Reston, VA: National Council of Teachers of Mathematics.

Good, T., Grouws, D., & Ebmeier, H. (1983). *Active mathematics teaching*. New York: Longman.

Kennedy, M. M., Birman, B. F., & Demaline, R. E. (1986). *The effectiveness of Chapter 1 services*. Washington, DC: U.S. Department of Education.

Knapp, M. S., St. John, M., Zucker, A. A., Needels, M., & Stearns, M. S. (1987). *Opportunities for strategic investment in K-12 science education: Options for the National Science Foundation*. Menlo Park, CA: SRI International.

McKnight, C. C., Crosswhite, F. J., Dossey, J. A., Kifer, E., Swafford, J. O., Travers, K. J., & Cooney, T. J. (1987). *The underachieving curriculum: Assessing U.S. school mathematics from an international perspective*. Champaign, IL: Stipes.

National Council of Teachers of Mathematics. (1987). *Curriculum evaluation standards for school mathematics: Working draft*. Reston, VA: National Council of Teachers of Mathematics.

Oakes, J. (1985). *Keeping track*. New Haven: Yale University Press.

Peterson, P. L. (1988a). Teachers' and students' cognitional knowledge for classroom teaching and learning. *Educational Researcher*, *17*(5), 5–14.

Peterson, P. L. (1988b). Teaching for higher-order thinking in mathematics: The challenge for the next decade. In D. A. Grouws & T. J. Cooney (Eds.), *Perspectives on research on effective mathematics teaching*. Reston, VA: National Council of Teachers of Mathematics.

Porter, A., Floden, R., Freeman, D., Schmidt, W., & Schwille, J. (1988). Content determinants in elementary school mathematics. In D. A. Grouws & T. J. Cooney (Eds.), *Perspectives on research on effective mathematics teaching*. Hillsdale, NJ: Erlbaum; and Reston, VA: National Council of Teachers of Mathematics.

Ragosta, M., Holland, P.W., and Jamison, D.T. (1982). *Computer-Assisted Instruction and Compensatory Education: The ETS/LAUSD Study—Executive Summary and Policy Implications*. Princeton, NJ: Educational Testing Service.

Resnick. L. B. (1987a). *Education and learning to think*. Washington, DC: National Academy Press.

Resnick, L. B. (1987b). Learning in school and out. *Educational Researcher*, *16*(9), 9–12.

Romberg, T. A. (1988). Mathematics for compensatory school programs. In B. I. Williams, P. A. Richman, & B. J. Mason (Eds.), *Designs for compensatory education: Conference proceedings and papers*. Washington, DC: Research and Evaluation Associates.

Romberg, T. A., & Carpenter, T. P. (1986). Research on teaching and learning mathematics: Two disciplines of inquiry. In M. C. Wittrock (Ed.), *Handbook of research on teaching* (3rd ed.). New York: Macmillan.

Russell, S. J., & Friel, S. (1989, March). *Dimensions of reality in elementary math problems*.

Paper presented at the annual meeting of the American Educational Research Association, San Francisco.

Saxe, G. B. (1988). Candy selling and math learning. *Educational Researcher, 17*(6), 14–21.

Schram, P. W., Feiman-Nemser, S., & Ball, D. L. (1989, March). *Thinking about teaching subtraction with regrouping: A comparison of beginning and experienced teachers' responses to textbooks.* Paper presented at the annual meeting of the American Educational Research Association, San Francisco.

Stigler, J. W., & Perry, M. (1988). Cross-cultural studies of mathematics teaching and learning: Recent findings and new directions. In D. A. Grouws & T. J. Cooney (Eds.), *Perspectives on research on effective mathematics teaching.* Reston, VA: National Council of Teachers of Mathematics.

Stodolsky, S. (1985). Telling math: Origins of math aversion and anxiety. *Educational Psychologist, 20*(3), 125–133.

Part III

Toward Effective Instructional Strategies and Classroom Management

9

Effective Schooling for Disadvantaged Students

Jere E. Brophy

This chapter summarizes my thinking concerning the elementary schooling needs of disadvantaged students. It begins with assumptions about the needs of disadvantaged students and then identifies school- and classroom-level features believed to be supportive of the academic progress of these students.

ASSUMPTIONS ABOUT THE NEEDS OF DISADVANTAGED STUDENTS

I take the term "disadvantaged" to imply two things about a child's family background: (1) poverty and (2) gaps and limitations in what Hess and Shipman (1965) have called the "cognitive environment" in the home. I do *not* attach biological implications to the term, however, so it should not be taken to imply limited intellectual potential, sensory or motor deficits, or learning disabilities (where these problems exist in disadvantaged students, I would ascribe them to other causes rather than to their disadvantaged family circumstances). These assumptions imply that disadvantaged students are not qualitatively different from other students and thus do not need qualitatively different educational programs, but that these students are likely to need educational programs designed to compensate for the gaps and limitations in their cognitive environments outside school. These assumptions square with the findings of a great deal of aptitude-treatment interaction research that has practically never yielded significant disordinal interaction effects, but has often yielded significant ordinal interaction effects, indicating that students lower in entry-level achievement need more structured, intensive, and sustained instruction (but not an entirely different kind of instruction) than students higher in entry-level achievement (Cronbach & Snow, 1977; Doyle & Rutherford, 1984).

Disadvantaged backgrounds limit students' readiness for school activities in both quantitative and qualitative ways (Hess, 1970). The quantitative limitations are associated with the poverty factor: compared to more advantaged age peers, disadvantaged students typically have less access to books and educational games and toys in the home and less exposure to out-of-home educational experiences such as vacation travel or trips to zoos and museums. Although the universality of television has probably reduced the impact of this factor somewhat, it remains true that children from more advantaged circumstances typically accumulate a much richer and more varied fund of background experiences from which to draw on at school than disadvantaged children do. This means that assumptions about background knowledge built into school curricula may not hold up for disadvantaged students, so that teachers may frequently have to build readiness for lessons by supplying such background knowledge, preferably using actual objects or audiovisual aids to help make this input concrete for the students.

In addition to these quantitative limitations in disadvantaged students' funds of background experience, there are gaps and qualitative limitations in their development of cognitive and metacognitive tools for processing and making sense of their experience, transforming and storing this information in the form of codified knowledge, and accessing and applying it in relevant future situations. After a great deal of research and debate, we have come to see that certain cognitive and linguistic capacities (described by Piaget, Chomsky, and others) tend to develop universally and "automatically" in all cultures and family environments, but that development of other cognitive and linguistic capacities is much more dependent on exposure to particular kinds of modeling and experience. The latter capacities include those involved in making functional use of one's thought and language in the service of developing, storing, reorganizing, and applying the kind of formal, codified knowledge that is emphasized in schools. For a variety of reasons, disadvantaged children tend to have many fewer interactions with family members of the kind that develop and exercise their capacities to use thought and language for building knowledge. These interactions include shared activities built around games, songs, or books; questions and discussion about topics other than those connected with daily routines; socialization that emphasizes the reasons for demands in addition to the demands themselves; encouragement to pursue talents or interests; discussions of current events; and activities involving writing, drawing, or counting. In response to such cognitively stimulating activities, and in particular through the parent-child discourse that occurs in connection with them, children not only get exposed to objects, concepts, and vocabulary but also develop schemata or scripts that represent their knowledge of the structures and activity potentials embedded in particular situations and thus develop routines for responding to those situations (Brophy & Willis, 1981).

Most children from advantaged homes, for example, begin school already familiar with and positively oriented toward the process of reading and discussing the meanings of books, so that they are well prepared to engage in this activity comfortably and efficiently when it is introduced. For these children, reading activities are mostly inviting opportunities rather than threatening challenges. Disadvantaged students, however, lack well-developed scripts to provide a basis for easily assimilating such reading activities, so they must struggle to accommodate by figuring out what these activities are all about and how they are expected to respond to them. If they do not receive sufficient support to enable them to meet these challenges consistently without experiencing too much frustration, the ultimate result may be not just failure, but development of anxiety during or alienation from reading instruction.

Thus, compared to more advantaged students, disadvantaged students will need more explanation of the purposes of activities, more cognitive modeling of the processes involved in responding to them, more extensive scaffolding through shorter steps toward eventual independent and self-regulated performance, and more post-performance guided reflection designed to develop recognition of how the activity fits into the bigger picture, metacognitive awareness of the strategies involved in accomplishing it, and motivational appreciation of the accomplishment itself as a significant addition to the student's knowledge and skill (Brophy, 1988b). In combination, these features of instruction should help ensure that disadvantaged students not only acquire isolated bits of knowledge and skill but gradually integrate what they are learning and embed it within scripts that will allow them to access and apply it in the future.

SCHOOL-LEVEL FEATURES

Research on school effects has identified several characteristics consistently observed in schools that elicit good achievement gains from their students: (1) strong academic leadership that produces consensus on goal priorities and commitment to instructional excellence; (2) a safe, orderly school climate; (3) positive teacher attitudes toward students and positive expectations regarding the students' abilities to master the curriculum; (4) an emphasis on instruction in the curriculum in allocating classroom time and assigning tasks to students; (5) careful monitoring of progress toward goals through student testing and staff evaluation programs; (6) strong parent involvement programs; and (7) consistent emphasis on the importance of academic achievement, including praise and public recognition for students' accomplishments (Good & Brophy, 1986). I believe that these characteristics are important for the effectiveness of any school, but especially for schools serving primarily disadvantaged students.

Here, I would place special emphasis on a safe, orderly school climate, positive teacher attitudes toward and expectations for students, and strong parent involvement programs. I see these factors as linked. Padlocks, guards, and other access and control measures may be necessary in certain situations, but by themselves such control measures cannot guarantee safety, let alone sustain in students the implicit feeling of security that must be present on a continuing basis if the school is to function as an effective environment for learning. To do the latter, it will be necessary not only to keep out undesirables and control troublemakers, but also to forge a familial atmosphere within the school that promotes identification with it and a sense of responsibility to contribute to its well being. This is difficult to accomplish unless the teachers are not only well prepared as academic instructors but familiar and comfortable with the local people, language, and customs, and unless the school not only serves the children but actively involves their parents in a variety of ways. I do not think that it is necessary that the teachers be from the local area or of the same racial or ethnic background as the students (although it is helpful if many of them are), but I do believe that it is essential that the teachers feel comfortable with the students and their families and are able to relate to them in personalized and individualized ways (i.e., not just within their official role as the teacher and not in ways that connote prejudice or stereotyping).

Ideally, the school would function not merely as an academic institution but as a neighborhood hub that would serve multiple purposes and sustain a sense of community in its catchment area. Thus, in addition to typical lunch programs and parent-teacher organization (PTO) activities, the school might sponsor a special breakfast program for especially needy students, vision and hearing testing, preschool programs with emphasis on parent education along with quality child care, substance abuse programs, after-school and summer recreational programs, educational arrangements for pregnant girls or unwed mothers, neighborhood councils, and so on. In addition to the usual academic staff there would be at least one social worker to assist troubled families and possibly also a community outreach person who would develop and supervise special programs.

Teachers would make it their business to get to know parents, share information with them, and enlist their involvement with the school and support of its goals. At a minimum, this would include establishing appropriate routines (concerning bedtimes, homework, breakfast, clothing and grooming) to ensure that their children were ready for school each day, showing interest in their children's school experiences and reinforcing their accomplishments, and coming to parent conferences and major PTO events. Ideally, it would also mean volunteering to get involved in school activities and playing a more active role in the PTO.

Both school safety and the kind of familial atmosphere that I envision are promoted when each individual student feels that he or she has a place in the school, students know and are comfortable with most of their fellow students, and each student and his or her family are known to several staff members. All of this is much easier to accomplish when schools are small than when they are large, so I would recommend that such schools be designed for no more than four hundred or five hundred students, preferably fewer. I know that this is considered inefficient and I cannot prove it with data, but I suspect that, other things being equal, school size is probably the single most important factor determining the potential of a school to achieve significant success with primarily disadvantaged students.

CLASSROOM MANAGEMENT

Very clear and well-replicated findings about classroom management strategies that are linked in the short run to high rates of student time on task and in the long run to high achievement gain have emerged over the last twenty years. The findings of work by Kounin, Evertson, Emmer, Anderson, Doyle, myself, and others not only replicate but fit together well to form the basis for a systematic and empirically supported approach to classroom management that applies to schools serving primarily disadvantaged students as well as to other schools. This knowledge base has been reviewed at length by Brophy (1983) and by Doyle (1986). A briefer summary of the main findings and implications is given in Brophy (1988a).

Major elements to this proven approach include preparation of the classroom as a physical environment suited to the nature of the planned academic activities; development and implementation of a workable set of housekeeping procedures and conduct rules; maintenance of student attention to and participation in group lessons and activities; and monitoring of the quality of the students' engagement in assignments and of the progress they are making toward achievement of intended outcomes. These broad goals are accomplished through procedures and routines concerning such aspects as storing supplies and equipment, establishing daily routines, establishing general expectations and rules at the beginning of the school year, getting each class period started and ended, managing transitions between activities, keeping group activities going (once they are started) by stimulating involvement and intervening only in brief and nonintrusive ways if possible, giving directions for and getting the class started on seatwork assignments, and meeting the needs of individual students during times when one's attention can be safely diverted from instructing or supervising the work of the class as a whole. As a fundamental principle, successful teachers approach classroom management as a process of establishing and maintaining student engagement in academic lessons and activities rather than as a process of enforcing discipline by punishing misbehavior. The emphasis is on clarity in stating rules and expectations (including providing modeling, instruction, and practice opportunities whenever the students need to be taught, rather than merely told, what to do), followed up with appropriate cues and reminders. Penalties are imposed where necessary to compel compliance, but the emphasis is on obtaining student cooperation in establishing an effective learning environment rather than on threatening or punishing students to establish the teacher as an authority figure.

Besides managing classrooms in the relatively narrow sense of creating and maintaining an effective learning environment, teachers also socialize their students by influencing the students' attitudes, beliefs, expectations, or behavior concerning personal or social (including moral and political) issues. Socialization includes articulation of ideals, communication of expectations, and modeling, teaching, and reinforcing of desired personal attributes and behavior (done mostly with the class as a whole), as well as counseling, behavior modification, and other remediation work done with students who show poor personal or social adjustment (done mostly with individuals). I think that it is especially important in schools serving primarily disadvantaged students that teachers be willing to undertake such socialization in addition to instructing their students in the formal curriculum.

Unfortunately, there has been much less research on student socialization than on classroom management, so that no solid knowledge base exists to inform guidelines for practice. Still, it is possible to identify a coherent set of concepts and strategies for socializing students that (a)are shared in common by, and in effect reflect a consensus of, the majority of mental health professionals concerning principles of effective practice and (b) are suitable for use by teachers working under normal conditions. Thus, it is possible to identify a coherent conceptual base, if not an established knowledge base, by piecing together elements drawn from the literatures on child rearing, teaching through modeling, communicating expectations and social labels, cognitive behavior modification and strategy training, and crisis intervention and psychotherapy (Brophy, 1988a; Good & Brophy, 1987).

Key elements in such a systematic approach to student socialization include modeling and instruction, communication of positive expectations and social labels, and reinforcement of desired behavior. Modeling is important in two senses. First, teachers must practice what they preach if they are to maintain credibility with their students. Thus, they must routinely model the attributes that they portray as desirable for their students. Second, modeling is important as an instructional technique, especially cognitive modeling in which the teacher verbalizes aloud (so as to make visible to the students) the thinking involved in making decisions and the self-talk involved in regulating one's own behavior. Such cognitive modeling of social skills and strategies for managing frustration or conflict can be invaluable for students, especially those who do not get much of it at home.

Consistent projection of positive expectations, attributions, and social labels to the students is important in fostering positive self-concepts and related motives that orient the students toward prosocial behavior. In short, students who are consistently treated as if they are well-intentioned individuals who respect themselves and others and desire to act responsibly, morally, and prosocially are more likely to live up to those expectations and acquire those qualities than students who are treated as if they had the opposite qualities. This is all the more likely if their qualities and behaviors are reinforced, not so much through material rewards (although these may often be appropriate) as through expressions of appreciation and encouragement. Ideally, expressions of appreciation and encouragement will be delivered in ways likely to increase the students' tendencies to attribute their desirable behavior to their own desirable underlying personal traits and to reinforce themselves for possessing and acting on the basis of these traits. All of this is in contrast to projecting the idea that the students are inherently oriented toward undesirable behavior and must be held in check through surveillance and rule enforcement.

It is important that teachers exert their authority in ways that Baumrind (1971) calls authoritative (as opposed to authoritarian or laissez-faire). That is, it is important that teachers make sure that students understand the rationales underlying rules and expectations, not just the rules and expectations themselves. Teachers should take questions about their conduct guidelines as opportunities to elaborate on rationales by supplying objectively good reasons for behavioral demands, not respond to them defensively as threats to their authority. The larger point here is that teachers should be seeking to develop self-regulation in their students, rather than merely to control them through imposition of external authority (Brophy, 1985).

In addition to these skills for socializing the class in general, teachers will need to learn basic socialization and counseling skills for working with individual students, especially those who display chronic problems in personal development or social adjustment (Good & Brophy, 1987). Such skills include developing personal relationships with such students and reassuring them of continued concern about their welfare despite provocative behavior; monitoring them closely and intervening frequently (if necessary) but briefly and nondisruptively to keep them engaged in academic activities during class time; dealing with their problems in more sustained ways outside of class time; handling conflicts calmly without engaging in power struggles; questioning in ways that are likely to motivate them to talk freely and supply the desired information; using active listening, reflection, interpretation, and related techniques for drawing students out and helping them to develop better insight into themselves and their behavior; negotiating agreements and behavior contracts; insisting that students accept responsibility for controlling their own behavior while at the same time supportively helping them to do so; and developing productive relationships with the parents.

Finally, I believe that it is especially important for teachers working with primarily disadvantaged students to develop certain beliefs and attitudes in those students. One set of such beliefs and attitudes surrounds the purposes and functions of schooling. It is important that such students realize that schooling is not merely imposed on them but established and maintained for their benefit, and that the knowledge and skills they learn in school are empowering "tickets" to success in our society (especially now when high-paying, unskilled jobs are rapidly disappearing from the economy). A related set concerns awareness of the future and realistic planning for it (it would be nice to become rich and famous as a sports or entertainment star, but the odds are heavily against this; better to think in terms of doing well at school, going to college, and learning about less glamorous but more realistic career options).

Schooling is not just a ticket to social advancement, however, so another important set of attitudes and beliefs to cultivate surrounds the potential of schooling for broadening one's horizons and enriching one's quality of life. The students should be taught to appreciate and enjoy literature, the arts, museums, educational television, cultural events, and so on; to pursue their interests through reading and other information-gathering activities; to keep informed about and participate in discussions of current events; and in general, to be well-informed, critical-thinking, active citizens. What I have in mind here is not sermonizing or culturally insensitive inculcation in middle-class values, but instead, development of "scripts" for the enjoyment, appreciation, and enhancement of quality-of-life applications of schooling through cognitive modeling of the self-talk involved in such applications, structuring of activities and assignments designed to allow students to experience the benefits of these applications themselves, and consistent use of strategies for motivating students to learn during everyday teaching (instead of relying exclusively on extrinsic motivational strategies, and instead of simply assuming that motivation to learn will be present rather than realizing that it will need to be developed). Many disadvantaged students not only need to learn *that* applying knowledge and skills learned in school can be self-enhancing, but also need to learn *how* to make such applications and experience such benefits. Motivation to learn is discussed at length in Brophy (1987).

Finally, teachers will need to socialize the efficacy/competence/ internal locus-of-control aspects of student motivation. In part, this involves making sure that students experience success consistently by beginning at their level, moving in small steps, and preparing them sufficiently for each new step so that they can adjust to it without much confusion or frustration. By continually teaching in the zone of proximal development and providing sufficient scaffolding to ensure continuous progress without undue frustration, teachers provide natural conditions for development of a sense of competence or efficacy. It is helpful to build on this more directly, however, by teaching students strategies for setting goals, monitoring and adjusting (if necessary) their strategies for responding to tasks, and reinforcing themselves for their efforts and accomplishments. It also helps if teachers consistently emphasize the linkages between effort and outcome, portray effort as an investment rather than a risk, portray skill development as incremental and domain-specific rather than as limited by fixed general abilities, and focus on the individual student's continuous progress toward mastery rather than on comparisons with how other students are doing when giving feedback. Particularly discouraged students will need consistent expression of teacher acceptance and encouragement, extra assistance, and possibly special remedial socialization targeted to particular problems such as learned helplessness or test anxiety. These aspects of student motivation are also discussed at length in Brophy (1987).

GENERAL CHARACTERISTICS OF CURRICULUM AND INSTRUCTION

I believe that the teaching of disadvantaged students should be characterized by serious academic expectations and "complete lessons" carried through to include higher-order applications of the content, but also by limitation in the breadth of content addressed in order to allow for more depth in teaching of the content that is included (actually, it appears that instruction for *all* students needs to move in this direction from what is typical now, but these changes appear to be especially essential to the academic success of disadvantaged students). Three points need to be stressed to ensure that this recommendation for a reduced curriculum is not misunderstood. First, although there would be exposure to less material, there would be emphasis on mastery of the material that is taught and on moving the students through the curriculum as briskly as they are able to progress. Thus, I am recommending serious, thorough instruction in a reduced curriculum, not abandonment of serious attempts to teach. Second, the curriculum would be built around the most important knowledge and skills that disadvantaged students need to learn in order to succeed in our society, and it would be taught with appropriate attention to problem solving, decision-making, and other higher-order applications in addition to lower-level knowledge and skills. Instead of heavy concentration on worksheets or overly repetitious practice of relatively isolated skills, there would be a varied and integrated program featuring active instruction by the teacher and meaningful (i.e., not rote) learning by the students in the context of integration and application of skills (i.e., not just practice). Third, to the extent that the students made progress and became more like more advantaged or higher-achieving students, the instructional methods would evolve accordingly (e.g., less structuring, more challenge, etc.).

I see active instruction by the teacher as crucial here. Experience with mastery learning and other forms of so-called individualized instruction that minimize the teacher's instructional role and require the students to attempt to learn mostly on their own by working through programmed curriculum materials has shown that these approaches are less effective than teacher-led group instruction, especially for disadvantaged students (Good & Brophy, 1987). These approaches are based on unwarranted assumptions concerning students' abilities and motivation for such sustained materials-based learning; they fragment the curriculum into isolated bits; and they produce students who can pass criterion-referenced tests on part skills but cannot "put it all together" and apply the larger skills that they are supposed to be learning. Such approaches to instruction might be reasonably effective (although, I would argue, still far from ideal) for experienced learners with advanced independent learning skills and a great deal of background knowledge to draw upon, but they are ill-suited to the needs of young disadvantaged students.

What these students need, as process-outcome research (reviewed in Good & Brophy, 1986) has repeatedly shown, is a great deal of active instruction and guidance from the teacher. This does not mean extended lecturing, although brief teacher presentations of information and cognitive modeling of skill applications are important sources of input to the students. What it does mean is a great deal of teacher-led discourse surrounding the content, in which the teacher uses questions to stimulate the students to process and reflect on the content, recognize the relationships among and implications of its key ideas, think critically about it, and use it in problem solving, decision making, or other higher-order applications (Brophy, 1990).

This classroom discourse is not mere factual review or recitation featuring rapid-fire questioning and short answers, but instead is sustained and thoughtful examination of a small number of related topics, in which students are invited to develop explanations, make predictions, debate alternative approaches to problems, or otherwise consider the implications and applications of the content (i.e., not just to reproduce facts or practice skills). Some of the questions admit to a range of possible correct answers and some invite discussion or debate (e.g., concerning the relative merits of alternative suggestions for solving problems). In addition to asking questions and providing feedback, the teacher encourages students to explain or elaborate on their answers or to comment on classmates' answers, and also capitalizes on the "teachable moment" opportunities offered by student comments or questions in order to elaborate on the original instruction by correcting misconceptions, calling attention to implications that have not been fully appreciated yet, and so on.

Skills would be taught holistically within application contexts and in conjunction with content knowledge, rather than being practiced in isolation. Thus, most practice of reading skills would be embedded within lessons involving reading and interpreting extended text, most practice of writing skills would be embedded within activities calling for authentic writing, and most practice of mathematics skills would be embedded within problem-solving applications. Also, skills would be taught as strategies adapted to particular purposes and situations, with emphasis on modeling the cognitive and metacognitive components of the procedural knowledge involved and explaining the necessary conditional knowledge (of when and why the skills would be used). Thus, students would receive *instruction* in when and how to apply skills, rather than merely being exposed to opportunities for such application.

The goals of instruction—empowering students with accessible and usable knowledge—would drive the entire system, so that content would be selected with these goals in mind and both the content and the activities and assignments would be treated as means toward ends rather than as ends in themselves. Instruction would be planned around units or strands designed to culminate in integrated and applicable knowledge. Activities, assignments, and evaluation devices would be planned accordingly, so that they would incorporate a much greater range and variety of tasks than the familiar workbooks and curriculum-embedded tests that focus on recognition and recall of facts, definitions, and fragmented skills. In general, there would be alignment among curriculum goals (the intended outcomes, phrased in terms of student capabilities to be developed), the content selected for inclusion, the representation and organization of this content, the instructional methods and modes of teacher-student discourse, the activities and assignments, and the evaluation methods (Porter & Brophy, 1988).

Curriculum strands or units would be planned with appropriate scaffolding to ensure gradual transfer of responsibility for managing learning activities from the teacher to the student in response to growing student expertise on the topic. The teacher would provide a lot of information, modeling, and guidance through well-structured activities and assignments early in the unit, but would increasingly allow the students to work more independently (or in cooperation with peers) and with greater autonomy as the unit progressed.

Concerning settings for and delivery of instruction, I am in agreement with those who question the value of pullout instruction by special teachers for Chapter 1 students or students who have been assigned vague special education labels such as learning disabilities or minimal brain dysfunction.

Consequently, I would recommend eliminating as much as possible of the bureaucracy and nonfunctional "diagnostic" labeling associated with compensatory and special education, and instead attempting to maximize the time that students spend being actively taught and supervised by homeroom teachers. Classes would be small (class sizes of eight to twelve students might be achievable if money currently spent on specialists were spent instead on more homeroom teachers), homogeneous, and taught by a single teacher (no aides, pullouts, interruptions, etc.).

The teachers would be given special training in teaching a reduced curriculum in depth, with emphasis on cognitive modeling of strategies, sustained teacher-student discourse designed to produce conceptual understanding of and critical thinking about content, and follow through to a level of integration and application of learning that corresponds to the intended outcomes envisioned in the curriculum goals. Individualization would be accomplished primarily through tutorial elaborations on the group instruction rather than by relying heavily on independent work with curriculum materials or computer programs, and it would include attempts to capitalize on interests and strengths in addition to compensating for weaknesses.

THE READING PROGRAM

The reading program would incorporate the research-based principles identified in the report *Becoming a Nation of Readers* (Anderson, Hiebert, Scott, & Wilkinson, 1985). In particular, the emphasis would be on teaching reading as a sense-making process of extracting meaning from texts read for information or enjoyment. Thus, the design of the program would be driven by application goals, leading to an emphasis on reading and interpreting text rather than on isolated practice of fragmented skills. Time would not be wasted on so-called "readiness" skills that are not demonstrably related to progress in learning to read, so as to get more quickly to the process of reading. Important skills such as decoding, blending, and noting main ideas would be taught and practiced, but primarily within the context of application (reading for meaning).

The program as a whole would feature overall coherence that included not only integration of knowledge and skill components but appropriate balance and sequencing of components and an appropriate phasing out of old instructional emphases and phasing in of new ones in response to students' developing expertise. Phonics and blending, for example, would receive a great deal of emphasis in first grade but would be phased out by the end of second grade. The KEEP program (Au, Tharp, Crowell, Jordan, Speidel, & Calkins (1985) is one example of what I have in mind, although the elements that were built into it to adapt it specifically to disadvantaged native Hawaiian children would need to be eliminated or adjusted to adapt the program to the needs of disadvantaged children from different cultural backgrounds.

The teaching of reading would be characterized by what Duffy and Roehler (1990) call the teaching of skills as strategies. Skills would be introduced via explicit instruction that included not only explanations of the key features of the skills and their purposes and uses, but also cognitive modeling of the covert processes involved in using the skills to process and interpret text. This introductory explicit explanation and modeling would then be followed up during teacher-led group reading activities by what Duffy and Roehler (1987) call responsive elaboration—cues, reminders, reemphasis of key ideas, additional modeling, and elaborated explanations designed to be responsive to the particular forms of difficulty that students experience as they attempt to process and interpret the text. All of this instruction would be goals-driven in the sense that the teacher would keep in mind (and would make clear to the students) that the skills were being taught not as ends in themselves but as strategies for getting meaning from one's reading.

Activities and assignments would feature more reading of extended text and less time spent with skills worksheets than is currently typical. Also, besides working individually, students would often work cooperatively in pairs or small groups, reading to one another or discussing their answers to questions about the meanings or implications of the text. Students would frequently engage in the predicting, questioning, summarizing, and clarifying activities that are stressed in Palincsar and Brown's (1984) Reciprocal Teaching program, both in the small-group format developed for that program and in other formats and settings. In short, there would be considerable attention to developing metacognitive awareness of reading comprehension strategies in addition to teaching the strategies themselves.

There would be rich supplies, both in the classroom and in the school library, of suitable children's literature, as well as a strong emphasis on encouraging the students to read these books, both at school and at home. Besides poetry and literature, there would be a great deal of biography and of nonfiction material that would inform students about the physical and social world (thus reinforcing the science and social studies programs). Collections would not be limited to classical literature and books dealing with academic subjects, but also would include books on sports, entertainment, popular culture, hobbies, unusual people and events, and other topics that students would read mostly for enjoyment. Within limits, I would be more concerned about getting students into the habit of reading regularly than about what they read, because I believe that reading facility is built up most certainly, and at the same time in the most natural and "painless" way, through regular reading for information and enjoyment.

In these ways, I would want to make sure that the students came to understand several things that many students (especially disadvantaged students, and especially boys) do not sufficiently appreciate: (1) reading is a skill that has a great many applications in life, not just in school; (2) it is a tool for finding out information about the real world and for pursuing one's interests, not just for reading "stories"; (3) even when applied to fiction, reading need not be confined to the suburban happy talk of Dick and Jane or the childishness or prissiness of certain genres of children's literature—much fiction is gripping, realistic, thought-provoking, and so on.

THE WRITING PROGRAM

I would also want the writing program to be comprehensive, balanced, well-sequenced, and, above all, driven by goals phrased in terms of intended student outcomes. In this case, the goals would focus on teaching students to use writing for organizing and communicating their thinking to particular audiences for particular purposes, and skills would be taught as strategies for accomplishing these goals. Again, there would be explicit instruction and modeling concerning when, why, and how to use the skills, elaborated later during responsive feedback to students' composition efforts. Key basic skills such as printing and cursive writing would be taught explicitly and practiced to mastery, but as much of the practice as possible would be embedded within writing activities calling for composition and communication of meaningful content rather than fragmented as isolated skills practice. Also, as many of these activities as possible would involve "authentic" writing intended to be read for meaning and response, not mere copying or exercises focused on displaying skills for the teacher rather than on communication of meaning.

Composition would be taught not as an impersonal exercise in writing a draft that conforms to the formal requirements of some genre and then editing it for grammar and spelling, but as an exercise in communication and personal craftsmanship calling for planning, developing and revising an outline, developing and revising successive drafts for meaning, and then polishing into final form (Applebee, 1986; Bereiter & Scardamalia, 1987; Calkins, 1986). Thus, emphasis would be on the cognitive and metacognitive aspects of developing compositions, not just on formal requirements, writing mechanics, and editing.

Students' writing efforts would be appropriately scaffolded by teachers, not only through initial explicit explanation and modeling and follow-up responsive elaboration, but also through provision of sets of questions to guide planning efforts, outline forms, suggestions for recording and organizing ideas, and other forms of assistance such as those used by Englert and Raphael (1990) in their recent work. In helping students plan and work through successive drafts, teachers would concentrate first on purpose, audience, and content and organization of the ideas to be communicated, and only later on the fine points of mechanics or spelling. Students would eventually have to correct invented spellings and other misspellings, as well as mistakes in grammar and punctuation, but first would concentrate on shaping the basic text. When the text was ready for final editing, the teacher would note errors but encourage students to correct them on their own by referring to dictionaries. Equipping the classroom with enough computers to allow for teaching students to type and enabling them to enter penultimate drafts and edit them on the computer would be a nice addition to the writing program, although it would not be essential.

I would like to see frequent writing assignments for the same reason that I would want to get students to read regularly: Many writing skills will be developed relatively naturally and painlessly through frequent application. Not all such writing assignments need to involve formal composing that would have to be developed and edited to perfection; many could be brief assignments in which students would be asked to respond to questions, and their answers would be evaluated for their ideational content rather than for their formal aspects. Many of these might be linked to reading assignments, as when students would be asked to respond to questions about their comprehension or interpretation of text. Such writing assignments should occur not only in connection with stories read during reading instruction, but also in connection with science and social studies lessons, thus providing not only practice in writing but use of writing as a way to organize and retain content area learning.

Finally, I would like to see reinforcement of writing through preservation and display. This might be accomplished, for example, through having students keep journals, displaying their compositions in the classrooms or the halls, having them take compositions home to show and discuss with parents, and publishing classroom or school newsletters carrying items written by the students themselves.

THE MATHEMATICS PROGRAM

The mathematics program would also be driven by goals framed as intended student outcomes. In this case, the goals would focus on the development in students of mathematical "power" as it is defined by the National Council of Teachers of Mathematics (1988): Mathematical power refers to an individual's abilities to explore, conjecture, and reason logically, as well as to the ability to use a variety of mathematical methods effectively to solve nonroutine problems. This notion is based on recognition of mathematics as more than a collection of concepts and skills to be mastered; it includes methods of investigating and reasoning, means of communication, and notions of context. In addition, for each individual, mathematical power involves the development of personal self-confidence.

Once again, this implies a comprehensive, balanced, and appropriately sequenced program that not only integrates knowledge and skills instruction but teaches skills as strategies for solving problems and embeds most skills practice within problem-solving applications. Instead of attempting to work through a postulated linear hierarchy from isolated and low-level skills to integrated and higher-level skills, and only then attempting application, mathematics would be taught within an application context from the beginning, as in the Cognitively Guided Instruction program of Fennema, Carpenter, and Peterson (1990).

The program would emphasize teaching of mathematical concepts, not just mathematical operations, and both the concepts and the operations would be embedded in networks of knowledge structured around key ideas. Compared to what is typically done now, students would spend less time working individually on computation skills sheets and more time participating in teacher-led discourse concerning the meanings and implications of mathematical concepts and their application to problem solving. Teachers would explain and model the processes involved in mathematical reasoning applied to problem solving, and then would stimulate the students to engage in such reasoning themselves by suggesting and then debating the relative merits of alternative ways of solving realistic problems. In addition to the well-structured exercises found in typical math texts that merely require students to recognize and then plug in the correct algorithm, students would often be exposed to the kinds of ill-structured problems that occur in real life and require one to discover and invent ways of framing and solving the problem. Often such applications are multifaceted and can be approached in many different ways, thus providing opportunities to require students to integrate their mathematical learning and encourage them to generate and examine potential solution strategies. Teacher-led discourse surrounding such applications would involve sustained, thoughtful examination of a small number of related questions rather than fast-paced recitation of number facts, an emphasis on metacognition and heuristics in addition to algorithms, and a great deal of higher-order mathematical reasoning and problem solving. Examples of such lessons have been described by the authors of the Cognitively Guided Instruction program as well as by Lampert (1988, 1990) and by Stigler & Baranes (1988) (concerning mathematics instruction in Japan).

Leading mathematics educators argue that mathematics teaching needs to move in these directions for all students. I agree, but I would caution that in applying these ideas to the teaching of primarily disadvantaged students, it would be important to see that the basics are learned thoroughly, that the problems selected for discussion are ones that the students see as interesting and important for application to life outside of school, and that the concepts and operations chosen for emphasis in discussion of these problems focus on mathematical content that would be of relevance to a broad range of citizens, not just to mathematical specialists.

Finally, as with reading and writing, I would want to make sure that the students came to appreciate mathematics not just as an isolated school subject but as an important source of concepts and strategies that they will use for a variety of purposes in their lives, now and in the future. Thus, I would stress consumer and household applications, make students aware of the role that mathematics plays in a great range of careers, take advantage of opportunities to build mathematical applications into science and social studies activities (involving charts, graphs, etc.), and emphasize that mathematics is as important for girls as for boys (but that girls often opt out of it, and thus opt out of a great many career options, at the junior high school level because of mistaken beliefs that they don't need it or are not good at it).

RESEARCH METHODS

In closing, I have a few suggestions about research methods for identifying effective instructional programs serving disadvantaged students. First, we need studies that elicit more and thicker data from fewer sites rather than the opposite. If clear-cut success models can be identified, very thick description is needed of exactly how the schools or teachers involved accomplish their positive effects.

Second, although I believe that standardized test data are important, studies must include additional measurement designed to assess progress in developing conceptual understanding and higher-order application abilities. Also, in looking for success cases I would give particular weight to evidence of unusual effectiveness in the middle and upper grades. I think that we have had enough experience with the meanings of test scores now to know that it is possible to use drill methods to build seemingly impressive scores in the early grades on standardized tests that emphasize factual recognition and memory (but not comprehension or higher-order learning), only to see these scores begin to fade at third or fourth grade.

Third, data collection procedures should be comprehensive enough to allow assessment of the degree to which curriculum and instruction in reading, language arts, and mathematics reveals some of the key characteristics stressed above (driven by goals phrased in terms of intended student outcomes; revealing alignment among the goals, the content selection, the instructional content and methods, the activities and assignments, and the evaluation methods; skills instruction integrated with knowledge instruction and embedded within application contexts rather than fragmented as isolated practice). I expect that this kind of holistic and qualitative assessment would be much more useful than frequency counts of discrete teacher behaviors or placing unnecessarily heavy emphasis on measuring process variables such as time on task.

Finally, successful schools or classrooms should be identified on the basis of achievement measures and other outcome data rather than on the basis of high scores on classroom process measures. It is possible that the most effective classrooms will show average or even somewhat below average time-on-task measures, but nevertheless produce more achievement gain in the students. Thus, except as a curiosity that would require additional explanation when they are below average, time-on-task scores are not of primary relevance in identifying successful classrooms. I believe that they should be made relevant, however, to the identification of appropriate low-success comparison classes. It seems to me that the ideal comparison classes would be classes that had average or higher scores on gross measures of classroom management, student engagement, or time on task, but low scores on measures of achievement gain. In this way, the research can be designed to identify curriculum, instruction, and evaluation practices that distinguish teachers who are highly successful in eliciting achievement gains from teachers who are much less successful, within that subset of teachers who are reasonably effective classroom managers and enjoy the general cooperation of their students.

There doesn't seem to be much point in including burned-out teachers, chaotic classrooms, or otherwise obviously malfunctioning classrooms in a research study, because we already know going in what the key problems are in these classrooms. Furthermore, their inclusion in research limits our ability to find out what makes the best teachers so effective (to find this out, we need to compare the best teachers with typical teachers, not with the worst teachers). In short, I am suggesting here that research be designed not so much to investigate classroom management in detail but to study restricted samples of teachers who are generally effective classroom managers who emphasize academic goals and keep their students engaged in academic activities most of the time. Then, if classrooms can be found within this restricted sample that differ considerably in degrees of success achieved on student outcome measures, it will become possible to identify the qualitative aspects of curriculum and instruction that explain these differential outcomes.

REFERENCES

Anderson, R., Hiebert, E., Scott, J., & Wilkinson, I. (1985). *Becoming a nation of readers*. Washington, DC: National Institute of Education.

Applebee, A. (1986). Problems in process approaches: Toward a reconceptualization of process instruction. In A. Petrosky & D. Bartholomae (Eds.), *The teaching of writing*. Eighty-fifth Yearbook of the National Society for the Study of Education. Chicago: University of Chicago Press.

Au, K., Tharp, R., Crowell, D., Jordan, C., Speidel, G., & Calkins, R. (1985). The role of research in the development of a successful reading program. In J. Osborn, P. Wilson, & R. Anderson (Eds.), *Reading education: Foundations for a literate America* (pp. 275–292). Lexington, MA: Lexington Books.

Baumrind, D. (1971). Current patterns of parental authority. *Developmental Psychology Monograph, 4* (No. 1, Part 2).

Bereiter, C., & Scardamalia, M. (1987). An attainable version of high literacy: Approaches to teaching higher-order skills in reading and writing. *Curriculum Inquiry, 17*, 9–30.

Brophy, J. (1983). Classroom organization and management. *Elementary School Journal, 83*, 265–285.

Brophy, J. (1985). Classroom management as instruction: Socializing self-guidance in students. *Theory Into Practice, 24*, 233–240.

Brophy, J. (1987). On motivating students. In D. C. Berliner & B. Rosenshine (Eds.), *Talks to teachers*. New York: Random House.

Brophy, J. (1988a). Educating teachers about managing classrooms and students. *Teaching and Teacher Education, 4*(1), 1–19.

Brophy, J. (1988b). Research linking teacher behavior to student achievement: Potential implications for instruction of Chapter 1 students. *Educational Psychologist, 23*, 235–286.

Brophy, J. (Ed.). (1990). *Advances in research on teaching. Vol. 1: Teaching for meaningful understanding and self-regulated learning*. Greenwich, CT: JAI Press.

Brophy, J., & Willis, S. (1981). *Human development and behavior*. New York: St. Martin's Press.

Calkins, L. (1986). *The art of teaching writing*. Exeter, NH: Heinemann.

Cronbach, L., & Snow, R. (1977). *Aptitudes and instructional methods*. New York: Irvington.

Doyle, W. (1986). Classroom organization and management. In M. C. Wittrock (Ed.), *Handbook of research on teaching* (3rd ed.). New York: Macmillan.

Doyle, W., & Rutherford, B. (1984). Classroom research on matching learning and teaching styles. *Theory Into Practice, 23*, 20–25.

Duffy, G., & Roehler, L. (1987). Improving classroom reading instruction through the use of responsive elaboration. *Reading Teacher, 40*, 514–521.

Duffy, G., & Roehler, L. (1990). The tension between information giving and mediation: Perspectives on instructional explanation and teacher change. In J. Brophy (Ed.), *Advances in research on teaching. Vol. 1: Teaching for meaningful understanding and self-regulated learning*. Greenwich, CT: JAI Press.

Englert, C., & Raphael, T. (1990). Developing successful writers through cognitive strategy instruction. In J. Brophy (Ed.), *Advances in research on teaching. Vol. 1: Teaching for meaningful understanding and self-regulated learning*. Greenwich, CT: JAI Press.

Fennema, E., Carpenter, T. P., & Peterson, P. L. (1990). Learning mathematics with understanding: Cognitively guided instruction. In J. Brophy (Ed.), *Advances in research on teaching. Vol. 1: Teaching for meaningful understanding and self-regulated learning*. Greenwich, CT: JAI Press.

Good, T., & Brophy, J. (1986). School effects. In M. C. Wittrock (Ed.), *Handbook of research on teaching* (3rd ed.). New York: Macmillan.

Good, T., & Brophy, J. (1987). *Looking in classrooms* (4th ed.). New York: Harper & Row.

Hess, R., & Shipman, V. (1965). Early experience and the socialization of cognitive modes in children. *Child Development, 36*, 869–886.

Hess, R. (1970). Social class and ethnic influences on socialization. In P. Mussen (Ed.), *Carmichael's manual of child psychology* (3rd ed., Vol. 2). New York: Wiley.

Lampert, M. (1988). Connecting mathematics teaching and learning. In E. Fennema, T. Carpenter, & S. Lamon (Eds.), *Integrating research on teaching and learning of mathematics*. Madison: National Center for Research in Mathematical Sciences Education, University of Wisconsin.

Lampert, M. (1990). Choosing and using mathematical tools in classroom discourse. In J. Brophy (Ed.), *Advances in research on teaching. Vol. 1: Teaching for meaningful understanding and self-regulated learning*. Greenwich, CT: JAI Press.

National Council of Teachers of Mathematics. (1988). *Curriculum and evaluation standards for school mathematics*. Reston, VA: Author.

Palincsar, A., & Brown, A. (1984). Reciprocal teaching of comprehension-fostering and monitoring activities. *Cognition and Instruction, 1*(2), 117– 175.

Porter, A., & Brophy, J. (1988). Good teaching: Insights from the work of the Institute for Research on Teaching. *Educational Leadership, 45*(8), 74–85.

Stigler, J., & Baranes, R. (1988). Culture and mathematics learning. In E. Rothkopf (Ed.), *Review of research in education* (Vol. 15). Washington, DC: American Educational Research Association.

—— 10 ——

Classroom Tasks: The Core of Learning from Teaching

Walter Doyle

To provide a provocative starting point for discussion of effective academic instruction for disadvantaged students, I have chosen to begin with a basic conception of the "treatment" in classrooms, a conception that places *classroom tasks* at the core of an understanding of how teaching effects occur. Once this conception is outlined, I will summarize what is known about (a) the educative consequences of different types of tasks; and (b) the instructional and managerial processes associated with task accomplishment, especially in classroom populations with a high concentration of disadvantaged students. Along the way, I hope to forge an integration of several lines of inquiry—curricular, cognitive, instructional, motivational, and managerial—that have addressed aspects of teaching. Although the path is not always clear at present, I remain convinced that an integration

I would like to acknowledge the help received from conversations with Kathy Carter, Jill Keller, and Mary Rohrkemper. The opinions expressed, however, are my own.

around a treatment framework is likely to generate *analytical categories* that are useful in understanding significant features of instructional practice in classrooms.

TASKS AS CLASSROOM TREATMENTS

For the past several years, my colleagues and I have argued that the tasks students accomplish in classrooms are the necessary and proximal "causes" of student learning (see Doyle, 1983; Doyle & Carter, 1984; as well as Blumenfeld, Pintrich, Meece, & Wessels, 1982; Cornbleth & Korth, 1983). Students learn, in other words, from the tasks they accomplish in classrooms, and what they actually learn depends upon what they do to accomplish these tasks. If there are no tasks, then no amount of instructional technique or motivation strategy or management procedure can foster learning.

The concept of "task," originally derived from studies of cognition (Anderson, Spiro, & Montague, 1977; Klahr, 1976), calls attention to the assignments students are given and to the way in which the products students generate in response to these assignments are judged by the teacher. In more analytical terms, a classroom task has the following features:

1. *A product*, such as words in blanks on a worksheet, answers to a set of test questions, an oral report in class, or an original essay.
2. *Operations to produce the product*, for example, copying words off a list, remembering words from previous lessons, applying a rule (such as "Distributive expressions—anyone, each one, nobody—take singular verbs") to select appropriate words, or formulating original sentences to compose a descriptive paragraph.
3. *Resources*, such as notes from lectures, textbook information, conversations with other students, or models of finished products supplied by the teacher.
4. *The significance or "weight"* of a task in the accountability systems of a class; for example, a warm-up exercise in mathematics might count as a daily grade whereas a unit test might equal 20 percent of the grade for a term.

The concept of "task," in other words, captures four aspects of work in a class: a goal state or end product to be achieved; a problem space or set of conditions and resources available to accomplish the task; the operations involved in assembling and using resources to reach the goal state or generate the product; and the importance of the task in the overall work system of the class.

Within this framework, teaching is mediated by task effects. Teachers affect what students learn by describing specifications for assignments, providing explanations about the processes that can be used to accomplish work, serving as a resource while students are working, and managing accountability for products. The central element in teaching, however, is the way teachers define and structure the work students are to do.

The task framework for interpreting instructional research grew initially out of an attempt to construct a treatment theory for research on teaching. Such a theory was considered essential to understanding how students learned from teaching in classrooms and to counteracting a simplistic empiricism in which discrete and narrowly defined variables or indicators were often seen as the "causes" of student learning, presumably in some mechanistic and additive ways. As work in this area progressed, however, it soon became clear that the concept of task captured the *curriculum in motion* in classrooms (see Doyle, 1986a). The curriculum exists in classrooms, in other words, as a bundle of tasks. In structuring and enacting tasks, a teacher translates the official or intended curriculum into concrete events for students and thus creates a context for interpreting information during class sessions and for thinking about subject matter. In sum, the task framework brought the curriculum into research on teaching by capturing it as a classroom process.

Before exploring the instructional and managerial dimensions of classroom tasks, I would like to dwell for a moment on some basic curriculum issues concerning the educative consequences of different types of academic tasks.

TASKS THAT ARE EDUCATIVE

Most of the studies I have been associated with indicate that a majority of classroom tasks for advantaged as well as disadvantaged students can be accomplished by memorization or routine computational algorithms rather than by understanding and problem solving (see Doyle & Carter, 1984; Doyle et al., 1985). Many advocates of various forms of direct instruction (including mastery and cooperative-learning designs) argue that precisely this type of "basic" curriculum is a prerequisite for success on more advanced, higher-order tasks, especially for disadvantaged students in the lower elementary grades (see Rosenshine & Stevens, 1986). Indeed, most approaches to the education of disadvantaged students are predicated on a model that assumes a necessary progression from "facts" to thinking and problem solving. Conventional wisdom has it that low-achieving students have not acquired the entering capabilities and perhaps lack the inclinations needed to accomplish academic tasks on their own. As a result, they need strong direct instructional support in the form of explicit goals, a carefully planned sequence of small steps through the curriculum, frequent testing and feedback, and supplemental or "compensatory" instructional time. Moreover, a curriculum geared to knowledge structures and understanding is inappropriate for low-achieving students, at least until they have mastered "basic" skills.

Yet many content specialists disagree with the fragmentation inherent in this approach to basics. The requirement to translate curriculum into a sequence of small, explicit steps limits the kind of knowledge that can be conveyed to students (see Jackson, 1985) and represents content as discrete skills rather than as a semantic network of information structures and processes (see Romberg & Carpenter, 1986). As a result of this fragmentation of curriculum, students do not acquire an adequate semantic framework to give meaning to the discrete pieces of content they encounter. But efficient thought requires a coherent mental representation, and it is precisely this coherence that is lost in fragmented remedial programs (see Calfee & Drum, 1986). As a result, programs for the disadvantaged often do not enable students to apply their skills in complex situations that differ from the constrained instructional context in which they were acquired. In other words, little transfer from remedial settings to regular classrooms occurs.

A similar argument can be constructed from study of grouping for instruction. Grouping, both within and between classes, often leads to curriculum differentiation. Students in high-achieving groups have many opportunities for self-direction and self-pacing in structuring their own tasks and approaches to learning. Students in low-achieving groups are typically relieved of the responsibility to structure their learning because tasks are simplified and instructional prompting is high. Thus, low-achieving students have fewer chances than their higher-achieving peers to experience knowledge domains in their full richness of meaning—to read or to do mathematics. Moreover, the rules for behaving in low-achieving groups are often different from those in higher-achieving groups. In the end, low-achieving students have little opportunity to learn how to participate independently in regular school work (see Eder, 1982).

The central point here is that *instructional differentiation often results in an unintended curriculum differentiation* and this latter differentiation can defeat the long-term goal of empowering disadvantaged students to participate successfully in regular classroom settings. Certainly there is evidence that mastery programs can improve the performance of low-achieving students on standardized tests. To an ever-increasing extent, however, this accomplishment is being criticized on the grounds that the content represented in standardized test items is an inadequate representation of knowledge structures in various disciplines. Thus, test performance does not necessarily approximate true achievement in a knowledge domain. Moreover, high performance on standardized test items may be symptomatic of *either* understanding of a knowledge domain *or* training to the test. In the latter case, test performance is illusory because it does not reflect empowerment in the knowledge structures required to do academic work. Indeed, it may well be that the problems of sustaining effects in the education of disadvantaged students can be traced to the failure of mastery programs in establishing an adequate semantic context for understanding and using intellectual skills.

A forceful argument in this regard has recently been advanced by Resnick (1987) in a review of what we know about learning to think. She argues that higher-order thinking—a nonalgorithmic, interpretive, constructivist process—is basic to learning in all curricular domains. In her words,

> The most important single message of modern research on the nature of thinking is that the kinds of activities traditionally associated with thinking are not limited to advanced levels of development. Instead, these activities are an intimate part of even elementary levels of reading, mathematics, and other branches of learning—when learning is proceeding well. In fact, the term "higher-order" skills is probably itself fundamentally misleading, for it suggests that another set of skills, presumably called "lower order," needs to come

first. This assumption—that there is a sequence from lower-level activities that do not require much independent thinking to higher-level ones that do—colors much educational theory and practice. Implicitly, at least, it justifies long years of drill on the "basics" before thinking and problem solving are demanded. Cognitive research on the nature of basic skills such as reading and mathematics provides a fundamental challenge to this assumption. Indeed, research suggests that failure to cultivate aspects of thinking . . . may be the source of major learning difficulties even in elementary school. [P. 8]

In elaborating her argument, Resnick maintains that such basic subjects as reading and mathematics are essentially tasks of constructing or inventing meaning through inferential and interpretive processes. Approaches to instruction that do not activate these processes of constructing meaning ignore the most important aspects of reading and mathematics. Resnick concludes that "processes traditionally reserved for advanced students—that is, for a minority who have developed skill and taste for interpretive mental work—might be taught to all readers, including young children and, perhaps especially, those who learn with difficulty" (p. 12).

In summary, the traditional behavioral view that complex learning is an accumulation of small components is being challenged by constructivist theories that emphasize meaning and invention. A strong argument is being made from cognitive and curricular theories that drill on skills isolated from their knowledge domains is unlikely to produce understanding, retention, and flexible application to novel circumstances. At worst, such representations of the curriculum are potentially miseducative.

In the next section I examine the instructional, motivational, and managerial aspects of enacting educative tasks in classrooms.

ENACTING ACADEMIC TASKS IN CLASSROOMS

From cognitive and curricular perspectives, the fundamental teaching issue is how to create classroom conditions in which disadvantaged students can learn to do academic work, that is, to construct meaning from school tasks. In this chapter, I examine various aspects of the problem of designing instruction that preserves and promotes meaning in classroom learning.

Curriculum Effects in Research on Teaching

Findings from descriptive and experimental studies in the process-product tradition have called attention to time, engagement, management practices, and direct instruction as features or indicators of effective teaching (for reviews, see Brophy & Good, 1986; Rosenshine & Stevens, 1986). At a very general level, the teaching model suggested by these findings is relatively straightforward: Engagement correlates with achievement and, thus, teaching practices (e.g., setting rules, explaining clearly, monitoring, providing feedback, holding students accountable) that establish and maintain engagement are likely to be effective. But the engagement-achievement connection implies curriculum effects. And such effects are large in process-product studies. In the first place, the findings were obtained in specific content areas, that is, primarily from the teaching of basic skills to disadvantaged students in early elementary grades. Second, content coverage, as measured by such indicators as opportunity to learn, curriculum pace, and academic engaged time, had strong empirical support in this research.

These curriculum effects point to the importance of the match between the taught curriculum and the tested curriculum. Indeed, little connection between teaching events and measures of student outcomes can be expected if content is not common across these two domains. This statement implies that the identification of any teaching effects in process-product research is dependent upon the nature of the criterion test (see Walker & Schaffarzick, 1974). In other words, the theory of the content embedded in the criterion test will operate as a screen to select classes that embody a corresponding theory of the content.

The following example, drawn from an analysis by Green, Harker, and Golden (1986), illustrates clearly this correspondence effect (see Doyle, 1986b). The cases analyzed were two versions of the "same" lesson—a reading and discussion of a study called *The Way the Tiger Walked* (Chacones, 1970)—taught by two primary grade teachers to equivalent groups of six students selected from their own classes. These cases were chosen from a larger sample of eleven teachers who taught the same lesson. Data consisted of a videotape and transcript of each lesson, a copy of the story, and transcripts of post-lesson retellings of the story by students. The last data set was used as an achievement measure in comparing the relative effectiveness of the teachers.

There were substantial differences between the two teachers in outcomes and in the ways the lessons were taught. Teacher G's students had the highest ranking of the eleven groups on the story-retelling task. Teacher S's students, on the other hand, ranked eighth among the eleven groups. At a process level, Teacher G conducted a two-phase lesson in which students were first introduced to the book (cover picture, title, title page, illustrator, and dedication) and then led through a reading-discussion of the story itself. A large majority of the teacher's questions and statements served to focus students on the content of the book. The lesson was goal-directed throughout and content coverage was high. Teacher S conducted a four-phase lesson in which students were first shown animal cut-outs and asked to tell all they knew about the animals. The teacher then entered a some-what bumpy transition phase to shift students' attention to the story while they continued to make spontaneous comments about the animals. The third phase was the reading and discussion of the story, and the fourth was a more general discussion phase. During the third phase—the actual reading and discussion of the story—spontaneous comments about animals were frequent and the lesson was not tightly focused on the story itself.

Specific contrasts in talk between the two lessons are instructive. Teacher G had more new questions, rephrased questions, and total group questions than Teacher S. Teacher G also talked twice as much as students, whereas Teacher S had a nearly equal distribution of teacher and student talk. Teacher S also permitted students to initiate spontaneous talk more often, had more clarifying cycles to determine what students meant, and repeated the same question to several students more often than Teacher G. In addition, Teacher S had more control moves and more student bidding for turns than Teacher G. Finally, the tone of Teacher S's class was less serious and more gleeful than Teacher G's class.

These contrasts suggest that Teacher G taught a teacher-led, group-focused lesson directed to the content of the story itself. Teacher S, in turn, taught a loosely structured lesson focusing on individual students and their personal knowledge about animals. The key point for present purposes, I would argue, is that reading was represented in quite different ways across these two lessons. Reading was depicted in Teacher G's class as a process of extracting and rehearsing information from a text and in Teacher S's class as a process of updating personal knowledge. One could easily build a case, I suspect, that the theory of reading in Teacher S's lesson has potentially more long-term consequences for reading achievement than that reflected in Teacher G's lesson. At the same time, a teacher following Teacher S's theory is not likely to obtain high recall of the details of a story and the class is likely to be more difficult to manage because of the diversity of relevant interests and comments.

I dwell on this illustration to underscore the congruence between conception of effective teaching and theories of content. Enacting some theories of content may not produce lessons that match the profile of a well-ordered, smooth-running class. Conducting well-ordered lessons may not allow one to represent some forms of content to students. From this perspective, the findings from process-product research suggest a mode of teaching suitable for performance on tasks embedded in standardized achievement tests. From a policy perspective, Madaus (1988) has forcefully argued that the use of such tests as the sole determinants of teaching and program effects can fundamentally distort and narrow the curriculum. I would argue that the imposition of teaching models selected on the basis of their effects on standardized test scores can have an identical effect.

The central issue for this chapter is that standardized tests are, in general, "ill suited to assessing the kinds of integrated thinking that we call 'higher order'" (Resnick, 1987, p. 47). And if, as argued earlier, such higher-order thinking is basic to school achievement, then models of teaching that predict standardized test scores are not necessarily suitable for the education of disadvantaged students.

Managing Academic Work

Before examining various teaching approaches in terms of their suitability for enacting educative tasks in classrooms, it is necessary to understand management processes in classrooms. Process-product findings underscored the importance of management in teaching (see Brophy & Good, 1986) and research on academic tasks has pointed to the strong connections between management and curriculum (see Doyle, 1986a). My own informal observations in classrooms also indicate that many low-achieving students have mastered the art of circumventing work altogether. They often look quite busy but seldom complete assignments.

In studies of academic tasks in classrooms, investigators have found that when students are assigned novel tasks, that is, assignments for which students are required to assemble information and operations from several sources in ways that have not been laid out explicitly in advance by the teacher (e.g., word problems in mathematics, writing projects in literature or social studies, or experiments in science), activity flow in the classroom is slow and bumpy and students directly and indirectly place pressure on teachers that shape the curriculum (see Davis & McKnight, 1976; Doyle & Carter, 1984; Doyle et al., 1985). In comparison to familiar work (i.e., tasks in which students use formulas or standardized procedures, such as grammar rules or mathematical computations, to generate answers to a set of problems), introductions to novel tasks are lengthy and work involvement and productivity are sometimes low. Moreover, rates for student errors and noncompletion of work are high when novel work is assigned. Finally, students sometimes respond to the ambiguity and risk involved in novel work by negotiating directly with teachers to increase the explicitness of product specifications or reduce the strictness of grading standards. In sum, novel work stretches the limits of classroom management and intensifies the complexity of the teacher's tasks of orchestrating classroom events.

Teachers sometimes respond to these pressures on work flow by excluding higher-level tasks from the classroom altogether. More often, however, they use two other strategies to manage academic work. The first involves redefining or simplifying task demands to make product specification more explicit and emphasize procedures for completing assignments (see Cornbleth & Korth, 1983; Doyle & Carter, 1984). When this happens, students' attention shifts from meaning and the underlying operations with content to correct answers and the completion of work (see Bennett, Desforges, Cockburn, & Wilkinson, 1984). As a result, the basic academic purposes of the curriculum are circumvented.

A second strategy involves softening accountability to reduce risk. Familiar work is usually subject to stringent accountability. Students are expected to hand in products of familiar tasks on time, and answers are judged strictly as correct or incorrect. When students are assigned novel tasks, accountability is often suspended or at least softened. The rules for grading are not especially explicit and they are not stringently applied to finished products. Moreover, students are often given repeated opportunities to obtain feedback before products of novel tasks are handed in for credit and bonus points are often used to supplement grades in this area. Such practices create surplus credit that appears to cushion the risk associated with novel work so that students will be encouraged to try these more challenging academic tasks.

The effects of management processes on curriculum are best understood within a model of classroom management that emphasizes action systems rather than rules and reprimands. Classrooms are crowded and busy places in which groups of students who vary in interests and abilities must be organized and directed in ways that maximize work involvement and minimize disruptions. Moreover, these groups assemble regularly for long periods of time to accomplish a wide variety of goals. Many events occur simultaneously, teachers must react often and immediately to circumstances, and the course of events is frequently unpredictable. Teaching in such settings requires a highly developed ability to manage events.

Traditionally, "misbehavior" has been the dominant theme in discussions of classroom management. This emphasis is understandable since the need for management and discipline is most apparent when students are misbehaving. Yet, order in classrooms is not a consequence of reactions to misbehavior but a condition established and sustained by the way a teacher organizes and guides a complex system of classroom activities and academic work. Moreover, the effectiveness of interventions to restore order when misbehavior occurs depends upon the existence of structures of orderliness in the first place. To understand management, therefore, it is necessary to examine what teachers do to structure and monitor classroom events before misbehavior occurs.

From an organizational perspective, the central unit of classroom order is the *activity*. An activity can be defined as a segment of time in which participants are arranged in a specific fashion and communication follows an identifiable pattern (see Gump, 1969). A segment of classroom time, such as a spelling test, writing lesson, or study period, can be described in terms of (a) its temporal boundaries or duration; (b) the physical milieu, that is, the shape of the site in which it occurs, the number and types of participants, the arrangement of participants in the available space, and the props or objects available to participants; (c) the behavior format or program of action for participants; and (d) the focal content or concern of the segment.

The concept for "program of action" is key to modern understandings of classroom management and order. Each activity defines a distinctive action structure that provides direction for events and "pulls" participants along a particular path at a given pace (see Gump, 1982). In seatwork, for example, students are usually expected to work privately and independently at their desks, attend to a single information source such as a textbook or worksheet, and finish within a specified time. In whole-class discussion, on the other hand, students are expected to speak publicly and monitor information from multiple sources. To say a classroom is orderly, then, means that students are *cooperating in the program of action defined by the activity a teacher is attempting to use.* Misbehavior, in turn, is any action by students that threatens to disrupt the activity flow or pull the class toward an alternative program of action. If order is not defined in a particular setting, that is, if an activity system is not established and running in a classroom, no amount of discipline will create order.

Major findings from research on classroom activities, most of which has been conducted in elementary classes, can be summarized as follows (for details, see Doyle, 1986a):

1. Activity types are systematically related to the behavior of students and thus place different classroom management demands on teachers. In a study of third-grade classes, Gump (1969) found, for instance, that involvement was highest for students in teacher-led small groups and lowest for pupil presentations. Between these extremes, engagement was higher in whole-class recitation, tests, and teachers' presentations than in supervised study and independent seatwork.

2. The physical characteristics of a classroom, including the density of students, the arrangement of desks, and the design of the building (open space vs. self-contained) also affect the probability of inappropriate and disruptive behavior as well as the difficulties a teacher encounters in preventing or stopping such behavior (Gump, 1982; Weinstein, 1979). In general, the more loosely structured the setting and the weaker the program of action, the higher the probability that inappropriate behavior will occur. Similarly, the greater the amount of student choice and mobility and the greater the complexity of the social scene, the greater the need for overt managing and controlling actions by the teacher (Kounin & Gump, 1974).

3. The type of work students are assigned affects classroom order. When academic work is routinized and familiar to students

(e.g., spelling tests or recurring worksheet exercises), the flow of classroom activity is typically smooth and well ordered. When work is problem-centered, that is, students are required to interpret situations and make decisions to accomplish tasks (e.g., word problems or essays), activity flow is frequently slow and bumpy. Managing higher-order tasks requires exceptional management skill.

Establishing Classroom Activities

Recent classroom studies have shown that the level of order created during the first few days of school reliably predicts the degree of student engagement and disruption for the rest of the year (see Emmer, Evertson, & Anderson, 1980). Most studies indicate that successful classroom managers rely on three basic strategies to establish order at the beginning of the year: simplicity, familiarity, and routinization (for a summary, see Doyle, 1986a). Early activities, in other words, have simple organizational structures that are typically quite familiar to students (e.g., whole-class presentations and seatwork rather than multiple small groups). The first assignments, in turn, are easy for the students to accomplish in relatively short periods of time and have clear specifications. Moreover, they are often based on work the students can be expected to have done the previous year. A significant chunk of the management task, then, is solved by selecting appropriate activities and assignments for the opening of school. Proper selection is supplemented by routinizing the activity system for the class (see Yinger, 1980). Teachers repeat the same activity forms for the first weeks to familiarize students with standard procedures and provide opportunities to rehearse them. This routinizing of activities helps sustain classroom order by making events less susceptible to breakdowns because participants know the normal sequence of action.

Monitoring and Guiding Classroom Events

Monitoring plays a key role in establishing and maintaining classroom activities. Teachers must be aware of what is going on in a classroom, while attending to two or more events at the same time (see Kounin, 1970). The content of monitoring—what teachers watch when scanning a room—includes at least three dimensions. First, teachers watch *groups*, that is, they attend to what is happening in the entire room and how well the total activity system is going. Localized attention to individual students must be scheduled within the broader framework of the group activity. Second, teachers watch *conduct* or *behavior*, with particular attention to discrepancies from the intended program of action. This enables teachers to recognize misbehavior early, stop it before it spreads, and select the appropriate target for intervention. Third, teachers monitor the *pace, rhythm,* and *duration* of classroom events. Several studies have shown that pace, momentum, and rhythm are key factors in maintaining an activity in a classroom (Arlin, 1982; Erickson & Mohatt, 1982; Gump, 1969). Excessive delays in the flow of classroom events or abrupt shifts in direction are often associated with inappropriate or disruptive student behavior.

Obviously, situational factors influence the monitoring and guiding processes in classroom management. The more complex the arrangement of students in a class and the greater the demands on the teacher as an actor in the activity system, the more difficult monitoring and cueing become and, thus, the greater the probability of a breakdown in order.

In summary, teaching in classrooms demands an ability to predict the direction of events and make decisions rapidly. For this reason, management is fundamentally a cognitive activity based on a teacher's knowledge of the likely trajectory of events in classrooms and the way specific actions affect situations (see Carter, 1985, 1986). Specific management skills are, for all practical purposes, useless without this basic understanding of classrooms.

Adventuresome Teaching and Learning

We have now reached a fundamental dilemma in teaching, and especially in the teaching of disadvantaged students. Cognitive and curricular research increasingly supports higher-order thinking as essential for achievement in all content areas. Yet classroom studies consistently point to the difficulties of enacting tasks involving such thinking in classroom environments. Students seldom struggle for meaning in accomplishing classroom tasks. Work is familiarized and proceduralized, and the meaning lies in the grades students receive rather than in the work itself. My own sense is that meaning is vulnerable in classrooms and that learning how to construct and enact a classroom curriculum for meaning is a fundamental engineering problem in the field today (Doyle, 1986b; see also Cohen, 1988).

Although I cannot claim to have solved this fundamental problem, I would like in this last section of the chapter to explore some lines of thinking that might enable us to work toward such a solution. This exploration is conducted around two basic themes that seem to run through research on teaching: explicitness and success.

Explicitness. Explicitness is a central dimension of teachers' explanations, assignments, prompting, and feedback in classrooms. Most instructional research indicates that a high degree of explicitness in defining goals, specifying assignments, explaining how work is to be accomplished, and providing guidance and feedback is required, especially in the early stages of learning or when working with novices or with students who lack academic skills. It is important to underscore that explicitness does not necessarily imply an emphasis on rote memorization or mindless drill and practice. Explicitness simply means that the teacher actively tells or shows students what they are to learn and how to use specific cognitive operations to accomplish work. For example, students can be told directly how to select the main idea of a passage or how to formulate a cause-and-effect argument. Indeed, many have argued that explicit teaching is appropriate, in principle, for comprehension, problem solving, and other complex forms of academic work for which the underlying processes can be explained or demonstrated by teachers and practiced by students (see Brophy & Good, 1986; Carnine & Stein, 1981; Collins & Smith, 1980; Pearson & Tierney, 1984; Rosenshine & Stevens, 1986). Some investigators have found that the modeling of the processes experts use in accomplishing tasks can help students acquire these processes in accomplishing their own tasks (see Scardamalia & Bereiter, 1985).

At the same time, too much explicitness about tasks can be counterproductive. A high degree of explicitness about operations to use in accomplishing work or about the character of the final product reduces the need for students to struggle with meaning, to make their own decisions about work, and generally to participate in generating their own knowledge in a domain. If, for example, the purpose of an assignment is to have students learn to interpret information or make decisions about how and when to use skills and strategies, then the task must be sufficiently ambiguous to leave room for students to exercise their own judgment. Moreover, intervention to help students complete their tasks must be sufficiently indirect not to take the work away from the students.

In addition, the teaching of specific strategies or operations must not be done in isolation from the knowledge that gives context and meaning to the processes. I remain convinced that the acquisition and utilization of information-processing strategies is fundamentally domain specific (Doyle, 1983). In other words, an understanding and flexible application of intellectual processes is knowledge driven, and problem-solving abilities are embedded in semantic knowledge of the structure and connectedness of a discipline (Resnick, 1987). To know what to do when, one must know the substance of a field. Without this context of knowledge, skills are highly abstract. Moreover, without a struggle for meaning and use, without the invention of the meaning of the strategy for oneself, the strategy is likely to remain the property of the teaching program rather than become the property of the student (see Rohrkemper, 1989). Under such circumstances, transfer and flexible adaptation to circumstances is unlikely to occur. We need to learn how to design tasks in which students can become familiar with a domain without resorting to rote memorization or meaningless procedures.

The management of explicitness can be a tricky business for teachers. Failure to provide adequate specifications for work, sufficiently clear explanations of what to do, or appropriate feedback for performance can make it impossible for students to accomplish tasks and can lead to the invention of erroneous strategies and understandings.

At the same time, overspecifying requirements and operations can restrict the range of opportunities students have to learn important aspects of the curriculum. Moreover, as suggested earlier, there are classroom pressures that impinge upon teachers and shape their explicitness during lessons. Studies of academic work suggest that ambiguous tasks are often unstable in classrooms (see Doyle & Carter, 1984). Management of the work flow is difficult when students are struggling with ambiguity. Errors increase and completion rates decrease. And some students are skilled at eliciting explicitness from teachers in order to circumvent task demands. Under such circumstances, teachers have a difficult time maintaining appropriate levels of explicitness in instruction.

Success. Some process-product researchers (e.g., Berliner, 1987) have celebrated the advantages of success as a predictor of achievement. Translated into practice, this faith in success has generally meant that the curriculum should be divided into small, easily accomplished steps so that movement through the curriculum occurs under conditions of continuous success. This conception, which has a family resemblance to earlier behavioral theories of shaping, is not supported by modern cognitive and curricular studies. Indeed, as noted earlier, such a fragmentation of curriculum can destroy meaning by isolating content and skills from the integrative knowledge structures within which they have significance. Moreover, tasks that are too simple obviate the need to struggle for meaning and thus to activate the affective and intellectual processes associated with goal-directed action, invention, and self-esteem (see Covington, 1984; Rohrkemper, 1989). Thus, from both motivational and intellectual perspectives, success is not, in itself, a suitable criterion for teaching. Educative tasks must be sufficiently complex and effortful to make construction of meaning possible. Indeed, Stodolsky (1988) found that engagement and challenge were related:

> We found that students were efficient—they attended to information when it was needed in the flow of instruction, and they listened to novel information. They were engaged by complexity, as they exhibited higher levels of involvement when asked to perform more intellectually complex activities than when given less challenging, simpler chores. [Pp. 2–3]

I will close with two illustrations in which attempts have been made to engage disadvantaged students in challenging academic tasks. The first is reciprocal teaching (Palinscar & Brown, 1984). In reciprocal teaching, four comprehension strategies are taught: summarizing the content of a passage, asking a question about the central point, clarifying the difficult parts of the material, and predicting what will come next. Initially, the teacher models these strategies by reading a short passage and illustrating the comprehension strategies aloud. Then, on the next passage the students begin to assume the teacher's role while the teacher provides prompts and guidance—a scaffolding to help students sustain the strategies. After several hours of practice, control of the strategies gradually shifts from the teacher to the students, during which time the teacher tries to match demands to ability and track the students' thinking as they acquire the skills. The results of this approach have been impressive.

The second example is the HOTS (Higher Order Thinking Skills) program developed by Pogrow and his associates (see Pogrow, 1987; Pogrow & Buchanan, 1985). In this approach, Chapter 1 students complete intellectually challenging computer games and instructional programs while engaged in conversations with teachers that focus on metacognitive dimensions of the tasks they are accomplishing on the computer. Instead of using direct instruction, teachers work to maintain proper levels of ambiguity so that students have to struggle with meaning and articulate ideas and strategies on their own. In addition, there are several strong motivational components in the program. Students have access to challenging tasks on attractive equipment rather than remedial texts and worksheets. Moreover, students are given special identity by being able to invite their classmates to the HOTS room to demonstrate the interesting things they are doing on the computers. Preliminary results indicate that this project is having dramatic effects on the achievement of Chapter 1 students.

SUMMARY

From a task perspective, students will learn higher-order thinking by accomplishing tasks in which such processes are used widely and frequently. The instructional problem is first to design such tasks and then enact them in the classroom. Cognitive and curricular research is beginning to provide useful information about the design of tasks that represent the curriculum in appropriate ways. Considerable work needs to be done, however, on how to establish and sustain such tasks in classroom environments. Herein lies the challenge for classroom research on the education of disadvantaged students.

REFERENCES

Anderson, R. C., Spiro, R., & Montague, W. (Eds.). (1977). *Schooling and the acquisition of knowledge*. Hillsdale, NJ: Erlbaum.

Arlin, M. (1982). Teacher responses to student time differences in mastery learning. *American Journal of Education, 90*, 334–352.

Bennett, N., Desforges, C., Cockburn, A., & Wilkinson, B. (1984). *The quality of pupil learning experiences*. Hillsdale, NJ: Erlbaum.

Berliner, D. C. (1987). In D. C. Berliner & B. Rosenshine (Eds.), *Talks to teachers*. New York: Random House.

Blumenfeld, P., Pintrich, P., Meece, J., & Wessels, K. (1982). The formation and role of self perceptions of ability in elementary classrooms. In W. Doyle & T. Good (Eds.), *Focus on teaching*. Chicago: University of Chicago Press.

Brophy, J. E., & Good, T. L. (1986). Teacher behavior and student achievement. In M. C. Wittrock (Ed.), *Handbook of research on teaching* (3rd ed.). New York: Macmillan.

Calfee, R., & Drum, P. (1986). Research on teaching reading. In M. C. Wittrock (Ed.), *Handbook of research on teaching* (3rd ed.). New York: Macmillan.

Carnine, D. W., & Stein, M. (1981). Strategy and Organizational Practice procedures for teaching basic facts. *Journal of Research in Mathematics Education, 12,* 65–69.

Carter, K. (1985). *Teacher comprehension of classroom processes: An emerging direction in classroom management research.* Paper presented at the annual meeting of the American Educational Research Association, Chicago.

Carter, K. (1986). *Classroom management as cognitive problem solving: Toward teacher comprehension in teacher education.* Paper presented at the annual meeting of the American Educational Research Association, San Francisco.

Chacones, D. (1970). *The way the tiger walked.* New York: Simon & Schuster.

Cohen, D. K. (1988). Teaching practice: Plus que ça change . . . In P. Jackson (Ed.), *Contributing to educational change: Perspectives on research and practice.* Berkeley: McCutchan.

Collins, A., & Smith, E. E. (1980). *Teaching the process of reading comprehension* (Tech. Rep. No. 182). Urbana: University of Illinois, Center for the Study of Reading.

Cornbleth, C., & Korth, W. (1983). *Doing the work: Teacher perspectives and meaning of responsibility.* Paper presented at the annual meeting of the American Educational Research Association, Montreal.

Covington, M. V. (1984). The self-worth dimensions of achievement motivation: Findings and implications. *Elementary School Journal, 85,* 5–20.

Davis, R., & McKnight, C. (1976). Conceptual, heuristic, and S-algorithmic approaches in mathematics teaching. *Journal of Children's Mathematical Behavior, 1* (Suppl. 1), 271–286.

Doyle, W. (1983). Academic work. *Review of Educational Research, 53,* 159–199.

Doyle, W. (1986a). Classroom organization and management. In M. C. Wittrock (Ed.), *Handbook of research on teaching* (3rd ed.). New York: Macmillan.

Doyle, W. (1986b). Content representation in teachers' definitions of academic work. *Journal of Curriculum Studies, 18,* 365–379.

Doyle, W., & Carter, K. (1984). Academic tasks in classrooms. *Curriculum Inquiry, 14,* 129–149.

Doyle, W., Sanford, J. P., French, B. S., Emmer, E. T., & Clements, B. S. (1985). *Patterns of academic work in junior high school science, English, and mathematics classes: A final report* (R&D Rep. 6190). Austin: University of Texas, Research and Development Center for Teacher Education.

Eder, D. (1982). Differences in communicative styles across ability groups. In L. C. Wilkinson (Ed.), *Communicating in classrooms.* New York: Academic Press.

Emmer, E. T., Evertson, C. M., & Anderson, L. M. (1980). Effective classroom management at the beginning of the school year. *Elementary School Journal, 80,* 219–231.

Erickson, F., & Mohatt, G. (1982). Cultural organization of participation structures in two classrooms of Indian students. In G. Spindler (Ed.), *Doing the ethnography of schooling.* New York: Holt, Rinehart and Winston.

Green, J., Harker, J., & Golden, J. (1986). Lesson construction: Differing views. In G. Noblit & W. Pink (Eds.), *Understanding education*. Norwood, NJ: Ablex.

Gump, P. V. (1969). Intra-setting analysis: The third grade classroom as a special but instructive case. In E. Willems & H. Rausch (Eds.), *Naturalistic viewpoints in psychological research*. New York: Holt, Rinehart and Winston.

Gump, P. V. (1982). School settings and their keeping. In D. L. Duke (Ed.), *Helping teachers manage classrooms*. Alexandria, VA: Association for Supervision and Curriculum Development.

Jackson, P. W. (1985). Private lesson in public schools: Remarks on the limits of adaptive instruction. In M. C. Wang & H. J. Walberg (Eds.), *Adapting instruction to individual differences*. Berkeley, CA: McCutchan.

Klahr, D. (Ed.). (1976). *Cognition and instruction*. Hillsdale, NJ: Erlbaum.

Kounin, J. S. (1970). *Discipline and group management in classrooms*. New York: Holt, Rinehart and Winston.

Kounin, J. S., & Gump, P. V. (1974). Signal systems of lesson settings and the task related behavior of preschool children. *Journal of Educational Psychology, 66*, 554–562.

Madaus, G. F. (1988). The influence of testing on the curriculum. In L. N. Tanner (Ed.), *Critical issues in curriculum*. Eighty-seventh Yearbook of the National Society for the Study of Education, Part 1. Chicago: University of Chicago Press.

Palinscar, A. S., & Brown, A. L. (1984). Reciprocal teaching of comprehension-fostering and monitoring activities. *Cognition and Instruction, 1*(2), 117–175.

Pearson, P. D., & Tierney, R. J. (1984). On becoming a thoughtful reader: Learning to read like a writer. In A. C. Purvis & 0. Niles (Eds.), *Becoming readers in a complex society*. Eighty-third Yearbook of the National Society for the Study of Education, Part 1. Chicago: University of Chicago Press.

Pogrow, S. (1987). *An overview of the techniques used in the HOTS program*. Tucson: University of Arizona.

Pogrow, S., & Buchanan, B. (1985). Higher-order thinking for compensatory students. *Educational Leadership, 43*, 40–43.

Resnick, L. B. (1987). *Education and learning to think*. Washington, DC: National Academy Press.

Rohrkemper, M. (1989). Self-regulated learning and academic achievement: A Vygotskian view. In D. Schunk & B. Zimmerman (Eds.), *Self-regulated learning and academic achievement: Theory, research, and practice*. New York: Springer-Verlag.

Romberg, T. A., & Carpenter, T. P. (1986). Research on teaching and learning mathematics. In M.C. Wittrock (Ed.), *Handbook of research on teaching* (3rd ed.). New York: Macmillan.

Rosenshine, B., & Stevens, R. (1986). Teaching functions. In M. C. Wittrock (Ed.), *Handbook of research on teaching* (3rd ed.). New York: Macmillan.

Scardamalia, M., & Bereiter, C. (1985). Fostering the development of self-regulation in children's knowledge processing. In S. F. Chipman, J. W. Segal, & R. Glaser (Eds.), *Thinking and learning skills: Vol. 2. Research and open questions*. Hillsdale, NJ: Erlbaum.

Stodolsky, S. S. (1988). *The subject matters: Classroom activity in math and social studies*. Chicago: University of Chicago Press.

Walker, D., & Schaffarzick, J. (1974). Comparing curricula. *Review of Educational Research, 44,* 83–111.

Weinstein, C. S. (1979). The physical environment of the school: A review of the research. *Review of Educational Research, 49,* 557–610.

Yinger, R. J. (1980). A study of teacher planning. *Elementary School Journal, 80,* 107–127.

— 11 —

Classroom Management and Instructional Strategies for the Disadvantaged Learner: Some Thoughts About the Nature of the Problem

Barbara Neufeld

I bring to the task of writing this chapter a firm belief that we know most of what we need to know about *formal teaching and learning* in classrooms to help disadvantaged children achieve in school. I am, therefore, impatient at the thought of yet more classroom research and uncertain that additional investigation of instruction and management practices will yield knowledge worthy of the time, effort, and expense. My stance is not anti-intellectual nor anti-inquiry. It is a function of my fear that as an educational community we are stalling; that we have knowledge and skill that we are not willing to act on because it would be difficult to do so. Or that we have knowledge that does not connect readily with policy; knowledge that might suggest changes that are beyond our political will as a nation.

We know, for example, that intelligent, well-educated teachers contribute to student learning. And it is no secret that cities, rural areas, and other areas that include large proportions of poor and minority children have difficulty recruiting and keeping what we consider our most talented teachers. Nor is it a secret that youngsters in these schools often pose educational and emotional challenges that teachers feel ill-prepared to handle and that lead them to cope by emphasizing lower-order skills and classroom control at the expense of education. A great part of the solution to poor academic achievement is better-quality teaching through better-educated teachers.[1] For the higher-order thinking skills and complex subject matter understanding we truly desire, *different* as well as better teaching is in order (Cohen, 1988). It is not clear, however, how we can translate this knowledge into practice.

I do not make the judgment about teaching quality solely on the basis of published research, although there is sufficient documentation with which to make that argument (Doyle, 1986, among others). It is a conclusion based on formal and informal observation in classrooms over the past five years and memories of my own teaching in the South Bronx and in New Haven in the late 1960s and early 1970s. I retain vivid images of dull classrooms, scenes of children and adults trying hard and getting nowhere meaningful. Frustration was a daily fact of life for teachers and children.

When I taught, basal reading groups, language experience charts, the Chandler and Bank Street reading series, individualized reading with trade books, and SRA came and went without impact on children's achievement. The principals (there were four of them in our school of 1,800 children) made sure that we planned for instruction in all required subject areas by collecting planbooks weekly and by

---

1. When I speak of the need for better-quality teaching, I refer to the quality of (1) the content under consideration, (2) the organization of learning opportunities, (3) the pedagogical strategies in use, and (4) the affective component of personal interactions between teachers and learners.

requiring a schedule that delineated how we allocated the instructional time available (1,550 minutes, as I recall) to various subjects. If they walked into a class at 10:30 on Tuesday, they could expect to see a social studies lesson in progress if that's what a teacher's time allocation plan described. Many classrooms were orderly; but few children or teachers got excited about and by learning. Standardized test scores were very low. In highly organized classrooms with caring teachers, achievement was dismal.

When I returned to inner-city elementary school classrooms in a number of states as a researcher several years ago, I was struck by how little had changed in the organization of schools, classrooms, and instruction. Teachers were still being asked to keep track of the minutes they spent on instruction in the various subject areas (only now it was part of a reform, not standard operating procedure). Textbooks were curriculum. Fragmentation and routinization—control strategies—were once again the latest route to the improvement of education for disadvantaged youngsters.

As a participant observer I experienced Madeline Hunter's approach to teaching through a five-day staff development program expertly delivered by Rob Hunter. Teachers applauded what they were learning and worked hard to incorporate the recommended teaching strategies into their repertoire of skills. When it was over, in classroom after classroom in states as different as Connecticut and Texas, teachers were saying "I like the way Tyrone is sitting," as they strove to have others follow suit. Advance organizers, objectives stated on the board, guided and independent practice in strict, undeviating order characterized classrooms. Careful organization through a standard lesson design, teacher-controlled use of time, central office control of curriculum coverage, pacing, and assessment characterized the classrooms I saw and those described by colleagues. Joy, creativity, and success, even on these limited terms, were rare commodities.

Lack of subject matter knowledge in mathematics and science, in particular, characterized far too much of the teaching that I saw. Teachers implemented well-organized mathematics lessons dealing with division of fractions without clearly understanding the concepts themselves. Children made mistakes that revealed where they misunderstood concepts; teachers failed to notice the thinking behind the mistakes, so they did not use children's errors to re-teach or teach differently the material under consideration. The form of lessons was as required by the latest staff development expert; content and meaning were often lacking. Children were remembering bits and pieces of information and computational strategies, some of which led to improved standardized test scores, some of which were wrong. Students wrote compositions that were pinned to bulletin boards so that they could be proud of their creative work—a testament to positive reinforcement. All of them were on the same assigned, narrow topics, such as "my favorite food," or "our trip to the newspaper." What were children learning from these lessons? What would they find compelling, I wondered, about the possibilities of learning from the opportunities they had in school? What did all of this effort, motion, and good intention have to do with education? What did we want children to be able to know and do at the end of this kind of educational experience? Why did educators think this new order was an improvement?

Just as we know that we need teachers who know their subject matter and how to teach it, we also know that organization, focus, and good use of time are important. But the valuable nuggets of information and skill that are embedded in the recent research on teaching have been transformed into the time and motion routines of schools. More than other reform efforts—open classrooms and progressive education ideas, in particular—the most recent strategies for improved teaching fall into the mainstream patterns already in place. As such, their weak points are exaggerated by the extant system. They have been turned into mechanical, standardized practices that fit well into our factory model of schooling. Far from providing teachers with a knowledge base that can underpin a professional practice of teaching, as used in too many elementary schools for disadvantaged children, they substitute form for thought.

Besides the well-studied areas of classroom management, curriculum, and instructional strategy, other issues are intimately related to students' ability to learn in schools, but remain out of mainstream efforts to improve students' achievement. In mentioning these, I am not minimizing the need for intelligent, well-educated teachers who know their subject matter and know how to teach it with pedagogics that go beyond the fragmented, decontextualized effective teaching strategies. I am choosing to focus elsewhere because there are additional, critical issues that have direct bearing on academic achievement and the impact of academic instruction, which are usually treated as tangential to instruction, or as merely providing difficult conditions under which instruction and learning must proceed. I want to suggest that these factors might well be thought of as integral to learning; that they may contribute far more to learning outcomes than does the choice of a particular instructional strategy. As such, they are important to the study of academic achievement for disadvantaged children.

I want to bring to the forefront ideas about (1) cultural differences (Au & Jordan, 1981; Delpit, 1986, 1988; Erickson, 1986, 1987; Rodriguez, 1982), (2) the influence of the "caste-like" status of black and some Spanish-speaking people (Fordham, 1988; Ogbu, 1987), and (3) the social distance between the culture of the home and the school (Comer, 1980a, 1986, 1988a & b) as factors with a profound influence on academic learning, as factors that ought to be included as central to any study of academic instruction for the disadvantaged. I will do this by talking briefly about the emotional cost of "making it" in mainstream schools if one is a member of a "caste-like" minority, the kinds of cultural differences that can interfere with learning, and the developmental differences between some minority and mainstream children when they enter school. Then I will highlight the School Development Program in New Haven to suggest school changes that can facilitate student learning by responding to children's social, developmental, and educational needs through a decentralized governance structure.

CULTURAL DIFFERENCES/DIFFERENCES IN STATUS

A growing number of academicians and practitioners are paying attention to the dilemmas that face disadvantaged children because they come to school well entwined into a community that they value and that is different from the mainstream community that structures educational settings and interactions (Comer, 1980a & b, 1988a & b; Delpit, 1988; Fordham, 1988; Ogbu, 1987). In the case of black and Hispanic children, that community may not share with the mainstream community the view that schooling is an avenue to economic and social success. Ogbu (1987) explains that years of oppression and lack of access to mainstream institutions have led black and some

Hispanic people to develop a culture that operates *in opposition* to the white culture. Accepting school, a prime mainstream institution, would be in conflict with maintaining the distinct, separate, and oppositional black community. Others (Erickson, 1986, 1987, and Comer, 1980a & b, 1988a & b) stress the cultural differences that exist between minority children and the mainstream culture rather than the accumulated impact of years of skewed power relations that have kept minority families in a subservient position. They point out (1) the difficulties that minority children have making sense of what is demanded of them in schools, (2) the negative impact of their lack of understanding on the adults in the schools, and (3) the lack of skill at home to help them bridge the differences.

Whichever the explanation, and it is feasible that both are correct for communities as diverse as the black and Hispanic communities, children find themselves in an organization that they do not understand well, that is not much like home in the interactional patterns and values that prevail, and that aims to prepare them for a world they do not feel is or can be theirs. It is a world in which they frequently do not succeed from the outset.

As early as age eight, at the developmental stage when they are decreasing their dependence on adults, disadvantaged minority children begin to attend to differences between themselves and the mainstream and they become more aware of their inability to succeed well at school tasks. Their separation from dependence on adults includes separation from the adults at school and the goals of academic success that they see as both unattainable and inappropriate (Comer, 1988a). Even at that young age, were they to choose to succeed in school, the choice would "[exact] a high price: such a choice means rejecting the culture of one's parents and social group" (Comer, 1988a, p. 46). No one should expect any child to choose school given these stakes.

Fordham (1988) describes the similar quandary in which older black students find themselves. She describes how they come to associate their future with that of their group and the mismatch between the group orientation of their community and the individual orientation of the school:

> Black children learn the meaning of fictive kinship from their parents and peers while they are growing up. It appears, moreover, that they learn it early enough, and well enough, so that they even tend to associate their life chances

and "success" potential with those of their peers and other members of the community. The collective ethos of the fictive-kinship system is challenged by the individual ethos of the dominant culture when the children enter school, and when the children experience the competition between the two for their loyalty. For many Black adolescents, therefore, the mere act of attending school is evidence of either a conscious or unconscious rejection of the indigenous Black American culture. [P. 57]

Using the words of three female and three male students who have chosen to be successful in school, Fordham describes their solution to the dilemma posed by choice. Becoming "raceless" is one strategy with which academically successful minority students accomplish and then cope with their success. Fordham writes:

High [Black] achievers often make choices that either put social distance between them and their peers or undermine group solidarity. They do not appear to believe—nor does their experience support—the idea that they can truly be bicultural and actualize what Edwards (1987) describes as their "crossover dreams"—the widely touted dreams of wealth, fame, and fortune. Instead, their experiences, both in and out of school, support the value of appearing raceless to their teachers and other adults in the school context . . . both male and female students . . . believe that school and schooling are the primary means of achieving vertical mobility for Black Americans in the existing social system. [Pp. 79–80]

She suggests that this is a pragmatic strategy but one that pits the student and individual mobility against the collective good of the black community as a cultural group. Students' words movingly describe the cost of their choices.

Rodriguez (1982), in his autobiographical account of the process and impact of becoming successful in school, approaches the same difficult choices from a different angle. He talks about the uses of language and the jarring differences between the private language of home and the public language of the school for the Spanish-speaking disadvantaged child. His comments are reminiscent of the trying experiences of many generations of immigrants who chose to join the mainstream:

There is something called bilingual education—a scheme proposed in the late 1960s by Hispanic-American social activists. . . . It is a program that seeks to permit non-English-speaking children, many from lower class homes, to use their family language as the language of school. . . . I hear them and am forced to say no: It is not possible for a child—any child—ever to use his family's language in school. Not to understand this is to misunderstand the public uses of schooling and to trivialize the nature of intimate life—a family's "language." [Pp. 11–12]

Each of these individuals argues that in one way or another, there is a high social and personal price to pay for adopting the mainstream habits and values that make it possible to succeed in school and beyond. They suggest that students are not merely passive recipients of teachers' pedagogical strategies, but rather are active participants in decisions about learning.

These analyses suggest strongly that to consider academic instruction and classroom management as if they were mere technical issues, as if they were about ways of controlling students who do not know how to behave in school or who lack the intellectual wit to deal with complexity, is to miss something essential about the emotional, affective, wrenching experience and hard choices that disadvantaged children face alone every day. To separate academic instruction from its social, contextual component is to seek improvements based on at least a partial misconstrual of the problem.

A primary reason for my success in the classroom was that I couldn't forget that schooling was changing me and separating me from the life I enjoyed before becoming a student. (Emphasis in the original.) That simple realization! For years I never spoke to anyone about it, never mentioned a thing to my family or my teachers or classmates. From a very early age, I understood enough, just enough about my classroom experiences to keep what I knew repressed, hidden beneath layers of embarrassment. Not until my last months as a graduate student, nearly thirty years old, was it possible for me to think much about the reasons for my academic success. Only then. At the end of my schooling, I needed to determine how far I had moved from my past. The adult finally confronted, and now must publicly say, what the child shuddered from knowing and could never admit to himself or to those many faces that smiled at his every success. [Rodriguez, 1982, p. 45]

Some might argue that what Comer, Rodriguez, and Fordham describe has been the case for all minorities, that previous generations of immigrants did indeed have to give up their native language and aspects of their culture in order to make it in America. Certainly generations of children did just this and did it with their parents' encouragement. It was not without pain, for parents or for children. What is different for the disadvantaged today, especially those who are Native American, black, and/or Spanish-speaking, is their enduring low social status in the nation, a situation over which they have had little control, little ability to change. Rodriguez (1982) talks about having to have a public language and a public identity. He had a vision of the possibility of a valued public identity if he gave up his private one. For too many of the disadvantaged, the possibility of a valued public identity still seems like a pipe dream. Thus, there is no compensation in sight for what they will surrender by assuming the public life and values of the school. Or so they think.

Rodriguez also points out the importance of his parents' assent to his learning English. They sanctioned his adoption of the mainstream by agreeing to use English at home. That connection between home and school, the authority of the school and teachers, seems rare today. Comer (1988c) tells the story of a first grader who listened to his teacher tell of the class rules on the first day of school and then raised his hand to say that his mother had told him he did not have to do anything the teacher told him! Parents' responses can make it even more difficult for children to be successful in school.

Rodriguez and Fordham describe children who saw what was required and had the personal qualities necessary to make difficult decisions. They saw what they had to do and they were able to take advantage of what the school had to offer. They are a minority within a minority. Countless other students see what is required and choose not to make the sacrifice; even more probably do not understand the situation they are in and the choices that are available.

There are children who are failing to learn because the interaction patterns required of structured lessons are at odds with those required of their home culture and, for one reason or another, they cannot figure out what is required by the teacher. The Kamehameha Early Education Project (KEEP) in Hawaii is cited frequently as an example of how correction of a cultural mismatch in interaction style had a profound impact on students' ability to learn to read in first grade (Erickson, 1986, 1987; Au & Jordan, 1981). Adjustments in permissible speech patterns and turn-taking enabled children to use existing material to learn to read with no change in the reading materials. There are other examples of cultural mismatches whose correction led to important achievement increases.

One can look at KEEP as an elegant, parsimonious intervention that makes it possible for children to learn to read and maintain their culture. However, those for whom education is acceptance of the oppressor's culture may not find such shifts beneficial. Rodriguez' insight into the fundamental nature of education—that it changes people and takes them from the private to the public domain—is still going to be an issue for those who want to become a part of the economic mainstream and simultaneously remain within the private, cultural enclave. It will be more of an issue for those whose identity is connected to *not* being part of the economic and social mainstream.

Finally, the instructional lesson of KEEP is not that basal readers are the best way to teach reading, but rather that whatever pedagogics teachers choose, they must be sensitive to the match and mismatch between the instructional demands and the normal interaction patterns of the children in the classroom. If KEEP had been trying to implement a trade book approach to reading, it might have looked for interference from other aspects of children's normal interaction patterns, not only those that were important given the structure of "reading groups." Efforts to make interaction patterns explicit and provide a way for children to use what they know as well as broaden their repertoire of skills in order to have access to the academic curriculum of the school might be characteristic of some effective instructional strategies. Delpit asks that schools teach children "the content that other families from a different cultural orientation provide at home . . . ensuring that each classroom incorporate strategies appropriate for all the children in its confines" (1988, p. 286). Some of that content will be mainstream interaction patterns.

DEVELOPMENTALLY RESPONSIVE SCHOOL ORGANIZATION

James Comer argues explicitly for the school to take on the roles of teaching mainstream social interaction skills to disadvantaged children and helping to build strong connections between the school and the home. Through the School Development Program (SDP), a school improvement strategy that uses child development and mental health concepts to orient the actions and activities of school faculty and staff through the locally constituted School Governance and Management Team (SGMT) and the Mental Health Team (MHT), he involves parents "so that they can support the kids even though [those kids are] growing away from the style and experience of the parents" (1986). The MHT and SGMT have distinct and significant roles in the SDP. Rather than summarize them, I quote from the Program Description (Comer, 1986).

1. *The Mental Health Team*
   a. works with the governance and management body [formerly the SPMT] to enable it to base its academic, social climate, and staff development programs on mental health, child development principles;
   b. facilitates the many interactions between parents and school staff to improve the social climate and cooperation throughout the school community;
   c. works with classroom teachers and parents to identify children who need special services;
   d. sets up individualized programs for children with special needs, using the school's special education facilities and staff and other school-based or outside services as needed;
   e. works with classroom teachers to develop classroom strategies to prevent minor problems from becoming major;
   f. offers ongoing consultation to all school staff to bridge the gap between special education and general classroom activities;
   g. provides consultation and training workshops to staff and parents on child development, human relations and other mental health issues.
2. *The School Governance and Management Body [SPMT].* The school governance and management body includes the school principal, a mental health team member and representatives selected by teachers and parents. This group:
   a. meets on a regular basis to carry out systematic school planning, resource assessment and mobilization, program implementation and program evaluation and modification;
   b. establishes policy guidelines in all aspects of the school program—academic, social and staff development;
   c. works closely with the parent group to plan an annual school calendar to integrate social, academic and staff development functions;
   d. works to facilitate social skill development and academic learning.

For the last twenty years, James Comer (1980b) has worked from a set of assumptions about what influences the academic and social success and failure of minority disadvantaged children, arguing that primary attention to the technical aspects of teaching and learning ignores significant features of learning encounters that are essential for success. Learning, he asserts, takes place in relationships. He diagnoses school failure as related to the failure of personal relations between children and adults in school (a failure that is not always intentional) and argues for a parental role for teachers:

> The effort to limit the role of the teacher and the school to academics is one of the primary reasons America's great experiment in education—the effort to educate more than the intellectual elite and economically privileged—has been less successful than it might have been. [Comer, 1988b, p. 34]

> By focusing solely on academic changes, the schools have ignored the affective domain—the crucial relationships that students need to grow and learn. We

remain mired in a mechanical approach to learning. It's one that has never served our children well—and in today's world dooms many of our students to failure. [Comer, 1988b, p. 39]

Comer urges attention to child development, to affective aspects of learning, to the relationships in which learning occurs, and to the need "for teachers and school people to again serve as parent surrogates." Comer's suggestion for improving academic achievement is the reorganization of schools so that their faculties can support the social and emotional growth of students "and in turn, academic learning" (Comer, 1988b). (Lipsitz [1984] makes a similar point with respect to middle schools.) He argues that "the failure to bridge the social and cultural gap between home and school may lie at the root of the poor academic performance of many of these [poor, minority, disadvantaged] children" (Comer, 1988a).

Comer talks about the differences in development and values that occur particularly in poor, marginal black families that lead their children to arrive at school without the mainstream values and social skills, for example, skills of negotiation and compromise, that they will encounter and need there. He writes:

Such lack of development or development that is at odds with the mainstream occurs disproportionately often among children from the minority groups that have had the most traumatic experiences in this society: Native Americans, Hispanics and blacks. The religious, political, economic and social institutions that had organized and stabilized their communities have suffered severe discontinuity and destruction. Furthermore, these groups have been excluded from educational, economic and political opportunity. [Comer, 1988a, p. 45]

He believes schools should explicitly teach children what they need to know and that such instruction can be good education. He, his colleagues, and parents developed a social skills curriculum that embeds social skills in the context of subjects that children need to know: "politics and government, business and economics, health and nutrition, and spiritual and leisure activity." In this program,

Children learned how to write invitations and thank-you notes, how to serve as hosts, how the body functions, how to write checks, how to plan concerts, and so on. Each activity combined basic academic skills with social skills and an appreciation of the arts. These activities were an immediate and dramatic success. [Comer, 1988a, p. 48]

Readers may disagree with Comer's acceptance of the mainstream culture and the power relationships implicit and explicit in teaching children to fit into it (1980a). His argument is that while schools are mainstream organizations and while access to the mainstream of America requires school success, teaching children explicitly what they need to know in order to succeed is a sensible strategy. And teaching children these social skills has been accompanied by reduced tensions in schools and significant increases in academic achievement that have been sustained over time. This strategy may be related to Delpit's (1988, p. 283) comment regarding "the culture of power," in which she states, "If you are not already a participant in the culture of power, being told explicitly the rules of that culture makes acquiring power easier." The School Development Program aims to make the rules explicit.

Chubb's (1988) work in a broader array of secondary schools supports Comer's view of the importance of effective school organization and parental involvement for student achievement. While school practices—graduation requirements, homework assignments, emphasis on writing and effective disciplinary practices—"yielded only the slightest improvements in achievement," organizational qualities that led faculty to talk about the school as if it were a family and parental involvement were associated with better academic achievement. "The largest estimated influence on the effectiveness of school organization is the role of parents in the school. All other things being equal, schools in which parents are highly involved, cooperative, and well-informed are more likely to develop effective organizations than are schools in which parents do not possess these qualities." The second most important determinant of school organization, and therefore effectiveness, was the influence of administrative superiors over policy and personnel. Schools worked better as organizations when the principal was powerful relative to the superintendent and other central office personnel. One might question the cause and effect relationship in these findings, something that Chubb does not address in this chapter. However, Comer's work in New Haven, because it was an intervention, sheds light on the question. He *created* (among other things) greater parent involvement and one result was a climate in which improved academic success was an outcome.

CONCLUSION

Suppose we already know all we need to know about the technical aspects of instruction for disadvantaged learners. Suppose that we have gone as far as we can in describing the discrete features of direct instruction, wait time, higher-order questions, classroom organization, for example, that make a difference to learning. Suppose that we have exhausted the possibilities for examining fragments of teaching acts and associating them with specific learning outcomes in children. If this were the case, what would we hope to gain from yet another study of classroom management and instructional strategies for the disadvantaged learner? What else would we need to know about the change from the intended to the enacted to the received curriculum? Certainly, we do not need another study of fidelity of implementation. Nor will it help us to know that teachers are street-level bureaucrats who must apply broad policies—curriculum and acceptable teaching techniques—to their unique settings under conditions of uncertainty. We know quite a lot about the importance of teachers who are reasonably organized about instruction and who can maneuver between a variety of teaching strategies depending on the material under consideration and the students who are attempting to learn it. We know about individual differences and the dilemmas of heterogeneous classrooms whatever the dimensions of the heterogeneity. And we know about problems associated with diversity and quality in the faculties that teach in inner-city and poor rural schools. These critically important, but nonattractive teaching positions do not draw or retain the best of our teaching force.

But somehow, through all of our research and efforts to improve education for the disadvantaged, we have had only minimal success. Over the last twenty or so years, we have learned a great deal about teaching and learning, tried a number of innovations in curriculum and instruction, and yet, despite some small progress, we have reaped too little for our efforts. Maybe what we have learned is necessary but not sufficient.

Without disregarding the contribution of the large body of research on classroom management and instruction, I have taken this opportunity to raise the possibility that we ought to look for characteristics, criteria, and models of management and instruction for academic subjects in nontraditional places, that is, in the improvement of the interpersonal relations between students and teachers, between home, students, and school, and in the social interaction skills necessary for success in school for children who, for one reason or another, do not come to school with them. Perhaps we ought to remind ourselves that learning is fundamentally accomplished in the context of relationships. Most teaching and school effectiveness/ improvement efforts are based on input-output models that tend to construe teaching and learning as primarily technical tasks that involve, for example, matching appropriately organized material with the right teaching techniques. Grounded in reinforcement and learning theory, these more common approaches aim to set up conditions that increase the probability of learning. They have not always paid much attention to what was happening in the learner's mind as a result of the social context in addition to the instructional strategy. What I have tried to insert into our thinking about improvement of education for the disadvantaged is the idea that children are actively constructing the world of school in which they spend their time and that the interpersonal relationships in schools and between homes and schools must be healthier before improvements in teaching and learning can occur; that what mediates between the stimulus and the response—the interpersonal and social relationship as well as the teacher's skill and knowledge—is fundamental to the enterprise, to the probability that learning will occur.

REFERENCES

Au, K. H., & Jordan, C. (1981). Teaching reading to Hawaiian children: Finding a culturally appropriate solution. In H. T. Trueba, G. P. Guthrie, & K. H. Au (Eds.), *Culture and the bilingual classroom: Studies in classroom ethnography* (pp. 139–152). Rowley, MA: Newbury House.

Chubb, J. E. (1988, Winter). Why the current wave of school reform will fail. *The Public Interest, 90,* 28–49.

Cohen, D. K. (1988). *Teaching practice: Plus que ça change* (Issue Paper 88-3). East Lansing: Michigan State University, NCRTE.

Comer, J. P. (1980a, March). The education of inner-city children. *Grants Magazine, 3*(1), 20–27.

Comer, J. P. (1980b). *School power: Implications of an intervention project.* New York: Free Press.

Comer, J. P. (1986, August). A prescription for better schools: An interview with Dr. James Comer. *CDF Reports, 8*(4), 1–6.

Comer, J. P. (1988a). Educating poor minority children. *Scientific American, 259*(5), 42–48.

Comer, J. P. (1988b, January). Is "parenting" essential to good teaching? *Families and Schools,* 34–39.

Comer, J. P. (1988c, Fall). Presentation at the Citywide Educational Coalition, Boston, MA.

Delpit, L. D. (1986). Skills and other dilemmas of a progressive Black educator. *Harvard Educational Review, 56*(4), 379–385.

Delpit, L. D. (1988). The silenced dialogue: Power and pedagogy in educating other people's children. *Harvard Educational Review, 58*(3), 280–298.

Doyle, W. (1986). Vision and reality: A reaction to issues in curriculum and instruction for compensatory education. In B. J. Williams, P. A. Richmond, & B. J. Mason, *Designs for compensatory education: Conference proceedings and papers.* Washington, DC: Research and Evaluation Associates.

Erickson, F. (1986). Qualitative methods in research on teaching. M. C. Wittrock (Ed.), *Handbook of research on teaching* (3rd ed.). New York: Macmillan.

Erickson, F. (1987, December). Transformation and school success: The politics and culture of educational achievement. *Anthropology & Education Quarterly, 18*(4), 335–356.

Fordham, S. (1988). Racelessness as a factor in black students' school success: Pragmatic strategy or pyrrhic victory? *Harvard Educational Review, 58*(1), 54–84.

Lipsitz, J. (1984). *Successful schools for young adolescents.* New Brunswick, NJ: Transaction Books.

Ogbu, J. U. (1987). Variability in minority school performance: A problem in search of an explanation. *Anthropology & Education Quarterly, 18*(4), 312–334.

Rodriguez, R. (1982). *Hunger of memory.* Boston: David R. Godine.

———12———

Instructional Strategies and Classroom Management

Heather McCollum

The focus of this chapter is on what has been learned about instructional strategies, viewed generically, and approaches to managing classrooms. I will review evidence that generalizes across subject matter areas regarding what teachers do to organize and manage instruction. Other chapters (see Chapters 4 and 8) focus on what is taught (and how) in specific content areas (literacy and mathematics). The distinction between generic and content-specific instructional practices is not always easy or useful to maintain. Nonetheless, a sufficient body of general knowledge about teaching practices has been developed to warrant reviewing them separately from classroom management approaches.

The literature sheds light on two problems that confront all teachers, regardless of the subject matter they are teaching:[1]

---

1. Much of the pertinent research, in fact, takes neither management nor instructional strategy as a primary focus, but instead provides important insights on

(1) *Instructional strategy:* How to arrange learning tasks, convey instruction to students, and facilitate the learning activities of groups and individuals.

(2) *Classroom management*: How to create and maintain order.

The concept of "management" in the classroom is intimately connected to instruction; the relationship works both positively and negatively. Put simply, effective instruction cannot occur without a minimum degree of order, and order cannot be maintained without a viable instructional program that keeps students engaged. As one scholar put it, "good management implies good instruction, and vice versa" (Brophy, 1982), but the relationship between the two is not completely symmetrical. For learning purposes, all students ideally should be fully engaged in the task at hand, while order often exists with a fair amount of "passive nonengagement" (Doyle, 1986a). Nonetheless, the reciprocal relationship is a powerful one: order is necessary to get work accomplished, but the way work gets organized is often determined by the demands of maintaining order. Effective classroom management thus involves cooperation with the teacher's agenda, rather than a simple absence of chaos.

My focus is on instructional and management approaches that appear to work well with disadvantaged populations, to the extent that evidence exists to support such claims. Although all teachers face structural problems of management and instructional organization, those who deal with concentrations of disadvantaged students are likely to encounter particular challenges. For this reason, I attempt here to delineate the processes in all classrooms, with a view toward isolating those factors that might be more pronounced in settings for pupils "at risk."

---

them through the investigation of other variables, such as particular teacher behaviors or the pattern of communication. As a result, the studies described here come from a variety of different theoretical perspectives.

CHARACTERISTICS OF CLASSROOMS SERVING DISADVANTAGED STUDENTS

Several features exist in every classroom regardless of size, grade level, or student characteristics (Doyle, 1977, 1980). These elements, which create structural constraints on what occurs in these settings, include the following:

- *Multidimensionality.* Classrooms are places where many things go on at different levels, with a limited amount of resources and an unlimited range of individual preferences and personal objectives. Choices must be made constantly.
- *Simultaneity.* A lot of things happen at once, and teachers are responsible for tracking as many of these as possible.
- *Immediacy.* The pace of events is very rapid, and teachers have little time to reflect before reacting to the constant demands of an ever-changing context.
- *Unpredictability.* Much of what happens in classrooms is unexpected; it is never possible to determine in advance how students will react to planned events, and there are continual distractions and interruptions.
- *Publicness.* All classroom events happen in front of an audience, with clear implications for students' perceptions of teachers' management skills when mistakes are made, along with the attendant likelihood of contagious disruption.
- *History.* Classes meet regularly over a period of time and accumulate patterns of interaction (often set early in the year) that tend to influence future events.

All of these interactional factors take place in a structural environment that is generally beyond the control of the participants, with certain restrictions on physical space. Although spatial arrangements have shown little correlation with achievement patterns, there is some evidence that density and "traffic design" influence attitudes and behavior (Silverstein, 1979; Weinstein, 1979).

Not all classrooms have the same number of individuals in them, but these variations in class size do not have clear implications for instruction. One research review asserts that achievement gains are most apparent when the class consists of ten to twenty students (Glass

& Smith, 1978), and Cooper (1986) showed that class size may be a more significant determinant of achievement in low-SES/low-ability classrooms than in others. Others find such direct correlations misleading: one view holds that the effects of class size are important only in that they constrain group formation and, as a result, instructional organization (Barr & Dreeben, 1983). From this perspective, class size by itself is not as significant as the size of the low-aptitude contingent in the group. Thus, both physical space and class size may be variables that are either facilitating or limiting, depending on other class characteristics.

Classrooms that serve disadvantaged students share all of these structural characteristics, but they are likely to be marked in varying degrees by conditions that pose particular management and organizational challenges to the teacher. These conditions are most pronounced in classrooms serving high concentrations of these children, especially in inner-city settings:

- *The physical condition.* The appearance of such classrooms tends not to be good, and the equipment within such rooms often shows the effects of restricted maintenance budgets or vandalism.
- *Instructional materials.* Limited resources are also reflected in poor and inadequate teaching materials (textbooks, supplies, audiovisual equipment).
- *Proportion of nonmainstream students.* The classroom population tends to have a high proportion of nonmainstream students, thus raising issues of cross-cultural communication and minority-majority relations for both teachers and students.
- *Student diversity.* The mixture of student abilities, ethnic/linguistic backgrounds, and special needs is often extremely diverse, and becomes more so at higher grade levels (unless tracking or other forms of homogeneous grouping intervene) as the achievement gap widens.
- *Use of supplementary services.* Students in the classroom typically receive some of their instruction in one or more supplementary rooms, located elsewhere in the school building.
- *Variability in the classroom population.* The cast of characters on any given day, and across the year, is variable, because of relatively high student and teacher absentee rates, student mobility, and teacher turnover.

Although there is much variation across classrooms serving disadvantaged students, it is reasonable to assert that teachers and learners alike face a more difficult job in these settings. The learning environment is likely to be less predictable, more multidimensional, with more immediate and adverse consequences for ineffective instructional or management approaches.

WHAT TEACHERS DO TO ORGANIZE AND DELIVER INSTRUCTION

In organizing and delivering instruction, teachers do at least the following: (1) arrange the grouping of students (if, indeed, they establish subgroups within the classroom), (2) structure participation and communication, (3) adopt an approach to delivering lessons, and (4) structure academic tasks for students. Together, these constitute the generic instructional "strategy" underlying the teachers' attempts to achieve instructional goals. (Other strategic decisions are more content-specific, as discussed in Chapters 4 and 8.)

The teacher may not use the same instructional strategy for all members of the class. Consequently, teachers must always consider how much, and how, to adapt the strategy to student differences—a crucial set of decisions in situations where student differences are pronounced, as in many classes serving disadvantaged students. In addition, teachers may alter their strategies according to subject matter, learning objective, and stage within the process of pursuing a specific learning objective. Scholars have examined these processes extensively and have often directed their research toward issues related to teaching disadvantaged students.

Instructional strategies are both a way of conveying curriculum and a tool for managing order. The need to maintain order—under a variety of circumstances—influences decisions about instructional organization in many ways. There are also a number of external constraints at work in designing instruction that have clear repercussions on the resulting curriculum. The following are instructional choices that are controlled by the teacher.

Grouping for Instruction

One of the most common ways of designing instruction to meet the diverse needs of the student population is to divide the class into instructional groups of various kinds. In the United States, this practice occurs on a number of institutional levels: by the formation of homogeneous classes, by tracking into college preparatory and general curricula, by the establishment of separate academic and vocational secondary schools. Of most interest here for elementary and middle grades is the use of within-class instructional groups, with an emphasis on the implications for low-achieving students.

Ability grouping has a long historical tradition in U.S. schooling and typically has been justified by two assumptions: that better instruction is achieved by reducing diversity in the target group, and that homogeneous groups are better suited to individualized instruction (Barr & Dreeben, 1983). Whereas there has always been controversy over the social consequences of "tracking" (sorting age cohorts into groups that experience different curricula), there has been less resistance to the notion of within-class sorting.

Many observers question the efficacy of within-class ability grouping, from the standpoint of low-achieving students. Because disadvantaged students fall disproportionately into the low-achievement category in typical schools, these concerns are especially germane. Most of the concern over the effects of ability grouping derives from the assumption that different groups receive different kinds—and perhaps quality—of instruction. There are more implications of grouping, as well, for instructional groups are a primary means by which students evaluate and rank each other (Cohen, 1984). Thus, the effects of low-ability groupings extend well beyond the specific learning tasks and help determine the students' perceived academic competence and status among peers. Ultimately, their possibilities for peer interaction are affected, which, in turn, limits the kinds of learning experiences students have.

In terms of more direct effects on achievement, the literature is difficult to summarize because of the enormous variety of variables analyzed and types of group situations chosen for investigation. However, there is a fair amount of consensus regarding the negative effects of tracking over the long term on the achievement, self-esteem, and educational aspirations of low-ability students (Gamorans, 1987; Oakes, 1985). Researchers who have summarized a variety of evidence have reached mixed conclusions about ability grouping in the earlier grades. One review finds positive effects of ability grouping on mathematics achievement for low achievers, though inconclusive results for reading (Slavin, 1987). On the other hand, a review of 217 studies of both tracking and within-class grouping found that the slight evidence for the improvement of high-ability students in grouped situations was more than offset by the negative results for middle and low-achieving students (Persell, 1977). Reviews of papers on within-class grouping agree with this assessment (Hallinan, 1984; Wilkinson, 1986).

The reasons for this result are less clear. Reasons suggested by researchers include the fact that there is often a failure to adjust materials and strategies to the various levels as much as might be theoretically possible (Johnson, 1970), and that, although misclassifications often occur, group placement tends to be permanent rather than flexible (Good & Brophy, 1984). Some research (e.g., McDermott, 1976; Eder, 1981; Alpert, 1974; Allington, 1983) concludes that students' learning is limited in some degree by the kind of instruction they receive in low-ability groups (see Chapter 4 for a more extended discussion of this point with regard to reading instruction). The ultimate question, for which there is no satisfactory resolution, is this: Is the restricted teaching that low-achieving students receive in ability-grouped instruction *appropriate* to their level of proficiency (Wilkinson, 1986)? There seems little doubt that many aspects of the curriculum that are currently considered desirable, especially involving higher-order thinking skills (see Chapters 4 and 8), are systematically excluded from the curriculum offered low-ability groups.

Structuring Participation and Communication

Because speech is the medium through which much teaching and responding take place, the amount of learning that occurs in the classroom depends to a great extent on the way the teacher structures verbal participation—that is, defines the rights and obligations of participants with respect to who can say what, when, and to whom (Cazden, 1986). Relevant research has concentrated on the relative balance of "teacher talk" and "student talk," the quality of communication, teacher questioning, and teachers' reactions to student responses. Additional work has examined how students determine the implicit rules for appropriate speech.

One aspect of classroom communication that has been investigated in depth is the amount and kind of "teacher talk." It has become common wisdom that, in most classrooms, teacher talk accounts for more than half of normal interaction; this in turn means that each pupil generally speaks for less than 1/30 of the time the teacher spends speaking. Attempts to correlate the amount of talk to outcomes such as achievement have had very mixed results. After reviewing dozens of studies, Dunkin and Biddle (1974) concluded that the quantity of teacher talk in itself constitutes an extremely weak variable, and more attention needs to be paid to the quality of this talk.

Research on the quality of classroom communication suggests that teachers' interaction patterns vary with the context (small group vs. whole class, etc.) (Levine & Mann, 1981), and that their affective reactions to students help determine which students get called on most often (Carew & Lightfoot, 1979). Some rather consistent findings demonstrate that the ability level of the student is a factor in how much interaction takes place: teachers call on high achievers more often and tend to give them a longer time to respond (Rowe, 1969). Research on the rates of interaction between the teacher and both high- and low-ability students (Brophy & Good, 1970) found that, whereas there were few differences in *quantity* of talk, the *quality* varied considerably: teachers were more likely to (1) praise high achievers, (2) criticize low achievers, (3) persevere with high achievers who answered "I don't know," and (4) give up more easily on the same response from a low achiever. Later work (Good & Brophy, 1984), however, indicates that there is considerable variation among teachers in this kind of differential treatment.

Some evidence links the number, type, and timing of teacher questions to academic learning outcomes. Although, once again, attempts to correlate achievement directly to types of questions (fact vs. complex, etc.) have shown inconclusive results (Dunkin & Biddle, 1974), there is some agreement that the frequency of questions is related to learning (Brophy & Evertson, 1976; Soar, 1973). This relationship may be due to the fact that high rates of academic questions imply good instructional organization and management, as well as the probability that active teaching, rather than simple presentation of information, is taking place (Good & Brophy, 1984). These authors have reviewed research on teacher questioning and have compiled some guidelines based on the work of Grossier (1964):

Good questions are clear, purposeful, brief, natural and adaptable to the level of the class, and thought provoking. Types of questions to avoid because they tend to lead to nonproductive student responses include (1) yes-no questions, (2) tugging questions (pumping the student when he/she doesn't know the answer), (3) guessing questions, and (4) leading questions (rhetorical: "Don't you agree?"). Research also shows that wait time after questions is generally too short, and that it should optimally be extended from the average one second to three to five seconds (Rowe, 1974). This practice appears especially significant in achieving higher-level cognitive outcomes, and for generally maximizing student engagement (Tobin & Capie, 1982). However, prescribing a particular length of wait-time is probably less important than tailoring the wait-time to the complexity of the questions asked. Moreover, the wait-time pattern across a set of questions related to an intended learning outcome is more meaningful than the wait-time for any particular questions.

Teachers' reactions to student responses to questions depend to some extent on pupil socioeconomic status (SES) (Brophy & Good, 1986). Although feedback is important, it is generally not necessary to praise correct answers, since this may be intrusive. However, when praise is useful, it is usually specific rather than global and is geared toward anxious, low-SES students rather than more independent, assertive, or high-SES students.

Participation rules are not necessarily communicated explicitly (Erickson & Shultz, 1977). Research on "contextualization cues"—the ways in which participants (and researchers) determine the implicit rules for appropriate speech—has laid the foundation for a number of studies on conflicting communication styles among cultural subgroups. Differences have been observed in such behaviors as children's ways of showing attention and understanding through nonverbal behavior such as gaze and nodding (Erickson, 1979) and differences in the ways turn-taking rules are understood (Watson-Gegeo & Boggs, 1977). This line of research is particularly important in investigating disjunctures between home and school; it sheds light on how some cultural differences may interfere with students' ability to perform academic tasks.

These aspects of classroom communication—teacher questioning, teacher reaction to student responses, and contextualization cues—are the components of conversations that take place between students and teachers, or among students. Note that the research reviewed here leaves out one important factor: the content of classroom discourse. Research that is more grounded in particular subject areas argues that sustained discourse that engages students in particular issues or questions of content is an extremely important part of effective instruction (see Chapters 4 and 8).

Adopting an Approach to Delivery of Lessons

There have always been debates over which instructional delivery approaches are most effective: whole-class recitations, individualized seatwork, small-group instruction. Not surprisingly, there are no clear answers; instead, the evidence seems to point to a more general conclusion: regardless of the type of instruction, the quantity of time spent pursuing academic work is the key component of achievement (Brophy & Good, 1986). Although the significant variables are content coverage and academically engaged minutes, a number of instructional options may achieve these ends (Rosenshine, 1979).

There is a fair amount of data on the relationship between engagement and the instructional arrangements in "typical" classrooms. Gump's (1967) study of a third grade found that engagement was highest for students in teacher-led small groups, and least for pupil presentations; in between were recitations, tests, and teacher presentations, which in turn were higher in involvement than supervised or unsupervised seatwork. Kounin (1970) found that involvement was highest in recitations and lowest in seatwork; studies reviewed by Rosenshine (1983) show similar differences between recitations and seatwork and demonstrate further that involvement during seatwork is even lower in classes where it is used often. Croll and Moses (1988) found in observations of thirty-two classrooms that classes that had higher levels of whole-class interaction had higher levels of engagement at all times, including individualized segments.

Four delivery approaches have received considerable attention because they purport to both encourage high levels of engagement and offer special benefits for disadvantaged students: mastery learning, direct instruction, cognitive modeling and explicit teaching, and cooperative and team learning. Their actual payoff for disadvantaged students is a matter of considerable debate. Moreover, the ultimate value of engagement depends on the instructional objectives and academic tasks in which students are engaged.

Mastery Learning. The approach known as "mastery learning" has provoked some controversy in recent years. This approach, which features cycles of teaching, testing, reteaching, and retesting, was designed specifically with low achievers in mind. Although some studies show that mastery learning does increase the amount of basic skills learned (Block & Burns, 1976; Guskey & Gates, 1985), many questions surround this conclusion. For example, most of the results are shown for short lesson units (a week or less). Furthermore, it does not appear that the goal of reducing time required to learn higher-level skills is actually achieved, and the approach seems far more difficult to orchestrate in inner-city schools with high student-teacher ratios, high absenteeism, and less time for teacher planning (Brophy, 1986). The main problem with mastery learning may be that the approach involves too much time working with materials and too little time working with teachers (Brophy, personal communication).

Direct Instruction. The most heated debate in this area revolves around the role of "direct instruction" approaches in increasing student achievement. Simply put, direct instruction means that (1) tasks are carefully structured, (2) students are explicitly told in small steps how to accomplish the tasks, (3) students are guided through the process and given a number of opportunities to practice the skills, and (4) assessment and feedback are frequent and consistent (Doyle, 1983). A number of researchers believe that this is the best system for all students, and particularly for disadvantaged students. I use the term to refer to a class of teaching approaches that derive from the original Follow Through model of the same name.

There are reasons for doubting that this category of approach handles all instructional goals equally well. A number of researchers (e.g., papers by Calfee, Doyle, Romberg, and Zumwalt in Williams, Richmond, & Mason, 1986) express concern over the level of skills learned in this format, and whether or not such skills are likely to transfer to more independent strategies. Other evidence suggests that improvements in students' conceptual abilities are positively correlated with opportunities to work with others, to use trial and error, and to make mistakes on their own, as opposed to lessons in which the teacher closely monitors the student's response (Cohen, 1988). Furthermore, the research showing positive gains through direct instruction is focused exclusively on achievement test scores, ignoring a broad range of educational goals such as creativity, independence, curiosity, self-concept, and attitude toward school and learning, all of which are better served by more varied approaches (Peterson, 1979).

While direct instruction is actually a teaching *method* and as such is not tied to any curriculum choice (such as discrete skill learning), its emphasis on drill and practice has made it particularly well suited to skill acquisition. It should not be confused, however, with the more general findings related to "active teaching" strategies derived from process-product research. This approach has found much more empirical support among researchers. Active teaching relies on a great deal of teacher-guided activity, but is adaptable to a variety of curriculum goals. While he does not encourage the use of the original direct instruction system, Brophy (1986) states that the best way to increase achievement gains for Chapter 1 students is to maximize the time spent in active teacher-led instruction and supervised practice. He argues that although variation in format is important, active teaching is always a key ingredient of effective instruction.

Cognitive Modeling and Explicit Teaching. Whereas an exclusive reliance on direct instruction approaches limits the kinds of learning that may occur, active and explicit teaching of certain things—especially mental processes—may have a particular payoff for disadvantaged students. Although the point is discussed in more detail with reference to particular content goals (e.g., reading comprehension, mathematics problem solving) in Chapters 4 and 8, I lay out the underlying generic argument here. Certain cognitive and linguistic capacities tend to develop universally; others are more dependent on exposure to particular types of modeling and experiences (Chapter 9). Included among the latter are a variety of schemata, "scripts," and verbal mediation strategies that are associated with success in school. Middle-class children are much more likely than others to learn these skills at home. Children from other backgrounds—in particular, working-class minority students—need to be explicitly taught the content and verbal strategies necessary to become part of the dominant culture in the school (Delpit, 1988). Instruction for disadvantaged students thus requires a great deal of "cognitive modeling," in which strategies for various types of learning tasks are demonstrated to students directly and related explicitly to other activities and skills. In this way, the emphasis is on developing metacognitive awareness as opposed to isolated, fragmented skill repetition. Although explicit teaching and modeling are necessary in the early stages of teaching a unit or skill, the teacher must eventually cede control of the learning process as students become more capable of applying modeled strategies and constructing knowledge on their own (Chapter 10).

Cooperative and Team Learning Arrangement. Unlike direct instruction, another category of approaches gives a substantial degree of control to students, who act as a resource for each other's learning. Much recent attention has been focused on cooperative and team learning, arrangements that generally involve heterogeneous groups who work together on tasks. There are different types of cooperative arrangements, some incorporating competitive elements, but as a class of instructional arrangements, several conclusions can be drawn about them. While such small groupings may be complex and difficult to orchestrate (Brophy & Good, 1986), they have been shown to have very positive effects on achievement, particularly for lower-ability students, and on achieving social goals such as intercultural understanding and friendliness in heterogeneous groups (Cohen, 1988). Evaluation of this type of arrangement over several years indicates that in many situations cooperative learning is more effective than traditional approaches in increasing basic achievement outcomes, including performance on standardized tests of mathematics, reading, and language (Slavin, 1987).

Structuring Academic Tasks

In addition to arranging groups, structuring participation, and adopting an instructional delivery approach, teachers structure the academic tasks their students perform. In this respect, decisions about instructional strategy merge with decisions about the content of instruction, which are discussed extensively in Chapters 4 and 8. At this point, however, it is useful to review the underlying conceptualizations, both to anticipate the later discussion and to provide further perspective on the debate about alternative instructional delivery approaches.

The Relationship between Academic Tasks and Teaching Approaches. The academic "task" is a useful analytical category for looking at instructional strategies and their outcomes (Doyle, 1983). In this view, understanding what students actually learn entails an examination of what they do to accomplish classroom tasks, in terms of both assignments given and the way the teacher evaluates outcomes. The concept of "task" comprises four aspects of instruction: (1) a goal state or end product, (2) a problem space or set of conditions and resources available to accomplish the task, (3) the operations involved in assembling and using resources to reach the goal or generate the product, and (4) the importance of the task in the overall work system of the class (Chapter 10). By using this concept in analyzing instructional strategies, it is possible to capture the *curriculum in motion* (Doyle, 1986c), as opposed to isolating discrete indicators of strategies that appear to correlate with achievement in all situations.

This notion—the idea of curriculum as a "bundle of tasks"—can be used to examine suitable strategies for varying levels of academic difficulty. Different types of academic tasks—memory, procedural or routine, comprehension or understanding, and opinion—make varying cognitive demands and may benefit from different teaching approaches. Although researchers have been trying to elucidate the various cognitive processes involved in expert writing, reading, or mathematics in order to teach these processes directly, there are a number of reasons why the original direct instruction model is inappropriate for many of these "skills." First, the cognitive processes involved are difficult to communicate in understandable ways to students at certain developmental or ability levels. Second, many of the relevant cognitive processes simply are not understood. Third, many important academic tasks, such as writing and mathematics, involve skills on a number of different levels simultaneously (Doyle, 1983). This does not mean, however, that active teacher-directed instruction has no place in teaching these cognitive processes.

Different instructional strategies may be equally successful in accomplishing the same learning task, according to Corno and Snow (1986). In their view, a variable amount of mediation is necessary in learning to either "short-circuit" or "activate" students' own cognitive processes, depending on ability levels. Low-ability students generally require more mediation for skill learning. Corno and Snow note that whereas teacher-directed instruction generally facilitates learning for disadvantaged students by mediating and controlling activities, heterogeneous groups like those in cooperative learning arrangements transfer some of the mediation function to higher-ability students, who then serve as "substitute teachers."

To the extent that teacher-directed instruction coincides with curricular choices favoring the teaching of discrete skills, much may be lost in excessively controlled instructional arrangements for lower-ability students (Doyle, 1979). Chapter 1 programs, in this view, are likely to concentrate on instructional processes at the expense of the knowledge domains necessary to give meaning to discrete skills. Although direct instruction might be appropriate, it is essential for teachers to create connections and help develop semantic frameworks and schemata that will form the basis for more independent thinking (Doyle, 1986b).

Negotiating Academic Demands. The teacher is not alone in structuring academic tasks. Classroom discourse and the expectations for academic work are jointly "constructed" by both students and teacher. A two-year study of participation structures found that students can in fact constrain the range of choices available to the teacher, thus helping to determine the way in which teaching is done (Dorr-Bremme, 1982). The same teacher was observed with different groups of children, and the behavior of the group had consequences for the way the teacher structured classroom talk. Compared to the first-year group, the teacher believed that the second-year group tended to discuss topics that she regarded as less valuable, and videotape analysis revealed that the teacher was more active with this group in directing topics, keeping the students on the subject, and intervening with questions and comments.

This is not to imply that a symmetrical relationship exists: that is, teachers have the responsibility and challenge to impose their instructional agenda on the class and elicit cooperation from students in so doing. Nonetheless, students are not passive actors in this process and their influence on the classroom agenda, though often subtle, can be substantial.

Recent "interpretive" anthropological research has provided a large amount of information about how meaning is constructed in the classroom and the ways in which students and teachers collectively alter the classroom situation by acting on their various understandings of the situation. This perspective has enabled us to see the subtle ways in which students themselves influence the amount and kind of academic work that is accomplished (Woods, 1978). Analyses of the "improvisational character" of the classroom indicate that much of what goes on there is beyond the control of the teacher and is contingent on many other variables, not the least of which is student cooperation (Erickson, 1982a; Griffin & Mehan, 1979).

Long-term ethnographic research (e.g., Everhart, 1983, in a junior high school) provides many insights into the dynamics of the constant negotiations over what gets learned. Although teachers may be primarily responsible for decisions about what constitutes "knowledge," students have almost infinite potential to offer resistance and thus determine the pacing of the curriculum and what actually gets accomplished.

One scholar (Doyle, 1983) offers a powerful argument about the way this process operates. All academic work is evaluated by the teacher in some way and therefore entails a certain amount of ambiguity and risk, with more difficult assignments occupying the high end of this continuum. Students tend to resist those at the high end ("understanding") and show a preference for the low end (memory, routine tasks). Students use order as a bargaining chip to lower the stakes in terms of the risk involved. They develop various strategies to minimize the risk to themselves: they restrict output, demand clarifications, or lobby for more lenient evaluation criteria.

Other studies confirm this phenomenon. Jorgenson (1977) found that students' behavior improved when they were assigned reading below their measured ability; Davis and McKnight (1976) observed high-ability secondary students who actively resisted attempts to increase academic demands; and Carter and Doyle (1982) found that tasks involving higher-order skills, such as expository writing, were much more difficult for the teacher to orchestrate while procedural tasks involving recall were conducted relatively smoothly.

This research has clear implications for instructional strategies in classrooms. For learning to occur, a delicate balance must be achieved between challenge and opportunities for success (Brophy, 1987). Moreover, if it is true that student pressure for stability and routine is usually evident (Doyle, 1983), then when management concerns are paramount, teachers are more likely to reduce academic demands in response. This is particularly significant for classes with high proportions of disadvantaged students, where successful management is likely to be more problematic.

ADAPTING INSTRUCTIONAL STRATEGIES TO STUDENT DIFFERENCES

Whatever the instructional strategy, many researchers have focused on the student characteristics that are seen to mediate effectiveness of instructional strategies. Differences in culture, ability, socioeconomic status, and language may have powerful effects on teaching and learning.

Once again, there is little consensus on the need to account for cultural and economic differences in designing instructional strategies. One view asserts that very little research has suggested the need for qualitatively different forms of instruction for students who differ in aptitude, achievement level, socioeconomic status, or learning style (Brophy, 1986). However, the same author also suggests that disadvantaged students may need more of what is recommended for all students: more control and structuring, more drill and practice, smaller steps, and more feedback. Others believe that disadvantaged students come to school without the cognitive schema to handle schoolwork, and therefore need more explicit metacognitive training (see Porter and Brophy, Chapters 5 and 9, respectively). Others (e.g., Passow, 1986) respond that far too little research attention has been directed toward understanding the types of differences that affect learning and that the literature that does exist points clearly to unique instructional needs.

This debate is highly complex and resists simple answers. Even among those researchers who emphasize the significance of differences, there is little agreement about how classroom practice should take them into account. There is no question that teachers themselves adapt their strategies to perceived differences among their students; some of this is necessary in any successful approach, and will often be based on experience rather than theory. In the case of reading groups, for example, it appears that teachers' differential treatment of high- and low-ability students is based on a mixture of teacher training, messages drawn from curriculum materials, and the received wisdom about what students need that is prevalent in "teachers' culture" (Cazden, 1986; Hargreaves, 1980). Skilled teachers appear to move constantly back and forth along a continuum of instructional mediation, depending on the perceived student need (Corno & Snow, 1986).

In terms of direct correlations with achievement, a number of studies show differences in instructional effectiveness according to student SES (Brophy & Good, 1986). These studies have focused on a limited range of variables and have been used to justify direct instruction approaches.

- In Soar and Soar's (1979) study of high-SES students in grades three and six, achievement correlated positively with indirect instruction for high-SES students, while a low-SES fifth-grade class showed higher achievement as a result of recitation, drill, and narrow teacher questions.
- Stallings and Kaskowitz's (1974) evaluation of Follow Through classes showed that greater gains were made by students who spent more time working with the teacher than on independent work.
- Brophy and Evertson (1974) found in the Texas Teacher Effectiveness Study that high-SES students needed intellectual stimulation, while low-SES students needed manageable assignments and supervision, the opportunity to answer a larger percentage of questions effectively, and an instructional strategy that emphasized smaller steps, practice, redundancy, and encouraging praise rather than challenge. However, they note that these findings do not represent a dichotomy but rather the need for different proportions of the same strategies. Thus, as low-SES students begin to function like high-SES students, it is necessary to adjust instructional methods accordingly.

This body of research has focused on other aspects of instruction besides delivery approach. In a study of junior high schools, Evertson, Anderson, Anderson, and Brophy (1980) found that greater gains for low-SES students corresponded to friendliness and acceptance on the part of the teacher, along with opportunities for self-expression. This finding is consistent with a growing body of literature on the need for a more personalized approach in educating disadvantaged students. A number of programs found to be unusually effective with this population have included efforts to make the student feel more at home in the school by helping teachers to understand students' cultural experiences and creating bonds between students, parents, and the school (Comer, 1988). Efforts by teachers to develop a familial atmosphere that promotes identification with the school and to relate to their students in individualized ways has a particularly important role in "personalizing" instruction (Chapter 9). Good teachers in minority communities establish meaningful interpersonal relationships that earn their students' respect while maintaining clear authority (Delpit, 1988).

The information available on those cultural differences that do not necessarily coincide with SES (such as ethnicity or native language) is more difficult to quantify, but there is an increasing awareness that they may need to be addressed in order for successful schooling to take place in a rapidly changing demographic climate (Erickson, 1982b).[2]

Knowledge about effective practice to improve performance of different cultural groups presents a difficult dilemma. Although many argue that we must understand how these differences affect achievement, there is always a possibility that such information will encourage more cultural stereotypes that may inhibit rather than facilitate learning. Pursued with good intentions, instructional differentiation may nonetheless result in curriculum differentiation—thus defeating a central goal of empowering disadvantaged students (Doyle, 1986b). The most important question remains whether differential treatment is helpful individualization or detrimental bias (Cazden, 1986). The larger issue, from this perspective, lies in examining programs that boost achievement through culturally appropriate strategies, thus alleviating the dissonance between home and school. It is not clear at this point precisely what the role of the school should be in maintaining such continuity, or where to break it in order to prepare students for the larger society.

WHAT TEACHERS DO TO FACILITATE ORDER

Research on classroom management, which has traditionally focused on disruptive student behavior out of the academic context in which it occurred, has increasingly shifted toward (1) a view of management and order as being closely connected to academic and instructional strategy and (2) "preventive" rather than "remedial" approaches to establishing orderly classrooms. There appears to be

---

2. According to recent estimates, the school-age population will be one-third minority by the year 2000 (ACE, 1988; Hodgkinson, 1985).

wide consensus nowadays that these perspectives hold the keys to effective classroom management.

The principal problem for the teacher is that of creating and sustaining an order in the classroom that is appropriate to the instructional goals being addressed. What constitutes "order" in classrooms is contingent on a number of factors: academic content, learning goals, instructional format. Teachers allow, for example, more unstructured interaction in subjects like social studies than in reading or mathematics (Stodolsky, 1981) and tend to intervene more often for misbehaviors in whole-class recitations than in reading groups (Gump, 1967). Different amounts of disruptive behavior tend to occur in various instructional arrangements. Silverstein (1979) found that inappropriate behaviors (such as unnecessary movement, shouting, and fighting) occurred more often during seatwork or silent reading than during whole-class formats, where disruption was relatively infrequent. Similarly, Kounin (1970) found that deviance occurred four times as often in seatwork as in recitations. The challenge for the teacher as classroom manager is to anticipate the situations in which disorder occurs, while allowing for order that is appropriate to the nature of the work being done.

Preventive and Remedial Approaches

Discussions of classroom management distinguish approaches aimed at forestalling inappropriate behavior from those that concentrate on remediating misbehaviors. The distinction derives in part from work over a decade ago that found no differences between good and poor managers in the types or prevalence of their behaviors aimed at handling disruptions (Kounin, 1970). Rather, the two groups differed in their capacity to establish a situation in which disruptive behaviors were unlikely to occur at all. A number of studies (e.g., Evertson & Emmer, 1982) have since confirmed this research, and the emphasis in both research and training has shifted definitively toward preventive group management and advance planning.

A prominent model of classroom management in this tradition revolves around the establishment of what is called the "primary vector"—a program of action in the classroom that includes a strong academic component (Doyle, 1986a). When the focus of interaction is on the substance of lessons, the primary vector is strong and the environment is orderly. When competing interests overrule the primary vector—as when instruction is poor or when students are either unable or unwilling to adapt to the level of the lesson—the teacher must work that much harder to restore order.

Occasionally, individual misbehaviors occur when the classroom is otherwise functioning smoothly, and teachers must respond to these as well. In Doyle's terms, misbehavior is any set of behaviors by one or more students that is perceived by the teacher to initiate a vector of action that competes with or threatens the primary vector of action at a given moment; such behaviors need to be dealt with, because they tend to be both public and contagious.

When behaviors that do not suit the task and context occur, teachers have a number of options. Many disciplinary "systems" have been developed in recent years, and teachers may be trained in one or more of them. Some reviews of one of the better-known systems—behavior modification—have suggested that the usefulness of such approaches as token economies and contingency management in normal classrooms is limited (Dunkin & Biddle, 1974; Lahey & Rubinoff, 1981). Because reinforcement techniques have been criticized for replacing intrinsic motivation with external rewards, the most positive directions for classroom management in this area involve systems for developing social skills and self-control (Brophy, 1982). One of the most effective ways of teaching these strategies is similar to that used for good instruction: teacher modeling of appropriate behaviors and ways of dealing with frustration and conflict (Chapter 9). However, good prevention may not obviate the need for remedial attention to disruptive behavior when it occurs; behavior modification strategies using home-based reinforcement or group contingencies, for example, can be effective when preventive strategies are insufficient.

There is very inconsistent evidence on other models designed to improve classroom discipline on an individual basis—for example, therapeutic interventions by schools as well as by the individual teacher, such as Teacher Effectiveness Training (T.E.T.) or Assertiveness Training. The important thing seems to be not what specific model or technique is used, but rather whether the teacher assumes responsibility for the discipline problems that arise and devises long-term, solution-oriented approaches to them (Brophy & Rohrkemper, 1981).

When and how teachers intervene during instances of misbehavior has consequences for overall management effectiveness. Successful managers are able to anticipate misbehavior and react appropriately early on (Emmer, Evertson, & Anderson, 1980). Successful interventions tend to be brief and do not interrupt the flow of interaction (Erickson & Mohatt, 1982). Attempts to investigate how teachers make their decisions to intervene show that these choices are made on the basis of knowledge of who is misbehaving, where the misbehavior is, and when it occurs; in short, responses are tailored to individual situations (Cone, 1978). Skillful teachers apparently learn the configuration of events in the classroom to enable them to make complex decisions about when to interrupt to repair order (Doyle, 1986a). In this way, effective interventions are inserted into the flow of the activity without becoming themselves distractions and detracting from the primary vector of classroom action.

Establishing and Maintaining Order

A range of activities appears to facilitate order in classrooms. One of the more negative ways in which order is maintained has been discussed above: negotiation with students to reduce academic demands. More constructive strategies are described below.

Research has increasingly demonstrated the importance of advance planning and organization in establishing a smoothly run classroom, and the early sessions of the school year are crucial in setting the stage (Ball, 1980; Doyle, 1979). An analysis of junior high and elementary classrooms has found that effective managers at both levels were more successful at establishing rules and procedures at the beginning of the year, and rules generally were part of concrete and explicit systems (Emmer et al., 1980). Successful managers lose little time in organizing, and have activities carefully planned even on the first day (Evertson & Emmer, 1982). Other studies indicate that when work systems were successfully established early in the year, by November teachers could devote more time to individual students while less successful managers were still focusing on disruptive behavior (Doyle, 1984).

In addition to early organization, a number of more ongoing teacher characteristics have been found to correlate with effective management and student engaged time. Kounin (1970) observed clear differences among teachers on a number of group management skills: (1) "withitness," in which teachers communicate to students that they are aware of all the various events that are happening at once; (2) "overlappingness," in which they respond to different simultaneous events; (3) smoothness and momentum of lessons; (4) group alerting and accountability; and (5) challenge arousal and variety in lesson materials. The importance of these behavioral dimensions has been reinforced by later research. For example, "withitness" appears to correlate positively with achievement (Brophy & Evertson, 1976); others (Copeland, 1983; Schumm, 1971) have found that situational awareness and "overlappingness" in teachers predict the acquisition of classroom management skills.

Creating "Definitions of the Situation"

For management techniques to be effective, students must have a clear understanding of the operating system at work. Teachers' success in maintaining an orderly and productive environment depends in part on creating and reinforcing a "definition of the situation" in which appropriate behavior is likely to occur.

This view has long been recognized by scholars studying classroom management. Waller's classic study (1932) of the sociology of teaching pointed to the importance of reciprocal meanings on the part of students and teachers: "We may see the whole process of personal and group conflict which centers about the school as a conflict of contradictory definitions of situations" (p. 297). From this perspective, the need for clarity and explicitness in organizing classroom rules makes eminent sense: it increases the likelihood that the various participants will understand order in consistent ways. A key to developing a workable definition of classroom order is for the teachers themselves to have what Spady and Mitchell (1979) call an "effective organizing perspective." Without such a consistent global view on the part of the teacher, it is unlikely that students will be cooperative.

This type of consistent understanding is important to achieve in all classrooms, but there may be particular problems in establishing it in classrooms serving disadvantaged students. From one perspective, order is held in place by a sufficient redundancy in the cues by which participants tell each other what is appropriate. A lack of congruence between these understandings is more likely when the teacher is a member of the majority group and the students' cultural background is different (Erickson, 1982a). Research on question-answer sequences in lessons demonstrates the possibility of miscommunication as a result of different cultural expectations about classroom discourse

(Mehan, 1979)—for example, in this study, students who offered and received help from one another were viewed by other students as "showing laudable concern for others" or as "cheating," depending on these students' cultural background. Other research demonstrates that the appropriateness of humor and mock aggression in talk depends on the different cultural assumptions of individuals engaged in conversation (Lein, 1975). In general, when students act on their definitions in ways that the teachers do not understand—both at the level of interaction and in broader assumptions about appropriate role relationships between adults and children—the teacher is likely to find their actions confusing or threatening, and this response in turn increases the likelihood of developing an adversarial relationship (Erickson, 1986).

EFFECTIVE CLASSROOM MANAGEMENT AND INSTRUCTION FOR DISADVANTAGED STUDENTS

The literature reviewed here shows that, in general, the most effective instructional strategies for all types of students simultaneously increase the amount of student engagement and establish order.

Effective Instructional Strategies

One attempt at summarizing the vast literature on instructional strategies (Brophy, 1986) has developed the following comprehensive list of what is known about effective instruction for disadvantaged students:

- The amount these students learn is related to the opportunity to learn, whether in time or content coverage.
- Achievement is maximized when teachers emphasize academic instruction as a major part of their role, expect students to learn, and allocate most of the available time in class to academic activities.
- Academically engaged time depends not only on allocated time but on effective management strategies.
- Students achieve more when they spend most of their time being

taught or supervised by teachers rather than working on their own or not working at all.

- Achievement is maximized when teachers not only actively present material to their students, but structure it by means of overviews, advance organizers, outlines, attention to main ideas, signalling transitions, and reviews.
- Achievement is maximized when content is logically sequenced and contains enough redundancy to allow linkages to be made between segments.
- Achievement is higher when teachers make clear presentations in precise language.
- Achievement is correlated with teacher enthusiasm in presenting material.
- Teacher questions should be reasonably difficult (approximately 75 percent correct response rate), with wait times geared to question complexity, and should involve all students in the early grades.
- In reacting to student responses, teachers should acknowledge correct answers, explain when answers are partially incorrect, attempt to elicit some response, and discourage irrelevant questions.
- Achievement is higher when seatwork assignments are varied and challenging, but appropriate for student ability.
- For smaller groups of disadvantaged students, such as in some Chapter 1 programs, individualized instruction may increase achievement.

The list serves to organize some salient points in a vast literature, but it has three important shortcomings. First, the list itemizes behaviors out of context of their instructional goals. It may be more appropriate for certain instructional goals for teachers to refrain from giving students advance organizers, outlines, and so forth. Second, all of these findings have used only achievement test gains as the outcome measure. A number of researchers have disputed the usefulness of this approach (Peterson, 1979; Zumwalt, 1986). Third, most of these conclusions are correlational, and in many ways it would be a mistake to assume one-way causality and develop teacher training or policy prescriptions based on these assumptions. Much of the evidence we have reviewed has emphasized the reciprocal influence of both teacher and students in classroom interaction, and many of these results may reflect far more complex, contextually contingent processes. For example, the research shows that frequency of teacher questions correlates positively with student achievement. It would be unfortunate to train all teachers in "frequent questioning" techniques when it may be true that high-achieving students cause teachers to ask more questions.

Effective Classroom Management

There is more consensus on what constitutes good management and how to achieve it than on effective instructional strategies. The most important conclusion that emerges from the research points to the significance of prevention over remediation. Research during the last twenty years has clearly established that some approaches are more effective than others and, in particular, that the key to successful management is *preventing problems before they occur* (Good & Brophy, 1984). The research summarized above also supports the following conclusions:

- Effective managers establish the rules and procedures of the classroom early in the year, and are more explicit in communicating them.
- Good managers consistently monitor compliance with rules.
- Good managers have more detailed and consistent accountability systems, keep better track of student assignments, and give clearer descriptions of the evaluation system.
- Good managers are clearer at communicating information, directions, and objectives.
- Good managers are also good instructional organizers in that they waste little time getting prepared or in transitions, keep the momentum in lessons, and maximize student engagement.
- Successful managers seem to "have eyes in the back of their heads," and demonstrate what Kounin categorized as "withit" and "overlapping" behaviors.
- Skillful managers are perceptive about classroom context and events and by using this information are able to develop activities that keep the flow going with minimal interruptions.

It is important to reemphasize in a discussion of effective management techniques what may appear obvious: that success does not depend entirely on teacher skills but is also a function of the characteristics and motivation of the students. Some researchers have attempted to measure the impact of student ability and interest in schoolwork directly. Metz (1978) analyzed interactions in high- and low-ability classes taught by the same teachers and found that there were more similarities in degree of order among different teachers working with students in the same track than in the same teacher working with different tracks. In other words, the student population had a clear influence on effectiveness. She also found that the tone of both high- and low-ability classes was set by a few active students, while the rest remained relatively passive.

That said, it is also clear that there are in fact differences among teachers who are given identical groups. For example, Campbell (1974) found marked differences in management success among the mathematics, science, and English teachers given the same low-ability group. Kounin (1983) found that student engagement in classes of the most successful managers was 98.7 percent, compared with a low of 25 percent for teachers who were struggling. In other words, some teachers are simply more effective at establishing an orderly environment, regardless of the student composition of the class.

Doyle (1986a) has summarized some of the important dynamics at work in typical well-managed classrooms:

- Classroom management is fundamentally a process of solving the problem of obtaining cooperation in classrooms rather than the problems of misbehavior or student engagement.
- Order in classrooms is defined by the strength and durability of the program of action embedded in the activities teachers and students engage in together as they accomplish work.
- A program of action, and thus classroom order, is jointly constructed by teachers and students in settings of enormous complexity.
- Programs of action in classroom activities are defined by both the rules for social participation and the demands for academic work.
- Order in classrooms is context specific and held in place by balancing a large array of forces and processes.
- The key to a teacher's success in management appears to be his or her (a) understanding of the likely configuration of events in a classroom and (b) skill in monitoring and guiding activities in light of this information. [Pp. 423–424]

Finally, it would be inappropriate to assume that orderly classes are always instructionally effective. Strategies that maximize order, although effective in terms of teacher survival, are all too common with large proportions of disadvantaged students. Previously mentioned research on interactions in reading groups shows that in some cases certain management tactics, such as prompting performance and group alerting, interfere with low-ability students' possibilities of learning to read (Allington, 1980; McDermott, 1976). Brophy (1983) and Good (1981) have each shown how low-ability students are given fewer opportunities to respond in whole-class formats. It seems apparent that some teachers may address management concerns by excluding potentially disruptive students from the action entirely; in these situations, well-managed classrooms are not necessarily high-achieving classrooms even when overall engagement rates are high (Doyle, 1986a). Moreover, it is clear that disadvantaged students disproportionately suffer from such compromises.

SUMMARY: PRINCIPLES GUIDING EFFECTIVE INSTRUCTION IN CLASSROOMS SERVING DISADVANTAGED STUDENTS

Although there is much that is not understood about effective instruction in classrooms serving disadvantaged students, several themes emerge from the literature reviewed in this chapter. The themes can be grouped under three headings: (1) the role of teacher-directed instruction, (2) differential treatment of student differences, and (3) the academic basis for classroom management and instructional strategies.

The Role of Teacher-Directed Instruction

A conventional wisdom has grown up over the last several decades regarding the most effective instructional strategies for disadvantaged students, and especially for the low-achieving members of this student population. Based in large measure on research regarding direct instruction approaches, teaching strategies that combine an active, directive role for teachers with a curriculum emphasizing discrete, sequential basic skills have come to be seen as effective for this student population. These strategies are characterized by (1) a directive role for teachers, who remain in continuous control of student learning activities; (2) careful structuring of tasks to present material in small, incremental steps combined with rapid pacing of instruction; (3) explicit teaching of new skills with a great deal of guidance by the teacher; (4) lots of opportunity to practice skills; and (5) frequent assessment and feedback to students.

The literature suggests the following conclusion about this class of instructional strategies: While they appear to produce measurable increases in disadvantaged students' achievement, at least in basic skills, they may have important limitations in the range and richness of curriculum they can convey. This category of approaches appears to solve the problem of obtaining student cooperation in the classroom by maintaining tight control over learning activities. However, as a result, students need to exercise their own judgment less and have less need to think learning tasks through for themselves. As a result, this approach to teaching may well limit student learning of higher-order skills.

These limitations do not appear to apply to the broader category of "active teaching." Active, explicit teaching may be especially useful in many situations; for example, in modeling cognitive processes, in communicating school culture to students who are unfamiliar with it, in the initial stages of establishing classroom order, and so on. In addition, active teaching can be usefully complemented by approaches that encourage (and structure) students' interaction with each other (e.g., in structured cooperative learning arrangements), which can bring about effective learning of basic skills, along with higher-order skills and affective/social skills. The important thing appears to be to bring about the right balance of teacher direction and student direction.

All told, the evidence suggests that instructional approaches that include a large amount of teacher guidance and involvement in student learning are well suited to a variety of curricular goals. By contrast with other classes of approaches that minimize teacher-directed instruction—for example, those that rely on independent interaction with materials—active teaching has been shown to be more effective.

Differential Treatment of Student Differences

The presence of disadvantaged students in classrooms brings two kinds of student differences into play that raise profound questions for teachers as they design and implement instructional strategies. First, how should the instructional strategy accommodate the students' differences in linguistic and cultural background? Second, how does the teacher instruct the large numbers of students from this population who do not achieve well in their academic work? The literature offers only partial answers. The primary themes are these:

- Instructional strategies that make some effort to bridge the gaps between student background and the school culture have a better chance of success. For example, "personalizing" teaching, which communicates to students care and respect for their backgrounds, works particularly well.
- Ability grouping of low-achieving students appears to be dysfunctional for many of them (although it may facilitate the teaching of higher-achieving children)—it too easily becomes a permanent tracking mechanism, whether or not it is intended to be that.
- Without necessarily being aware of it, teachers tend to act differently with lower-achieving students, and their actions (e.g., types of questions asked, frequency of questions, nature of response to student answers) tend to limit these students' instructional experience.
- Too much differentiation of the curriculum to accommodate the special needs and characteristics of a particular group of students risks inviting stereotyping and limiting the curriculum.

Academic Basis for Classroom Management and Instructional Strategies

The point may seem obvious, but a generation of research on generic instructional variables (on which I have concentrated in this chapter) may have obscured the following principle: The success of instructional strategies and of approaches to classroom management cannot be divorced from the academic goals and content of instruction. This theme has more specific implications:

- Maintaining appropriate order in the classroom learning environment depends in part on the academic tasks in which students are engaged and on a "preventive" approach to establishing order from the outset. The nature of academic tasks affects how much students are challenged and also prompts them to negotiate with the teacher over the difficulty of academic demands, which poses a problem of order for the teacher.

- Instructional delivery approaches influence the structure of curriculum that can be taught: mastery learning and direct instruction approaches, for example, lend themselves more readily to the teaching of discrete "basic" skills, which they seem to do with some efficiency, than to helping students develop their analytic abilities or other "higher-order" skills (this theme is explored more extensively and specifically in Chapters 4 and 8, which deal with particular content areas).

But the most important implication is that effective instruction cannot be reflected adequately in generically framed management or strategy variables. We can gain from this literature some overarching principles about teacher behavior and the arrangement of classes that affect learning in the classroom. But beyond that, we can say little about the effective teaching of reading, writing, or mathematics, without reference to the content considerations discussed in other chapters of this book.

A central finding of the literature reviewed in this chapter provides a good example of this point. The research makes it clear that maximizing engaged learning time is a major determinant of student achievement. Thus, the research establishes what can be thought of as a basic condition of learning. But much of the research reviewed here makes little attempt to answer the question: Engaged in what? Engagement in repetitive discrete skill-building leads to learning experiences and outcomes that are profoundly different from engagement in a varied and more challenging curriculum aimed at a variety of curricular goals. The challenge for future research lies in connecting what has been learned about basic conditions for learning with the emerging insights into the teaching of particular kinds of content.

REFERENCES

ACE (American Council on Education). (1988). *One-third of a nation*. Washington, DC: Author.

Allington, R. L. (1980). Teacher interruption behaviors during primary grade oral reading. *Journal of Educational Psychology, 72,* 371–377.

Allington, R. L. (1983). The reading instruction provided readers of different reading abilities. *Elementary School Journal, 83*(5), 549– 559.

Alpert, J. (1974). Teacher behavior across ability groups: A consideration of mediation of Pygmalion effects. *Journal of Educational Psychology, 66,* 348–353.

Ball, S. J. (1980). Initial encounters in the classroom and the process of establishment. In P. Woods (Ed.), *Pupil strategies: Explorations in the sociology of the school.* London: Croom Helm.

Barr, R., & Dreeben, R. (1983). *How schools work.* Chicago: University of Chicago Press.

Block, J., & Burns, R. (1976). Mastery learning. In L. Shulman (Ed.), *Review of research in education* (Vol. 4). Itaska, IL: Peacock.

Brophy, J. (1982). *Classroom organization and management.* East Lansing, MI: Institute for Research on Teaching.

Brophy, J. (1983). Research on the self-fulfilling prophecy and teacher expectations. *Journal of Educational Psychology, 75*(5), 631–661.

Brophy, J. (1986). Research linking teacher behavior to student achievement: Potential implications for Chapter 1 students. In B. I. Williams, P. A. Richman, & B. J. Mason (Eds.), *Designs for compensatory education: Conference proceedings and papers.* Washington, DC: Research and Evaluation Associates.

Brophy, J. (1987). Synthesis of research on strategies for motivating students to learn. *Educational Leadership, 45*(2), 40–48.

Brophy, J., & Evertson, C. (1974). *Process-product correlations in the Texas Teacher Effectiveness Study: Final report* (Research Report 74–4). Austin, TX: University of Texas, R&D Center for Teacher Education.

Brophy, J., & Evertson, P. (1976). *Learning from teaching: A developmental perspective.* Boston: Allyn & Bacon.

Brophy, J., & Good, T. (1970). Teachers' communications of differential expectations for children's classroom performance: Some behavioral data. *Journal of Educational Psychology, 61,* 365–374.

Brophy, J., & Good, T. (1986). Teacher behavior and student achievement. In M. C. Wittrock (Ed.), *Handbook of research on teaching* (3rd ed.). New York: Macmillan.

Brophy, J., & Rohrkemper, M. (1981). The influence of problem ownership on teachers' perceptions of and strategies for coping with student problems. *Journal of Educational Psychology, 73*(3), 295–311.

Calfee, R. (1986). Curriculum and instruction: Reading. In B. I. Williams, P. A. Richmond, & B. J. Mason (Eds.), *Designs for compensatory education: Conference proceedings and papers.* Washington, DC: Research and Evaluation Associates.

Campbell, J. R. (1974). Can a teacher really make the difference? *School Science and Mathematics, 74,* 657–666.

Carew, J. V., & Lightfoot, S. L. (1979). *Beyond bias: Perspectives on classrooms.* Cambridge, MA: Harvard University Press.

Carter, K., & Doyle, W. (1982, March). *Variations in academic tasks in high- and average-ability classes.* Paper presented at the annual meeting of the American Educational Research Association, New York.

Cazden, C. (1986). Classroom discourse. In M. C. Wittrock (Ed.), *Handbook of research on teaching* (3rd ed.). New York: Macmillan.

Cohen, E. G. (1984). Talking and working together: Status, interaction, and learning. In P. Peterson, L. C. Wilkinson, & M. Hallinan (Eds.), *The social context of instruction: Group organization and group processes.* New York: Academic Press.

Cohen, E. G. (1988). *On the sociology of the classroom.* Stanford, CA: Center for Educational Research.

Comer, J. P. (1988). Educating poor minority children. *Scientific American, 259*(5), 42–48.

Cone, R. (1978, March). *Teachers' decisions in managing student behavior.* Paper presented at the annual meeting of the American Educational Research Association, Toronto.

Cooper, H. M. (1986). Chapter 1 programs reduce student-to-instructor ratios but do reduced ratios affect achievement? In B. I. Williams, P. A. Richmond, & B. J. Mason (Eds.), *Designs for compensatory education: Conference proceedings and papers.* Washington, DC: Research and Evaluation Associates.

Copeland, W. D. (1983, April). *Classroom management and student teachers' cognitive abilities: A relationship.* Paper presented at the annual meeting of the American Educational Research Association, Montreal.

Corno, L., & Snow, R. E. (1986). Adapting teaching to individual differences among learners. In M. C. Wittrock (Ed.), *Handbook of research on teaching* (3rd ed.). New York: Macmillan.

Croll, P., & Moses, D. (1988). Teaching methods and time on task in junior classrooms. *Educational Research, 30*(2), 90–97.

Davis, R. B., & McKnight, C. (1976). Conceptual, heuristic, and algorithmic approaches in mathematics teaching. *Journal of Children's Mathematical Behavior, 1*(Suppl. 1), 271–286.

Delpit, L. D. (1988). The silenced dialogue: Power and pedagogy in educating other people's children. *Harvard Educational Review, 58*(3), 280–298.

Dorr-Bremme, D. W. (1982). *Behaving and making sense: Creating social organization in the classroom.* Unpublished doctoral dissertation, Harvard University (UMI # 82-23, 203).

Doyle, W. (1977). Paradigms for research on teacher effectiveness. In L. S. Shulman (Ed.), *Review of Research in Education, 5,* 163–169.

Doyle, W. (1979). Making managerial decisions in classrooms. In D. Duke (Ed.), *Classroom management.* Seventy-eighth Yearbook of the National Society for the Study of Education, Part 2. Chicago: University of Chicago Press.

Doyle, W. (1980). *Classroom management.* West Lafayette, IN: Kappa Delta Pi.

Doyle, W. (1983). Academic work. *Review of Educational Research, 53,* 159–199.

Doyle, W. (1984). How order is achieved in classrooms: An interim report. *Journal of Curriculum Studies, 16*(3), 259–277.

Doyle, W. (1986a). Classroom organization and management. In M. C. Wittrock (Ed.), *Handbook of research on teaching* (3rd ed.). New York: Macmillan.

Doyle, W. (1986b). Vision and reality: A reaction to issues in curriculum and instruction for compensatory education. In B. I. Williams, P. A. Richmond, & B. J. Mason (Eds.), *Designs for compensatory education: Conference proceedings and papers.* Washington, DC: Research and Evaluation Associates.

Doyle, W. (1986c). Content representation in teachers' definitions of academic work. *Journal of Curriculum Studies, 18,* 365–379.

Duke, D. (1982). *Helping teachers manage classrooms.* Alexandria, VA: Association for Supervision and Curriculum Development.

Dunkin, M. J., & Biddle, B. J. (1974). *The study of teaching.* New York: Holt, Rinehart & Winston.

Eder, D. (1981). Ability grouping as a self-fulfilling prophecy: A microanalysis of teacher-student interaction. *Sociology of Education, 54,* 151–173.

Emmer, E., Evertson, C., & Anderson, L. (1980). Effective classroom management at the beginning of the school year. *Elementary School Journal, 80* 219–231.

Erickson, F. (1979). Talking down: Some cultural sources of miscommunication in inter-racial interviews. In A. Wolfgang (Ed.), *Research in non-verbal communication.* New York: Academic Press.

Erickson, F. (1982a). Classroom discourse as improvisation: Relationships between academic task structure and social participation structures in lessons. In L. C. Wilkinson (Ed.), *Communicating in the classroom.* New York: Academic Press.

Erickson, F. (1982b). Taught cognitive learning in its immediate environment: A neglected topic in the anthropology of education. *Anthropology and Education Quarterly, 13,* 149–180.

Erickson, F. (1986). Qualitative methods in research on teaching. In M. C. Wittrock (Ed.), *Handbook of research on teaching* (3rd ed.). New York: Macmillan.

Erickson, F., & Mohatt, G. (1982). Cultural organization of participation structures in two classrooms of Indian students. In G. Spindler (Ed.), *Doing the ethnography of schooling.* New York: Holt, Rinehart & Winston.

Erickson, F., & Shultz, J. (1977). When is a context? Some issues and methods in the analysis of social competence. *Quarterly Newsletter of the Institute for Comparative Human Development, 1*(2), 5– 10.

Everhart, R. C. (1983). *Reading, writing, and resistance: Adolescence and labor in a junior high school.* Boston: Routledge & Kegan Paul.

Evertson, C., Anderson, C., Anderson, L., & Brophy, J. (1980). Relationships between classroom behaviors and student outcomes in junior high mathematics and English classes. *American Educational Research Journal, 17,* 43–60.

Evertson, C., & Emmer, E. (1982). Effective management at the beginning of the school year in junior high classes. *Journal of Educational Psychology, 74,* 485–498.

Gamorans, A. (1987). The stratification of high school learning opportunities. *Sociology of Education, 60*(3), 135–155.

Glass, G., & Smith, M. (1978). *Meta-analysis of research on the relationship between class size and achievement.* Boulder, CO: University of Colorado, Laboratory of Educational Research.

Good, T. (1981). Teacher expectation and student perceptions: A decade of research. *Educational Leadership, 38,* 415–422.

Good, T., & Brophy, J. (1984). *Looking in classrooms* (3rd ed.). New York: Harper & Row.

Griffin, P., & Mehan, H. (1979). Sense and ritual in classroom discourse. In F. Coulmas (Ed.), *Conversational routine: Explorations in standardized communication situations and prepatterned speech.* Janua Linguarum. The Hague: Moulton.

Grossier, P. (1964). *How to use the fine art of questioning.* New York: Teachers' Practical Press.

Gump, P. V. (1967). *The classroom behavior setting: Its nature and relation to student behavior (Final report)* (ERIC No. ED 015 515). Washington, DC: U.S. Office of Education, Bureau of Research.

Guskey, T. R., & Gates, S. L. (1985, March/April). *A synthesis of research on group-based mastery learning programs.* Paper presented at the annual meeting of the American Educational Research Association, Chicago.

Hallinan, M. (1984). Summary and conclusions. In P. Peterson, L. C. Wilkinson, & M. Hallinan (Eds.), *The social context of instruction: Group organization and group processes.* New York: Academic Press.

Hargreaves, D. H. (1980). The occupational culture of teachers. In P. Woods (Ed.), *Teacher strategies: Explorations in the sociology of the school.* London: Croom Helm.

Hodgkinson, H. (1985). *All one system: Demographics of education, kindergarten through graduate school.* Washington, DC: Institute for Educational Leadership.

Johnson, D. (1970). *The social psychology of education.* New York: Holt, Rinehart & Winston.

Jorgenson, G. W. (1977). Relationship of classroom behavior to the accuracy of the match between material difficulty and student ability. *Journal of Educational Psychology, 69*(1), 24–32.

Kounin, J. (1970). *Discipline and group management in classrooms.* New York: Holt, Rinehart & Winston.

Kounin, J. (1983). *Classrooms: Individuals or behavior settings?* (Monographs in Teaching and Learning, No. 1). Bloomington, IN: Indiana University, School of Education.

Lahey, B. B., & Rubinoff, A. (1981). Behavior therapy in education. In L. Michelson, M. Hersen, & S. M. Turner (Eds.), *Future perspectives in behavior therapy.* New York: Plenum Press.

Lein, L. (1975). You were talkin' though, oh yes, you was: Black migrant children: Their speech at home and school. *Anthropology and Education Quarterly, 6*(4), 1–11.

Levine, H., & Mann, K. (1981, April). *The "negotiation" of classroom lessons and its relevance for teacher decision-making.* Paper presented at the annual meeting of the American Educational Research Association, Los Angeles.

McDermott, R. P. (1976). *Kids make sense: An ethnographic account of the interactional management of success and failure in one first-grade classroom.* Unpublished doctoral dissertation, Stanford University.

Mehan, H. (1979). *Learning lessons: Social organization in the classroom.* Cambridge, MA: Harvard University Press.

Metz, M. (1978). *Classrooms and corridors.* Berkeley, CA: University of California Press.

Oakes, J. (1985). *Keeping track: How schools structure inequality.* New Haven, CT: Yale University Press.

Passow, A. H. (1986). Curriculum and instruction: Reactions. In B. I. Williams, P. A. Richmond, & B. J. Mason (Eds.), *Designs for compensatory education: Conference proceedings and papers.* Washington, DC: Research and Evaluation Associates.

Persell, C. (1977). *Education and inequality: The roots and results of stratification in America's schools.* New York: Free Press.

Peterson, P. (1979). Direct instruction reconsidered. In P. Peterson & W. Walberg (Eds.), *Research on teaching: Concepts, findings, and implications.* Berkeley, CA: McCutchan.

Romberg, T. A. (1986). Mathematics for compensatory school programs. In B. I. Williams, P. A. Richmond, & B. J. Mason (Eds.), *Designs for compensatory education: Conference proceedings and papers.* Washington, DC: Research and Evaluation Associates.

Rosenshine, B. V. (1979). Content, time, and direct instruction. In P. L. Peterson & H. J. Walberg (Eds.), *Research on teaching.* Berkeley, CA: McCutchan.

Rosenshine, B. V. (1983). Teaching functions in instructional programs. *Elementary School Journal, 83,* 335–351.

Rowe, M. (1969). Science, silence, and sanctions. *Science and Children, 6,* 11–13.

Rowe, M. (1974). Wait-time and rewards as instructional variables, their influence on language, logic, and fate control: Part 1, Wait-time. *Journal of Research in Science Teaching, 11,* 81–94.

Schumm, R. W. (1971). *Performances on multiple attention measures as a predictor of the classroom management proficiency displayed by student teachers.* Unpublished doctoral dissertation, Indiana University, Bloomington.

Silverstein, J. M. (1979). *Individual and environmental correlates of pupils' problematic and nonproblematic classroom behavior.* Unpublished doctoral dissertation, New York University.

Slavin, R. E. (1987). Cooperative learning and the cooperative school. *Educational Leadership, 45*(3), 7–13.

Soar, R. S. (1973). *Follow Through classroom process measurement and pupil growth (1970–71, final report).* (ERIC No. ED 033 749). Gainesville, FL: University of Florida, Institute for Development of Human Resources.

Soar, R. S., & Soar, R. M. (1979). Emotional climate and management. In P. Peterson & H. Walberg (Eds.), *Research on teaching: Concepts, findings, and implications.* Berkeley, CA: McCutchan.

Spady, W. G., & Mitchell, D. E. (1979). Authority and the management of classroom activities. In D. Duke (Ed.), *Classroom management.* Chicago: National Society for the Study of Education.

Stallings, J., & Kaskowitz, D. (1974). *Follow Through classroom observation evaluation 1972–1973* (SRI Project URU-7370). Stanford, CA: Stanford Research Institute (now SRI International).

Stodolsky, S. S. (1981, April). *Subject matter constraints on the ecology of classroom instruction.* Paper presented at the annual meeting of the American Educational Research Association, Los Angeles.

Tobin, K., & Capie, W. (1982). Relationships between classroom process variables and middle-school science achievement. *Journal of Educational Psychology, 74,* 441–454.

Waller, W. (1932). *The sociology of teaching.* New York: Wiley.

Watson-Gegeo, K. A., & Boggs, S. T. (1977). From verbal play to talk story: The role of routine in speech events among Hawaiian children. In S. Ervin-Tripp & C. Mitchell-Kernan (Eds.), *Child discourse.* New York: Academic Press.

Weinstein, C. S. (1979). The physical environment of the school: A review of the research. *Review of Educational Research, 49*(4), 557–610.

Wilkinson, L. C. (1986). Grouping low-achieving students for instruction. In B. I. Williams, P. A. Richmond, & B. J. Mason (Eds.), *Designs for compensatory education: Conference proceedings and papers*. Washington, DC: Research and Evaluation Associates.

Williams, B. I., Richmond, P. A., & Mason, B. J. (1986). *Designs for compensatory education: Conference proceedings and papers*. Washington, DC: Research and Evaluation Associates.

Woods, P. (1978). Negotiating the demands of school work. *Journal of Curriculum Studies, 10*, 309–327.

Zumwalt, K. (1986). Curriculum and instruction: Reactions. In B. I. Williams, P. A. Richmond, & B. J. Mason (Eds.), *Designs for compensatory education: Conference proceedings and papers*. Washington, DC: Research and Evaluation Associates.

Part IV

The Big Picture: New Perspectives on Academic Instruction for the Children of Poverty

School and Community Influences on Effective Academic Instruction

Patrick M. Shields,
with the assistance of
Debra M. Shaver

The interaction among teachers, students, and curriculum described in earlier chapters takes place within a broader environment that supports or constrains academic learning. School-level factors, in particular, powerfully influence classroom instruction. Beyond this, both the classroom and the school are affected by the community they serve and by the broader professional and institutional environment (e.g., the school district and state education agency). In this chapter, I describe each of these environments and discuss their relationships to effective instruction for disadvantaged students. The focus is on those findings that have the clearest and strongest implications for what goes on in classrooms and for the academic learning that results from formal schooling.

THE SCHOOL ENVIRONMENT

Classroom instruction and academic learning are facilitated or constrained most immediately by the context of the school. The relationship between school characteristics and the nature of teaching and learning varies across schools and classrooms; yet, evidence from two decades of research—much of which has been carried out in elementary schools serving significant concentrations of disadvantaged students—points to a number of school factors that go far to shape the climate and activities of the classroom (see Purkey and Smith, 1983, for a review).

First and foremost, *the school constitutes an environment in which meaningful teaching and learning are (or are not) allowed to take place.* Students and teachers must be able to reach their classes safely, be reasonably free from interruption, and have access to sufficient materials to carry out their academic tasks. Schools that have proven effective for disadvantaged students are characterized by active steps to ensure that teachers have adequate and uninterrupted time for instructional activities. Extracurricular, recreational, athletic, and administrative activities are considered secondary to direct academic teaching and learning (Brookover, Beady, Flood, Schweitzer, & Wisenbaker, 1979; Rosenshine & Berliner, 1978; Stallings, 1980; Tomlinson, 1981). Within this setting, discipline for those who disrupt the school climate is firm and consistent (Edmonds, 1979; New York City Board of Education, 1979; Rutter, Maughan, Mortimore, Ouston, & Smith, 1979; Tomlinson, 1981; Weber, 1971).

This research does not suggest, however, that effective instruction takes place in schools in which teachers, afforded sufficient uninterrupted time and materials, work in isolation from one another. Rather, *effective schools are characterized by a significant degree of cross-classroom coordination and articulation of instruction-related activities* (M. Cohen, 1983; Phi Delta Kappa, 1980; Stallings, 1979). Such coordination provides students a coherent and consistent academic experience, one that is cumulative over time as they move across grades and classrooms.

Such coordinated efforts appear most effective when they are comprehensive, encompassing instructional objectives and strategies, curricular content, and student assessment mechanisms. The development of whole-school efforts depends, in part, on the staff's agreement about a set of clear and commonly shared goals and objectives for the school's instructional program (Behr & Bachelor, 1981; Blumberg & Greenfield, 1980; Doherty & Peters, 1981; Edmonds, 1979; Saronson, 1971). A clearly articulated and commonly understood direction for the school, then, facilitates the coordination of curricula and instructional efforts across classrooms and grades (Armor et al., 1976; Little, 1981). A set of common goals also lays the groundwork for the creation of a regular system of monitoring and evaluation of student progress in relationship to these goals (Edmonds, 1979; New York City Board of Education, 1979; Venezky & Winfield, 1979; Weber, 1971).

Cross-classroom and cross-grade articulation gain added importance as administrators and teachers implement instructional strategies that have gained currency in recent years—strategies that include peer and cross-age tutoring, certain forms of cooperative learning, and the provision of supplementary in-class services for special populations (Smith & O'Day, 1988). In particular, current efforts to reduce the fragmented instructional experience of students receiving supplementary program services require significant interaction among teachers from different classrooms and programs (Gartner & Lipsky, 1987; Shields, Jay, Parrish, & Padilla, 1989). The mechanisms that make such coordination possible, that allow teachers time and authority to plan integrated efforts, need to be established at the school level.

Another related finding of this literature is that in schools in which disadvantaged students perform well, *the shared goals and objectives of the school staff—which allow for such coordinated efforts—are oriented toward increased academic achievement.* These schools are infused with an ethos in which student learning considerations are the most important criteria in making both administrative and instructional decisions (Armor et al., 1976; Berliner, 1979; Brookover et al., 1979; California State Department of Education, 1977; Edmonds, 1979; Purkey & Smith, 1983; Rutter et al., 1979; Weber, 1971). This focus on academics is guided by the basic assumption that all students can and will learn, given the proper guidance and assistance, and is especially important in schools serving disadvantaged students. Similarly, administrators believe that teachers can teach, and teachers and aides believe that they can meet the challenge to teach students (Austin, 1979; Brookover et al., 1979; Dornbush & Scott, 1975; Edmonds,

1979; Lipham, 1980; Purkey & Smith, 1983). In the classroom, the school ethos is reflected in a sharp focus on academic learning and high expectations for all students, regardless of their backgrounds.

Finally, this research suggests that *a strong instructional leader is necessary to facilitate the development of clear goals, the creation of mechanisms that allow for collegial planning and coordinated action, and the nurturing of an academically oriented climate.* Typically (but not always) the school principal is the one who works to focus staff and student efforts on academics, create a supportive administrative and organizational structure for academic endeavors, and foster a positive school climate conducive to learning (Armor et al., 1976; Brookover et al., 1979; California State Department of Education, 1977; Edmonds, 1979).

Although many researchers have noted methodological and conceptual shortcomings in the effective schools research (see, for example, Cuban, 1984; Rowan, Bossert, & Dwyer, 1983), these diverse studies have painted a remarkably consistent portrait of schools that work for disadvantaged students. Taken together, the findings from this research underscore the central role that the school can play in fostering academic achievement. At their best, schools can provide teachers with the time, autonomy, support, and opportunities for collegial interaction and planning necessary to craft and carry out effective classroom practice (Little, 1981). Similarly, schools can offer students an environment in which expectations for academic progress are unambiguous and high, while providing the respect and support required to meet those expectations.

THE FAMILY AND COMMUNITY ENVIRONMENT

The creation and maintenance of a strong, academically oriented school ethos depends in part on the extent to which such values are shared by students, their families, and the broader school community. Effective instruction is hardly possible if students actively resist learning; also, students' meaningful participation in school typically requires support and assistance from home. In this chapter, I discuss the relationship between the family and community environment and effective classroom instruction.

For decades, we have had convincing empirical evidence of the powerful influence of student background on academic achievement

(Coleman et al., 1966; Jencks et al., 1972). In fact, much of the research on effective schooling that I have reviewed has examined school and teacher effects while controlling for what are perceived to be the robust but nonmanipulable factors associated with students' social and economic characteristics (Good & Brophy, 1986). However, many researchers argue that instead of controlling for social status, we should explicitly examine the relationship between students' backgrounds and the norms, values, and routines of the school and classroom (e.g., Cummins, 1986; Diaz, Moll, & Mehan, 1986; Heath, 1983). Only with such an understanding, they argue, can we design more effective instructional practices that build on students' strengths while compensating for their weaknesses.

This line of research is premised on a recognition that all students arrive at school with a set of school-relevant characteristics, including patterns of discourse, spoken and written language codes, ways of interacting with adults and peers, perceptions of the purpose of schooling, and attitudes toward their likelihood of success in school (Delpit, 1988; Heath, 1983; Ogbu, 1978). For all students, these culturally generated characteristics help to explain how they interpret and react to what takes place in the classroom. For many students, the learning skills and cognitive strategies they have acquired outside school are readily applicable to the demands and routines of the school experience. For other students—many of them nonwhite and non-middle-class—the skills and strategies they have learned to get along in their own communities often prove ineffective in meeting the demands of the school setting (Comer, 1988). In the case of some economically disadvantaged students from nonmainstream backgrounds, this mismatch between their home culture and that of the school is exacerbated by a lack of school-relevant experiences (e.g., exposure to books) and opportunities to engage in cognitive processes typically called for in school (e.g., building generalized analytical categories) (Heath, 1983).

The mismatch may also extend to school-related values. In large part, students' views of schooling are shaped by the values toward school and achievement present in the home. Studies have shown this to be true for successful middle-class students (Bloom, 1985) as well as for poor students struggling to escape the ghetto (Clark, 1983). Yet, families from disadvantaged communities do not always share the same values as the school (Comer, 1980, 1988; Matute-Bianchi, 1986; Ogbu, 1978). Although the overwhelming majority of parents want their children to succeed, parents vary significantly in the amount of support they are able or willing to provide and in the extent to which they believe in and trust the schools. At the extreme, parents identify the school as an antagonist, as illustrated by an account of an inner-city student who arrived at school to inform the teacher, "Teacher, my mama said I don't have to do anything you say" (Comer, 1988). More commonly, parents may not understand the norms and procedures of the school and feel alienated from it (Comer, 1980; Cummins, 1986).

This mismatch between aspects of the home and school cultures can have a number of negative consequences. Because some students come to school unprepared to tackle certain types of academic tasks, they begin to fall behind their peers in the early grades. Students may also face school failure as a consequence of being unable to make sense of school norms, values, and expectations and to respond appropriately. Heath (1983), for example, has documented classrooms in which both black and white students from working-class families were unable to decipher teachers' indirect requests for adherence to an unstated set of rules and so were not able to act in ways consistent with their teachers' expectations. Similarly, the mismatch can interfere with learning as teachers misinterpret students' speech or actions. For example, some teachers misinterpret black children's use of Black English Vernacular as evidence of a decoding problem and so focus their teaching to remediate decoding difficulties that do not exist (Burke, Pflaum, & Krafle, 1982). In a separate study, Au and Jordan (1981) showed that a number of the difficulties Polynesian students experienced in learning to read were related to teachers' ignorance of the students' basic cultural norms regarding turn-taking.

The initial problems that disadvantaged students experience are often exacerbated over time as they fail to pick up skills they may need later on, and as their attitudes toward school become less and less positive. If students are consistently given the message that there is something wrong and dysfunctional about their ways of acting and communicating, they can come to lose faith in their own abilities (Ogbu, 1978). Moreover, a continued disjuncture between the values of a student's home and community and those of the school may lead the student to reject the school's values and begin to identify himself or herself in opposition to the predominant culture of the school (Willis, 1977). Assuming a stand "in opposition," students begin to define success as *not* doing well in school, *not* carrying books, *not* dressing "properly," *not* completing assignments, and the like (Matute-Bianchi, 1986). Some researchers argue that minority students begin to develop such a culture of resistance as early as preadolescence as they struggle to develop individual identities (Comer, 1988).

This literature, then, points to a complex and dynamic conception of disadvantagement. Students can be disadvantaged both because they come to school less than well prepared and because school staff fail to diagnose and address their particular difficulties. Similarly, some students are disadvantaged both because their patterns of behavior, language use, and values do not match those of the school setting and because teachers and administrators fail to adapt to and take advantage of the cultural strengths students do possess. Over time, these phenomena can create a negative cycle of failure and despair, culminating in students' turning their backs on schooling and dropping out.

This same line of research, however, also suggests that this cycle can be broken, or need not even begin, if administrators and teachers take steps to minimize the cultural incongruities between students' homes and schools. Such steps involve developing instructional programs that incorporate the life experiences and skills that students bring with them to the classroom in order to provide those students with the skills and strategies they need to succeed in the broader society (Delpit, 1988). From this perspective, effective instruction should integrate specific school concepts and the everyday life experiences of the students (Cazden, 1986; Tharpe, 1988). The goal here is to recognize the existence and value of the students' cultural backgrounds and to adapt instructional and administrative strategies to the extent necessary for students to acquire needed life skills.

Specifically, *the research suggests that effective instruction for disadvantaged students involves allowing students to use their own life experiences as starting points for learning.* Students are able, for example, to read more, read faster, and make fewer errors if the reading material is relevant to their religion (Lipson, 1983), their ethnicity (Schreck, 1981), and their nationality (Pritchard, 1987). Similarly, studies of instruction for Latino students have found that the most effective teachers regularly encourage students to use their personal experiences to make sense of classroom content (Diaz, Moll, & Mehan, 1986; see also Chapter 3).

To be able to build on their personal experiences, *teachers must allow students opportunities for active participation in the class.* Research suggests that teachers should not rely solely on the direct transmission of information—a process that often confines students to a passive role. Rather, students need opportunities for active participation and knowledge generation, a finding with broad applicability across all types of classrooms, but especially important for disadvantaged students (E. Cohen, 1988). Research on cooperative and small-group learning has demonstrated the value of active student learning (E. Cohen, 1984; Slavin, 1986).

In some cases, *effective instruction will require teachers to adapt instructional activities to the cultural characteristics of the students.* Research has shown that students learn better if the questions teachers ask reflect the predominant patterns of questioning in their students' community (Heath, 1983). Similarly, Au and Jordan (1981) report increases in student reading achievement among native Hawaiian children after rules about turn-taking were adjusted to the students' home culture.

School staff can also help to bridge the gap between the culture of the home and that of the school by *helping parents to devise effective ways of helping their children in school-related activities at home.* Research has demonstrated convincingly that even parents with minimal formal education can be taught a variety of techniques (e.g., reading to their children, tutoring them in different subject areas, and allowing their children to read out loud) that lead to increased school achievement (Clarke-Stewart, 1983; Lazar & Darlington, 1978). Although much of this research has been done with very young students, studies have also shown that parents can be trained to offer upper-elementary students instructionally related support at home that results in higher achievement (Barth, 1979).

A final strategy that research has found effective in bridging the home/school gap *involves various methods of bringing parents into the school building.* Studies have shown an association between student achievement and a wide variety of efforts that allow parents to participate meaningfully in in-school activities (Leler, 1983). One particularly effective strategy is training parents to tutor or work with their own children in class (Becher, 1984). Studies have demonstrated that such programs can be successful regardless of parents' socioeconomic status (Shields & McLaughlin, 1986; Shields & David, 1988). In fact, one study that included a nationally representative sample of students found that the effects of maternal education and other status variables on a child's achievement were mediated almost entirely by the extent of the mother's involvement in school activities. That is, the study found that social status affects student achievement only through its effect on parental involvement (Stevenson & Baker, 1987). Similarly, studies of effective schools for disadvantaged students have found them to have strong programs of parental involvement (Chubb, 1988).

Taken together, these findings suggest that teachers and administrators can do much to address the needs of students disadvantaged by a mismatch between their home and school cultures. Generally, effective instruction appears to require a recognition and integration of students' cultural diversity so that teachers can build on students' experiences as a way of teaching the concepts and skills the students will need to succeed. Thus, the research suggests, effective instruction involves allowing students the opportunity to participate actively in class and to use their own life experiences as the foundation for actively constructing meaning and knowledge in the school setting. Furthermore, efforts to reduce the home-school mismatch can also be aided by strategies that "bring the school into the home" (by getting parents involved in instructional activities at home) and that "bring the home into the school" (by getting parents involved in the school site).

Efforts to increase the understanding and support between home and school are especially important in the most disadvantaged communities, where school staff are likely to have mixed expectations of students and parents are likely to have fewer positive experiences with formal educational institutions. In these situations, home-school cooperation can help create a school climate that is both sensitive to the students' backgrounds and driven toward high expectations for academic achievement. Most of all, parents' active involvement sends an unambiguous message to the student that school is important. Parental values become increasingly important as a student enters the upper elementary grades and begins to make more overt choices about his or her participation in schooling. In the absence of an early message from home concerning the value of school and ongoing efforts by school staff to remain sensitive to and supportive of the community, many students from disadvantaged backgrounds decide to opt out of school (Fordham, 1988; Matute-Bianchi, 1986; Willis, 1977).

THE PROFESSIONAL AND INSTITUTIONAL ENVIRONMENT

Finally, both school and classroom instructional activities take place within a broader professional and institutional environment. District policy and practices heavily influence school and classroom practice, as do numerous state-level decisions. Testing and textbook policies, in particular, affect much of what teachers do in the classroom.

Legal responsibility for K-12 education rests at the school district level, and district-level policies can do much to promote effective classroom practice. It is at the district level that decisions are made about the incentives and resources teachers require to do their jobs effectively (Cuban, 1984), and it is district policymakers who establish the mechanisms for information sharing and collaboration among schools and teachers and who provide opportunities for needed staff development (David, 1989b). In particular, the extent to which schools are afforded the autonomy to develop appropriate instructional strategies for their student population depends on a devolution of authority from the district level (Purkey & Smith, 1985). Research has shown that district policies that give school staff responsibility for budgeting, staffing, and curricular decisions can increase teachers' motivation, help to develop a sense of professionalism among school staff, and produce effective changes in instructional practices (David, 1989a; Rosow & Zagar, 1989).

This body of research suggests that district policies are most effective in fostering improved classroom practice when they facilitate alliances with the community, the school board, and school staff. The greatest results occur when all the parties share the same goals and feel some level of responsibility for meeting those goals. The creation of such alliances generally requires strong district-level leadership, typically a superintendent who serves as both an instructional and a political leader (Hill, Wise, & Shapiro, 1989).

State legislators, governors, chief state school officers, and state departments of education are also playing an increasingly important role in influencing local educational practice. In part, this trend reflects the greater share of educational expenses now borne by state governments (U.S. Department of Education, 1988); in part, it reflects the nationwide educational reform movement that has motivated even those states that traditionally had remained quiescent in the field of education to take active steps to promote more effective schooling at the local level (Timar & Kirp, 1987). Along with greater state financial and political involvement in education have come increased state guidelines and mandates concerning curricula, textbooks, and testing. Increasingly, school and classroom decisions about appropriate practices are defined in large part in response to state curricular and testing policies (see, for example, Knapp et al., 1986).

As states have become more active in the educational arena, their efforts have often promoted school improvement because they have brought increased funds, political clout, and technical assistance to local educators' efforts. State agencies can serve an important role in coordinating the flow of communication and information about effective practices and in encouraging the development of problem-solving coalitions through the state (David, 1989b). Yet states, like districts, can also impede local improvement efforts and tie the hands of teachers. In particular, states can limit local efforts through restrictive regulations and an overreliance on test results (see Odden and Anderson, 1986). The increased use of tests, often resulting from state requirements or pressure, is having a profound effect on instructional activities. As standardized tests take on increased salience in an era of accountability, the traditional role of curriculum is being increasingly performed by testing as teachers begin to teach more and more "to the test" (Popham, Cruse, Rankin, Sandifer, & Williams, 1985). The creators of tests, rather than curriculum developers or teachers, become the arbiters of what should be taught (Madaus, 1988).

SUMMARY: ENVIRONMENTS THAT SUPPORT THE ACADEMIC LEARNING OF DISADVANTAGED STUDENTS

I conclude this chapter, then, with the message that although the ingredients for effective instruction of disadvantaged students are found within the confines of the classroom, the interaction between and among teachers and students is constrained and influenced by factors in the broader environment. First, school-level factors facilitate or limit effective classroom practice. Good classroom practice turns in part on an orderly school climate, well-coordinated curricula and instructional strategies, and an overall atmosphere characterized by a concern for academic excellence and high expectations for all students. Such a climate is particularly important in schools for disadvantaged students, which are too often typified by disorder, a lack of discipline, little academic orientation, and low expectations.

Second, classroom practice is powerfully influenced by the families and communities from which students come. The creation and maintenance of a climate of achievement in schools requires students and parents to share values, and effective instruction requires that students actively try to learn. Research suggests that classroom instruction for disadvantaged students should be particularly sensitive both to compensating for students' weaknesses and to providing students the opportunity to build on their own personal experiences as they learn needed skills. Similarly, research suggests that effective school environments are created in part by responding to the needs of students' families and by building networks of support between home and school. Such support is especially important in signaling to disadvantaged students that the school is valued by teachers and parents alike.

Finally, teachers and administrators in schools that serve disadvantaged students require both autonomy and support from state and district education agencies. Schools need assistance in the implementation and use of evaluations; in gaining access to, and support for, appropriate staff development activities; and in the identification, use, and modification of appropriate instructional materials. At the same time, school staff—especially those in schools that serve disadvantaged students and that often receive categorical program funds— need sufficient autonomy and freedom from restrictive state or district rules and regulations to develop and implement effective instructional strategies tailored to the specific settings in which they teach.

REFERENCES

Armor D., Conry-Oseguera, P., Cox, M., King, N., McDonnell, L., Pascal, A., Pauly, E., & Zellman, G. (1976). *Analysis of the school preferred reading program in selected Los Angeles minority schools.* Santa Monica, CA: Rand.

Au, K. H., & Jordan, C. (1981). Teaching reading to Hawaiian children: Finding a culturally appropriate solution. In H. T. Trueba, G. P. Guthrie, & K. H. Au (Eds.), *Culture and the bilingual classroom: Studies in classroom ethnography* (pp.139–152). Rowley, MA: Newbury House.

Austin, G. R. (1979). Exemplary schools and the search for effectiveness. *Educational Leadership, 37*(1), 10–12, 14.

Barth, R. (1979). Home-based reinforcement of school behavior: A review and analysis. *Review of Educational Research, 49*(3), 436–458.

Becher, R. M. (1984). *Parental involvement: A review of research and principles of successful practice.* Washington, DC: National Institute of Education.

Behr, G., & Bachelor, B. (1981). *Identifying effective schools—A case study involving black racially isolated minority schools and instructional accomplishments/information systems.* Los Alamos, CA: SWRL Educational Research and Development.

Berliner, C.D. (1979). Tempus educare. In P. Peterson and H. Walberg(Eds.), *Research on Teaching.* Berkeley, CA: McCutchan.

Bloom, B. S. (Ed.). (1985). *Talent in young people.* New York: Ballantine.

Blumberg, A., & Greenfield, W. (1980). *The effective principal.* Boston: Allyn & Bacon.

Brookover, W. B., Beady, C., Flood, P., Schweitzer, J., & Wisenbaker, J. (1979). *School social systems and student achievement: Schools can make a difference.* New York: Praeger.

Burke, S. M., Pflaum, S. W., & Krafle, J. D. (1982). The influence of Black English on diagnosis of reading in learning disabled and normal readers. *Journal of Learning Disabilities, 15*(1), 19–22.

California State Department of Education. (1977). *School Effectiveness study: The first year.* Sacramento: California Department of Education, Office of Program Evaluation and Research.

Cazden, C. (1986). Classroom discourse. In M. Wittrock (Ed.), *Handbook of research on teaching* (3rd ed.). New York: Macmillan.

Chubb, J. E. (1988, Winter). Why the current wave of school reform will fail. *The Public Interest*, No. 90.

Clark, R. M. (1983). *Family life and school achievement: Why poor black children succeed or fail.* Chicago: University of Chicago Press.

Clarke-Stewart, A. K. (1983). Exploring the assumptions of parent education. In R. Haskins and D. Adams (Eds.), *Parent education and public policy.* Norwood, NJ: Ablex.

Cohen, E. G. (1984). Talking and working together: Status, interaction, and learning. In P. Peterson, L. C. Wilkinson, & M. Hallinan (Eds.), *The social context of instruction: Group organization and group processes.* New York: Academic Press.

Cohen, E. G. (1988). *On the sociology of the classroom.* Stanford, CA: Center for Educational Research at Stanford, School of Education, Stanford University.

Cohen, M. (1983). Instructional management and social conditions in effective schools. In A. Odden & L. D. Webb (Eds.), *School finance and school improvement: Linkages for the 1980s.* Fourth Annual Yearbook of the American Educational Finance Association. Cambridge, MA: Ballinger.

Coleman, J. S., Campbell, E. Q., Hobson, C. J., McPartland, J., Mood, A. M., Weinfeld, F. D., & York, R. L. (1966). *Equality of educational opportunity.* Washington, DC: U.S. Government Printing Office.

Comer, J. P. (1980). *School power: Implications of an intervention project.* New York: Free Press.

Comer, J.P. (1988). Educating poor minority children. *Scientific American, 259*(5), 42–48.

Cuban, L. (1984). Transforming the frog into a prince: Effective schools research, policy, and practice at the district level. *Harvard Educational Review, 54*(2), 129–151.

Cummins, J. (1986). Empowering minority students: A framework for intervention. Harvard Educational Review, 56(1), 18–36.

David, J. L. (1989a). *Restructuring in progress: Lessons from pioneering districts.* Washington, DC: National Governors' Association.

David, J. L. (1989b). Synthesis of research on school-based management. *Educational Leadership, 46*(8), 45–53.

Delpit, L.D. (1988). The silenced dialogue: Power and pedagogy in educating other people's children. *Harvard Educational Review, 58*(3), 280–298.

Diaz, S., Moll, L. C., & Mehan, H. (1986). Sociocultural resources in instruction: A context-specific approach. In California State Department of Education, *Beyond language: Social and cultural factors in schooling language minority children* (pp. 187–230). Los Angeles: Evaluation, Dissemination and Assessment Center, California State University.

Doherty, V., & Peters, L. (1981). Goals and objectives in educational planning and evaluation. *Educational Leadership, 38*, 606–611.

Dornbush, S., & Scott, W. R. (1975). *Evaluation and the exercise of authority.* San Francisco: Jossey-Bass.

Edmonds, R. R. (1979). Effective schools for the urban poor. *Educational Leadership, 37*(1), 15–18, 20–24.

Fordham, S. (1988). Racelessness as a factor in black students' school success: Pragmatic strategy or pyrrhic victory? *Harvard Educational Review, 58*(1), 54–84.

Gartner, A., & Lipsky, D. K. (1987). Beyond special education: Toward a quality system for all students. *Harvard Educational Review, 57*(4), 367–395.

Good, T. L., & Brophy, J. E. (1986). School effects: In M. L. Wittrock (Ed.), *Handbook of research on teaching* (3rd ed.). New York: Macmillan.

Heath, S. B. (1983). *Ways with words.* Cambridge: Cambridge University Press.

Hill, P. T., Wise, A. W., & Shapiro, L. (1989). *Educational progress: Cities mobilize to improve their schools.* Santa Monica, CA: Rand.

Jencks, C. S., Smith, M., Ackland, H., Bane, M. J., Cohen, D., Gintis, H., Heyns, B., & Michelson, S. (1972). *Inequality: A reassessment of the effect of family and schooling in America.* New York: Basic Books.

Knapp, M. S., Turnbull, B. J., Blakely, C. H., Jay, E. D., Marks, E. L., & Shields, P. (1986). *Local program design and decisionmaking under Chapter 1 of the Education Consolidation and Improvement Act.* Menlo Park, CA: SRI International.

Lazar, I., & Darlington, R. (1978). *Lasting effects after preschool.* Ithaca, NY: Cornell University.

Leler, H. (1983). Parent education and involvement in relation to the schools and to parents of school-aged children. In R. Haskins & D. Adams (Eds.), *Parent education and public policy.* Norwood, NJ: Ablex.

Lipham, J. A. (1980). Change agentry and school improvements: The principal's role. *Interorganizational arrangements for collaborative efforts: Commissioned papers.* Portland, OR: Northwest Regional Educational Laboratory.

Lipson, M. Y. (1983). The influence of religious affiliation on children's memory for text information. *Reading Research Quarterly, 18*(4), 448– 457.

Little, J. W. (1981). *School success and development: The role of staff development in urban desegregated schools. Executive summary.* Washington, DC: National Institute of Education.

Madaus, G. (1988). The influence of testing on the curriculum. In L. N. Tanner (Ed.), *Critical issues in curriculum.* The Eighth Yearbook of the National Society for the Study of Education. Chicago: University of Chicago Press.

Matute-Bianchi, M. E. (1986, November). Ethnic identities and patterns of school success and failure among Mexican-descent and Japanese-American students in a California high school: An ethnographic analysis. *American Journal of Education, 95,* 233– 255.

New York City Board of Education. (1979). School improvement project: The case study phase. In A. W. Block (Ed.), *Effective schools: A summary of research.* Arlington, VA: Educational Research Service.

Odden, A., & Anderson, B. (1986). How successful state education improvement programs work. *Phi Delta Kappan, 67*(8), 582–585.

Ogbu, J. U. (1978). *Minority education and caste: The American system in cross-cultural perspective.* New York: Academic Press.

Phi Delta Kappa. (1980). *Why do some urban schools succeed?* Bloomington, IN: Author.

Popham, W. J., Cruse, K. L., Rankin, S. C., Sandifer, P. D., & Williams, P. L. (1985). Measurement-driven instruction: It's on the road. *Phi Delta Kappan, 66*(9), 628–635.

Pritchard, R. (1987). *The effects of cultural schemata on reading processing strategies.* Unpublished doctoral dissertation, Indiana University, Bloomington, IN.

Purkey, S. C., & Smith, M. S. (1983). Effective schools—A review. *Elementary School Journal, 83*(4), 427–452.

Purkey, S. C., & Smith, M. S. (1985). School reform: The district policy implications of the effective schools literature. *Elementary School Journal, 85*(3), 353–389.

Rosenshine, B. V., & Berliner, D. C. (1978). Academic engaged time. *British Journal of Teacher Education, 4,* 3–16.

Rosow, J., & Zagar, R. (1989). *Allies in educational reform: How teachers, unions and administrators can join forces for better schools.* San Francisco: Jossey-Bass.

Rowan, B., Bossert, S. T., & Dwyer, D. C. (1983). Research on effective schools: A cautionary note. *Educational Research, 12*(4), 24–31.

Rutter, M., Maughan, B., Mortimore, P., Ouston, J., & Smith, A. (1979). *Fifteen thousand hours: Secondary schools and their effects on children.* Cambridge, MA: Harvard University Press.

Saronson, S. B. (1971). *The culture of the school and the problem of change.* Boston: Allyn & Bacon.

Schreck, J. (1981). *The effects of contents schema on reading comprehension for Hispanic, black, and white cultural groups.* Unpublished doctoral dissertation, University of Illinois, Urbana, IL.

Shields, P. M., & David, J. L. (1988). *The implementation of Family Math in five community agencies.* A report for the EQUALS Program at the Lawrence Hall of Science, University of California, Berkeley.

Shields, P. M., & McLaughlin, M. W. (1986). *Parent involvement in compensatory education programs.* Stanford, CA: Center for Educational Research at Stanford, School of Education, Stanford University.

Shields, P. M., Jay, E. D., Parrish, T. B., & Padilla, C. L. (1989). *Alternative programs and strategies for serving students with learning disabilities and other learning problems.* Menlo Park, CA: SRI International.

Slavin, R. E. (1986). *Ability grouping and student achievement in elementary schools: A best evidence synthesis.* Baltimore, MD: Center for Research on Elementary and Middle Schools, Johns Hopkins University.

Smith, M. S., & O'Day, J. (1988). *Teaching policy and research on teaching.* Stanford, CA: Stanford University.

Stallings, J. A. (1979). *How to change the process of teaching basic reading skills in secondary schools: Executive summary.* Menlo Park, CA: SRI International.

Stallings, J. A. (1980). Allocated academic learning time revisited, or beyond time on task. *Educational Researcher, 9,* 11–16.

Stevenson, D. L., & Baker, D. P. (1987). The family-school relation and the child's school performance. *Child Development, 58,* 1348–1357.

Tharpe, R. (1988, February 26). *4V + 2K = A formula for minority student success.* Presentation at the first Stanford Centennial Conference on Educating Children at Risk, Stanford University, School of Education.

Timar, T. B., & Kirp, D. L. (1987). Educational reform and institutional competence. *Harvard Educational Review, 57*(3), 308–330.

Tomlinson, T. M. (1981). The troubled years: An interpretive analysis of public schooling since 1950. *Phi Delta Kappan, 62*(5), 373–376.

U.S. Department of Education. (1988). *State education statistics supplement: Student performance and resource inputs.* Washington, DC: Author.

Venezky, R. L., & Winfield, L. F. (1979). *Schools that succeed beyond expectations in reading* (Studies on Education Tech. Rep. No. 1). Newark: University of Delaware. (ERIC Document Reproduction Service No. ED 177 484).

Weber, G. (1971). *Inner-city children can be taught to read: Four successful schools* (Occasional Paper No. 18). Washington, DC: Council for Basic Education.

Willis, P. (1977). *Learning to labor: How working-class kids get working-class jobs.* Lexington, MA: D. C. Heath.

——14——

Alternatives to Conventional Wisdom

Michael S. Knapp and Brenda J. Turnbull

The research evidence reviewed in this book leads to an overall conclusion that much recent thinking about the education of disadvantaged students has been flawed. This thinking, which we call conventional wisdom, itself represents an advance beyond an earlier stage of educational practice that tended simply to ignore the plight of disadvantaged students. The conventional wisdom has some strengths as a basis for curriculum and instruction. Nevertheless, the most recent scholarly analysis suggests that further modifications in thinking and practice are needed.

What is the conventional wisdom? Stated oversimply, it focuses on "disadvantaged learners'" deficits and sets forth solutions in the form of principles of curriculum organization, instructional approach, classroom management, and instructional grouping:

- *View of disadvantaged learners:* An emphasis on disadvantaged learners' lack of information and intellectual facility.
- *Curriculum organization:* A model of the curriculum in mathematics

and literacy that emphasizes sequential mastery of discrete skills ordered from "the basics" to higher-order skills.

- *Instructional approach:* A high degree of teacher-directed instruction, in which the teacher presents material and supervises students closely, designed to maximize engaged learning time and the frequency of feedback to students.
- *Classroom management:* An approach to classroom management built on generic principles for maintaining classroom order, to be applied uniformly across content areas.
- *Arrangement of instructional groups:* Instructional arrangements that are grouped or tracked by students' ability, not only within class, but also through supplemental programs for children with the greatest educational need.

We do not suggest that this way of thinking must be discarded, although some researchers advocate doing so (for example, see Chapter 3). Our review of the research base indicates that there is this to be said for the conventional wisdom: Applied skillfully, it tends to result in good student performance on current standardized tests, especially the tests administered in the elementary grades that emphasize basic skills. This is not a trivial outcome; it is more desirable than the performance now seen in many high-poverty schools. Many classrooms now fall far short of effectively implementing the conventional wisdom, and they might benefit from doing so.

Nevertheless, this formula for effective academic instruction may not succeed in meeting all educational goals for disadvantaged—or any—youngsters. In particular, there is increasing reason to believe that it may place an unintended ceiling on the learning of the disadvantaged student population—for example, by repetitively exposing them to an impoverished "basics only" curriculum and nothing more.

Assessing the merit of the conventional wisdom is an important emerging issue for regular classroom instruction and compensatory education programs alike. Compensatory education programs represent major investments by the federal and state governments in the education of disadvantaged students. The federal Chapter 1 program is a case in point. Aimed at low-achieving students in schools with higher-than-average poverty, Chapter 1 is deeply rooted in the conviction that these students need something extra. Local Chapter 1 programs have increasingly relied on a general model that exposes students to intense doses of instruction in basic skills, often in small, teacher-directed groups of students who have similar achievement levels. The program does yield achievement gains for participants (Office of Educational Research and Improvement, 1986). However, the disappointing fact that Chapter 1 students' achievement does not tend to catch up with that of their peers has begun to stimulate a reexamination of the typical instructional premises for the program. Increasingly, Chapter 1 policymakers want to implement new ideas about how federal aid can make a difference in the education of disadvantaged students. New legislation stresses the need to improve students' performance in "more advanced skills." Communication between regular and supplemental teachers is now a mandated priority.

For both compensatory and regular classroom instruction in high-poverty schools, this book is intended to contribute to the vigorous search for feasible improvements on the conventional wisdom. The goal is to find better ways of designing elementary-level instruction for disadvantaged students. Our focus is at the classroom level, because we believe that good curriculum and instruction are essential and within the power of teachers and principals to achieve.

A CRITIQUE OF CONVENTIONAL WISDOM

Taken together, the chapters in this book present a broad and provocative critique of conventional wisdom regarding curriculum and instruction for the children of poverty. In particular, this critique addresses current thinking and practice along five dimensions: (1) the underlying conception of the "disadvantaged" learner, (2) the sequencing and challenge of the curriculum, (3) the role of the teacher in instruction, (4) the relationship of classroom management to academic tasks, and (5) the degree and nature of curricular differentiation to accommodate different levels of student proficiency. For quick reference, the critique and alternatives are summarized in Table 14–1.

Table 14-1
Conventional Wisdom and Alternatives

Conventional Wisdom	Alternatives
1. *View of disadvantaged learners:* An emphasis on learners' deficits—that is, what the "disadvantaged" student lacks in knowledge, intellectual facility, or experience	• An emphasis on the knowledge students *do* bring to school • Explicit teaching of how to function in the "culture" of the school
2. *Curriculum organization:* Curriculum that teaches discrete skills in a fixed sequence from "basic" to "higher-order" skills	• Early emphasis on appropriate "higher-order" tasks • Extensive opportunities to learn and apply skills in context • An emphasis on meaning and understanding in all academic instruction
3. *Instructional approach:* Exclusive or heavy reliance on teacher-directed instruction	• A combination of teacher-directed and learner-directed instruction
4. *Classroom management:* Classroom management principles uniformly applied across the school day so as to forestall disorder in the classroom	• Variation in classroom management approaches depending on the kind of academic work being done
5. *Arrangement of instructional groups:* Long-term grouping of students by achievement or ability	• Some use of grouping arrangements that mix ability levels • More flexibility in grouping arrangements

THE CONCEPTION OF THE "DISADVANTAGED" LEARNER

Conventional Wisdom

A great deal of research and practice has been predicated on the assumption that "disadvantaged" students are deficient in ways that influence their performance in school (see Chapter 9).

A corollary assumption is that disadvantaged students' families have given them a bad start in life. These assumptions, in effect, locate the problem in the learner and his or her background.

A Critique

These conventional assumptions can be criticized on two general grounds. First, stereotypic ideas about the capabilities of a child who is poor or who belongs to an ethnic minority will detract from an accurate assessment of the child's real educational problems and potential. Second, by focusing on family deficiencies, the conventional wisdom misses the strengths of the cultures from which many disadvantaged students come. This is not to say that dysfunctional families do not exist in poor communities; indeed, such families represent a serious social problem. However, focusing only on the possibility of family dysfunction may obscure the larger picture of a community's culture and its strengths.

Researchers have pointed out the adverse consequences of these conceptions (Chapters 3 and 6 are especially articulate on this point). They include (1) low expectations for what these students can accomplish in academic work, (2) failure to examine carefully what the schools do that exacerbates (or facilitates the solution of) these learning problems, and (3) misdiagnosis of the learning problems these students face (e.g., interpreting dialect speech patterns as decoding errors).

An Alternative View

A growing body of research provides different conceptions of disadvantaged students that help educators avoid these adverse consequences (Delpit, 1988; Heath, 1983; Ogbu, 1978). The central idea is that the disadvantaged child brings to school speech patterns, cognitive experiences, and behavior patterns that do not match the way things are done in school. These students face a difficult learning task—that of learning the culture of the school and at the same time mastering academic tasks. While recognizing that there may be gaps in the disadvantaged student's experience (e.g., limited exposure to print, if not more serious gaps in family support for schooling), the educator builds on the child's experience base and at the same time challenges children to expand their repertoire of experiences and skills.

This perspective gains further support from a decade or more of cognitive research and related theories of learning that have profoundly shaped thinking about education and teaching in recent years. Put simply, these theories picture the learner as an active constructor of knowledge and meaning rather than a passive recipient of information and skills (Linn, 1986). Furthermore, this line of research has demonstrated that the beginning or "naive" learner, before and during schooling, develops theories about the way the world works as actively as the advanced or expert learner: these theories often misrepresent the world and resist alteration. Although this research has yet to focus on disadvantaged students per se, it implies that they, like anyone else, come to school with more sophistication and more active, inquiring minds than deficit models may presume. That is not to say that disadvantaged students arrive at school on an equal footing with their advantaged counterparts. But they have done a great deal of learning when they come and have more capacity for academic proficiency than is often recognized.

To summarize the alternative to the conventional wisdom, evidence suggests that disadvantaged students will be better able to meet the academic challenge of school if the following principles are followed (Comer, 1988; see also Chapters 3 and 11).

- Teachers know and respect the students' cultural/linguistic background and communicate this respect in a personal way to the students.
- The academic program allows and encourages students to draw and build on the experiences they have, at the same time that it exposes them to unfamiliar experiences and ways of thinking.
- The assumptions, expectations, and ways of doing things in school—in short, its culture—are made explicit to these students by teachers as they explain and model these dimensions of academic learning.

SEQUENCING AND CHALLENGE IN THE CURRICULUM

Conventional Wisdom

Conventional approaches to fashioning curricula for disadvantaged students—and indeed for "slow" learners of any kind—follow from the conception of the student as an individual with critical skill and knowledge deficits. Such curricula are characterized by two basic traits (see Chapter 10). First, these curricula tend to break up reading, writing, and mathematics into fixed sequences of discrete skills, ordered from the simplest (the "basics") to the more complex ("higher-order skills"). Second, instruction typically emphasizes developing mastery of these skills by linear progression through the curricula. By this line of argument, children who haven't mastered spelling, for example, are not thought ready to write stories. Or, in mathematics lessons, practical problems involving multiplication are not introduced until the students can do paper-and-pencil multiplication problems, to say nothing of knowing their multiplication tables. Rigid sequencing appears in curricula at all elementary grade levels.

Not only are many mathematics textbooks, basal reading series, and district curriculum guides built on these assumptions, but also the supplemental programs designed for low-achieving disadvantaged students are especially likely to reflect this basic model of curriculum. From one point of view, this way of building curricula makes good sense. It helps to isolate basic skills that are assumed to be the critical deficiency in the disadvantaged student's repertoire; it provides a clear structure for learning; it facilitates the charting of students' progress; and it provides regular and supplemental instructional programs a common vocabulary for diagnosing what low-achieving students need.

A Critique

Despite these advantages, there is broad agreement across experts in the content/skill areas reviewed in this book that these curricular assumptions are critically limited in several respects (see Chapters 1, 5, and 9). They tend to (1) underestimate what students are capable of; (2) postpone more challenging and interesting work for too long, and in some cases forever; (3) fail to provide a context for learning or for meaningfully employing the skills that are taught; and (4) even reinforce academic failure over the long term. The *students* are literally charged with putting the pieces together into an integrated and useful base of knowledge, and, more often than not, they don't. In the view of many experts, this approach to curriculum lacks both coherence and intellectual challenge for students who experience it.

An Alternative

Assuming that the academic program for disadvantaged students should convey more than discrete basic skills, the available evidence suggests the following principles (see Chapter 2 regarding reading;

Chapters 5 and 7 regarding mathematics). More effective curricula should

- Balance routine skill learning with appropriate novel and complex tasks from the earliest stages of learning.
- Provide a context for skill learning that establishes clear reasons for needing to learn the skills, affords opportunities to apply the skills, and helps the student relate one skill to another.
- Focus on meaning and understanding from the beginning—for example, by orienting instruction toward comprehending reading passages, communicating important ideas in written text, or understanding the concepts underlying number facts.
- Influence attitudes and beliefs about the academic content areas, as well as skills and knowledge.
- Eliminate unnecessary redundancy in the curriculum (e.g., repeated instruction in the same mathematics computation skills year after year).

THE ROLE OF THE TEACHER IN INSTRUCTION

Conventional Wisdom

Since the mid 1970s, efforts to define appropriate models for instructing disadvantaged students have been dominated by a class of teaching approaches that we refer to as "direct instruction" (by this term, we mean instructional approaches that emulate the model of the same name that was part of the Follow Through Planned Variation Experiment in the early 1970s). Although there are variations among them, these approaches typically feature (1) teacher-controlled instruction, with considerable time spent presenting lesson material and directly supervising students' work; (2) extensive opportunities for practice and frequent corrective feedback; (3) a careful structuring of academic tasks so that content can be introduced in small, manageable steps; (4) rapid pacing; and (5) whole-group or homogeneous-group formats. For various reasons, this class of approaches lends itself particularly well to the teaching of the linear, discrete skills-oriented curricula discussed above.

We distinguish direct instruction from what has been described more generically as "active teaching"—that is, instruction in which "students spend most of their time being taught or supervised by their teachers rather than working on their own (or not working at all)" (Brophy & Good, 1986). Both direct and active instruction emphasize direct teacher control of learning activities in the classroom. However, unlike direct instruction, active teaching does not presuppose any particular type of academic task, pacing, or grouping.

The research evidence supporting various elements of direct instruction indicates that for disadvantaged populations, it enhances some kinds of academic learning, in particular, those involving discrete basic skills (see Chapter 12).

A Critique

There is growing dissatisfaction about the ability of this category of approaches to convey more integrated and challenging curricula to students. First, students do not need to do much thinking for themselves when the teacher breaks the learning task into small, manageable steps and explains how to accomplish each step. Second, some important academic learning goals don't lend themselves to small, manageable steps. Third, students can easily become dependent on the teacher to monitor, motivate, and structure all aspects of the work they do.

The criticisms of direct instruction are both about the pedagogical technique and the type of curriculum with which it is often associated. Consequently, not all of the same conclusions can be drawn about active teaching viewed more broadly. However, some of the same objections have been raised, among them the potential danger of dependence on the teacher or lack of opportunity for learners to exercise initiative in structuring academic tasks for themselves, or developing novel solutions to problems.

An Alternative

In this area, current research does not support abandoning the conventional wisdom but instead suggests balancing it with different approaches. Work on the teaching of learning strategies and other aspects of classroom practice gives reason to believe that a balance of teacher-directed instruction and learner-directed instruction has more to offer the education of disadvantaged students, especially if the goal is to engage students in curricula that are more intellectually challenging (see Chapter 12). The trick is to strike the right balance between teacher direction and student responsibility, so that students understand what they are doing (and why) and that, over time, their capacity for self-regulated learning increases.

Beyond a few general principles, it is difficult to suggest specific practices without reference to the particular subject matter that is to be conveyed through instruction. Recent research has shifted the focus of attention from the search for generic principles of good instruction (for disadvantaged students or any other population) to the identification of subject-specific principles. There, much work remains to be done to identify pedagogy appropriate to subject-specific instructional goals.

Evidence suggests that the following principles aim at an appropriate balance between teacher-directed and learner-directed instruction (Chapters 2, 9, and 12 deal with this issue). Teachers should

- Teach explicitly the underlying thinking processes along with skills—for example, by modeling the cognitive process involved when interpreting a story problem in mathematics or trying to understand the author's point of view in a piece of literature.
- Within sequences or units of instruction, and across the school year, gradually turn over responsibility for the learning process to the students as they become more capable of constructing knowledge and applying modeled strategies on their own.
- Encourage students to use each other as learning resources and structure their interaction accordingly, as in many cooperative or team learning arrangements.

THE RELATIONSHIP OF CLASSROOM MANAGEMENT TO ACADEMIC WORK

Conventional Wisdom

Conventional wisdom holds that a uniform structure provides students with clear expectations and guidance regarding interactions with teachers and other students. All classrooms present the teacher with a problem of establishing and maintaining order, and this is especially true in classrooms that serve large numbers of disadvantaged students. The management problems in such classrooms confront teachers forcefully as the year begins, and invite solutions that impose a uniform—sometimes rigid—structure.

To an extent, well-established principles of "good" classroom management have been developed that implement this view (Brophy, 1986). These principles combine good prevention, chiefly through tone-setting and the development of routines early in the year, with appropriate remediation as disruptive behavior occurs.

A Critique

This way of thinking about classroom management leaves out one critical element: the relationship between classroom management and the actual academic work that goes on in the room (Chapter 10 argues this point persuasively). This relationship is not necessarily problematic or complex when the work itself is routine and oriented toward basic skills instruction. But when more challenging curricula are introduced, this approach to classroom management can become increasingly unsatisfactory. Project learning in mathematics, for example, may involve simultaneous student groups engaged in projects that, together, increase the level of noise and activity in a room beyond what is conventionally considered optimal.

An Alternative

A better perspective on classroom management retains two elements of the conventional wisdom: (1) establishing general ground rules at the beginning of the school year and (2) maintaining order over time through vigilant monitoring and ongoing problem solving on the part of the teacher, as he or she anticipates challenges to, or distractions from, the primary program of action in the classroom. But this perspective encourages teachers to find a new basis for order in the classroom that emanates as much as possible from academics rather than generic rules, incentives, and consequences for misbehavior. Specific ways of doing this will vary across grades.

In general, then, classroom management should be intimately linked to the nature of the academic work being done. From this perspective, teachers can most effectively manage instruction if they do the following (see Chapters 10 and 12).

- Set expectations for classroom order that are appropriate to the academic work at hand, within broad boundaries established for overall behavior in the room. Students need to be taught explicitly that noise levels, the degree of movement around the classroom, and so forth can vary, and under what circumstances.
- Anticipate resistance to the novel and unfamiliar work that is necessarily a part of a more challenging curriculum.
- Plan a strong "program of action," rooted in interesting and engaging academic activities.

ACCOMMODATING DIFFERENCES IN STUDENT PROFICIENCY

Conventional Wisdom

Several common arrangements for instructing diverse groups place low-achieving children together and separate them from those who do better. Three are especially pervasive: (1) ability-based reading groups in the primary grades; (2) formal or informal tracking in literacy or mathematics instruction in the upper elementary grades; and (3) group-based supplemental services (e.g., Chapter 1 pullout instruction) in both literacy and mathematics. These arrangements have special relevance for classrooms and schools serving large concentrations of disadvantaged students. Here, differentiated arrangements appear to solve a fundamental instructional problem—that of matching students with appropriate learning tasks.

A Critique

Differentiated arrangements may, however, create or exacerbate other problems (Chapter 12 discusses evidence in relation to this point). Most important, low-achieving students tend to become permanently segregated in these groupings or tracks. To make matters worse, determinations of "low achievement" are not necessarily reliable, which means that students' academic abilities can be misdiagnosed. This happens all too often when ethnic or linguistic features (e.g., dialect speech or limited English proficiency) are misinterpreted as signs of low ability. In addition, some of these arrangements create groupings of convenience—for example, four to six poor readers in a

Chapter 1 reading room drawn from two or three different classrooms—that may not be particularly effective from the students' point of view. Furthermore, segregation in lower-track groups carries with it a visible stigma that contributes to certain students' being labeled "dummies," not to mention the more limited curricula that are sometimes offered such groups.

Still, the research evidence on the efficacy of ability-grouped learning arrangements for low achievers is mixed (consider evidence from research syntheses by Slavin, Hallinan, Persell, and Wilkinson, reviewed in Chapter 12). Some reviews find positive effects, while others find harmful or inconclusive influences of such arrangements on academic outcomes.

An Alternative

Research evidence does not warrant doing away with ability-based differentiation altogether (e.g., Slavin, 1986). Under some conditions, its effects are positive. However, schools and teachers should at least consider adopting the following principles:

- Use (1) heterogeneous grouping, such as cooperative and team learning, and (2) more flexible and temporary ability-grouped arrangements.
- Integrate supplementary assistance, such as Chapter 1 instruction, as much as possible into mainstream classroom activities and/or provide supplementary instruction at times that do not require students to be away from activity in their main classrooms.
- Maximize individual help to low-achieving students on an ad hoc basis rather than in long-term group-based arrangements.

STANDARDS FOR CURRICULUM AND INSTRUCTION IN MATHEMATICS AND LITERACY

The preceding discussion suggests alternative conceptions of the learner, the curriculum, and instructional practice that apply across all subject areas in elementary schools. Guiding these conceptions is a conviction that disadvantaged students are capable of much more than is typically expected of them and that schools can organize themselves to demand high academic performance from them (Calfee, 1986). There is evidence on which to base this conviction—ranging from advances in understanding of student cognition to dramatic demonstrations of results such as the performance of inner-city youths on Advanced Placement calculus tests (Mathews, 1988). The upshot is to assert that the ultimate criterion for curriculum and instruction offered disadvantaged students is whether it promises to impart the analytical and communicative skills and knowledge necessary for full participation in a technological society.

Such an aspiration takes on more concrete meanings when one shifts to a more specific focus on mathematics and literacy curricula, and how they should be taught to elementary school children. Based on our review of literature and expert opinion, certain attributes of "good practice" can be suggested in each subject area. Although there are parallels across areas, the particulars will differ for mathematics instruction and for the teaching of literacy (reading and writing).

These conceptions of good practice reflect both the findings of research and the judgment of relevant professional communities, as expressed by such documents as *Curriculum and Evaluation Standards for School Mathematics* (by the National Council of Teachers of Mathematics) or *Becoming a Nation of Readers* (by the Center for the Study of Reading, the National Academy of Education, and the U.S. Department of Education). We state these standards below in brief, global terms; the reader is referred to corresponding sections in the companion volume for a more detailed treatment of each.

Mathematics

Regarding mathematics curriculum and instruction, the following are widely held to be important ingredients for effective elementary *curriculum* in schools serving disadvantaged students:

- An emphasis on the understanding of mathematical concepts that are part of computation, symbols, mathematical problem-solving, and so on.
- Reduced emphasis on computational skills in the upper elementary grades, especially when taught out of context.
- A broader range of other mathematical topics including at least geometry, estimation, probability, and statistics, which are covered in greater depth for mastery rather than touched on for "exposure."

- Opportunities to apply mathematical ideas and skills to novel problems and real-life situations.
- Less redundancy in curricula across grades.

In implementing curricula of this sort, there is widespread agreement that good mathematics *instruction* for this and other student populations involves

- Explicit teaching of mathematical problem-solving strategies.
- Teacher-student and student-student discourse about mathematical ideas or skills and their applications to life experience.
- Multiple representations of mathematical ideas and operations, including graphical displays and manipulatives.
- Experience with educational technologies as mathematical problem-solving tools (in particular, desktop computers and hand-held calculators) and with other appropriate tools or materials useful for problem solving.
- Some opportunities for project-based learning of mathematics.

Literacy

Recent conceptions of good literacy teaching stress the integration of language arts leading to a broadly based ability to communicate and understand written language.

While separate (though related) standards can be suggested for curriculum and instruction in reading and writing, two overarching standards apply to the relationship between these two aspects of language arts:

- Effective language arts curricula for disadvantaged students seek to impart a broadly based ability to communicate with and understand written language, rather than a more limited "functional literacy."
- Reading and writing should be taught in a way that meaningfully relates the two to one another, rather than treating them as separate, unrelated "subjects."

Given overall standards guiding the teaching and learning of literacy skills, parallel standards can be suggested for curriculum and instruction focused on reading and writing.

Reading. Good reading *curriculum* for disadvantaged elementary school students, as viewed by many contemporary reading scholars, is characterized by

- Emphasis on meaning, that is, on comprehending what is read, employing the full range of cues (phonemic, contextual, knowledge-based) as aids to "constructing" meaning.
- Less emphasis on the teaching of discrete coding skills in isolation from their use, as children move up through the grades.
- Exposure to a wide range of appropriate text, including children's literature.
- Reading material that reflects and respects the life experiences and backgrounds of the students.

While a variety of teaching approaches have value in conveying this kind of curriculum to students, it is widely believed by experts that reading *instruction* for disadvantaged students should include

- Opportunities to engage in extended silent reading of appropriate texts from the earliest stages in learning how to read, rather than after the "basics" have been mastered.
- Teacher-student and student-student discourse about the meaning and interpretation of material that has been read, as well as its relevance to students' life experiences.
- Explicit teaching of comprehension strategies through means such as cognitive modeling.
- The chance to relate reading to other uses of language, in particular, written and oral expression.

Writing. An emerging conception of a good writing *curriculum* for this student population parallels that for reading in many respects. Such a curriculum

- Emphasizes meaningful written communication.
- Deemphasizes the learning of written language mechanics (spelling, punctuation, grammar, etc.) in isolation from the act of communicating in writing.
- Draws on students' experiences and knowledge, as well as on other realms of experience less familiar to students.
- Introduces students to processes of writing and the skills appropriate to each stage in the writing process.

To impart this kind of curriculum to disadvantaged students, language arts *instruction* should

- Provide frequent opportunities to write text from the earliest stages, rather than after the "basics" have been mastered.
- Engage in discourse with and among students about the meaning of what they have written.
- Expose students to various genres, such as narrative, descriptive, and persuasive writing.
- Create the conditions that encourage the use of written language for meaningful communication.

PUTTING NEW CONCEPTIONS INTO PRACTICE: A ROLE FOR CLASSROOM-BASED STUDIES

These standards and the conceptions of curriculum and instruction on which they rest are not easily realized in practice and are not yet widespread in the nation's schools. But a process of reevaluation and change is under way in many schools that may bring these conceptions of curriculum and instruction into wider use, appropriately balanced with principles from the conventional wisdom.

Classroom-based studies have a central role to play in this process of change. Several other categories of research that do not focus primarily on curriculum and instruction in the classroom have important contributions to make, as well, to an overall understanding of disadvantaged students and the education they receive. In particular, cognitive research is helping to establish how learners construct knowledge in particular subject areas (e.g., Kintsch & Van Dijk, 1978; Larkin, 1980; Scardamalia & Bereiter, 1986; Schoenfeld, 1983); studies of the learner's home environment and the relationship between it and school are illuminating how these factors affect children's education; research on effective schools has pointed out important principles of instructional leadership and school organization (Purkey & Smith, 1983; see also Chapter 13); and investigation of education policy systems and the reform process are helping to understand the environments in which classrooms are situated. Classroom-based inquiry can draw on all of these lines of research, even though its findings are not primarily about student cognition, home-school relations, effective schools, or policy systems. Most important, classroom-based studies can help to translate other research into terms that can guide curricula, classroom practice, and instructional interventions.

The usefulness of classroom-based studies to practitioners and policymakers, however, depends heavily on whether the study designs reflect an understanding of the change process. What we have learned to date from investigations of intervention programs and the change process itself can help inform the design and dissemination of further classroom-based research.

CONTRIBUTIONS OF RESEARCH TO CHANGES IN INSTRUCTIONAL PRACTICES

Two decades of attempts at improving schools have underscored several simple facts: The instructional programs in the school are not quickly or easily changed, nor are changes necessarily improvements. Practices take root over many years and are the result of many forces, among them resource constraints, the nature of available teaching materials, prevailing ideas in the professional community, and kinds of training and support available to teachers.

Research on innovations, school improvement, and the implementation of intervention or reform programs helps identify what it takes to change educational practices. Several principles have particular bearing on the role and usefulness of classroom-based studies.

Superficial Changes Are Popular and Common

Although research findings may be announced with much fanfare, their effects on schools are typically modest. Even when the findings can be turned into practical guidelines, many of the realities in schools reinforce the status quo and lead to the adaptation and dilution of planned changes. The sweeping curricular reforms envisioned in the 1950s and 1960s, for example, found eventual realization in most schools as nothing more than a series of high-quality conventional textbooks (Cuban, 1989; Atkin & House, 1981).

Critics of the way this nation often goes about educational reform have pointed to the problem of faddism (Slavin, 1989). For curriculum supervisors, staff developers, and many superintendents, the professional incentives favor being up to date and pursuing the latest educational buzzwords—not making a long-term commitment to the effective implementation of a few more solidly conceived changes. Thus, school districts may be subject to endless cycles of partially adopting one new educational model, only to abandon it when the next model begins to dominate professional conversations. In this situation, savvy teachers simply go through the motions of complying with each new idea and continue to teach more or less as they always have.

This tendency represents a real danger for the future success of the alternative ideas about curriculum and instruction discussed in this report. These principles and standards, like many others in education, can be turned into catch phrases with little real substance. Already, "higher-order skills" are coming into vogue. Classroom-based studies and the dissemination efforts based on their findings must look for ways to resist the most superficial versions of these findings.

Local Leadership Makes a Difference in the Implementation of Innovative Ideas

Research on the change process shows that, despite the tendency toward diluting or even subverting a planned change, commitment at the district or school level can lead to effective implementation (Huberman & Miles, 1983; McLaughlin, 1987). Thus, if new ideas are persuasive to key people in districts and schools, they may have better prospects of implementation. Among these key people are superintendents and principals, who can use their line authority both to coerce change (which research shows to be an effective and even necessary step in many cases) and to provide support in the implementation process (necessary in virtually all cases).

Other key people are the supervisors of curriculum and staff development, whose job is to keep the school district up to date with professional trends. When these people are able to work on well-conceived agendas for change and take a long-term perspective, their effects on classroom practice can be powerful. Their involvement can be an important resource for improvement.

Teachers Attend Best to Practical Ideas

Theoretical breakthroughs may be of professional interest to many teachers, but actual implementation of research findings is greatly enhanced by translating the theory into practical advice. Teachers do search for new knowledge that will improve their craftsmanship. They welcome knowledge that has passed the test of acceptance by other teachers and that they consider likely to benefit their students (Huberman, 1985; Louis & Dentler, 1988). Like anyone else, they are not eager to overhaul their entire approach to their work; small-scale additions to their repertoire are the easiest to absorb. Again, there is a danger for ideas like those in this report: Principles that suggest fundamental changes in conventional wisdom may be turned into rather trivial prescriptions that can coexist alongside conventional teaching approaches.

WHAT CLASSROOM-BASED STUDIES CAN OFFER

Taking these principles into account, we see three ways that classroom-based studies can contribute to improving curriculum and instruction for disadvantaged students: (1) document more precisely the range of practices now in place, (2) demonstrate what is possible, and (3) show how the school and district environment can stimulate and sustain (or inhibit) classroom practices.

Documenting the Range of Practices Now in Place

Though we know a good deal about the nature of curriculum and instruction in typical schools serving disadvantaged children, our sources of information are largely broad-brush statistical portraits (e.g., from the National Assessment of Educational Progress) or case studies of a particular subject, grade level, or type of setting (e.g., Anyon, 1981). Studies have yet to describe, intensively and comprehensively, the elementary curriculum in mathematics and literacy across grades 1 through 6 in schools serving large concentrations of disadvantaged children. What is more, research has not yet studied systematically the instruction for this population at the classroom level in schools that vary across performance levels.

The key questions to be answered concern the degree to which teachers vary their approaches to teaching disadvantaged students by subject area, by type of student population, and by school setting. In addition, although we are aware that the curriculum is likely to be more restricted in settings with high concentrations of these students, we need to know in detail how it is restricted—that is, what does and doesn't get taught in the curriculum as a whole (which combines both regular and supplemental instruction).

Demonstrating What Is Possible

Documenting the range of current practices does not tell us much about what is possible to accomplish in these kinds of classrooms. Demonstrating—and extending the conception of—what is possible is doubly important because so many people believe that challenging curricula and instruction, however desirable, are beyond the reach of most classrooms and most students in these schools, a conviction that educators' painful experience and dismal test results may appear to bear out.

Demonstrating what is possible can be done in several ways. Studies of natural variation (of which the Study of Academic Instruction for Disadvantaged Students is one example) can identify exemplary practices that have developed over time at the initiative of teachers and schools, sometimes with resources and the involvement of outsiders. Planned variation studies, experimental studies (e.g., assessments of schools in the Success for All program carried out by Johns Hopkins University), and demonstration projects (e.g., the Ford Foundation's support for improved mathematics curriculum for upper elementary disadvantaged students) can put in place a preconceived improvement program and seek to demonstrate its efficacy through comparative research designs (Slavin et al., 1989; Silver, 1989).

Both modes of investigation support "existence proofs": They show that a great deal more can be accomplished under difficult educational circumstances. Furthermore, they can show how it was accomplished.

Understanding How the School and District Environment Influences Academic Instruction in the Classroom

A third goal is equally important for classroom-based studies. In addition to showing the range of current classroom practice and demonstrating what can be done at that level, investigations need to identify the links between effective classroom practice and the environment surrounding the classroom. It is especially important to trace the connections between classroom practice and elements of the school, district, community, and policy environment that define, constrain, or support academic instruction. Understanding these connections is essential both to explain why things are the way they are and to help educators or educational policymakers know how to encourage effective classroom practice in other schools.

Existing research at the school level provides some understanding of these conditions. For example, we know that the school environment should place value on academic work, maintain high expectations for all students in their academic learning, insist on an appropriate level of order in the school as a whole, and provide adequate resources (see Chapter 13) (e.g., library materials for literacy instruction; computer software and hardware for mathematical applications). However, studies have not always carefully traced the links between these elements of the school environment and what takes place in classrooms, although recent work suggests important linkages:

- Analyses of the profession of teaching and the restructuring of schools suggest the value of a supportive professional environment for teachers, consisting of access to colleagues and expert advice, sufficient autonomy to develop solutions to the various problems posed by instructing this student population, and professional development activities that help to put new ideas in front of teachers.
- In the same vein, researchers have learned some things about the "policy environment" created by district, state, and federal requirements, expectations, and programs. Existing research suggests that for academic instruction in classrooms to flourish, the policy environment must be committed to high-quality academic instruction for all students, avoid unnecessary constraints on teachers, and provide the requisite resources for their work.

The key questions for studies at the classroom level concern the way in which actions in the school, professional, or policy environment, guided by these kinds of principles, effect changes in the classroom. Furthermore, the full extent of environmental influence on academic instruction in classrooms serving large numbers of disadvantaged students has yet to be appreciated. Many of these influences may stem from the actions of well-meaning educators and the policies or programs they create to improve the situation. Many programs in place today are based on the conventional wisdom, discussed earlier in this volume, which may be limiting the potential effectiveness of these classrooms. Careful examination of the ways these policies and programs do or don't support effective curriculum and instruction can do much to guide future improvement efforts, both by identifying misguided or counterproductive policies and by pointing the way toward more helpful ones.

A MODEST ASPIRATION FOR THE IDEAS IN THIS BOOK

Applying the ideas summarized in this chapter means going beyond what is assumed to be "best practice" in many quarters. It would be a mistake, however, to take the ideas we have presented as a new received wisdom about curriculum and instruction for the children of poverty. There is still much to be learned about how to translate these general principles into specific practices that work in various settings. For reasons that are obvious, that translation process will be difficult, long term, and uncertain.

Transcending current conceptions of best practice means more work by both practitioners and researchers. Only by careful documentation, demonstration, natural variation studies, and experimental investigations will researchers, in collaboration with practitioners, be able to extend our understanding of what is possible. Only through constant experimentation and refinement will practicing teachers find ways to adapt challenging and coherent curricula to the variety of classroom settings in which the children of poverty are concentrated. The same approaches may not work in a rural Appalachian classroom serving poor white children, an inner-city classroom with predominantly black children, or a classroom combining immigrant and refugee children from multiple language groups. In addition, there is much still to be learned about the environment for curriculum and instruction—that is, the structures of the school and the teaching profession, the frameworks of district and state policies, and the kinds of resources that best support the approaches we are discussing here.

Tackling this ambitious agenda is worth doing only if we accept the premise that the children of poverty have potential for academic learning that is not fully realized. We believe they do. The search for more effective curricula and instruction for these children must go forward. Not doing so amounts to writing off a substantial segment of the student population.

REFERENCES

Anyon, J. (1981). Social class and the hidden curriculum of work. *Journal of Education*, *162*(1), 118–132.

Atkin, M., & House, E. (1981). The federal role in curriculum development, 1950–1980. *Educational Evaluation and Policy Analysis*, *3*(5), 5–36.

Brophy, J. (1986). Research linking teacher behavior to student achievement: Potential implications for Chapter 1 students. In B. I. Williams, P. A. Richmond, & B. J. Mason (Eds.), *Designs for compensatory education: Conference proceedings and papers*. Washington, DC: Research and Evaluation Associates.

Brophy, J., & Good, T. (1986). Teacher behavior and student achievement. In M. C. Wittrock (Ed.), *Handbook of research on teaching* (3rd ed.). New York: Macmillan.

Calfee, R. (1986). Curriculum and instruction: Reading. In B. I. Williams, P. A. Richmond, & B. J. Mason (Eds.), *Designs for compensatory education: Conference proceedings and papers*. Washington, DC: Research and Evaluation Associates.

Comer, J. (1988). Educating poor minority children. *Scientific American*, *259*(5), 42–48.

Cuban, L. (1989, February). *Helping policymakers become streetwise: The art of changing schools*. Stanford, CA: Stanford University.

Delpit, L. D. (1988). The silenced dialogue: Power and pedagogy in educating other people's children. *Harvard Educational Review*, *58*(3), 280–298.

Heath, S. (1983). *Ways with words*. Cambridge: Cambridge University Press.

Huberman, M. (1985). What knowledge is of most worth to teachers? A knowledge-use perspective. *Teaching and Teacher Education*, *1*(13), 251–262.

Huberman, M., & Miles, M. (1983). *Innovation up close: A field study in twelve school settings*. Andover, MA: The Network.

Kintsch, W., & Van Dijk, T. A. (1978). Toward a model of text comprehension production. *Psychological Review*, *85*, 363–394.

Larkin, J. (1980). Models of competence in solving physics problems. *Cognitive Science*, *4*, 317–345.

Linn, M. (1986, May). *Establishing a research base for science education: Challenges, trends, and recommendations*. Berkeley, CA: Lawrence Hall of Science/University of California at Berkeley.

Louis, K., & Dentler, R. A. (1988). Knowledge use and school improvement. *Curriculum Inquiry, 18*(1), 33–62.

Mathews, J. (1988). *Escalante: The best teacher in America*. New York: Holt, Rinehart and Winston.

McLaughlin, M. (1987). Learning from experience: Lessons from policy implementation. *Educational Evaluation and Policy Analysis, 9*(2), 171–178.

Office of Educational Research and Improvement. (1986). *The effectiveness of Chapter 1 services*. Washington, DC: U.S. Department of Education.

Ogbu, J. (1978). *Minority education and caste: The American system in cross-cultural perspective*. New York: Academic Press.

Purkey, J. C., & Smith, M. S. (1983). Effective schools—A review. *Elementary School Journal, 83*(4), 427–452.

Scardamalia, M., & Bereiter, C. (1986). Research on written composition. In M. C. Wittrock (Ed.), *Handbook of research on teaching* (3rd ed.). New York: Macmillan.

Schoenfeld, A. (1983). Beyond the purely cognitive: Belief systems, social cognitions, and meta cognitions as driving forces in intellectual performance. *Cognitive Science, 7*, 329–363.

Silver, E. (1989). *Improving mathematics education for educationally disadvantaged middle school students—Brief project summary*. Pittsburgh, PA: Learning Research and Development Center/University of Pittsburgh.

Slavin, R. E. (1986). *Ability grouping and student achievement in elementary schools: A best evidence synthesis*. Baltimore, MD: Center for Research on Elementary and Middle Schools, Johns Hopkins University.

Slavin, R. E. (1989). PET and the pendulum: Faddism in education and how to stop it. *Phi Delta Kappan, 70*(1), 752–758.

Appendix

Study of Academic Instruction for Disadvantaged Students

Because the material in this book was produced as a first step for the Study of Academic Instruction, it may be useful for the reader to understand what the study team has set out to do and how we are going about it. In this appendix, we discuss the study's setting and focus, as well as the basis for determining the effectiveness of instruction. Following that, we note the primary features of the study's design and the kinds of contributions it will make to knowledge in the field.

THE SETTING FOR THE STUDY: SCHOOLS SERVING HIGH CONCENTRATIONS OF POOR STUDENTS

A study of academic instruction for "disadvantaged" students needs to begin with a definition of the population of students in question. Our focus is on children whose families live in poverty—a condition associated with a high risk of school failure. This group includes many children who have a home language other than English, and their limited proficiency in English is also associated with a risk of failure in school.

Rather than studying the problems that children of poverty face in whatever schools they attend, we are examining classrooms in schools that serve high concentrations of poor children. Research shows that children in such schools face a double disadvantage, related to their own poverty and that of the group: low achievement is most likely among children who attend schools serving large numbers of children from poor families. This fact reinforces our conviction (see Chapters 13 and 14) that research in such settings must focus on approaches to instruction, the curriculum, and the school as a whole. In practice, then, this will be a study of high-poverty classrooms and schools. Most, but not all, of the students attending these schools will themselves come from poor families.

The schools in this study's sample reflect the urban, suburban, and rural settings in which many of the nations poor children are educated: all are neighborhood schools, though many have specialized programs that attract some students from outside the neighborhood attendance area. Reflecting a range of effectiveness, from adequate to outstanding, the classrooms in these schools will afford us the chance to investigate how teachers implement various approaches to curriculum and instruction for disadvantaged students.

THE FOCUS OF THE STUDY: CURRICULUM AND INSTRUCTION AT THE CLASSROOM LEVEL

The study focuses on curriculum and instruction in the classroom. It describes the body of content and skills that students are expected to master; it will also examine the instructional behaviors and academic tasks that structure students' experience in the classroom. This focus reflects our assumption that curriculum and instruction are major (though not sole) determinants of the quality of education received by poor children. In choosing this focus on curriculum and instruction, we are giving less emphasis to other lines of research noted earlier in this report (e.g., on student cognition, the child's home environment) that also offer plausible explanations for educational problems.

The study's purview is still broad. As this book illustrates, much has been learned and written about effective curriculum and instruction. Prior research gives us frameworks for examining what is taught and how it is taught in literacy and mathematics, as well as for examining more general approaches to classroom management.

THE BASIS FOR DETERMINING THE EFFECTIVENESS OF CURRICULUM AND INSTRUCTION

In addition to describing the curriculum and instruction found in a sample of classrooms, this study will arrive at judgments of effectiveness. To do so, we must make assumptions about what constitutes a valid measure of effectiveness. We assume that students' performance and gains on standardized tests, measured over an academic year and a calendar year, are data that will help us distinguish classrooms and schools in which students learn more or less, but are not by themselves sufficient measures of the extent to which new standards of curriculum and instruction are achieved.

We are well aware of the limitations of standardized test scores—for example, that they underrepresent the learning of higher-order skills, a key dimension of the complaints over conventional "good teaching" for disadvantaged students. We are therefore using four other measures:

1. A test of mathematical problem-solving specially designed to look at higher-order thinking.
2. Analysis of student writing samples.
3. Teacher judgments about student competence and mastery of the reading, writing, and mathematics curricula.
4. Analysis of the degree to which the practices and curricula we observe conform to research-based standards of effective practice.

We are thus assuming that no single measure fully captures the quality of curricula and instruction, and are therefore using these alternative measures to provide a more complete picture of learning outcomes.

OVERVIEW OF STUDY DESIGN

The kind of study we are undertaking enables us to investigate curriculum and instruction intensively at the classroom level and relate patterns of enacted curriculum to student outcomes. The key features of our study design are as follows:

- The fifteen elementary schools in our sample are located in six districts in three states (California, Ohio, and Maryland): within these schools a total of eighty-five classrooms and approximately two thousand children (per year) are included in the investigation.
- Using data collected through teacher and student interviews, observation, teacher logs, and inspection of materials, we will describe the curriculum and instruction in these classrooms.
- We will test children in literacy and mathematics skills at the beginning and end of two consecutive school years, following each of three cohorts (grades 1, 3, and 5) through that grade and the next.
- Drawing on both student performance and expert theory about curriculum and instruction, we will analyze qualitatively and quantitatively the effectiveness of the curriculum and instruction experienced in classrooms under study.

WHAT THE STUDY WILL CONTRIBUTE

In analyzing the data from observations and interviews, we will be able to discern examples of both conventional and alternative approaches to defining the problems of disadvantaged learners, selecting and sequencing curriculum topics, balancing teacher-directed and student-directed instruction, and so forth. Thus, our analysis will help us to assess different views about what works in curriculum and instruction for classrooms with high concentrations of disadvantaged students. It will contribute to the reexamination of the conventional wisdom and the search for alternatives, as discussed in the concluding chapter of this book.

The reports to emerge from the study are meant to accomplish three analytic goals. First, the reports will describe what is taught in reading, writing, and mathematics, and the manner in which these subjects are taught, in schools serving large concentrations of disadvantaged students. The practices found in the sample schools, although not statistically representative of all schools with high concentrations of disadvantaged students, will illustrate variations and typical patterns in teachers' expectations and content knowledge, the use of time in the classroom, curriculum content, instructional strategies and grouping, school facilities, and interactions among teachers and with the community.

Second, the reports will identify effective practices in these subject areas, with reference both to student learning outcomes and to current standards of "good practice." Here we will investigate classrooms that exemplify the conventional wisdom in particular respects and classrooms that are trying alternatives. We will compare classrooms along many dimensions, including the degree of emphasis on skills versus applications, curricular integration within and across subject areas, the proportion and uses of teacher-directed instruction, discourse about content, grouping techniques, and the teaching of thinking strategies. Student performance on several measures will form one basis for drawing comparative conclusions, although we will emphasize the use of diverse standards in this regard.

A third goal will be to identify policies and procedures at the school and district levels associated with the presence of effective practices. In particular, we hope to shed light on the role that district and school leaders can play, the influences of staff development, and the effects of policies regarding testing, discipline, curricular standards, promotion, and other matters that impinge on the classroom.